Social Media in the Workplace:
A Handbook

Social Media in the Workplace: A Handbook

Chris Bryden
Barrister, 4 King's Bench Walk

Michael Salter
Barrister, Ely Place Chambers

JORDAN PUBLISHING

Published by Jordan Publishing Limited
21 St Thomas Street
Bristol BS1 6JS

Whilst the publishers and the author have taken every care in preparing the material included in this work, any statements made as to the legal or other implications of particular transactions are made in good faith purely for general guidance and cannot be regarded as a substitute for professional advice. Consequently, no liability can be accepted for loss or expense incurred as a result of relying in particular circumstances on statements made in this work.

Please note that on occasion strong or obscene language is cited in this book where extracts from case reports are reproduced. Such language is included for contextual and illustrative purposes only and is not condoned by the authors or publisher.

British Library Cataloguing-in-Publication Data

A catalogue record for this book is available from the British Library.

ISBN 978 1 84661 898 7

Typeset by Letterpart Ltd, Caterham on the Hill, Surrey CR3 5XL

Printed in Great Britain by Hobbs the Printers Limited, Totton, Hampshire SO40 3WX

PREFACE

4 And they said, 'Come, let us build ourselves a city, and a tower whose top is in the heavens; let us make a name for ourselves, lest we be scattered abroad over the face of the whole earth.'

5 But the Lord came down to see the city and the tower which the sons of men had built.

6 And the Lord said, 'Indeed the people are one and they all have one language, and this is what they begin to do; now nothing that they propose to do will be withheld from them.

7 Come, let Us go down and there confuse their language, that they may not understand one another's speech.'

8 So the Lord scattered them abroad from there over the face of all the earth, and they ceased building the city.

9 Therefore its name is called Babel, because there the Lord confused the language of all the earth; and from there the Lord scattered them abroad over the face of all the earth.

Genesis 11:4–9

Communication is the defining achievement of human society, and social media may be its apotheosis. Social media platforms are deeply rooted in the human desire to connect and to communicate. It is the first truly global active method of mass communication. The culmination of millennia of theory and invention has resulted in the instantaneous ability to share views or thoughts with the world at large, and immediately receive commentary, criticism, praise and opprobrium. Famous names, ancient and modern, have contributed to this process, from the programmable mechanical devices of Hero of Alexandria, the mechanical calculator of Blaise Pascal, the mechanical computer of Charles Babbage, to the algorithmic developments of digital computation pioneered by Alan Turing and the development of Colossus. Building on such work, Ferranti and IBM separately created commercial machines capable of then-astonishing computing power. From valves to transistors to integrated circuits, computers as we know them developed and refined. The US, UK and France developed linked networks of machines through ARPANET, the precursor to the internet as we know it, in the 1960s and 1970s. The foundations of social media were laid by Sir Tim Berners-Lee and the creation of the world wide web and the concept of web pages in 1989. After centuries of development, these tools were quickly harnessed by visionaries and entrepreneurs to create social media as we know it today.

Even prior to the advent of the world wide web, the newly created internet was being used for personal and social interaction over vast distances. As early as the 1970s, passive message posting was available on primitive bulletin boards. Delphi, now Delphi Forums, was established in 1983. Web-based forums developed in around 1994. Social media as we now know it grew out of precisely such boards.

In October 2003, Mark Zuckerberg wrote the code for Facemash. After this was shut down, he coded thefacebook.com. Within a month, half of the undergraduates at Harvard were members. By July 2010 it had 500 million members. By October 2012 that number had passed a billion. It now has brand recognition up there with the most famous companies, and a vast stock market valuation, empowering it to grow, develop, and move into more and more socio-internet areas. The first tweet was sent by Jack Dorsey on 21 March 2006: 'Just setting up my twttr'. 400,000 tweets were posted per quarter in 2007; 100 million in 2008; and 50 million tweets per day by 2010. By September 2013 this had grown to 400 million tweets per day, with 200 million users. Even less successful mediums, such as MySpace and FriendsReunited, have entered the popular consciousness and merely act to bolster existing social media platforms.

By contrast, the Gutenberg printing press, developed in around 1440, took 60 years to produce between 8 and 20 million books. It took another 100 years before the presses had produced 200 million books, leading to Francis Bacon declaring that the printing press was an invention that had changed the world. Whilst undoubtedly true, social media has in a fraction of the time had arguably just as great an impact and will continue to do so in more and more advanced forms potentially for decades or centuries to come.

Social media has certainly changed the modern workplace. It opens up new markets, but also gives rise to new risks. Employees previously vented their grievances in the kitchen, the watercooler or the pub after work. This had the advantage of being limited in scope, time and reputational risk. No longer. An employee with a social media account can now broadcast their grievance to the world at large. Even if regretted and deleted the morning after, retweets, copied posts and forwarded emails will ensure that the unwise interaction remains in the ether, effectively unremovable. The risk to employers of the proliferation of social media is significant, and it is essential that employers take such steps as they can to protect themselves from claims, whether of unfair dismissal, harassment, victimisation, defamation or from third parties. This book explores the issues that the modern employer may find itself facing from a legal perspective. It is intended to be a guide for employers and managers seeking to understand the effects of social media on their relations with employees and more widely, and to take protective steps proactively to insulate themselves from the problems that the use of social media can cause.

As may become apparent, a significant number of the reported cases have included posts or other communications via social media containing strong language and obscenities. Indeed, it is often the case that the nature of the language expressed in such posts is a core reason for the invocation of disciplinary or other procedures. Given that this is the case, extracts from case-law cited in this book are reproduced in their original form and thus include in all their glory the infelicitous and colourful language deployed, for the purpose properly of illustrating the principles considered.

Chris Bryden and Michael Salter

September 2015

ACKNOWLEDGEMENTS

Chris would like to thank his numerous supportive colleagues and very generous and understanding clerks, the combination of which has enabled the writing of this book; and in particular his civil and employment clerk, Hilary Foster. Chris also thanks his wonderful parents and of course the most important thing in the world, his beautiful wife (and proof-reader) Anna.

Michael thanks his mum and dad, his clerks, the very special Boris and Brian and his wonderful partner, Clare, without whose support this would not have been possible.

ABOUT THE AUTHORS

The authors are both practising barristers, working in the field of employment law, harassment and civil law. Having originally met at the Chambers of Jane Rayson, 2 Gray's Inn Square, they have gone on to build successful and promising careers in their respective areas.

Chris Bryden was called to the Bar by Gray's Inn in July 2003. Chris is a tenant of the Chambers of Timothy Raggatt QC, 4 King's Bench Walk. Chris studied jurisprudence at Magdalen College, Oxford and gained an LLM from University College, London thereafter, studying corporate insolvency, advanced trusts and equity and corporate law. Prior to beginning his pupillage he worked for a year in the litigation department of the Treasury Solicitor. He undertakes advocacy and advisory work in various areas of the law, with a particular interest in employment, family, housing, PI and general common law and Chancery cases. In particular, Chris is interested in the interplay between different legal areas, and is frequently instructed to advise or act in cases which involve disparate fields, as he is recognised as an expert in numerous fields of work. Chris regularly lectures in various fields of law to solicitors, employers and the third sector, and has a prolific output of journal articles and commentary, writing for the *New Law Journal, Solicitors Journal* and Lexology.com amongst other works. Chris has a reputation as a fearsome advocate and is often called upon to take cases which require his special brand of assertiveness.

Michael Salter was called to the Bar in 1999 and is a tenant at Ely Place Chambers. He holds a first class degree in law and went on to study the BCL at Brasenose College, Oxford. Michael specialises in all aspects of employment, commercial and general common law, with a particular interest in cases involving harassment and stalking. Michael is an external examiner at the University of Law, has also taught Evidence to undergraduates at King's College, London and sits as a part-time employment judge. He is appointed to the *New Law Journal* panel of expert authors and regularly writes and lectures on employment-related topics. He is listed in the *Legal 500* and in the upcoming edition of *Chambers and Partners Guide to the Legal Profession* as a leading junior in employment law.

Chris and Michael are co-authors of *I CAN see you: Harassment and Stalking on the Internet*, published in the *Journal of Information and Computer Technology Law* in 2011 and both have a strong practical and academic interest in the legal issues surrounding harassment and stalking. They have also presented a paper at the IADIS Conference held in Rome in July 2011 building on their conclusions, and which was published in the October 2012 *International Journal of Distributed Systems and Technologies*: 'Cyberstalking in the UK: Analysis and Recommendations', IJDST 3(4), 34-51 Oct–Dec 2012. Their academic interest has led to their being called to provide evidence to Parliament during the Select Committee stage of consideration of amendments to the Protection from Harassment Act 1997, and they have presented numerous seminars to leading organisations within the field. Their involvement in particular with the *New Law Journal* has led to their publication of a significant number of articles relating to social media and in particular its impact in the field of employment.

Michael and Chris work closely with the National Centre for Cyberstalking Research, based at the University of Bedfordshire, as well as the Cyber Stalking Unit established by Collyer Bristow. They are also affiliated with the National Stalking Training Academy, which provides training and awareness of the risks posed by cyberstalking. In November 2011, both Chris and Michael were appointed visiting Fellows of the University of Bedfordshire, as part of their ongoing work with the National Centre for Cyberstalking Research. Chris and Michael are each able to accept instructions both from solicitors and from members of the public pursuant to the Bar Public Access scheme, which Chris has been accredited to provide training to members of the Bar since January 2011. Both Michael and Chris are regularly instructed by clients seeking to protect themselves from issues arising out of social media.

CONTENTS

TABLE OF CASES

References are to paragraph numbers.

TABLE OF STATUTES

References are to paragraph numbers.

TABLE OF STATUTORY INSTRUMENTS

References are to paragraph numbers.

CHAPTER 1

INTRODUCTION

1.01 The current 21st century workplace is a very different environment to that of even a decade ago. The world wide web forms a backdrop to everyday working life. The internet connects us all; social media segues almost seamlessly between personal and professional lives, sometimes with damaging consequences for employer, employee or both. The strength of English common law lies in its adaptability in the face of previously unconsidered behaviour. Since the advent of the world wide web into mainstream usage in the early 1990s English law has adapted to the new challenges produced by this massive new forum. Internet connectivity in the UK has become the norm and communication over the internet by way of email is ubiquitous. Instant messaging and forum posting are also commonplace, as are the exponentially-expanding social media sites such as LinkedIn, Twitter, Facebook, Instagram and numerous others, with more in use or in development on an ever-changing basis. The challenges of this vast electronic system to law enforcement became clear in such fields as money scams (a simple development from old-fashioned postal scams), illegal pornography and other obscene materials (dealt with by direct legislation that applied equally to the internet) and, more recently, terrorist activities. However, perhaps the greatest single effect that this vast inter-connectivity has had on the law is in the field of employer–employee relations and the various permutations of that relationship.

1.02 The purpose of this book is to provide an overview of the various legal issues that can arise in the workplace out of the use and application of social media. The main social media platforms remain LinkedIn, Twitter and Facebook, but new entrants are emerging all the time. WhatsApp is overtaking text messaging. Snapchat allows the sharing of photographs which are then swiftly deleted (a potentially significant risk to an employer). Instagram runs the risk of the posting of proprietary material. The focus of this book is on the workplace, though social media permeates just about every area of law. This book will consider the legal ramifications of this interconnectivity in the context of the workplace and the effect on business and employee relations; analyse the application of the law to the use of social media in the workplace; provide employers with guidance as to their IT and social media policies; and provide a guide to professionals and those responsible for employees. It is important however to bear in mind just how large a role social media plays in the lives of numerous individuals. Whilst this book will touch on issues such as intellectual property and the criminal aspects potentially arising out of social media abuse, it is intended primarily to be a Handbook for employers, particularly those involved in the training and management of staff, and for their advisors. Its focus therefore is on the preventative steps that can be taken by employers to safeguard themselves and their employees from risk. Such risks include employee behaviour via social media that could give rise to disciplinary or dismissal procedures, or which might impact on other employees; the need to safeguard data and the extent to which employers are able to monitor social media usage by their employees; and the risks that social media poses in respect of other claims, such as pursuant to the Protection from Harassment Act 1997. The fundamental message of this book can, however, be encapsulated in the exhortation to employers to ensure that they have a social media policy in place, which is regularly reviewed, and of which employees are aware.

1.03 Thus, whilst at first glance the effect of social media on workplace relations might seem obvious, a deeper consideration demonstrates that there are numerous potentially identifiable effects. From an employee disciplinary point of view, social media may come into play when an employee is found to have posted derogatory comments about the company on the internet; to have leaked confidential information; or to have behaved in a way that brings the company into disrepute. The latter could include internal behaviour, such as the sharing of inappropriate material via email, or external behaviour such as posts on forums, Facebook, Twitter or other sites, either from an official company account or from a personal account. Different considerations may apply to these circumstances, but the reputational damage to the employer may be the same. Such behaviour might even give rise to vicarious liability for harassment of a third party against the employer. Social media therefore impacts upon companies and organisations in multifarious aspects, from reputational and customer-focused involvement to internal disciplinary matters.

1.04 Given how embedded social media now is in our everyday lives, it is impossible in a work of this nature to cover every aspect of the law in this regard. As is evident from the title, this work aims to cover the major aspects of social media from a legal perspective arising in the workplace, from an employer-focused analysis. However, as already noted, this work will also touch on other aspects including the criminal and family law, as these may also have relevance to a corporate entity whose employee involves it inadvertently in his dispute in the family or criminal courts. The principal focus, however, is on the primary effect of social media on the employer–employee relationship and its effect on disciplinary and dismissal procedures. As a result, much of this work considers the need for appropriate policies to deal effectively with social media in the workplace, from recruitment through to employment and if necessary dismissal. It includes consideration of case-law arising out of social media-related dismissal, and useful tips for HR practitioners and employment lawyers involved in such cases. Consideration is also given to circumstances in which an employer may be concerned as to its personal liability for acts of employees in the social media field as well as the need to protect its reputation both against malicious posts and the actions of employees who may appropriate social media accounts for which they have previously been responsible after their dismissal. The intention of this work is to provide detailed and relevant guidance to identified issues,as well as practical assistance for HR and legal practitioners dealing with this ever-developing and highly pertinent area of employment law.

1.05 It is likely that the principal social media sites used by employees will be the major platforms: Facebook, Twitter and LinkedIn. However, new social media platforms are launched on almost a weekly basis. Social media is ever-changing and will continue to revolutionise the way that companies communicate with their customers and how employees interact with their colleagues, friends and peers. The following table seeks to set out the potential risks arising out of social media for employers, and to demonstrate that those risks are stark.

	Confidentiality	Harassment	Copyright	Defamation	Reputational Damage
Twitter	X	X	X	X	X
Facebook	X	X	X	X	X
LinkedIn	X	X	X	X	X
Snapchat	X	X	X	X	
MySpace	X	X	X	X	X
Flickr	X		X		
Google+	X	X	X	X	X
Instagram	X	X	X		
Tumblr	X	X	X	X	X
Pinterest	X	X	X	X	X
Ask.fm	X	X	X	X	X

The above table demonstrates the risks of social media across a range of legal disciplines.

1.06 As already noted, the aim of the authors is not to add to the corpus of academic criticism of the jurisprudence in this area. We have previously written extensively as to the perceived problems arising out of the converging views as to the balance between freedom of speech on the internet and the protection of individual rights.

1.07 There is a powerful belief amongst internet activists that, because of the extra-national existence of the world wide web, freedom of expression should not be a qualified right, but instead an absolute right. This would mean that the various checks and boundaries that apply to, for example, the print and broadcast media, are not applicable to cyberspace. John Gilmore, a founding member of the Electronic Frontier Foundation[1] is regularly quoted as stating that 'the Internet interprets censorship as damage and routes around it'. This is not a universally held point of view, and is not borne out by English judicial decisions. However the statement does encapsulate the commonly held view that anyone should be free to say or do anything on the internet, and that attempts to regulate will fail, as the internet will find a way around any perceived block on the right to free expression. Were such a position to prevail, the online world would be unregulated. In reality however, the jurisprudential position has increasingly developed, as will be seen later in this book, to provide a remedy to a wronged employee, often against his employer.

1.08   There has been judicial recognition of this view in the American courts. In *ACLU v Reno*[2] Judge Dalzell stated that:

> 'as the most participatory form of mass speech yet developed, the Internet deserves the highest protection from government intrusion. Just as the strength of the Internet is chaos, so the strength of our liberty depends upon the chaos and cacophony of ... unfettered speech'.

This is a dangerous point of view, and one that has not broadly speaking been recognised by the courts of England and Wales, as will be seen by the later analysis of case-law. Freedom of speech is an important right, but the European Convention of Human Rights properly marks it as a qualified right, afforded less protection than the vaunted First Amendment. This may explain the divergence between European and US jurisprudence, together with broader provisions protecting American employees in respect of concerted action; this will be considered in greater detail at a later stage of this work.

1.09   Rather, this work is intended to be a composite practical starting point for employers and their advisors in respect of the numerous potential risks posed by social media in the workplace, together with a guide to minimising the risk of the employer finding itself in need of further advice, by taking preventative and pre-emptory steps to manage problems before they arise. The intention is to provide a guide to the most common areas where liability may arise, whether to an employee, a third party, or otherwise.

1.10   The book is therefore split into four parts. The first chapters (Chapters 2–5) will consider the framework surrounding the most common issues arising out of social media in the workplace. This will include the use of social media in recruitment of prospective employees; ongoing monitoring of existing employees; disciplinary and dismissal procedures. The second part of the book (Chapters 6–10) will consider more unusual but still highly relevant potential legal issues, including third party harassment, intellectual property and defamation and reputational damage. The third part of the book draws together a number of other non-specific issues, future developments and general

---

[1]   www.eff.org.
[2]   521 US 844 (1997).

conclusions, and the final part of the book gives practical guidance in the form of model policies, flowcharts and statutory resources.

CHAPTER 2

SOCIAL MEDIA AND INTERNET USE AT WORK: AN OVERVIEW

INTRODUCTION

2.01　The circumstances in which IT is involved in the everyday workplace are myriad. It is likely that the vast majority of employees will make use of computerised technology as part of their daily tasks. In addition it is likely that a number of employees will be engaged in online endeavours as part of their role, be it maintaining a web presence, engaging with customers over social media such as Facebook, Twitter or LinkedIn, or simply responding to queries via email. IT now pervades the office environment in a way unimaginable even 20 years ago. In addition, most employees will carry around with them highly sophisticated computer technology in the form of a mobile telephone, whether a personal device or company issue. The computing power contained within these devices is phenomenal. Mobile telephony has morphed from a mechanism to make voice calls into a device that holds far more computing power than a mainframe server from seven years ago. The primary purpose of these devices is now internet connectivity. The use of smartphones as data devices first, voice-communication devices a distant second, demonstrates how far the internet has permeated into our day-to-day lives. The reality of the modern work environment is that employees are likely in any event to have access to social media during breaks or during the course of the working day generally, with constant data streams keeping them connected, with Facebook, Twitter, Snapchat and many other apps continually updating and being updated. Access to the internet is all-pervasive and in practice extremely difficult to control, even were an employer to consider such control desirable. Thus a practical employer will wish to put in place policies that seek to regulate use of the internet and social media in various contexts.

2.02　Putting in place a policy to regulate personal use of the internet and of social media during working hours is a relatively simple endeavour, though enforcing the same may not be. Some companies operate filters to prevent access via an installed browser to certain categories of website or to block access to social media during working hours. Others monitor employee internet search history. Failure to comply with a policy on internet usage is likely to be a disciplinary offence. However many companies allow their employees to use the internet freely, particularly during breaks; and preventing an employee from accessing the internet via a personal smartphone or tablet is in practice very difficult. Such workplaces will likely have a policy that expressly allows limited use of the internet for personal purposes during working hours. However many companies will have blurred the distinction between personal and business usage by having a presence on social media, often managed by employees. Further, the advent of smartphones, meaning that social media can be accessed at all times, can lead to obvious monitoring difficulties. It is therefore apposite to consider the various situations in which issues can arise out of employee use of the internet and social media at work.

2.03 This chapter will therefore consider various examples of IT and social media use at work and explore situations that may arise, together with an analysis of a number of relevant cases. The following chapter will then go on to consider ways in which employers can mitigate risk and concern arising out of employee interaction with social media.

EXAMPLES OF INTERNET AND SOCIAL MEDIA USE

2.04 The general usage of IT systems for record-keeping, word-processing, databases and the like does not fall within the scope of the issues considered in this book. Rather, the focus is on those areas of IT and social media use that are likely to give rise to issues in the workplace that may lead to tribunal or court claims or disciplinary or dismissal issues. It is necessary to consider firstly types of issues arising out of general internet usage and then to go on to consider matters arising out of the use of social media in the workplace.

Internet usage

2.05 The immediate issues of internet usage raising concerns are likely to involve the inappropriate use of the facilities provided. This could include the visiting of pornographic or other inappropriate sites; the use of forums or other web-based bulletin boards to post aggressive, defamatory or other material; use of company resources (including employee time) on personal web usage, such as internet shopping; the use of the internet to assist or defect to competitors, and the misuse of email. The latter in particular may well pose a heightened risk to a company, though a well-drafted policy should set out the extent to which employees can use the internet and company email for personal use.

2.06 Employers may, for example, want to consider what sites are appropriate for work; whether it should be necessary for blocking software to be deployed or to operate a trust system; and whether automatic site blocking may impinge on particular tasks that may arise from time to time. For example, a firm may wish to impose a ban on visiting certain sites, but may need to use them from time to time for research. A policy dealing with the visiting of particular sites will need to be regularly updated, given the fluid nature of the world wide web.

Social media

2.07 Issues arising out of social media will likely fall in part within similar considerations to the general usage of the internet. The particular difficulty from an employer's perspective of the use of social media is that its interactive nature may give rise to disciplinary or liability issues with significant ramifications for a company's reputation, whereas the passive use of the internet in breach of policy, such as the use of inappropriate or pornographic websites, or a misuse of employee time on, for example, eBay, is far more reactive. Whilst equally inappropriate, the fall-out from such misuse is likely to be confined internally, though may involve outside parties if, for example, inappropriate emails or images are being shared outside of the company. In the main, however, this sort of misuse is likely to cause limited damage to an organisation. Social media interaction, however, may result in defamatory or harassing postings, issued in the name of a company account, or defamatory or inappropriate commentary being posted, or racist or sexist language, being sent out on an active basis to multiple recipients, and remaining as part of the company's digital footprint in a way that may be impossible to erase. There is therefore a significant issue arising out of active engagement with the internet and social media, which may require a specific policy and other steps being put in place to ensure that as far as is possible the liability of the employer is restricted and the actions of an employee engaging in active online activity can be dealt with appropriately. No policy can entirely prevent the reputational damage that a misguided or malicious tweet can cause, but it may assist in inculcating a culture whereby employees pause for thought before committing damaging material to the social ether, or enable a company to manage the situation appropriately by a swift and justified dismissal for breach of a clear policy. The existence of such a policy can therefore be used *ex post facto* as a damage-limitation exercise, to mitigate damage that has been done, where its primary preventative purpose has not been successful.

MONITORING INTERNET USAGE AT WORK

2.08 One of the controls that an employer may wish to introduce is the monitoring of internet usage, including access to social media, by employees at work, or from work equipment. The extent of such controls can vary, and can be active or passive. For example, an employer may simply forbid employees from using the internet during working hours or from work equipment at any time, for anything other than work-related usage. Such a policy, however, is both Draconian and extremely difficult to enforce; Draconian because many employees will consider that they should be able to browse websites during breaks, and difficult to enforce as it requires compliance with the policy. In addition, control over access to smartphones is likely to prove impossible.

2.09 Alternatively, an employer could rely upon software to block access to sites such as Facebook, Twitter or other specified sites, together with the more usual standard blocks on pornography and other similar sites. However such blocks will potentially cause difficulty through their blanket nature as they may restrict access to a site legitimately required for work purposes. Such a policy is in any event only as good as the software installed to enforce it; and given the rapid evolution and development of the world wide web, will require ongoing active management. It also gives no control or insight into usage of sites that are not blocked, nor in respect of emails.

2.10 It is possible for companies to utilise software that blocks emails containing inappropriate terms. However, while such software has become increasingly sophisticated, it remains a blunt instrument, potentially blocking emails with no malicious purpose.

2.11 The examples considered above are variations of a passive monitoring policy. The flaws in such policies are that they rely either on employee discipline or 'blunt-instrument' software blocks, and will likely cause resentment amongst the workforce as well as potential legitimate difficulty in accessing sites that are blocked despite not containing prohibited material. An active monitoring policy might instead involve the random or constant monitoring of internet usage, browsing history, emails and social media. The nature and extent of any such policy will depend upon a consideration of whether its aims are reasonable and legitimate.

GENERAL CONSIDERATIONS

2.12 A full consideration of employee monitoring and surveillance is outside the scope of this book and the interested reader should consider the forthcoming *Employee Surveillance* (Jordan Publishing, due early 2016) by the authors for comprehensive guidance in this regard. What follows amounts to a summary of the important issues arising in respect of such monitoring in the context of this work.

2.13 An employer is entitled to have a policy that allows for the reasonable monitoring of internet usage by an employee. Guidance in this regard has been issued by the Information Commissioner's Office in Part 3 of the Employment Practices Code.[1] The Code notes that the Data Protection Act 1998 does not prevent monitoring of employees, but any such monitoring must be done in a way that is consistent with that Act's requirements. In essence this requires that the benefits arising from that policy outweigh any adverse impact. This balance applies both to systematic and to occasional monitoring and is referred to in the code as 'impact assessment'. Such assessment should identify the purposes behind the monitoring arrangement and the benefits it is likely to deliver; identify any likely adverse impact of the monitoring arrangement; consider alternatives to monitoring or different ways in which it might be carried out; take into account the obligations that arise from monitoring; and judge whether monitoring is justified.

---

[1] https://ico.org.uk/media/for-organisations/documents/1064/the_employment_practices_code. pdf retrieved 27-1-15.

2.14 It is also noted in the Code that Art 8 of the European Convention on Human Rights (respect for private and family life) will apply. This also requires a balance between the legitimate expectation for employees to have their personal lives kept private and their entitlement to a degree of privacy in the workplace, against legitimate business reasons of the employer. It is therefore necessary for an employer who wishes to monitor his workforce to have in place a clear and justified policy for monitoring employees, and it is wise to carry out a formal or informal impact assessment prior to its implementation.

2.15 The code gives a number of examples of what 'Monitoring' might include, and notes that there is no particular definition of the same. These examples include:

- random opening of individuals' emails to look for evidence of malpractice;
- using automated checking software to check on the sending or receiving of inappropriate emails; and
- examining logs of websites to check that individual workers are not downloading pornography.

2.16 Thus, so far as the Information Commissioner's Office is concerned, 'monitoring' of employees online, so long as the same can be justified as being legitimate and reasonable, can take many forms. This issue will be looked at in further detail in Chapter 3.

EMAIL USAGE: SPECIFIC ISSUES

2.17 The case of *Williams v Leeds United Football Club*,[2] highlights the issues that can arise from inappropriate usage of corporate emails. The case is important for a number of reasons. It has made headlines due to the high profile nature of the parties. From a legal perspective, however, it is of interest for two main reasons: firstly, the fact that the misconduct in question was discovered only 5 years after it had occurred, and after notice of redundancy had been given; and secondly, for its consideration of the applicability of the employer's email and IT policy. It is instructive to consider the case to highlight the approach of the courts to employee email misuse.

2.18 The facts of the case are relatively straightforward. Evan Gwyn Williams was employed as the technical director of Leeds United from August 2006, having previously worked for Chelsea Football Club. His salary with Leeds was £200,000 per annum, terminable on 12 months' notice. The agreement was oral – there was no written contract of employment in place. In summer 2013, Mr Williams was identified as being at risk of redundancy following a restructuring that had been carried out. He was given written notice on 23 July 2013 of his termination. Leeds contended that his initial contractual agreement had ended after 5 years (in August 2011) and from that time he was employed

---

[2]   [2015] EWHC 376 (QB) (19 February 2015).

on the terms of the standard senior management contract, which provided a notice period of 3 months. This point was not pursued at trial, because, as transpired, Mr Williams was summarily dismissed shortly thereafter. The subtext appears to be that Leeds determined to find another method of getting rid of Mr Williams and therefore carried out investigations. Following the giving of notice, Leeds had as a result discovered that on 28 March 2008 Mr Williams had forwarded to Mr Dennis Wise, of Newcastle United, an email which stated 'Looks like dirty Leeds!!' and which contained a PowerPoint presentation containing pictures of women's breasts and genitalia. Mr Williams at trial accepted that the photographs were vulgar, and that some were obscene. Lewis J agreed.

2.19 As a result of this discovery, the day after written notice had been given, Mr Williams was invited to a disciplinary hearing on 29 July 2013. He did not attend, and was found to have committed gross misconduct as a result of his having forwarded the email. Reference was made in the findings to Leeds' internet policy, which specifically prohibited transmitting by email words or pictures that were obscene, lewd or pornographic, or which could amount to harassment. An appeal hearing upheld the findings.

2.20 It was later discovered that the email had been forwarded by Mr Williams to two other people, one of whom was a junior employee of Leeds. That employee was a Ms Lamb, who, it is noted at para 20 of the judgment, was the most junior member of staff, and half the age of Mr Williams. The explanation given by Mr Williams was that Ms Lamb was a keen Leeds fan, and would as such appreciate the 'play on words' in the email. The reason given for Mr Williams' belief that this young female employee would find this amusing was that, since the 1970 Chelsea–Leeds FA Cup final, Leeds had had a reputation for dirty playing. This was an explanation that Lewis J found was 'frankly, not credible'.

2.21 An issue at trial was whether Leeds knew of the emails at the time notice was given, and further whether Leeds were actively trying to find reasons to dismiss for misconduct, to get out of paying notice pay. Lewis J found in respect of the latter that such a decision had been taken, and that senior staff knew it, and that it was a breach of contract. As to the former, whilst Lewis J found that there was an active search for misconduct, the emails were not known of at the time of giving notice.

2.22 The claim brought by Mr Williams was for damages for wrongful termination. He claimed unpaid salary, unpaid pension and damages for the loss of other contractual benefits, together with a statutory redundancy payment. Leeds defended, inter alia, on the basis that Mr Williams had breached the implied term of trust and confidence by forwarding on the email. Mr Williams contended that his actions were not sufficiently serious to amount to a repudiatory breach.

2.23 Lewis J reviewed the law relating to the implied term of mutual trust and confidence, and found that, viewed objectively, the conduct did amount to a breach. This may not seem to be a surprising conclusion, and Lewis J set out a number of reasons, including the seniority of Mr Williams, the fact that the images were obscene, the potential for a claim for harassment by sending the email to Ms Lamb, the nature of the business of Leeds and the potential for adverse publicity, together with the fact that no reasonable explanation for the forwarding of the email had been given. These reasons are important, as they demonstrate the danger of damage that can be caused to an employer by a misuse of electronic equipment. A claim by Ms Lamb could well have been against both Mr Williams and Leeds, who as a result could have been found to be vicariously liable for its employee's actions. Having made a clear finding, Lewis J went on to refute the arguments put forward on behalf of Mr Williams.

2.24 There was an internet policy in place, but it was argued that that internet policy had not in fact been provided to Mr Williams; and, further, that the internet policy itself referred to such matters as being 'serious disciplinary matters' which should, it was argued, therefore be treated as 'serious' not 'gross' misconduct, for which summary dismissal should rarely be a sanction. That such a submission was made demonstrates the need for a clear policy which cross-references to disciplinary policies. These submissions were dealt with shortly by Lewis J. The judge held that notwithstanding the policy had not been provided, it should have been obvious that the email system should not be used to send obscene and pornographic images; and that the 'serious disciplinary' argument was a mistaken understanding of the policy. It is interesting to note that the judge treated as a matter of common sense the fact that such emails should not be sent. It is however worth noting that, in the absence of a policy and in a workplace where such emails were common, such a view might not have prevailed. The possibility for such an argument, with potentially damaging evidence being given in an employment tribunal of the culture in a given workplace, where, for example, pornography is tolerated, is clearly of reputational concern. The case does highlight that notwithstanding that the policy was not known of by Mr Williams, a sensible approach is likely to be taken to such issues. However had the conduct been less stark, it is likely that the existence or otherwise of a policy would have mattered more than in the event it did.

2.25 The decision is not, on the facts, surprising. The case is however a salutary reminder that employees may treat their work email accounts as 'private', with potentially devastating effects for employers. In the worst-case scenario, Leeds could have found itself subject to a claim by Ms Lamb and potentially other employees, and, in the absence of an appropriate policy, would have drawn speculation that at the least it tolerated such behaviour in the workplace.

2.26 Surfcontrol, an email and internet blocking company, commissioned in 2004 a survey of 350 companies in the United Kingdom, the United States and Australia, to consider misuse of employee email, and in particular the practice of sending pornography. The survey was conducted by Dr Monica Whitty, of the school of psychology at Queen's University, Belfast. That survey returned results which should be of significant concern to employers:

- when asked whether employees had used work email to send sexual material to a colleague, 28% of respondents answered affirmatively, and 3% said they did so daily;
- when asked whether employees had used work email to send such material outside of the workplace, 31% had done so, 4% daily;
- 28% of employees had downloaded pornographic material at work;
- 51% of employees had been exposed to sexual material at work by someone else who had downloaded it.

2.27 It is possible that changing social norms have altered these statistics so that there is greater understanding of the unacceptability of such usage at work. However, the *Williams* case suggests that such issues still prevail. The recent dismissal of three judges by the Lord Chancellor for misuse of work IT to access pornography likewise provides anecdotal evidence that such risks for employers continue to persist.

SOCIAL MEDIA: SPECIFIC ISSUES

2.28 The following section will consider a number of specific issues arising out of social media use at work, by way of illustration. The themes developed will then be considered in further detail in later chapters.

Personal vs professional social media use

2.29 Social media and IT use is likely to break down into two categories: professional use and personal use. However there may be an overlap between these two categories as the distinction between personal and private use of IT and social media is increasingly blurred. Employees are often encouraged to join social media networks such as LinkedIn or Twitter, or to promote company news or products through their personal accounts. Alternatively, an employee may monitor and run a Facebook or Twitter page that is set up to promote the business, on behalf of their employer. In such circumstances it may be difficult to monitor the distinction between personal and business use and to know where to draw the line between the two.

Who owns a social media account?

2.30 The question of who 'owns' social media accounts, and therefore has the right to retain the followers and contacts of those accounts, is a vexed question with no straightforward answer. As a starting point, many social media providers stipulate that they own the account. The true dispute over ownership however is likely to arise between employer and employee when the employee leaves the company in question. It might initially appear to be common sense that where an employee has been posting or tweeting on behalf of the employer, the employer retains the rights to that account. However there is little to stop an employee simply changing, for example, the handle of an 'official' twitter account which they have set up and for which they have the password, to the name of the competitor organisation to which they have defected, potentially opening up to that new employer hundreds of established business leads together with goodwill generated. This argument might be especially powerful where the employee has set up the account in their own time, or in a quasi-official capacity without express instruction to do so.

2.31 The question of ownership in this situation has as yet no definitive answer. In America litigation on precisely this issue was instituted in 2011 in the so-called *PhoneDog* case, *PhoneDog v Kravitz*,[3] which settled in early 2013. PhoneDog brought a claim against Mr Kravitz, who had previously been an employee and amongst other things was responsible for the company's Twitter account. The claim involved some 17,000 followers of the Twitter account, which Mr Kravitz 'retained' after the termination of his employment. The company claimed $340,000 by way of damages for misappropriation of trade secrets, intentional interference with their business, negligent interference with prospective economic advantage and conversion (the latter claim being in relation to the Twitter handle when it was changed from @phonedog_noah to @noahkravitz). The claim included quantifying the value of each Twitter follower at $2.50 per month. The settlement is confidential, but the Twitter account and followers were retained by Mr Kravitz.

2.32 No precisely comparable issue has arisen in any reported case before the courts of England and Wales, but there are signs that the courts will apply existing legal principles to cases involving social media. Thus, for example, in *Hays Specialist Recruitment (Holdings) Ltd v Ions*[4] an English court required at a pre-action stage the disclosure of LinkedIn contacts, where the defendant was suspected of inviting contacts made at his previous employer to join his account for the purposes of the establishment of a competitor business. His authorisation to use his employer's contact email details to do this did not extend beyond his employment. In *Eagle v EdComm*,[5] a US case, an employer appropriated a LinkedIn account and altered it to add the profile of the new CEO, but did not erase the details of the former CEO entirely. Dr Eagle won but received no damages, as she could not prove loss. The determinative feature in her case was the lack of a social media policy allowing the company to act as it did. And in *Whitmar Publications Ltd v Gamage & Ors*[6] injunctive relief was sought and granted where employees setting up in competition had used LinkedIn groups operated by their employer.

---

[3]   No 11-03474 (ND Cal) 8 November 2011.
[4]   [2008] EWHC 754 (Ch).
[5]   12 March, 2013.
[6]   [2013] EWHC 1881 (Ch).

2.33 Given the uncertainty over ownership and control of social media accounts, particularly those operated by employees even when under the employer's brand, it is important that employers consider what protection they can provide for themselves. To this end, Chapter 10 considers the use of policies and restrictive covenants to ensure as far as is possible that employees do not leave with valuable contacts and high profile social media accounts, which can then be subverted to their own ends.

Dismissal for personal use

2.34 In certain circumstances, an employer may seek to discipline or dismiss an employee for their conduct outside of work hours, relating to the use of only personal social media accounts, and in respect of posts conducted out of working hours. Such an action might be appropriate where the interactions of the employee are such as to bring the company into disrepute or otherwise adversely affect its business. An example of this occurring can be found in the case of *Game Retail Ltd v Laws*,[7] which illustrates the risks that can arise through unfettered social media use.

2.35 Mr Laws was an employee of Game Retail Limited, which operates a number of shops selling computer games and other such products. Its business model depends at least in part upon promotion of its products over the internet and over social media. His role at the relevant time involved him having responsibility as a risk and loss prevention investigator for around 100 stores based in the North of England. Mr Laws joined Twitter and opened his own account in a personal capacity. He followed the accounts of those stores for which he was responsible, specifically in order to monitor their tweets, to check for inappropriate activity. This was considered to be part of his employed role. Eventually, Mr Laws followed around 100 store accounts, and some 65 were following him back. It appeared that one store had tweeted that Game shops ought to be following Mr Laws, which was considered to be an important factor by the employment tribunal.

2.36 On or around 18 July 2013, a store manager brought to the attention of a regional manager the contents of tweets being posted by Mr Laws, from the same personal account, followed by a number of the stores. Following an investigation by Game, 28 of the tweets posted by Mr Laws were identified as being offensive. The character of these tweets did not relate in any way to the job performed by Mr Laws, or to his employment. Rather, they were said to involve foul language and derogatory references to, amongst others, 'fucking robbin bastard' dentists, Newcastle FC supporters, 'twats in caravans' and 'golf geeks'. Whilst it was clear that these tweets had nothing to do with the role that Mr Laws was employed in, or had any relation to Game, the company was concerned about reputational damage. The conclusion of the investigation was that the tweets were in the public domain, clearly accessible by stores, and that some were abusive. Disciplinary action was recommended. Mr Laws was

---

7   [2014] UKEAT 0188_14_0311 (3 November 2014).

suspended on 23 July 2013 and was invited to a disciplinary hearing to meet a charge of gross misconduct. It was observed in the covering letter that 'whilst this is your personal Twitter account and you do not specifically affiliate yourself to the company on that account, you also use your account to monitor Twitter activity from the company's stores that you are responsible for in your capacity as risk officer'. At the hearing, Mr Laws contended that he had not consented for managers to encourage other managers to follow him. He was dismissed, which was upheld on appeal. He brought a claim for unfair dismissal.

2.37 As is well-established, in order for a dismissal to be fair the employer must establish an acceptable reason for dismissal and the tribunal must conclude that the dismissal was fair in the circumstances under the Employment Rights Act 1996. The test to be applied in respect of the latter limb is whether the employer's actions, including its decision to dismiss, fell within the band of reasonable responses which a reasonable employer could adopt: *Iceland Frozen Foods Ltd v Jones*.[8] The tribunal is not to substitute its own view for that of the employer and decide what the 'right' approach should have been, but rather to ask whether it was reasonable for the employer to take the decision:

> Since the present state of the law can only be found by going through a number of different authorities, it may be convenient if we should seek to summarise the present law. We consider that the authorities establish that in law the correct approach for the industrial tribunal to adopt in answering the question posed by section 57(3) of the 1978 let is as follows.
>
> (1) the starting point should always be the words of section 57(3) themselves;
> (2) in applying the section an industrial tribunal must consider the reasonableness of the employer's conduct, not simply whether they (the members of the industrial tribunal) consider the dismissal to be fair;
> (3) in judging the reasonableness of the employer's conduct an industrial tribunal must not substitute its decision as to what was the right course to adopt for that of the employer;
> (4) in many (though not all) cases there is a 'band of reasonable responses to the employee's conduct within which one employer might reasonably take one view, another quite reasonably take another;
> (5) the function of the industrial tribunal, as an industrial jury, is to determine whether in the particular circumstances of each case the decision to dismiss the employee fell within the band of reasonable responses which a reasonable employer might have adopted. If the dismissal falls within the band the dismissal is fair: if the dismissal falls outside the band it is unfair.

2.38 At first instance, the employment judge found that the decision to dismiss did not fall within the range of reasonable responses open to Game. This was firstly, he found, because the Twitter account was not opened as part of Mr Laws' job but principally to communicate with acquaintances outside of work, using his own mobile phone, and concerning matters nothing to do with work; secondly because the relevant offending material was tweeted in his own

---

[8]   [1983] ICR 17.

time and not during work hours; and thirdly, because explanations were given by him to contextualise some of the offensive tweets. Paragraph 13 of the EAT judgment reproduces the EJ's analysis of a sample of the offensive tweets, which make for interesting reading, but which are clearly nothing to do with Mr Laws' job or work. The employment judge also noted that it had not been established that any member of the public or of Game's staff had seen the offensive tweets other than one manager and the complainant; there was no link between Mr Laws and Game that viewers of the relevant posts could have drawn; and that there was no specific clause in the disciplinary policy that demonstrated that offensive or inappropriate use of social media in private time could amount to gross misconduct.

2.39 Game appealed, and argued that the employment judge had erred both in having substituted his own view and in reaching a conclusion that was perverse. The EAT allowed the appeal. It was noted that this appeared to be the first EAT decision concerning dismissal for misuse of Twitter. However the EAT noted that, notwithstanding the subject-matter of the appeal, the issues in the appeal amounted in effect not to new considerations but rather to an application of the well-established principles of substitution and perversity to the decision reached on the facts by the employment judge. On those issues, the EAT held that the EJ had failed to engage properly with Game's case, and that it was wrong to suggest that followers of Mr Laws were restricted to social acquaintances. Mr Laws must have known that the offensive tweets were going out to all of his followers, which included 65 stores, and any customers that also followed him.

2.40 The EAT confirmed that private usage was not an irrelevant question and that there is a balance to be drawn between the desire of the employer to remove or reduce reputational risk and the right to freedom of expression. 'Generally speaking', said the EAT, 'employees must have the right to express themselves, providing it does not infringe on their employment and/or is outside the work context. That said, we recognise that those questions might themselves depend on the particular employment or work in question'. The EJ had not properly tested the question of whether this was truly a case of private usage, in a case in which 65 stores followed and 100 were followed; privacy settings had not been engaged by Mr Laws to restrict his tweets only to those users following him. Mr Laws had encouraged stores to follow him by re-tweeting a store manager's exhortation to follow him. The EJ had allowed his own focus to prevent him from engaging with a point of concern: the offensive messages going to the stores that followed Mr Laws. This was a substitution of what was relevant, or alternatively was perverse. It was also inconsistent to find that no-one was offended, when it was known that a complaint had been made, this also being a substitution. Finally, it was also perverse or an error of substitution, to hold that nothing derogatory of the respondent or that might reveal that he was an employee of Game, had been posted.

2.41 In *The British Waterways Board (t/a Scottish Canals) v Smith (Unfair Dismissal: Reasonableness of dismissal)*,[9] the Employment Appeal Tribunal (sitting in Edinburgh, the Honourable Lady Stacey presiding), a decision of the Employment Tribunal below that the dismissal of Mr Smith for posts made on Facebook was unfair, was overturned. The case is of importance, as the EAT confirms the view expressed in *Game Retail Ltd v Laws*[10] that there is no need for the creation or implementation of special rules in cases involving social media, and that the ordinary principles of law developed by the tribunals fell to be applied in such cases.

2.42 Mr Smith worked for the British Waterways Board, as part of what the Employment Tribunal had found as a fact was 'not a happy team'. He raised a grievance, stating that he was stressed and felt bullied. He was referred to Occupational Health, which found that his symptoms were entirely work-related.

2.43 Mr McRoberts, a supervisor of Mr Smith, had come across various Facebook posts made by Mr Smith. These included:

(i) chipper training today and supposed to go home after it wanker supervisor told the trainer to keep us as long as he could the fuckers don't even pay u for this shit;

(ii) hard to sleep when the joys of another week at work are looming NOT;

(iii) ha what joy, 2 sleeps til back to my beloved work NOT;

(iv) good old bw cant wait to see all my friends again lol;

(v) going to be a long day I hate my work;

(vi) that's why I hate my work for those reasons its not the work it's the people who ruin it nasty horrible human beings;

(vii) why are gaffers such pricks, is there some kind of book teaching them to be total wankers;

(viii) on standby tonight so only going to get half pissed lol;

(ix) im on vodka and apple juice first time ive tried it no to shabby; and

(x) in response to the latter comments someone had noted the claimant was on 'floor alert' and asked if the claimant was going to let everyone drown, to which the claimant had responded 'just the cunts from Braid Square lol'.

2.44 Mr Smith admitted making the posts, but defended them as banter. He had not been drinking, and it was common practice to 'slag off' the person on standby. He also claimed that his privacy settings had been hacked, making his account public, and produced evidence of this change. An investigation recommended disciplinary proceedings.

2.45 No social media policy was in place, but there was a policy relating to internet and email use. In addition the following section was included:

The following activities may expose BW and its employees, agents and contractors to unwarranted risks and are therefore disallowed:-

9 [2015] UKEAT 0004_15_0308 (3 August 2015).
10 [2014] UKEAT 0188_14_0311.

- Any action on the internet which might embarrass or discredit BW (including defamation of third parties for example, by posting comments on bulletin boards or chat rooms) ...

2.46 Mr Smith accepted before the ET and the EAT that the policy could encompass personal posts in his own time from his own equipment, if his employer or his work was referred to. It is unfortunate that Mr Smith, who was in person at least before the EAT, did not take this point, as a ruling on the personal/private divide without a specific policy in place would have been instructive.

2.47 The disciplinary hearing found that the comments, whether true or not, had the potential to undermine confidence in Mr Smith and would have left the employer open to public condemnation. Mr Smith was summarily dismissed for gross misconduct. Other employees, who had also posted offensive material, were not dismissed, but the employer found that the distinction was that Mr Smith had been drinking, which he found to be the case. An appeal upheld the dismissal.

2.48 The Employment Tribunal found that the comments were offensive, but that the employer was not identified by the reference to 'bw' in the posts. It found that the decision to dismiss fell outwith the band of reasonable responses test, on the basis that the disciplinary panel did not consider the mitigation put forward by Mr Smith. The Tribunal held:

> We decided the decision to dismiss fell outside the band of reasonable responses: we were satisfied that no other reasonable employer would have dismissed in these circumstances given the historic nature of the comments, the mitigating factors and the fact the claimant had demonstrated in the three years since the comments had been made, that, in reality, he was not a risk and could be trusted in his work and whilst on standby. The respondent did not suggest there was any basis upon which to believe the claimant would reoffend: there had not been any further comments on Facebook regarding drinking on standby, and none of the supervisors on standby had raised any issues.

> We concluded the decision to dismiss in the circumstances fell outside the band of reasonable responses which a reasonable employer might have adopted. We decided the dismissal was unfair.

2.49 The EAT disagreed, finding that the Tribunal had erred by substituting its own view for that of the employer. They did not as a result need to go on to consider the alternative ground of perversity.

2.50 This decision is not in and of itself remarkable. It is referred to principally as a further decision by the EAT, following *Laws* that there is no need for special rules in social media cases. On the facts, that is clearly correct; this was a straightforward case turning on the s 98(4) test, where the Tribunal fell into the error of substitution. However, the fact that such substitution did occur is instructive. It is respectfully submitted that, had the case been presented by Mr Smith on other grounds, including the public/private nature of posts, the lack of a specific social media policy or training, and the question of harm, as opposed to risk, a determination that the dismissal was unfair might not have been so easily overturned. Where guidance is needed in particular is in respect of social media policies and training, given the conflicting case-law in this regard, as will now be considered.

2.51 In contrast to the views expressed in the decisions above, the case of *Smith v Trafford Housing Association*[11] is another case that received widespread publicity and that provides an informative lesson as to the risks on an employer acting on a social media posting that is not necessarily linked directly to work. Mr Smith worked for the housing association as a manager. In February 2011 he posted a link on his personal Facebook page but which stated the name of his employer, which linked to a story on the BBC News website relating to gay marriage. Along with the link he posted a personal comment, stating that this was an 'equality too far'. A work colleague complained, was found to have committed gross misconduct, and was demoted. He brought a claim for breach of contract and for breach of his Art 9 and 10 rights to freedom of expression. The latter breaches were struck out on the basis that the matter was a private law matter and the association was not a public body.

2.52 In respect of the breach of contract claim, the High Court found in favour of Mr Smith. They held that he had not committed a breach of contract, as he had not committed misconduct; he had not brought the association into disrepute as his Facebook wall was for personal purposes and did not hold itself out as being for work, despite the identifying of his employer; the posting did not bring the association into disrepute; and Facebook was not of a sufficient work-related context to activate the particular disciplinary policies of the Association, and the work colleagues who saw the post and engaged in discussion with Mr Smith chose to be his friends on Facebook. Mr Smith on the facts received only £98 in damages, being damages for wrongful dismissal over his notice period.

2.53 *Smith* is important, because it makes clear the approach of the High Court in considering the right to freedom of expression (following on from the *Trimingham* case, considered later in this work). It is important to bear in mind, however, that the *Smith* case was a case of breach of contract heard in the High Court. The contrast between the decision in *Smith* and that in *Laws* is of interest, and turns on the application of the range of reasonable responses test.

2.54 The context of most arguments relating to social media dismissals is likely to be a claim to the Employment Tribunal. It is notable that, in *Laws*, the EAT declined to give any specific guidance as to social media dismissals, instead simply applying the range of reasonable responses test. This appears to be consistent with the approach of tribunals previously. In the unreported ET case

---

[11] [2012] EWHC 3221.

of *Barnes & Carter v Greenacres School*[12] the dismissal of two special needs teachers for making inappropriate and unprofessional comments about students on Facebook was upheld. In *Crisp v Apple Retail (UK) Ltd*[13] Apple was able fairly to dismiss a worker who had posted derogatory comments about work and its products on Facebook, on the basis that its disciplinary and training policy covered the area. And in *Dixon v GB Eye Ltd*[14] an employee who posted whilst on suspension that her colleagues were 'the biggest bunch of wankers known to the human race! Full of gingers, fat wankers, sleazes, brown noses and cokeheads!' was fairly dismissed.

2.55 The reason for the apparent divergence between the High Court in *Smith* and the Employment Tribunals is that a decision to dismiss is a subjective decision. This is because it is not the tribunal's role to decide what it would have done had its members been sitting in the disciplinary hearing. Rather, it is the function of the tribunal to determine whether or not in coming to its decision the employer acted reasonably. As Pugsley J stated in *London Borough of Sutton v Kester*:[15]

> 'The substitution by a tribunal of its view of the matter, as opposed to looking at whether the respondent's actions were within the range of reasonable responses, is not an empty legalistic forma. It goes to the very heart of the function of a Tribunal. Tribunals have neither the experience or the expertise nor the information before them to assume the role of castigating employers, because the Tribunal would not necessarily have acted in that way. If Tribunals are to maintain their credibility with both employee and employer, they must show a suitable modesty about their role.'

2.56 This principle has been a clear aspect of employment law for some 30 years, following *British Home Stores v Burchell*,[16] and more recently in *Post Office v Foley*.[17] To avoid this great heresy requires a tribunal to confine itself, when considering the fairness of the dismissal under s 98(4) of the Employment Rights Act 1996, to focus entirely upon the three fundamental issues of: the reasonableness of the investigation; whether there was a genuine belief at the time of the dismissal which was held on reasonable grounds; and whether the dismissal was within the band of reasonable responses. It is clear that the tribunal is not to substitute its own evaluation of a witness or of the evidence of that witness, or its own take on written documents forming part of the trial bundle.

2.57 By applying the range of reasonable responses test, it is far more likely that a genuine dismissal will be upheld on the basis of the misuse of social media, particularly where a clear policy is in place. Other examples of a tribunal finding in favour of an employer include *Preece v JD*

---

[12] February 2012.
[13] ET/1500258/11.
[14] ET/2803642/10.
[15] UKEAT/0187/06/MAA (2006).
[16] [1978] IRLR 379.
[17] [2000] ICR 1283.

Wetherspoons plc,[18] where dismissal after inappropriate use of Facebook was considered reasonable, and *Weeks v Everything Everywhere Ltd*,[19] where a dismissal was found to be fair after a report by an employee of threats over Facebook following on from a complaint that that employee was being disparaging about his workplace. However this will not always be the case. In *Alan Blue v Food Standards Agency* a worker was unfairly dismissed after 'liking' a post on Facebook about his boss being attacked by a chair and in *Lake v Amey Services Ltd Sheffield*[20] an employee was unfairly dismissed after an 'inappropriate' Facebook post. It is notable that in both of these latter cases there was no relevant social media policy governing posts outside of work.

Pre-employment vetting

2.58 An increasingly important area of recruitment is a vetting of a potential employee by reference to their social media and general internet profile. It is becoming increasingly common for employers to conduct a cursory Google search and follow up results; other employers will commission specialist companies to provide background checks based on social media and other profiles. There have been instances of employees being refused job interviews as a result of their online profiles; alarmingly, there is evidence of employees being refused security-cleared work in situations where it has been determined from a social media footprint that they hold particular views, or even based on the nationality of their parents. The authors have dealt with cases where social media vetting has taken place to 'weed out' applicants due to their profiles, and the recent case of Paris Brown, the 17-year-old Youth Police Crime Commissioner forced to resign after a media furore relating to insulting tweets that she had posted between the ages of 14 and 16 that were considered homophobic and racist demonstrates the reputational effect of a social media history.

2.59 Guidance from the Information Commissioner's Office is clear that such checks should not be carried out on an arbitrary basis. There is a requirement that such screening is carried out only for specified and good reason, which is necessary and proportionate to achieve identified aims. Again, it is essential that a policy is in place to cover such matters. Companies should also make clear to potential employees that checks will be carried out and the reason for such checks, as well as the method by which such checks will be carried out. Checks should therefore be tailored to the role to be carried out and should be used only where there is no other method of verifying the matters in question. The next chapter will consider this topic in further detail, in the context of social media policies.

---

[18] ET/2104806/10.
[19] ET/2503016/2012.
[20] ET 1807678/2013.

CHAPTER 3

IT AND SOCIAL MEDIA POLICIES AND INTERNET MONITORING

INTRODUCTION

3.01 Whilst, as has been seen in the preceding chapter, the absence of an IT or social media policy does not of itself prevent a dismissal in obvious circumstances being fair (so that in the *Williams* case, the transmission of pornography via an employee email account was 'sufficiently serious'), given the myriad circumstances that may not be so self-evident it is clearly sensible for a policy to be put in place. Such a policy may allow the monitoring of IT and social media use; set out guidelines as to the use of social media during office hours, using office equipment and/or from official accounts or those clearly identifying the employer; deal with email usage and what is and is not appropriate, and otherwise regulate social media and IT usage. Chapter 13 of this book provides a template basic policy together with practical guidance as to what should be included and what should be the aims of the policy. This chapter will focus in greater detail on the theoretical and legal issues underpinning any such policy, together with considerations that should be borne in mind when developing such a policy.

SOCIAL MEDIA AND RECRUITMENT

3.02 It is increasingly common that employers will vet potential candidates via a search of their social media. The authors are aware of businesses across the spectrum, from FTSE 100 companies to small retail outfits, from Magic Circle solicitors firms to barristers' chambers, who have an official or unofficial policy of such vetting. This can range from a quick Google search and a check of Facebook, Twitter or LinkedIn, to the hiring of a specialist social media vetting firm to compile a full and in-depth profile of a candidate's social media profile. Careerbuilder.com, a recruitment website based in the United States but also operating in the United Kingdom, carried out a survey in 2014 of employers who had carried out checks of some form via social media.[1] The results were striking. 43% of prospective employers at least carried out a basic Google search of prospective candidates. Of those, 51% had found something online that had caused them not to hire a candidate, though 33% likewise said that

---

[1]   http://www.careerbuilder.co.uk/share/aboutus/pressreleasesdetail.aspx?sd=6 per cent2F26 per cent2F2014&id=pr829&ed=12 per cent2F31 per cent2F2014 (retrieved 30 May 2015).

they had found something that made them more likely to hire a candidate, showing the double benefit of carrying out research into prospective candidates.

3.03   Amongst reasons cited by employers for not hiring, the following (taken from the said survey) are notable:

- 46% of candidates posted inappropriate or provocative photographs or information;
- 41% of candidates posted references to drink or drug use;
- 36% of candidates were rude about their former employer or fellow employees;
- 28% of candidates had made discriminatory comments;
- 24% of candidates had shared confidential information relating to their previous employer;
- 22% of candidates had links to criminal behaviour;
- 21% of candidates had inappropriate user names.

3.04   Other notable concerns raised included the candidate who was actively involved in a demonic cult; the candidate who had sued his wife for shooting him in the head; the candidate who had bragged about his numerous drink-driving narrow escapes; and the candidate who featured a pig as his best friend. Whilst these examples are all taken from the United States, it is nevertheless highly likely that just as many issues of concern would be found from a similar survey in the United Kingdom. Indeed, what research there has been in the UK demonstrates this, as will be seen below.

3.05   What an employer can find online, a potential customer, or a competitor, or an ex-employee with a grievance can also find. It is therefore unsurprising that social media vetting is on the rise at the recruitment stage. The accessibility of sites such as LinkedIn provide a useful check for employers to determine whether qualifications or employment history have been exaggerated (though there is always the risk that such exaggeration has been used on such sites as well as on applications). However, given the desirability of a policy in respect of employee monitoring, is it likewise necessary to have a policy in respect of pre-employment social media vetting?

3.06   Guidance in this regard is available from the Chartered Institute of Personnel and Development (CIPD), the professional body for Human Resource Practitioners.[2] In that Guidance the CIPD contrasts the increasing public perception that employers when recruiting must behave ethically with the increasing emphasis on consideration of social media footprints by prospective employers. The CIPD considers that some 40% of prospective

---

[2]   December 2013, https://www.cipd.co.uk/binaries/pre-employment-checks_2013.pdf, (retrieved 30 May 2015, subscription only).

employers now utilise social media checks, a figure that will likely only rise. In addition, in August 2013 ACAS issued guidance[3] entitled 'The Use of Social Media in the Recruitment Process'.

3.07 The following factors, taken from the CIPD Guidance, are said to be the core aims for employers in conducting pre-employment checks, with which the authors respectfully agree and gratefully adopt:

- protect the organisation;
- protect clients and customers;
- be fair to all candidates;
- ensure non-discrimination and compliance with data protection law;
- rely on fact, not opinion;
- validate information to be relied on;
- ensure relevance to the post to be filled;
- see the candidate in the round;
- be transparent and open to candidates about the checking process.

3.08 According to the CIPD and their own research, some 6% of prospective employers 'always' make use of online profiles and social media presence in considering prospective employees, with a further 33% doing so from time to time. This fits in well with findings from the ACAS survey, again in 2013, which suggested that 45% of HR decision-makers were using social media to inform their decisions, and 40% who said that they would make greater use of them in the future. This contrasts with the findings of the ACAS research, which suggests that close to 100% of prospective employees believe that their social media footprint is considered by employers. The ACAS paper also cites a survey by Jobsite in 2012, which suggested that in terms of employers using social media sites for recruitment (though not necessarily for vetting), LinkedIn was by far the most popular site, followed by Facebook and then Twitter.

3.09 The CIPD notes that the law in this area is not as yet settled, and that there is a tension between a reasonable expectation of privacy and the usage of information which is readily available online. Attention is drawn to the eight principles set out in the Data Protection Act 1998 (Schedule 1), which provide in respect of the use of personal data:

1. Personal data shall be processed fairly and lawfully and, in particular, shall not be processed unless –

(a)   at least one of the conditions in Schedule 2 is met, and
(b)   in the case of sensitive personal data, at least one of the conditions in Schedule 3 is also met.

---

[3]   http://www.acas.org.uk/media/pdf/0/b/The-use-of-social-media-in-the-recruitment-process.pdf (retrieved 30 May 2015).

2. Personal data shall be obtained only for one or more specified and lawful purposes, and shall not be further processed in any manner incompatible with that purpose or those purposes.

3. Personal data shall be adequate, relevant and not excessive in relation to the purpose or purposes for which they are processed.

4. Personal data shall be accurate and, where necessary, kept up to date.

5. Personal data processed for any purpose or purposes shall not be kept for longer than is necessary for that purpose or those purposes.

6. Personal data shall be processed in accordance with the rights of data subjects under this Act.

7. Appropriate technical and organisational measures shall be taken against unauthorised or unlawful processing of personal data and against accidental loss or destruction of, or damage to, personal data.

8. Personal data shall not be transferred to a country or territory outside the European Economic Area unless that country or territory ensures an adequate level of protection for the rights and freedoms of data subjects in relation to the processing of personal data.

3.10   The reference in point 1 to the reasons in Schs 2 and 3 of the Act require one of the following considerations to be met. It is, however, important to note that the meeting of such condition is not a blanket allowance. Lawfulness is a necessary but not sufficient requirement. The overarching concept of fairness must also be satisfied:

- the individual whom the personal data is about has consented to the processing.
- the processing is necessary:
  - in relation to a contract that the individual has entered into; or
  - because the individual has asked for something to be done so they can enter into a contract.
- the processing is necessary because of a legal obligation that applies to you (except an obligation imposed by a contract).
- the processing is necessary to protect the individual's 'vital interests'. This condition only applies in cases of life or death, such as where an individual's medical history is disclosed to a hospital's A&E department treating them after a serious road accident.
- the processing is necessary for administering justice, or for exercising statutory, governmental, or other public functions; and
- the processing is in accordance with the 'legitimate interests' condition.

3.11   It is likely that the first and second of these points may (subject to fairness) potentially justify the processing of personal data in the context of a job application, but also highlight the need for a clear and cogent policy to address both the legality and the fairness of pre-employment vetting. In addition, the final point, legitimate interests, will probably be relevant to such investigations. The legitimate interests condition involves a balancing between the needs of the business with the rights of the subject. Clearly, the most straightforward method of putting in place a vetting process is to ensure that the process is proportionate and necessary, and that the subject is informed of and consents to, such vetting.

3.12 It is clear that there are competing legal aspects arising out of the active consideration of prospective employees. There is a balance between the lawful accessing of material freely available, and the reasonable expectation of privacy to which a candidate is entitled. The authors consider that it is sensible and highly desirable for any employee conducting more than a simple and cursory Google search (and even in those circumstances thought should be given) to have a written policy in place that is provided to prospective candidates in advance, setting out what steps the employer may take. It is notable that the ACAS study suggested that most social media research was conducted at the initial recruitment stage, rather than to screen and shortlist candidates. The authors consider that this is a trend which is in the process of reversing, with social media screening increasingly being deployed to shortlist candidates, and even to provide a final check against suitability prior to the hiring decision, given the increasingly pervasive ubiquity of social media profiles. Having had regard to the various suggestions of the CIPD and ACAS the authors consider that the following points are relevant in drawing up a policy relating to pre-employment vetting:

Do:	Don't:
Prepare and make available an appropriate, clearly drafted and comprehensive written policy	Indiscriminately Google some but not all candidates
Set out the basis upon which data mining or social media research will take place, including its restriction to open or freely available posts, tweets, blogs, profiles or similar	Create accounts for the purpose of friending or following prospective candidates so as to monitor their social media interactions which might otherwise not be accessible
Take note that existing discrimination policies and the law in general apply as much to cyberspace as in the kinetic world	Search through the photo archives or tags of (for example) only female candidates, or specifically look for characteristics such as age, race, sex, or disability unless there is a well documented and clear reason for the same

Do:	Don't:
Seek to corroborate information garnered online, or, if unable to do so, put concerns to the candidate together with the source material	Take as fact all that is gleaned from social media, or go on a fishing expedition by seeking to provoke a candidate online or their friends, followers or associates
Distinguish between the professional and the private: an unidentifiable profile posting about weekends out is very different to a work-linked account doing the same thing	Assume that a candidate having a personal and private life is not allowed his or her own views: work and personal are not the same thing
Consider personal data in so far as it is justifiably relevant to the prospective employment	Trawl for personal indiscretions or delve too deeply into personal matters
Ensure that all data mining is proportionate and appropriate	Collect more information than is reasonably necessary
Inform candidates of material gathered and afford them an opportunity to respond	Ambush candidates with photographs downloaded from social media
Consider that a candidate may simply not utilise social media or have an internet footprint	Assume that an absence of a social media profile means that a candidate is hiding or is in any other way deficient
Consider the proportionality of internet data mining against the role being recruited for	Forget the risk to corporate reputation from public social media posts
Consider training for decision-makers	Forget that the internet and social media are fast-changing and fail to adapt policies and practices accordingly

3.13   A survey carried out by ACAS and referred to in their 2012 paper noted above, found that 55% of HR decision makers did not have a policy. 37% did and 9% could not recall. The report concludes:

> 'There are also, however, a number of potential risks and costs associated with the use of social media for recruitment. There is the actual cost of dedicating resources to social media sites, as traffic can be significant and unpredictable. There are also issues surrounding the accuracy of the information gained by the use of social media tools – there is no guarantee that the information that individuals, or others, post on their SNSs is accurate.

There are also issues around the depth of the applicant pool that social media tools can access, giving rise to potential problems around diversity and discrimination, particularly in terms of reaching older candidates and those who are not as comfortable with using computers. This means that there are a number of legal aspects that employers should consider when thinking about using social media tools for recruitment. These include difficulties arising from HR decisions based on inaccurate information, issues related to employee privacy, equality and diversity and the use of standardised information about candidates. Furthermore, given the diversity of information about individuals available on social networking sites, it is difficult to see how this can be fairly compared.'

3.14   There is clearly a risk that employers, who discover information which relate to protected characteristics, may put the company at risk of a claim arising out of conscious or unconscious bias on that basis. There are also risks arising out of legitimate privacy expectations, and a further risk of a perception of bias towards those candidates that do (or do not) utilise social media. This again demonstrates the importance of a clear policy and recruitment training for those involved to ensure as far as is possible that such risks are identified and managed accordingly. A template policy can be found in Chapter 13 at the end of this book.

MONITORING POLICY

3.15   It is perfectly acceptable for an employer to have a policy that allows for the reasonable monitoring of internet usage by an employee, so long as the benefits arising from that policy outweigh any adverse impact. Whilst the Information Commissioners' Office Employment Practices Code[4] makes clear that there is a legitimate expectation for employees to have their personal lives kept private, and that employees are entitled to a degree of privacy in the workplace; so long as the policy is for legitimate reasons it will be acceptable. Therefore it is necessary for an employer who wishes to monitor his workforce to have in place a clear and justified policy for monitoring employees, with an impact assessment being carried out prior to its implementation. A good policy should set out for the employee the right of the employer to monitor all email and internet access, detail when and how work email, telephone and internet access may be allowed for personal use, and should also specifically state that an employee is not allowed to access, for example, pornographic or gambling websites from the work server, giving reasons for this. It is unlikely that a simple ban on, for example, 'offensive material' will be sufficiently specific. The policy should also set out guidelines for employee use of social media, both for business purposes and personally. A policy might, for example, forbid the use of Facebook and Twitter during business hours, or allow it only during specified breaks. Likewise, such policy might require that any personal use of social media should not link back to the company, so that personal Twitter accounts do not contain identifying features of the employer.

---

4   http://www.ico.gov.uk/for_organisations/data_protection/topic_guides/~/media/documents/ library/Data_Protection/Detailed_specialist_guides/the_employment_practices_code.ashx.

3.16   Monitoring of internet usage should not be used as a general 'snoop' but only for the purposes set out in the policy (such as ensuring that employees are not accessing or transmitting pornographic material). Personal information collected through monitoring should only be used outside of those purposes (such as, for example, ensuring that pornographic websites are not accessed) if it is clearly in the employee's interest to use it (for example a personal email which shows a risk of physical harm to the employee) or if no reasonable employer could be expected to ignore it (such as, perhaps, the posting of denigrating comments about the employer on web forums). Clearly personal emails, either sent to a work email account or via a personal email account, should not be accessed without good reason, and personal accounts should not be accessed save exceptionally.

3.17   Employers may find that Art 8 arguments are raised in respect of the monitoring of employee emails. Article 8 of the European Convention on Human Rights provides:

1. Everyone has the right to respect for his private and family life, his home and his correspondence.
2. There shall be no interference by a public authority with the exercise of this right except such as is in accordance with the law and is necessary in a democratic society in the interests of national security, public safety or the economic well-being of the country, for the prevention of disorder or crime, for the protection of health or morals, or for the protection of the rights and freedoms of others.

3.18   The right is a qualified right. In *Halford v United Kingdom*[5] the tapping of a work telephone used to make personal calls was a violation of Art 8 on the basis that no prior warning had been given, and as a result Ms Halford, a senior police officer, had a reasonable expectation of privacy. That right subsisted notwithstanding that the calls were made on a telephone provided by her employer:

> There is no evidence of any warning having been given to Ms Halford, as a user of the internal telecommunications system operated at the Merseyside police headquarters, that calls made on that system would be liable to interception. She would, the court considers, have had a reasonable expectation of privacy for such calls, which expectation was moreover reinforced by a number of factors. As Assistant Chief Constable she had sole use of her office where there were two telephones, one of which was specifically designated for her private use. Furthermore, she had been given the assurance, in response to a memorandum, that she could use her office telephones for the purposes of her sex-discrimination case [at 45].

3.19   The logic of the decision applies just as much to emails and other internet usage as to the telephone. That does not mean that postings on public fora such as Facebook or YouTube cannot be used as evidence in disciplinary

---

5   [1997] IRLR 471.

proceedings: see *Gill v SAS Ground Services UK Ltd*,[6] referenced above. *Halford* does quite clearly reinforce a point already made on numerous occasions: the need for a clear policy in respect of internet monitoring at work.

3.20 In addition, the Regulation of Investigatory Powers Act 2000 will apply to employee internet monitoring. RIPA renders unlawful a person who has the right to control a private telecommunications system, which would include email, to intercept a communication in the course of its transmission, unless the interception happens 'with lawful authority'. The Employment Practices Code suggests that a policy should set out the circumstances in which telephony and email (including personal access or devices) can be used. An interception of, for example, an email, will only be authorised, in accordance with the Lawful Business Practice Regulations 2000[7] where it is done to ascertain whether business standards or procedures are being complied with or for the establishing of the existence of facts, for national security purposes, to prevent or detect crime, to detect authorised use, or in respect of charity helplines. It is likely that it is only the former of these which will be applicable for the majority of businesses, and as a result it is essential that a clear policy is established prior to any internet monitoring that is carried out.

3.21 A good policy should therefore set out for the employee the rights that the employer reserves in terms of internet monitoring. Types of reserved rights might include:

- monitoring provisions for internet, social media and email usage;
- personal use: when this is allowed, to what extent, and what sites are prohibited, such as pornography;
- specific details of what is not allowed. Rather than simply referencing 'material which is likely to be found to be offensive' or words to like effect, it is sensible to spell out the aims and objectives. Pornography is inappropriate due to the risk of offence and as such it is not allowed. Gambling websites are prohibited due to the risks posed to the wellbeing of employees, and similar;
- the times or circumstances during which personal use of social media is permitted. This may also tie in with use of company social media sites;
- guidelines as to the extent to which purely personal accounts may be used to discuss or mention company business or to promote company activities.

3.22 A policy that requires access to personal Facebook or Twitter accounts, for example, is not likely in most cases to be defendable, as the need for such information is not necessary. However, if a disgruntled employee is tweeting or posting on their 'wall' information relating to the company, even out of hours, this may be a disciplinary offence, if a complaint is raised about it or the employer becomes aware in some other way. Reference to recent case-law

---

[6] ET/2705021/09.
[7] SI 2000/2699.

however demonstrates that this area is something of a minefield, as seen in the previous chapter. It is sensible to update disciplinary policies to make clear that inappropriate use of social media that brings the company into disrepute may be misconduct or gross misconduct, and any bullying over social media will not be tolerated. An employer can be held vicariously liable for workplace bullying or harassment of third parties, and if this occurs through a branded company account, the company may struggle to raise a defence. It is important also to note that 'fake' access to employee social media profiles, for example by posing as a friend or using subterfuge to gain access to an account, will likely be deemed to be a breach of the Data Protection Act 1998 and will be difficult to justify.

3.23 When the specifics of a social media policy are considered in the next chapter, a list of do's and don'ts also appears.

CHAPTER 4

DISCIPLINARY ISSUES AND INVESTIGATION

INTRODUCTION

4.01 Many organisations seek to restrict the coming together of an employee's personal and work life so as to ensure that employees act in a manner appropriate to the workplace during working hours, regardless of their interests, actions or behaviours outside of it. Whilst there was a clear differentiation between these two spheres in past generations the modern pervasive nature of technology and ease of communication means that a strict demarcation between the two is unobtainable and, in fact, may be counter-productive to the workforce and therefore the employer.

4.02 However, employers will be relieved to know that this does not mean that an employee is entitled to act as they would in their private life at work: an employer can dismiss for misuse on social media just as they can do for direct inter-personal vocal communication or for misconduct committed outside of work that impacts on the employer's ability to undertake their contract of employment. Social media does not change this. What it does do, however, is broaden the audience able to observe the misconduct and magnifies the potential for harm that can be caused thereby. The vast expanse of social media and the significant level of interconnectivity will necessarily increase dramatically the potential damage that can be visited upon the employer as a result of employee misconduct online. The risk of harm to employers is manifold: for instance there is the risk of being bound in contract to agreements the employer would rather wish to not be a party to, as a result of an employee unwisely agreeing a deal over social media; there is the risk that confidential information and material either disappears with a departing employee or becomes public knowledge; there is the risk of reputational damage being inflicted on the employer owing to comments by the employee; and there is a risk that social media profiles are subverted to the needs of a new employer. In addition, social media can engender claims by employees or third parties that they have been subject to unwanted attention amounting to an actionable claim, or of defamatory statements. Given that many employers entrust their professional social media accounts to relatively young employees, who may lack experience in the workplace, the issues that can arise out of misuse of social media are a significant potential risk.

4.03   These very real risks posed by social media to employers do not, however, abrogate the need for an employer to prove its case when considering the dismissal of an employee for misconduct arising out of social media use. The relatively permissive regime available to employers when considering a misconduct dismissal, as outlined in *BHS v Birchell*,[1] still holds sway, and lessons learned from the proceeding 30 years of employment litigation are still very much applicable. This is the case notwithstanding the relative novelty of social media, at least in respect of its ubiquity. As noted elsewhere, social media is treated jurisprudentially merely as a novel conduit for behaviour that is unacceptable. The fact that that behaviour is conducted over social media gives rise to certain legal considerations specific to the medium, but, in general terms, employment and civil law will treat social media as nothing other than an additional way in which behaviour can be conducted, though the risk of magnification of harm is increased due to the ability of commentary so easily to be replicated, reproduced, viewed and forwarded over the medium. Therefore, a dismissal arising out of misuse of social media will be fair where it falls within the range of reasonable responses open to the employer (s 98(4) of the Employment Rights Act 1996). The Employment Tribunal will not substitute its own view of what is reasonable, but will consider whether the decision taken by the employer was reasonable for it to have taken in the circumstances.

SCOPE

4.04   This chapter aims to consider in some detail the risks posed to employers by their employees misusing social media, in particular arising in the field of employment law. Examples from the growing body of case-law will be considered and the chapter will then address the issues that often arise when conducting disciplinary hearings into social media misuse. In addition, this chapter will seek to provide further guidance from an employment law-specific viewpoint as to the contents of any social media policy, building both on what has come before, and presaging the subsequent chapters (a model policy is provided within Chapter 13).

4.05   Despite the many opportunities that social media presents to employers, including the ability to have direct contact with customers and more actively to steer how its brand and image are seen, as with all technology, employers are understandably wary; the inevitable question that arises for employers is: 'how can use of this media be restricted to legitimate, work related, activities and how can its misuse be prevented and our risks minimised'. This question is not new and probably arose when telephones were introduced and certainly was considered by many employees more recently when the internet became a mainstream tool in most (if not all) offices. Social media is merely the latest development in the rise of interconnectivity and the world wide web. Employers have been adapting to this new way of reaching customers for decades now. In 2015, 15.2% of all retail transactions are conducted via the internet.

---

[1]   [1980] ICR 303, [1978] IRLR 379, [1978] UKEAT 108_78_2007, (1978) 13 ITR 560.

Increasingly, the internet is a tool for employers to promulgate their products to a wide audience. This is the case as much for retail as it is for the professions. The internet is here, and it has fundamentally changed the way that employers interact with their customers.

4.06 Such concern is not unsurprising given the potential exposure to liability and business risk which mass communication presents. Risks include the potential for disclosure of confidential and sensitive information, infringement of other parties' intellectual property rights and potential liability for defamation, harassment and discrimination. Gone are the days when a single point of contact controlled the employer's entire communications output: the partner who reviewed a firm's letters before they were posted, or a senior employee who was tasked with reviewing all communications on behalf of the employer, can no longer carry out such a task. Whilst some employers will still retain a communications team to handle the bulk of public messages, the reality is that a significant press release can be pre-empted by an eager employee sending a presumptive tweet. Nowadays responsibility for dissemination of the 'corporate message' and communications has effectively been delegated (without either the employer or the communications department necessarily having realised it) to any employee with any access to a computer or internet-enabled device (whether or not those machines are provided by the employer). To compound matters, the first, and often only, point of regulation of such a communication has been left to the employee themselves, who may have received no training or guidance on this topic. Thus the risk to any business is obvious, and the cynic may consider that such open access presents a perfect storm for misuse. To make the risks even starker, the time when communications which affect the employer can be sent is not restricted to the time that the employee is sat in the office, at work and potentially observed by their fellow employees. The 'always on' nature of the internet and particularly of social media means that employees can post social media messages, either formally or informally, at all times of day or night, during the working week or at weekends. These factors only heighten the risk (perceived or otherwise) posed by social media.

4.07 In addition, there is the real potential for the same social media site to be used by the employee for both work and personal usage, further greying the work/life divide, which in turn adds the variable of the potential for diverging understandings of what is an acceptable use of social media held by both the employer and employee. The blurring of the lines between workplace colleagues and Facebook friends, especially with a superior, also adds to the complexities. This is particularly the case where a senior subordinate feels able to use social media to behave inappropriately, due to social connections to a more senior manager. The inference to junior mutual connections may be that a level of informality that is not in fact acceptable is endorsed over social media, leading to the risk of misunderstanding or worse.

This may also be an issue in relation to employees who connect over social media with third parties. The recent media attention over the private LinkedIn message to the barrister Charlotte Proudman from the senior solicitor Alexander Carter-Silk, in which he commented upon her 'stunning' photograph on the site, demonstrates the risk of employees acting in ways that may be actionable. The risks of liability to or from third parties are considered elsewhere in this work.

4.08   The converging factors of delegation of regulation, ease, and availability of communication methods, combined with human nature of making errors and doing foolish or thoughtless things means that employers should seek to provide guidance to those who work with or for them as to their usage of social media whether or not the employer as an organisation embraces such social media: whether or not they have a Facebook page, Twitter feed or other social media presence. However, in order to be successful and attract and retain the best staff an employer needs to reflect modern expectations: just as a blanket prohibition on personal calls at work is likely to be seen as unsustainable and a barrier to employee retention and satisfaction, it is the authors' view that a blanket prohibition on social media use at work is equally unattractive, unsustainable and unenforceable, particularly for the latest generation of employees who have grown up with connectivity provided by social media and consider it a key part of their relationships and lives.

Harm and misuse

4.09   At the core of the case-law that has been developing in this area is, the authors believe, a distinction as to what the employer is seeking to control or regulate. When considering the form of guidance as to social media usage that the employer wishes to provide it is first vitally important for that employer to understand there are two separate (but, it is accepted, often related) legal concepts. These we term 'misuse' and 'harm'; the latter may follow from the former but it does not do so necessarily, and may be totally independent from any misuse. Further, 'misuse' can occur without any 'harm' being inflicted. As separate concepts they both must be understood and addressed as such in any policy that the employer wishes to put in place to regulate employee usage.

4.10   What then are these two separate concepts? 'Misuse' may conveniently be defined as the 'employee's improper behaviour'. It is easier for employers to regulate 'misuse' on machinery that the employer controls and owns and it is open to them to proscribe what will amount to misuse during the time the contract of employment operates. For instance an employer will find it easier legitimately to proscribe the sending of personal emails during working hours from a work PC or from using a mobile device at work during working hours and it is generally easier for an employer to discipline an office worker for viewing legal pornography (as opposed to, for example, child abuse images, which would likely in any situation amount to an offence of gross misconduct) during work hours or on a work machine outside of work hours than it would be for the employer to discipline the same employee for conducting that (legal) activity privately at home on their own computer or device: as there has been misuse of the employer's machinery. That is not to say, however, that employers are limited to proscribing misuse on work machinery only.

4.11 What, therefore, amounts to misuse? This really depends on the form of social media being used, as considered in Chapter 2. For communications technology, misuse could be any form of inappropriate communication: be it the dissemination of sexually explicit material, the expression of offensive views or the forwarding of client lists and pricing structures to other accounts in advance of leaving the current employment. Misuse of the internet can be accessing inappropriate sites, and in some circumstances could also be mere usage for personal reasons during work hours.

4.12 Some instances are not so clear-cut. In many organisations mere use of the internet is unlikely to amount to a misuse and so is unlikely to constitute misconduct that permits disciplinary sanction and therefore potentially dismissal. In any event even were it to do so there is a good chance that the dismissal may fall outside the band of reasonable responses (on which see the consideration below). However excessive use of the internet is likely to amount to a misuse. Where the line is to be drawn is hard to predict in general terms and one that needs to be considered in light of the particular business need of the organisation. Particular industries may be justified in blanket prohibitions whilst a sales office, for example, which might well require access to social media in order to carry out its function, may not. The self-regulating nature of office communications, whereby the message is sent out without passing through a communications officer, also renders the risk of misuse all the greater. Misuse therefore may well be a disciplinary offence, but is such due to the behaviour of the employee and only the employee. Misuse will normally be self-contained and will not have wider ramifications. Accessing a forbidden site (whether legal or illegal) will not in itself cause harm to the employer over and above the issue with the particular employee.

4.13 The concept of 'harm' in contrast is not so ambiguous. It has been long established that any actions 'of such a nature, whether done in the course of employment or outwith it, that reflect in some way upon the employer–employee relationship'[2] are capable of being regulated by an employer and may form a reason for dismissal of an employee. The fact that an action by the employee may give rise to a wider difficulty for the employer, such as active actionable posts, or the visiting of sites that are not only banned but illegal, may result in reputational embarrassment for the employer or claims against it. Cases involving harm are far more likely to give rise to a fair dismissal of that employee.

4.14 Over the years case-law has widened this consideration to include actions that harm the reputation of a business, cause a loss of trust and confidence held between an employer and employee or damage the relationships between employees. The ACAS Code of Conduct for Disciplinary and Grievances at

---

[2]   *Thomson v Alloa Motor Company Ltd* [1983] IRLR 403, EAT.

Work expressly makes the connection between conduct outside of work and the impact at work whilst identifying the distinction between 'misconduct' and 'harm', albeit in the context of criminal offences:

> if an employee is charged with, or convicted of a criminal offence this is not normally in itself reason for disciplinary action. Consideration needs to be given to what effect the charge or conviction has on the employee's suitability to do the job and their relationship with their employer, work colleagues and customers.

4.15   In the ACAS example, it is possible to categorise both harm and misuse. The misuse (misconduct) is the fact of the charge or conviction. The 'harm' is the question over the 'suitability [of the employee] to do the job, their relationship with their employer, work colleagues and customers'. The proliferation of IT and social media and the running together of the work and private life spheres of employees has not changed this distinction, but rather highlights the need for employers to be clear in their policies that actions damaging the employer/customer/employee relationships are prohibited and that this prohibition extends beyond working hours, beyond the physical confines of the office and transcends the medium of technology provided by the employer for the purposes of work. Actions that are harmful to the employer will be harmful whenever, wherever and however caused.

4.16   'Harm' is, therefore, potentially able to be caused by an employee at any time, and over many media. Even if an employer does not itself have a social media profile, its employees are more than likely to: be it a Facebook page, Twitter account or other forum for the posting of opinions and the interaction with strangers, colleagues, customers or the public at large. The need for specific regulation of such conduct is therefore necessary, as the employee's conduct may not otherwise always be caught by a 'standard' employee handbook and contract of employment.

4.17   As a result, employers should be aware that the implied contractual obligations of fidelity and confidentiality owed by an employee to an employer, can, if broken, amount to either 'misuse' or 'harm', or both. Much will depend on the circumstances. An employee who posts to an empty forum, or tweets malicious information to a tiny number of followers, may be 'misusing' social media, but not causing harm, though considerations of the risk of such material being discovered, or reposted, or otherwise becoming part of more mainstream media may well be relevant in considering what is a reasonable response. It is important, when considering disciplining an employee for social media interaction, to consider both elements – what is the alleged misuse, and what harm has been caused? It may be a disciplinary offence for an employee to misuse social media; but is it appropriate to dismiss where no harm has objectively been caused? Likewise, harm can be caused without misuse – an employee can be posting from an unaffiliated account in their personal time, but with potential ramifications for the company. The need for a clear policy to set out in detail what is and what is not misuse and what the consequences may be for both misuse and harm is of significant importance in determining whether an employee should be disciplined and what the consequences should be.

Examples of misuse	Examples of harm
Drunken but harmless tweets	Aggressive posts relating to customers or other employees in a personal manner
Genuinely held expressions of view inappropriately posted	Bigoted, offensive or grossly inappropriate material
Moans about work generally	Specific abuse of the company or named managers
Passionate debate	Twitter trolling with specific threats
Private emails or messages	Private emails or messages that become public
Visiting inappropriate websites	The fact of the visiting attracting the attention of the authorities
Accessing sites relating to protected characteristics	Posting information that amounts to discrimination

Disciplinary issues

4.18 The advent of social media has not made the law any more complex in this regard then it ever was, though misconduct over social media may make it more difficult for an employer to determine whether to take disciplinary steps or not. The Employment Tribunals in particular have simply applied existing legal principles to unfair dismissal cases and other aspects of the law. Focusing initially on unfair dismissal claims, the case of *British Home Stores v Burchell*[3] contains the seminal guidelines in misconduct cases:

> 'First of all, there must be established by the employer the fact of that belief [of the employee's guilt]; that the employer did believe it. Secondly, that the employer had in his mind reasonable grounds upon which to sustain that belief. And thirdly, we think, that the employer, at the stage at which he formed that belief on those grounds, at any rate at the final stage at which he formed that belief on those grounds, had carried out as much investigation into the matter as was reasonable in all the circumstances of the case.'

4.19 Accordingly, *Burchell* sets out three stages, namely:

- Did the employer believe the employee was guilty of misconduct;

---

[3]   [1978] IRLR 379.

- Did the employer have reasonable grounds for that belief;
- Had the employer carried out as much investigation into the matter as was reasonable in all the circumstances?

4.20 The decision to dismiss must also have been within the band of reasonable responses: s 98(4) ERA 1996. These stages will be considered in turn.

Genuine belief of guilt

4.21 At its most basic, this requirement means that the employer had misconduct (misuse, as well as harm, may, in particular circumstances amount to misconduct) as their reason for dismissing the employee and not some other (possibly prohibited) reason such as race, sex, age or any of the protected characteristics. It is the employer's duty to produce evidence which will prove the belief in guilt and if they fail here they will lose the claim. Once again, this requirement highlights the need for clear policies if evidence from social media is to be relied upon. Social media as an evidence-gathering tool is permitted. In *Gill v SAS Ground Services UK Ltd*[4] Ms Gill was absent from work unwell, and was receiving sick pay. However she repeatedly posted to Facebook during that period relating to her choreographing and other activities at London Fashion Week. This came to the attention of her employer as a fellow employee had printed out her Facebook posts and had provided these to her boss. Ms Gill contended that she was simply attending in a social capacity, in a manner consistent with her sick leave (she was due to have a minor operation). However in the course of the disciplinary process further evidence, which was publicly available, was obtained. This included a YouTube video of her receiving a bouquet of flowers on the catwalk, together with the suggestion that she had carried out some 300 auditions of hopefuls during her sick leave period. The evidence was not specifically trawled for, but rather came to light in the process of the existing investigation. There were no particular issues that arise from the medium by which the evidence was gathered in that case.

4.22 In cases where the employee is alleged to have misused the employer's IT facilities the genuine belief required of employers to satisfy *Burchell* is probably easily made out: eg documents showing the misuse of the computer, print-outs of the offending posts, images recovered from the hard-drive, telephone logs etc may all go to support the contention that the reason for dismissal was the genuine belief of the misconduct. Of course such material is also relevant as to the reasonable grounds derived from a reasonable investigation on which to have arrived at that belief.

4.23 It is, however, in the 'harm' claims where employers often fall foul. Historically, courts and tribunals have deprecated the use of 'loss of trust and

---

[4]   2705021/09.

confidence' as a universal catch-all for employers to dismiss employees: see, for instance, *Leech v Office for Communications*,[5] in which Mummery LJ stated:

> 'The legislation is clear: in order to justify dismissal the breakdown in trust must be a "substantial reason". Tribunals and courts must not dilute that requirement. "Breakdown of trust" is not a mantra that can be mouthed whenever an employer is faced with difficulties in establishing a more conventional conduct reason for dismissal ...',

though it is worth noting that in that case the finding of a fair dismissal was upheld.

4.24 It is perhaps unsurprising, therefore, to find a similar measure of caution being derived from some of the case-law involving social media where 'breach of trust and confidence' and 'bringing the employer into disrepute' have been relied upon by the employer as the reason for the dismissal. For example, in *Witham v Club 24 Ltd trading as Ventura*[6] the employer dismissed the claimant after a series of comments she made on Facebook. The employer considered that the majority of these comments related to work and brought the company into disrepute. So far this is the archetypal 'harm' based case discussed above.

4.25 However, in *Witham* no evidence was adduced to show that the employer had actually undertaken any investigation into the 'disrepute' the employee's actions were said to have brought the employer into, or what, if any, damage had been occasioned to its relationship with one of its clients. The dismissal was held to be unfair (albeit with a finding of contributory conduct of 20%). Contrast this decision to the more recent decision in the *Laws* case, considered above.

4.26 By way of a further example, in *Taylor v Somerfield*[7] eight people had viewed a video of the claimant and other employees fighting with plastic bags at work. The plastic bags were clearly branded with the logo of the employer, the supermarket Somerfield. Three of those eight were the disciplinary panel. The tribunal found that there was not a genuine belief of a reputational risk to the company, and accordingly the dismissal was unfair. Had a policy been in place, which covered misuse as well as harm, the outcome might well have been different.

4.27 These decisions can be contrasted with that of *Preece v J D Wetherspoons plc*[8] where the dismissal was found to have been fair owing to a breach of an clearly disseminated policy that prohibited

> acts committed outside of work ... which have an adverse effect bearing on the employee's suitability for the job, which amounts to a serious breach of trust,

---

[5] [2012] ICR 1269.
[6] 1810462/2010.
[7] ETS/107487/07.
[8] 2104806/2010.

which affects employee or customer relations or which brings the company's name into disrepute .... Any conduct resulting in a fundamental breakdown in trust and confidence ... failure to comply with the Email, internet and intranet policy.

4.28   Further the employer had a policy expressly covering the use of Facebook that prohibited conduct that is 'found to lower the reputation of the organisation, staff or customers and/or contravene the company's equal opportunity policy'. The case here was both a 'misuse' type case and a harm one: the entire Facebook conversation the claimant engaged in took place during work time but it is not clear whether the technology used was provided by the employer or was privately owned by the claimant. In any event, there was also clear evidence of the impact the discussion had as the daughter of the person referred to in the Facebook discussion complained to Wetherspoons a short while after the conversation took place. Accordingly, owing to the policies and the evidence of harm, if the Facebook conversation had taken place outside of work hours the outcome would have likely been the same.

4.29   A similar point was made by the EAT in *Game Retail Ltd v Laws*[9] (considered in Chapter 2 above) where there was clear evidence of at least one member of staff – the manager who reported the offensive tweets – finding Mr Laws' postings to be inappropriate and so the findings of the tribunal that there was no evidence of any member of staff having access to the material were perverse. This case can be characterised as a case where there was a clear risk of harm, even if that harm was not in fact caused, as opposed to a pure 'misuse' case, but it is likewise clear from *Preece* that misuse in itself can justify dismissal.

Belief based on reasonable grounds which result from a reasonable investigation

4.30   Again, misuse-type cases are easier to defend here: every action online has a record somewhere, usually the laptop's cache or hard drive, the network's server or the recipient of the email/tweet, or the social media profile itself. The gathering and retention of this material is likely necessarily a reasonable step to take in an investigation, particularly if the employer is protected by an appropriate policy. The gathering of such information from private profiles may be more difficult to do surreptitiously, for reasons discussed above, and therefore an employer is likely to come into possession of such material following a complaint.

4.31   It is, again, the 'harm' cases where employers are more likely to become unstuck: in *Witham* there was no enquiry made of the customer whom the employer thought would take negatively to the comments by Ms Witham. Accordingly, there was not a reasonable investigation into the allegation of bringing the company into disrepute; indeed, the tribunal notes that it was 'entirely unreasonable' (para 33) for the employer to not have obtained this

---

[9]   EAT 0188/14.

information. Of course, this puts any employer in an invidious position: if they raise the matter with the customer then there is a risk that the customer's attention has been drawn to it, but if the employer does not then there is the risk that the customer will come across it later.

4.32 How, therefore, should the relevant parties approach disciplinary proceedings involving social media? The issue is, it seems to the authors, firstly one of precision in what is being alleged: is it misuse or is it harm? Harm will likely involve evidence that the employer has been, or could have been, damaged by the action of the employee. This is particularly important in social media cases. As will be seen, much of the case-law, and particularly that which has developed in sympathetic common law jurisdictions, considers not just the actual harm that has been caused, but the *potential* for that harm. There will be numerous cases where the employee is accused of misconduct only. Many of these cases will turn on the terms of the policy and the s 98(4) consideration. However, where harm has been caused, it is likely to be more reasonable for an employer absent a policy to take disciplinary or dismissal steps. Once the nature of the conduct has been established then the issue turns to one of clarity of charge: an employer must formulate the charge accurately and clearly. The characterisation of the charge will identify the evidence that is necessary to support the claim. If the employer cannot, or will not, seek out that material which may support its charges as part of the investigation processes it should expect little sympathy from a tribunal.

4.33 There is a further distinction that appears clear from the case-law considered above: conduct that actually brings the employer into disrepute (*Preece* being an example) and conduct that has not, but that could bring the employer into disrepute (such as *Somerfield*). The case-law in this regard is not entirely clear, and much will turn on the evidence before the tribunal of the decision that the employer takes. In *Lake v Amey Services Ltd Sheffield*[10] (noted above) the claimant succeed in his claim for unfair dismissal, but with a 30% reduction for contributory fault. After responding to an incident he took a photograph on his personal phone and posted it to his Facebook page, considering that a sign at the scene of the incident was ironic. The respondent was identified in the comments, but only once. The account was private and no employees had access. It was accepted that there was no evidence of actual prejudice to the employer's reputation or to the consequent health and safety investigation. The respondent's concern can be summarised as 'once they are out there, there is no controlling them', in reference to the post. The claimant conceded that there was the potential for a risk to reputation, but the respondent had no evidence to put forward that this had in fact occurred. The tribunal found that, if the respondent had intended to include in the definition of 'gross misconduct' within its disciplinary policy the prospect of jeopardising its reputation, as opposed to actually doing so, it should have said so. Whilst accepting that the social media policy envisaged both potential and actual harm, there was no real awareness amongst employees of the policy. There was

---

[10]   ET 1807678/2013.

sufficient evidence of potential harm, but it was not reasonable in those circumstances to dismiss for gross misconduct given the wording of the policy, requiring actual harm. Ignorance of the social media policy was also powerful mitigation for dismissal on the ground of a breach of it, and as such it is important that employers ensure that their employees are aware of polices and have training as appropriate.

4.34 A clear policy that sets out the effect of misuse regardless of harm will clearly assist an employer in establishing social media interactions that could cause harm, even if there is no evidence that they have in fact done so. Many cases will be self-evident, such as *Williams*, where there was a clear risk of a harassment claim or reputational damage, but if the employer is unable to demonstrate such considerations in its decision-making process it may find itself in a position where the decision taken is found not to have been within the band of reasonable responses.

Reasonable responses

4.35 Section 98(4) of the Employment Rights Act 1996 provides:

'(4) In any other case where the employer has fulfilled the requirements of subsection (1), the determination of the question whether the dismissal is fair or unfair (having regard to the reason shown by the employer) —

(a)   depends on whether in the circumstances (including the size and administrative resources of the employer's undertaking) the employer acted reasonably or unreasonably in treating it as a sufficient reason for dismissing the employee, and

(b)   shall be determined in accordance with equity and the substantial merits of the case.'

4.36 Where the employer has been able to show a genuine belief of guilt and the tribunal are satisfied that the belief was based on a reasonable investigation the focus of the tribunal will turn to whether the decision to dismiss was one that a reasonable employer could have taken in these circumstances. It is accepted that there are a range of such responses in any given situation ranging from a warning to dismissal all of which may be appropriate.[11] It is not the tribunal's role to impose such sanction as it would have thought appropriate were it the employer; rather, it must look at whether a reasonable employer could have arrived at the decision that this particular employer did. This is necessarily a factually dependent issue, but the ACAS Guide suggests employers should consider a number of factors. For situations involving social media the relevant factors identified by the Guide include: what are the rules of the organisation; the penalty in other cases; whether other employees' conduct is also worthy of censure, and the individual circumstances of the employee. These are in effect the factors applied by the tribunal in the *Lake* case, and demonstrate the need for a clear and well-disseminated policy.

---

[11]   *Trusthouse Forte (Catering) Ltd v Adonis* [1984] IRLR 382.

4.37 At the most general level, the more senior the employee or more prominent their role, will be highly relevant when assessing a harm-type case and the damage caused to the employer. Notably though in *Lake*, as in a number of other cases considered herein, the long service of the employee and in particular the fact that he had had no real time to consider the social media policy, as he was not made specifically aware of its terms, were deemed to be 'powerful mitigation'. The failure of the employer to ensure that the employee was aware of what was deemed to be misuse and what was deemed to be harmful in a social media context was important; as will be seen this will not always be the case, but will always be an important factor.

4.38 Equally, the nature of comments made by an accused employee, which are the subject of the disciplinary process, will be of key importance. The line that seems to be developing between the acceptable and unacceptable appears to be becoming focused at the point where a general grumble ends and something more develops; a line is crossed into inappropriate behaviour or more general harm. As considered previously, social media does not change the fact of the wrong; rather it provides, due to the medium, a potential wider audience to hear or read the complaint. Unlike direct vocal communication many social media platforms contain privacy settings that limit the scope of who can read the message. Putting aside the obvious risk that the tweet or post is retweeted or reposted, with the potential for re-retweeting and the exponential growth of the recipients, all of which will have bypassed the originator's privacy settings (and thus are relevant to potential harm), employment tribunals have been slow to accept that a belief in the private nature of the tweet or post (even if genuinely held) will provide an excuse to the misconduct. In *Preece* the fact the claimant understood her posts to be private, owing to her mistaken belief over her Facebook privacy settings, was irrelevant. The tribunal in *Celestine v Anchor Trust*[12] noted that whilst the claimant's privacy settings did prohibit the viewing of her posts by anyone other than her friends the risk posed by the forwarding of comments bypassed these settings. This factor was expressly identified by the tribunal in *Preece*. However this can be contrasted by the decision in *Smith*, considered above, and further below, and with the possible treatment of private emails and private or direct messages, which, where they are intended to be and remain private, may be treated differently. However, where such a message is brought to the attention of the employer, a balance between Art 8 privacy rights and the harm that has actually been caused is likely to be carried out in the context of the s 98(4) exercise.

4.39 As is clear from the above considerations, privacy and freedom of expression necessarily engage issues under the Human Rights Act 1998 and a conflict between the rights contained within the European Convention of Human Rights and the contract of employment. Whilst the Human Rights Act 1998, which introduces the Convention into the law of England and Wales, applies to public authorities, tribunals and courts have an obligation under s 3

---

[12] 2389755/2011.

to ensure that they give effect to those rights contained within the Convention on Human Rights. Accordingly, indirectly, private employers will need to ensure their actions are in accordance with those rights. The most applicable of these rights is the right to private and family life (Art 8) and freedom of expression (Art 10).

4.40 Article 8 states:

> Everyone has the right to respect for his private and family life, his home and his correspondence.

4.41 Article 10 states:

> Everyone has the right to freedom of expression. This right shall include the freedom to hold opinions and to receive and impart information and ideas without interference by public authority and regardless of frontiers.

4.42 Both Arts 8 and 10 are qualified rights, and thus can be interfered with if the 'protection of the rights and freedoms of others' is at stake whilst the right to freedom of expression (Art 10, Sch 1) can be interfered with for the 'protection of the reputation or rights of others', and to prevent the disclosure of information received in confidence. In both cases, any limits on the right must be 'necessary in a democratic society', which means they must be proportionate in the circumstances. Clearly, therefore, the courts and tribunals of England and Wales will be required in appropriate cases to carry out a necessary balancing act between the qualified human rights of employees against the harm caused or potentially caused to their employer, and the reasonableness of dismissal.

4.43 In *Smith v Trafford Housing Association*[13] the High Court (considering a claim for wrongful as opposed to unfair dismissal) found that postings on Facebook by S, a manager at THA, about gay marriage being 'an equality too far', did not justify a finding of gross misconduct and a demotion, as there was no reputational damage caused to the employer – harm had not been caused, despite what appears to have been clear misuse. The High Court, at para 66, went on to state that whilst an employer could restrict or prohibit the conduct of the employee at work, it would be 'prima-facie surprising' to find a restriction being upheld in a personal or social context. Here the Code of Conduct which prohibited the promotion of political and religious views was held not apply to personal social media usage. *Smith* will be considered in greater detail in a later chapter.

4.44 The *Smith* decision should be contrasted with *Crisp v Apple Retail (UK) Ltd*[14] where the tribunal expressly rejected the respondent employer's contentions that the very fact of posting an item on Facebook meant the matter was in the public domain for all purposes. The tribunal found the claimant's

---

[13] [2013] IRLR 86.
[14] 1500258/2011.

argument that his dismissal was in breach of Art 8 was ill founded. It noted that the 'nature of the internet generally is that comments by one person can very easily be forwarded on to others'. The tribunal noted, however, that this was not a case where the employer had hacked into an employee's Facebook account, where the employee would have had a reasonable expectation of privacy. The claimant's arguments that his conduct was an embodiment of his freedom of expression also failed: Apple's conduct in limiting that right was, the tribunal found, expressly and clearly aimed at protecting its reputation.

4.45 A conclusion similar to *Apple* was reached in *Preece* where the tribunal rejected the claimant's contention that her discussion on Facebook received the protection of Art 10 of the ECHR. The tribunal found that, as this is a qualified right, and the employer's actions were justified under Art 10(2) on the grounds of the reputational risk to the employer, the employer was able to satisfy Art 10(2). That said, in *Whitham v Club 24 Ltd*[15] (the dismissal of an employee for making derogatory comments about her employer on Facebook, but which were of a relatively minor nature, was not reasonable in the circumstances and the dismissal was therefore unfair.

4.46 It is telling that in both *Apple* and *Preece* the relevant polices expressly set out the concern of the employer to protect its reputation. However, it is generally likely that this limitation on Arts 8 and 10 is likely to only apply where a complaint has been received by an employer as opposed to an unsolicited trawl by an employer of its employee's social media profiles conducted for no good reason. It is expected that such a trawl would fall foul of Art 8, unless there is a very clear policy in place and clear justification for it, as considered in Chapters 2 and 3 above.

4.47 The case-law demonstrates that other relevant factors will include the seriousness of the comment, whether the employing organisation is identifiable, whether a connection would be made between the comment and the employing organisation (*Trafford Housing*), whether the comment is workplace related as opposed to merely being between work colleagues (*Trafford Housing*), how many people saw the post (*Taylor*), whether (and how many) complaints were made (*Game*).

Personal vs private posts: what is the difference?

4.48 The case-law considered in this book seeks to draw a distinction between the personal and the private. This is an understandable distinction, given the importance of Art 8 rights in our jurisprudence. However, as will become clear from an analysis of the case-law both from England and Wales and the Commonwealth jurisdictions, the position is not as clear as might otherwise be implied. An employee posting from an official work Twitter account is unlikely to be able to expect, let alone assert, a reasonable expectation of privacy. What though of the employee who sends a private tweet from their locked personal

---

[15]   Unreported, ET/1810462/10.

account, disparaging of their workplace? Or the employee who posts on their Facebook wall, confident in the knowledge that their privacy settings restrict viewing to their select group of authorised followers? Or the employee who, from their personal email account, in their own time, and using their own equipment, sends to a friend an email intended to be private, which if it became public would cause their employer significant harm? Such an email might contain sensitive information or a significant personal attack on a colleague. If that email later becomes public, or is drawn to the attention of the employer, is the fact that harm is caused sufficient to make a dismissal reasonable?

4.49 The answer to these questions is predictable: it depends. As will be seen later in this work, there are cases in which employees have argued that their posts were private, or were limited to a small, private audience. The courts and tribunals have however become more knowledgeable about the facilities of social media as the jurisprudence has developed; some cases stress the fact that the risk to an employer of a post being retweeted or replicated may be sufficient reason for a dismissal to be reasonable. There is no reported case of which the authors are aware relating to purely private emails becoming public in this jurisdiction, but the forwarding of racist emails as part of a chain mail certainly can give rise to a dismissal (*Gosden*, below). However, a senior employee becoming aware of disparaging private emails about him only after hacking into an account is unlikely to give rise to circumstances allowing a fair dismissal. Each case will depend on its particular facts and whether the decision of the employer was reasonable, but it is important not to assume that Art 8 rights will protect social media posts. Certainly where harm, or the risk of harm, is caused or threatened, it is unlikely that this will be the case. When considering pure misuse cases, much will depend on the terms of the policy and what has been communicated to the employee. If in doubt, ensure that a policy is in place.

Policies

4.50 The importance of having a policy was underlined in *Lerwill v Aston Villa*[16] where the claimant's dismissal for intemperate posts on an unofficial fan forum was held to be unfair as there was no policy, and therefore no forewarning that the consequences of his posts (denying the authorship of an article that was attributed to him in his role as the club's historian), would amount to misconduct. Even though the club had requested that the employee only post on websites when the post concerned the club's history, this exhortation was not enough to amount to a warning of future conduct and consequences for the purposes of disciplinary action. The tribunal accepted that the club held a genuine concern as to its reputation and that Mr Lerwill was known to be its employee; his views would be treated as synonymous with those of the club. However it also accepted that Mr Lerwill was unaware of

---

[16]   Unreported, ET/1304758/10.

this. This decision is consistent with other decisions considered above and makes clear that there a tribunal will look to the policy in place when determining what is reasonable.

4.51 *Bates v Cumbria County Council and another*[17] is an interesting contrasting case in which a dismissal of a teacher who had accessed a dating site during working hours was found to be unfair. The claimant, Mr Bates, was the head of Religious Studies at Dowdales School. He joined an internet dating site, and was reported by a colleague for using the site on his school laptop during lessons. The head teacher was concerned that it was inappropriate for Mr Bates to be a member of such a site, as it could bring the school into disrepute: his profile could be seen by anyone over the age of 18. Following a check of computer usage by the school's IT technician, Mr Bates was found to have accessed the dating site for a period of some 15 seconds during lessons. He accepted that he had done so during a class, when his students had been watching a video. He was duly subjected to an investigation. A number of the issues subject of the investigation were recommended by the school's HR officer to be without evidentiary foundation and should be dropped. However the school went ahead with all allegations in a disciplinary process. It is not clear how extensive the school's internet policy was, but it was noted that it had been relaxed as teachers had suggested that, for example, access to YouTube was useful as a teaching tool. The case put to Mr Bates was that there was a risk that the reputation of the school could be put at risk if his dating website profile was discovered by the media. The issues relating to inappropriate use of the internet were found to be made out, and upheld on appeal.

4.52 The tribunal found that the dismissal had been unfair. It was concerned in particular that disciplinary allegations had been pursued that had no factual basis and which the HR officer had advised against; and found that the emotive views of the head teacher as to the appropriateness of dating websites had coloured the view of the disciplinary panel. The real reason for the dismissal was not misconduct but rather the desire of the head teacher to 'get rid' of Mr Bates, together with the views of some of the panel that dating websites were 'seedy'. It did however reduce the damages to be awarded by 15% for contributory fault.

4.53 The case has a sting in the tail; post-dismissal, Mr Bates was convicted of common assault on a former pupil. The case went to the EAT on grounds relating to the relevance of this to the assessment of damages, but the appeal did not have relevance to the dismissal itself.

4.54 The extent of the school's social media or internet policy is not clear. However the case is a useful reminder that the tribunal will consider the real reason for dismissal. Here, it was the view of the head teacher in respect of Mr Bates. That said, a clear policy dealing with such internet usage would likely

---

[17] Unreported ET/2510893/09.

have made the dismissal fair, which underlines the importance of ensuring that employers spell out what is and is not acceptable at work.

4.55 In contrast, the case of *Birchall v Royal Birkdale Golf Club*[18] demonstrates that a policy will not be necessary in cases of obvious internet misconduct. The Employment Tribunal considered a dismissal for reason of excessive personal internet use during working hours. Mrs Birchall was the assistant secretary to the club. She did not get on with her line manager, the club's secretary. In June 2008 she was given a final written warning for leaving work early, and for having accepted free accommodation from a hotel in return for her recommending that hotel to club members. This was the first time that she was disciplined by her employer.

4.56 Mrs Birchall then got into trouble for excessive personal use of the internet. The club did not have a written internet policy, but its general disciplinary policy did list 'inappropriate use of the internet' as an example of gross misconduct. There had been concerns previously that some staff were using the internet inappropriately, but at no time was a written policy in this regard established, and, whilst the informal position of the club was that there was a disciplinary distinction between 'reasonable' and 'excessive' use, this was not made clear to the staff.

4.57 The Club Secretary, Mr Gilyeat, instituted in 2009 a policy of monitoring staff computer use, and tracking software was uploaded to staff computers in January that year. This followed concerns that kitchen staff had been accessing pornography through work computers. After investigations, Mrs Birchall was informed that her internet use for personal purposes was excessive, being some three and a half hours over the five days of the monitoring period. She was disciplined and dismissed. An appeal was unsuccessful.

4.58 The Employment Tribunal found the dismissal to be fair. It determined that the real reason for dismissal was the internet usage, and not the difficulties that Mrs Birchall had with Mr Gilyeat. It found that, whilst there was no clear policy as to the use of the internet for personal purposes during working hours, the usage of Mrs Birchall had gone beyond 'reasonable use' and that the policy was not so vague as to be unreliable. It noted that a written internet policy would have been preferable but, on the facts, the dismissal was within the range of reasonable responses.

4.59 *Birchall* demonstrates an application of the 'common-sense' approach, notwithstanding the absence of a dedicated policy, and fits within the analysis of the *Williams* case. The conduct was sufficient to allow dismissal, regardless of a specific and communicated policy. However the decision jars somewhat with other decisions relating to social media, where the absence of a policy has been determinative. The lesson to be taken from the case is that where the misconduct is blatant, a dismissal is more likely to be justified. However, a clear

---

[18]   ET/2104308/09.

policy will avoid uncertainty and will ensure in so far as is possible that the risk of a finding of unfair dismissal on the facts is minimised.

4.60 On the assumption that there is a policy in place, at a fundamental level the policy must actually cover the wrong that is complained of. Again, once the distinction between 'misuse' and 'harm' has been identified the scope of the required policy becomes clearer and it becomes necessarily easier for an employer to distil its views on social media usage into a written policy. Equally, the shortcomings of any existing policy are exposed.

4.61 Disciplinary action will be permissible in situations where there is misuse and/or harm. However, the risk that employers face is for claims to be presented to employment tribunals or issued in the civil courts for breaches of employment rights if the employer has not acted as it should have. Effective action against an errant employee is more likely to succeed if there is clear guidance provided in advance by the employer.

4.62 Prohibiting misuse will be easier and is likely to require linking of the IT policy to the existing policies such as the misconduct policy, whistleblowing policy and equal opportunities policy. Managing harm is more involved, and is likely to involve the drafting and implementation of new paragraphs into existing policies. It will also involve consideration of where the particular risk for the particular employer lies. Some 'misuse' and 'harms' will overlap and are probably more obvious (eg the publication of discriminatory material is likely to be objectionable on both bases). The result will likely be that it is self-evident that the policy must set out that the employer will not tolerate the dissemination of, for example, material that discriminates or is offensive under the Equality Act 2010. But the growing body of case-law regarding social media shows that not all employers are highlighting the risk of harm-based conduct to their employees.

4.63 Because an employer's ability to prohibit 'harm'-based conduct will extend beyond the workplace, clear and unequivocal guidance will need to be provided to the employee to ensure they are aware of the more wide-ranging impact of the policy in this regard.

4.64 As with all policies there is not a 'one-size-fits-all' answer to that question, as much depends on the ethos and approach to social media by the employer (as this may influence the regulation of 'misuse' type matters). Generally, however, the policy should aim to inform the employee of the risks faced by the employer and themselves of social media misuse. The policy should be explicit on its application: both as to the platforms it covers as well as its impact on the employee's conduct outside of work. The policy in the case of *Celestine* contained clear indications:

> '... you must remember that customers, colleagues and management often have access to the on-line content if posted on sites such as Facebook ...

It is essential that employees using these sites realise any descriptions of themselves etc will be accessed by other people. These people may include other Anchor employees, customers, families or suppliers, comments and entries made on these sites have the potential to cause offence or concern. Finally, before you post something onto your site you should consider who will see what you write and the repercussions of publishing something inappropriate or that brings Anchor into disrepute will mean for you. This means publishing images, opinion, information that can be seen by more than friends and family and information originally intended just for friends and family can be forwarded on. If you are ever in doubt as to whether your comments will cause offence it is better not to post it.'

4.65 Obvious points to cover include the prohibition on dissemination of offensive material and the risk this poses to the employee for both criminal prosecution as well as internal disciplinary action.

4.66 The policy should make it clear that misuse of the system, even where there is no harm, may amount to misconduct and could give rise to performance-related issues. If usage is permitted but on a limited basis this should be explained. For instance, is it limited to during lunch breaks only or is it totally unlimited, subject to performance levels being maintained? If restrictions are to be placed on personal use then these should be spelt out in unambiguous terms: eg 'before 0900', 'after 1700', as opposed to undefined or subjective terminology that is open to different interpretations: 'outside core hours' or 'when not busy'.

4.67 The consequences of an outright ban should also be considered: not only does it not affect the out-of-hours posting, but also it is naïve to think that members of staff would not be tempted to tweet/post using their own mobile technology. Indeed, one question a court would ask is whether any such tweeting during work amounts to misconduct, let alone gross misconduct: simply because a disciplinary policy sets out often laudable aims it does not automatically mean that any potential breach of those aims can justify dismissal in every situation.

4.68 A useful contrast to *Williams* in the context of social media misconduct in sport, and which highlights the need for a court to consider carefully the culpability of a party, is *Mason v Huddersfield Giants*.[19] HHJ Saffman, sitting as a Judge of the High Court, considered a claim for wrongful dismissal by the claimant, Keith Mason. Mr Mason was a rugby league prop forward and had been under contract with Huddersfield until his dismissal for gross misconduct. After losing the final game of the season, Mr Mason undertook a significant drinking session, or, as the judge termed it, a 'communal bender', on what was known as 'Mad Monday'. A team-mate, Scott Moore, used the claimant's phone (unbeknownst to him) to take a picture of his anus. Mr Mason was subsequently informed of this by his friends.

---

[19] [2013] EWHC 2869 (QB).

4.69 Mr Mason returned home on Tuesday and had a bath. His girlfriend looked through his phone and found the photograph. She was informed by Mr Mason what it was, and took it upon herself without his knowledge to send it attached to a Tweet from his telephone. The tweet was addressed to @alleycat21, the Twitter handle of Mr Moore. The judge noted 'The effect of that, and I understand this to be common ground between the parties, is that it would have been seen by all the claimant's Twitter followers of which there are about 4,200 provided that they cared to access it'. As a matter of fact, this statement on its own is not necessarily correct. If the message was sent with Mr Moore's handle preceding the message, it would have been seen in their timeline only by those followers that Mr Mason and Mr Moore had in common, though it would have been available to be accessed by all of Mr Mason's followers. It is not clear from the judgment whether Mr Moore's handle did so precede the text of the tweet.

4.70 The tweet was subsequently deleted on Thursday, when, according to him, Mr Mason had sobered up. The defendant contended that it was deleted only after the intervention of Mr Mason's agent. This was however too late, as one of the club's sponsors had contacted the chief executive of the defendant on Tuesday evening and subsequently put his complaint in writing. Others, including the club's main sponsor, also complained.

4.71 After a disciplinary process, Mr Mason was dismissed. The club accepted that he had not taken the photograph; nor had he posted it. However:

> You were aware of the photo being on your account for a considerable period for time. Given that you have over 4000 followers you must have been aware that the image would have been viewed by a considerable number of people and of the effect it would have on the reputation of the club. The fact that you did eventually delete it is evidence that you aware that the image was both offensive and completely inappropriate. During the hearing you accepted that your profile made you a role model for the club and you understood the impact that the presence of such an image on your Twitter feed could have on the club. You also acknowledged that you had attended a social media presentation before the start of the season which stipulated how players use social media.

4.72 The judge considered the profile of Mr Mason, and the fact that, whilst his account was a personal account, it identified him as a Giants player. His profile was such that 'the claimant's Twitter account is inextricably linked to him in his role as a high profile player for the club evidenced by the fact that he had 4,200 followers and the claimant himself recognises that most were rugby, and in particular Giants, fans'. The judge went on to state:

> 'I am told but have not been shown any evidence that there is, in fact, a biography on his Twitter account describing the claimant as a Giants rugby player. That does not appear on any of the tweets that I have been referred to and there is no evidence that it appears on every tweet he sends. The evidence is however, that the club took advantage of those players who subscribed to Twitter by ensuring that they tweeted information about the club to their followers. Accordingly say the defendants a disreputable tweet brings the club into disrepute.'

4.73 The judge did not agree, and found that the dismissal was in fact wrongful. He relied upon the dictum of Lord Evershed, the Master of the Rolls, in *Laws v London Chronicle*:[20]

> 'The question must be whether the conduct complained of is such as to show the servant to have disregarded the essential conditions of the contract of service. One act of disobedience or conduct can justify dismissal only if it is of a nature which goes to show that the servant has repudiated the contract or one of its essential conditions and, for that reason therefore, I think what one finds in the passages which I have read that the disobedience must at least have a quality that it is wilful. In other words it connotes a deliberate flouting of the essential contractual terms.'

4.74 The judge concluded that the event could not be seen as a deliberate flouting of contractual obligations, or a flouting of essential contractual obligations. At best the claimant could have been said to have omitted to do something – remove the tweet, which he had not posted, including a photograph he had not taken, promptly. Importantly, he also held:

> '123. Furthermore and in any event I am not convinced that this tweet can be seen as being inextricably linked to the club. I accept, albeit that I have heard no real evidence of it, that the majority of the claimant's followers are Giants fans. I even accept that somewhere on his tweet account there is his biography in which he is described as a Giants player but I think it is very unlikely that any fan seeing this tweet and, assuming that they recognise it for what it is would assume that this tweet is condoned by the club. It seems to me that even the complainants who wrote in do not think that. None of them has complained about the club's conduct but rather they complain about Keith Mason's conduct. They themselves have drawn a distinction between the club and the individual.
>
> ....
>
> 125. It is also worth pointing out that this is the claimant's own Twitter account not a club Twitter account and he tended to use it for general social communications independent of his employment as well as tweeting the club's events or matters which may be of interest to Giants' fans.'

4.75 This decision appears initially to jar with the thrust of the other authorities referred to herein. The question of culpability however runs strongly through the *Mason* decision. Mason did not take the photograph. He did not send the tweet. He deleted the tweet 2 days later. The reputational damage from complaints appeared to be directed towards him, rather than the club. It also appears that, although social media training had been provided, the relevant misconduct policy was generic:

> 'You agree with the club that...
>
> ...

---

[20]   [1959] All ER 285.

(e) You acknowledge and agree that to preserve the good name and reputation of the club and the league that your conduct both on and off the field must be of the highest standard and that you must conduct yourself at all times both on and off the field in a manner which will uphold the good reputation of the club and the league and not bring the club or league into disrepute. And that if you breach this clause the club may take action against you independent of any action that the league may take against you under the regulations. If your conduct is such that, in the reasonable opinion of the club, the reputation of either the club or the league is or is likely to be harmed this could amount to gross misconduct which may lead to summary termination.'

Had the policy, for example, included a clause requiring the prompt deletion of any offensive social media posts immediately, the outcome might well have been different. Had Mr Mason posted the tweet, likewise, the outcome might have been different. The contrast between *Mason* and *Williams* though appears principally to be the deliberate action of the latter, as opposed to the omission of the former.

4.76　Other examples of the application of the reasonable responses test in a social media context include *Young v Argos Ltd*.[21] Ms Young was dismissed after she liked a comment referring to her manager as 'as much use as a chocolate teapot' and commented on her former colleague's escape. The dismissal was found to be unfair as it was outside the band of reasonable responses to dismiss as gross misconduct. The tribunal found that the 'liking' of the comment was no more than office gossip. A similar conclusion was reached by the Employment Tribunal in *Grant and Woods v Mitie Property Services (UK) Ltd*[22] where a decision to dismiss was outside the band of reasonable responses as, even though the misconduct in question was listed as a form of gross misconduct in the disciplinary policy, it did not mean that any listed transgression automatically meant that dismissal would follow. In *Mason v CXC Advantage Ltd*,[23] an email exchange with a client was suggested by the latter to be continued on personal email, which Ms Mason (no relation) provided. The client's managing director commented to the employer that the emails were getting 'pretty saucy'. As a result the employer asked for copies of the email. The client company refused, and the relationship broke down. Following disciplinary proceedings, in which Ms Mason was accused of bringing the reputation of CXC into disrepute, she was dismissed. Ms Mason brought tribunal proceedings and produced the emails, which were not in fact 'saucy'. However, notwithstanding the view of the tribunal that dismissal was 'harsh', the decision was upheld as being fair, as a genuine belief that inappropriate behaviour had taken place was attributed to the employer.

4.77　It is also important that employers do not jump to conclusions or make swift decisions without a proper investigation, simply because pressure is being brought to bear on them by customers or social media users more widely. In

---

[21]　(2011).
[22]　S/113536/08.
[23]　(unreported) ET/2203930/2013.

Mason it is clear from the judgment that the court considered that the process had been conducted with significant haste at least in part because of the complaints from sponsors. The 'twitterstorm' that ensued after the Nobel Prize winner Sir Tim Hunt made ill-advised comments appears to have prompted a manager from UCL to telephone his wife (also a scientist at the university) to tell him to resign or be sacked. The news story is still developing at the time of writing, but it appears that significant doubt is now cast on the accuracy of the initial reports which led to the furore. An employer who acts in haste to 'protect' their reputation risks a further backlash (as UCL has found) as well as the risk of a claim for constructive unfair dismissal in appropriate circumstances. Whilst there is an understandable desire for employers to move quickly to prevent a situation from causing significant reputational damage, the reality of social media is that what appears to be significant public outrage may in fact be the magnified views of a small grouping, who should not be entitled to dictate the disciplinary processes of the organisations upon which they choose to turn their fire.

4.78 A social media policy therefore needs to be actively and consistently policed and kept up to date, even more so with respect to an IT policy given the pace of technological advance. Further, it needs effectively to cross-refer to other policies the employer has in place, most notably the equal opportunities and disciplinary polices.

4.79 That said, clear and appropriate restrictions should be identified and incorporated into policies. These may reference confidential information, prohibitions on using other parties' intellectual property, and contain the more obvious restrictions on discrimination and defamation. A useful catch-all is to state that if the employee has any doubt they should ask! Note for instance the last sentence of the policy in *Celestine*:

> 'Whatever the ethos of the employer the policy should make it clear that material on the employer's computer system is owned by the employer and remains the employer's.'

4.80 A common failing of employers is to think that a policy alone is sufficient to protect them from risk: it is not. Adequate training is as important as the provision of the policy. The aim of training should be to highlight the risks faced by the employees (both criminal and in terms of their job security), to underline the standards of behaviour expected by employers (both at work and when away from work) and to ensure that the employee is aware of this.

4.81 Such training should take place on induction into the work force and should be evidenced by acknowledgment slips signed by the employee upon their commencing employment or attendance logs for training courses. A more tech-savvy method of ensuring the highlighting of the policy and its effect is to require employees to tick a box on a log-in screen indicating they understand that their conduct online is governed by the relevant disciplinary policies.

4.82 The employer will also be required to ensure associated training is carried out and awareness of the policy is highlighted, even more so as to ensure employees are aware of this interference with the employee's extra-curricular activities over social media.

4.83 Equally important is to ensure that employees who know that misuse is occurring or harm is being inflicted to the employer feel they can come forward to raise this. Express reference to the whistleblowing policy is encouraged.

Social media: how it can work

4.84 Social media will be of significant importance to many employers. According to a 2014 Ofcom report:

> Two-thirds (66%) of online adults say they have a current social networking site profile, unchanged since 2012 (64%). Nearly all with a current profile (96%) have one on Facebook, although the incidence of having only a Facebook profile has fallen to 43% in 2013 compared to 53% in 2012. Three in ten social networkers say they have a Twitter profile, and one in five say they have a YouTube (22%) or WhatsApp profile (20%). Social networking overall remains a popular pastime, with 60% of users visiting sites more than once a day, an increase from 50% in 2012, and with 83% of 16-24s doing so (69% in 2012).
>
> Twitter users are the most likely to say they follow friends (72%) and then celebrities (45%) and news (also 45%), followed by hobbies and interests (33%). On average, Twitter users say they follow 146 people or organisations, and have 97 followers.

4.85 As a result, companies and other employers are increasingly tapping into social media and establishing their own profiles. Employers need these profiles to be maintained, serviced and proliferated. Employers as a result are dependent on such employees far more than previously; even HR or communications departments used to dealing with the daily news cycle are often no match for the instantaneous effects of social media.

4.86 Companies and employers can deploy social media successfully and without problem. Many do. But when it goes wrong, the results for the company in terms of reputational damage can be significant. Whilst the existence of a social media policy will not prevent a disgruntled employee going rogue, it is at least likely to ensure that that employee can be dismissed fairly, and that the organisation can be vindicated in any tribunal hearing that ensues. There is little worse for the reputation of a company to be embarrassed firstly by a series of inappropriate tweets and then again by that employee winning a claim of unfair dismissal. The considerations set out above are designed to assist organisations in their planning, as far as is possible, for when social media goes wrong.

Conclusion

4.87 As will have been seen from the past four chapters, it is of critical importance that employers have carefully considered and tailored policies in place wherever social media or internet usage is envisaged. This is of particular importance where an employer intends to make use of information gathered from social media or internet usage for the purpose of pre-employment vetting or disciplinary procedures. The case-law in this area continues to develop and, whilst the EAT has made clear that it does not see a need to develop specific guidance in social media cases, it is clear that the factual matrix arising from such cases when applied to the range of reasonable responses test will in many cases turn on the extent to which behaviour is circumscribed by policies of which employees are made aware. There is also an apparent jurisprudential distinction between the treatment by the High Court of the facts in *Smith*, and other cases where personal use of social media has nevertheless led to dismissal. Some situations will be common sense, such as in *Williams*; others will be more nuanced, as in *Mason*. The starting point to any disciplinary process is to consider the policy in place and the potential for harm. Where harm can be shown, particularly where there is culpability, disciplinary sanctions or dismissal are more likely to be found to be reasonable. Even without culpability, a clear and detailed policy may well make a dismissal reasonable.

4.88 Employers should also beware the 'casual' Google search of a potential employee, particularly if the same could be said to be discriminatory in the course of a recruitment process. Again, it is important to put in place a policy and to apply that policy across the board. Employers otherwise risk potential litigation not just under the Equality Act 2010, but also in respect of the various data protection regimes.

Do	Don't
Have a specific social media policy, which is kept up to date	Simply use a cut and paste template without tailoring its terms to the specific workplace
Ensure that employees are aware of the policy and its terms	Assume that an employee will be held to terms that they may not have seen, particularly in 'borderline' cases
Consult on the implementation of the policy, and as appropriate provide training	Simply impose a policy
Take advice on the policy	Rely on the work experience lad to define 'social media'

Do	Don't
Carry out a thorough investigation on an open basis	Create a profile on social media for the sole purpose of connecting with an employee
Consider the effect of the misconduct: what harm has been caused, to the company and to other employees	Assume that any misuse of social media will make a dismissal a reasonable response
Consider the context of the misconduct when considering harm as above.	Assume that private use will never give rise to misconduct issues. Consider the context when determining whether misconduct and harm have occurred
Consider the extent of the harm caused and whether a proposed sanction in the circumstances is reasonable	Abrogate a decision on the circumstances to the wording of the policy
Take time to follow a fair process	Jump to conclusions based on perceived reputational damage

4.89 The next section of this book will go on to consider other applications of social media and the internet in the field of employment law and explore additional potential areas of liability, together with steps that employers can take in order to minimise any such liability. Many of the aspects discussed both above and below are contained within the draft policies in Chapter 13 of this work, which also includes flowcharts suggesting the courses of action that employers should take.

CHAPTER 5

WHISTLEBLOWING AND REGULATORY ISSUES

WHISTLEBLOWING

5.01 'Whistleblowing' is an important concept in employment law. The protections afforded to those who make protected disclosures (a defined by statute and considered in more detail below) in the public interest are quite rightly recognised as necessary and important. Once again, however, the permeation of social media throughout the traditional workplace gives rise to problems, potential claims and potential liability to an employer. This section will consider whistleblowing and related issues in the context of social media and identify the problems that can be caused for employers by the actions of their employees relating to whistleblowing. This work is not the place for a detailed exposition of the history of whistleblowing law, and a basic knowledge of the concepts is assumed. Essentially, a whistleblower is an employee or worker who makes a disclosure falling within the categories of protected disclosures in respect of certain information, in the public interest.

5.02 A person who makes a protected disclosure obtains the right not to suffer a detriment in employment.[1] That right applies not just to employees, but also to workers. The category of individuals who can potentially bring a claim for a detriment is therefore extremely wide, as it is not solely limited to those persons traditionally considered to be employed. Section 230 of the ERA 1996 sets out definitions of employee, contract of employment and worker as follows:

> (1) In this Act 'employee' means an individual who has entered into or works under (or, where the employment has ceased, worked under) a contract of employment.
>
> (2) In this Act 'contract of employment' means a contract of service or apprenticeship, whether express or implied, and (if it is express) whether oral or in writing.
>
> (3) In this Act 'worker' (except in the phrases 'shop worker' and 'betting worker') means an individual who has entered into or works under (or, where the employment has ceased, worked under)—
>
> (a)   a contract of employment, or

---

[1]   Employment Rights Act 1996, s 47B.

(b)   any other contract, whether express or implied and (if it is express) whether oral or in writing, whereby the individual undertakes to do or perform personally any work or services for another party to the contract whose status is not by virtue of the contract that of a client or customer of any profession or business undertaking carried on by the individual;

and any reference to a worker's contract shall be construed accordingly.

5.03 'Employment' is likewise defined for the purposes of the Equality Act 2010 as being 'employment under a contract of employment a contract of apprenticeship or a contract personally to do work'.[2] Both are clearly wide definitions. Contracts of employment are also sometimes referred to in older case-law as 'contracts of service'. This should be contrasted with 'contracts for services', which tends to relate to contractual agreements with self-employed providers of services. Self-employed providers will not have the protections afforded by the whistleblowing provisions, but there will often be a debate as to the status of the whistleblower – employee, worker, or self-employed. Only the first two categories will qualify for protection. The self-employed contactor, workers and employees will all have the benefit of the discrimination provisions (including harassment) considered elsewhere in this work, and the former may well also be able to rely on the principles of vicarious liability in terms of the PfHA 1997. Likewise, as will be seen later in this section as a result of the reversal of the *Fecitt* decision, the same approach is now taken in respect of victimisation as a result of the whistleblowing provisions by fellow employees, which is likewise unlawful and as a result can give rise to vicarious liability. Only employees will have the benefit of the protections afforded by the Employment Rights Act 1996 in respect of unfair dismissal, which may be a relevant factor when considering the ending of a working relationship following social media-related misconduct.

5.04 In order to establish that a person is an employee, the starting point is that there is a contractual relationship between them. Once this has been established, it is necessary to consider the basis of that contract. Establishing a contractual relationship should not in the ordinary course of events be a difficult task. An employer should have provided a contract of employment containing the various matters required by the Employment Rights Act 1996. In such circumstances it is unlikely that any dispute as to status will arise. However it is in those cases where there is no written contract, or a written contract that purports to establish a relationship different to the standard employer-employee model that difficulties may arise. Smaller employers, who may be more lax in their compliance, or those companies that have a large turnover of staff, should be particularly aware of the need to be clear as to the status of an 'employee', as the rights afforded to that individual will vary wildly dependent upon their true status. However for the purposes of the tortious social media liabilities considered in this work, it is likely that many of the provisions considered will in any event apply. Where the distinction may be

---

2   EqA 2010 s 83(2)(a).

highly material is when considering the risk of an unfair dismissal claim arising out of the application of a social media policy.

5.05 A problem may particularly arise in relation to agency temporary workers. In such circumstances, there is likely to be a contract between the agency and the worker, and the agency and the employer, but probably not between the worker and the employer. In such circumstances, who employs the 'employee'? If there is no contractual relationship between them, the worker cannot be an employee of the client: *Hewlett Packard Ltd v O'Murphy*,[3] and as such no employment rights arise. Successive tribunals have attempted to subvert this position. In certain circumstances, therefore, a contractual relationship can be implied through conduct, where it is necessary to do so: *James v Greenwich Borough Council*.[4] It is almost exclusively the case that in order to imply such a relationship identifiable words or conduct displacing the original agency contract need to be shown. As noted below, the Supreme Court in *Autoclenz Ltd v Belcher*[5] made clear that the question to be considered is the true agreement between the parties, with consideration to be given to the conduct of the parties to evidence this, together with inequality of the parties' bargaining power. Whilst tribunals are often keen to try to imply such a contract, the circumstances in which this test can be satisfied are relatively rare; however, employers should be careful in the language they use to agency workers or contractors to avoid this happening. It should be noted in any event, however, that an agency worker, even one who is supplied on a temporary basis and paid by the agency rather than the 'employer' who would properly be regarded as a user of his services, may still render the 'employer' liable for his actions by way of vicarious liability: *Mersey Docks and Harbour Board v Coggins and Griffiths (Liverpool) Ltd.*[6] The 'employer' may also be liable to the agency worker for any claims, such as under the PfHA 1997.

5.06 In any event the Agency Worker Regulations 2010[7] provide certain protections for agency workers by entitling them to equal treatment with comparable permanent workers after 12 weeks of employment. However, to qualify for unfair dismissal protection, agency workers will need to demonstrate that they have the status of employee.

5.07 Assuming a contractual relationship has been established, the next step is to determine the nature of that contract to determine the status of the worker. It has long been settled that the three irreducible elements of an employment contract are: (a) personal service; (b) mutuality of obligation; and (c) sufficient control.[8] Without one of these elements, the contract is not a contract of employment. However, the converse is not true; the presence of all three does

---

[3] [2002] IRLR 4.
[4] [2008] EWCA Civ 35.
[5] [2011] UKSC 41.
[6] [1947] AC 1.
[7] SI 2010/93 (in force from 1 October 2011).
[8] *Ready Mixed Concrete (South East) Ltd v Minister for Pensions and National Insurance* [1968] 2 QB 497.

not necessarily mean that the contract is one of employment. This depends on all of the other circumstances of the case. As already noted, the status of the 'employee' may be highly relevant when considering what potential statutory provisions will apply.

5.08 The obligation to provide work personally has been considered in some detail by the appellate courts. A provision in a contract that allowed the contractor to send a substitute where the worker was unable or unwilling to carry out the work themselves was incompatible with a contract of employment: *Express and Echo Publications Ltd v Tanton*;[9] however where the worker merely could not, as opposed to could not and/or did not want, to do the work, the personal service obligation will be satisfied: *James v Redcats (Brands) Ltd*.[10] A limited power to delegate also does not necessarily mean that the contract is not a contract of employment: *MacFarlane v Glasgow City Council*;[11] which defined the replacement clause in *Tanton* as being an extreme type of clause. In later cases the EAT has confirmed that, if there is clear express contractual terminology that does not impose personal obligations (so that, for example, a substitute can be sent), that term will be upheld unless it is a sham or there has been a variation: *Staffordshire Sentinel Newspapers Ltd v Potter*.[12] What is a sham has also been considered. In *Consistent Group Ltd v Kalwak*[13] the Court of Appeal held that to find a sham required a finding that both parties intended to paint a false picture as to the nature of their relationship. However in *Redrow Homes (Yorkshire) Ltd v Buckborough & Sewell*[14] the EAT contended that a sham could be found where both parties did not intend for the term to apply. In *Protectacoat Firthglow Ltd v Szilagyi*,[15] the Court of Appeal confirmed that there was no need for an intention to deceive a third party, and it was for the court to determine the true nature of the relationship, both at the time of the contract and as time goes by. Finally, in *Autoclenz v Belcher*,[16] the Supreme Court held that it was the reality of the arrangements between the parties, rather than the strict written terms of the contract, that mattered when determining the true nature of the parties' relationship. This illustrates a sensible move away from a focus on contractual terminology and formalities towards a consideration of what the parties' actual intentions are.

5.09 An example from the authors' own experience of such cases concerned a large number (around 23) of supposedly self-employed drivers of lorries transporting concrete. The contracts were ostensibly contracts for services; the drivers owned their own vehicles through hire-purchase agreements, and could, according to their contracts, send a replacement if they were unable to work shifts. However the requirements as to vetting for replacement drivers were

---

9   [1999] IRLR 267.
10 [2007] IRLR 296.
11 [2001] IRLR 7.
12 [2004] IRLR 752.
13 [2008] EWCA Civ 430.
14 [2009] IRLR 34.
15 [2009] EWCA Civ 98.
16 [2011] UKSC 11.

highly onerous and the replacement provisions were rarely relied upon. The Employment Tribunal concluded that they were employees. The result of this finding was a liability by the employer that cumulatively amounted to over £2m.

5.10   Mutuality of obligation requires that both parties have legal obligations towards each other for the duration of the contract. The Court of Appeal decision in *Quashie v Stringfellow Restaurants Ltd*,[17] that a lap-dancer was not an employee, as there was no contractual obligation on the club to pay her (as a result of the agreement that she had entered into) meant that there was no contract of employment, overturning the decision of the EAT.

5.11   The third element – control – is again a question of fact and degree. There must be control for there to be a contract of employment; but what amounts to sufficient control will depend on the circumstances of each case. These may include the status of the worker in the organisation; who provides the equipment and any subordinates; and many other potential factors.

5.12   Many workers engaged on what are at first glance contracts for services (ie the ostensibly self-employed) may in fact be held to be an employee upon an application to a tribunal. Given the rise in the use of peripatetic 'contractors' amongst many organisations, this gives rise to potential danger. A contractor may bring a claim seeking to contend that they were in fact an employee. This may then lead on to the establishment of employment rights which then results in a costly compensation bill. Employers must take care to treat contractors as such, and to resist the temptation to treat them as any other employee. This is particularly important when considering the various risks to employers referenced elsewhere within this work. A person treated as being self-employed (or as a worker) may be found to be an employee, thus giving rise both to potential employment remedies where, for example, workplace harassment has been alleged, or to vicarious liability for their actions, even in their own time, and even when considered to be self-employed. It is essential that employers ensure that their social media and other policies are provided to anyone working for or with them, and that appropriate training is provided even to apparently self-employed practitioners, so that in the event that they are ultimately found to be employees in the course of any claim, they are not able to claim ignorance of any policy, particularly one pertaining to reputation, in any unfair or wrongful dismissal claim. In any event, it is likely to be sensible for any employer to seek to bind their contractors and workers to the same terms, conditions and policies as their employees, due to the risk of inappropriate social media behaviour by such contractors. It will also be sensible to ensure, as with employees, that contractors likewise surrender any social media accounts that they have built during the scope of their contract.

5.13   A dismissal of an employee where the reason or, if more than one reason, the principal reason for the dismissal is a protected disclosure is automatically

---

[17]   [2012] EWCA Civ 1735.

unfair and there is no two-year (or other) period before an employee qualifies for such rights. Further the termination of a worker's contract (though not the termination of the contract of a self-employed contractor) on grounds of the protected disclosure is an act of detriment. The status of a person providing services to an employer is therefore of significant importance, particularly in a social media context, as will be seen below.

5.14 When considering a claim arising out of a whistleblowing complaint, it is important to bear in mind that not just any disclosure will qualify as being potentially a protected disclosure. A qualifying disclosure[18] is information that, in the reasonable belief of the disclosing worker, falls into one of the following categories:

- a criminal offence has been, is being or is likely to be committed;
- a person has failed, is failing or is likely to fail to comply with a legal obligation to which he is subject;
- a miscarriage of justice has occurred, is occurring or is likely to occur;
- an individual's health and safety has been, is being or is likely to be endangered;
- the environment has been, is being or is likely to be damaged; or
- information tending to show one of the above has been, is being or is likely to be concealed deliberately.

5.15 Disclosures that relate to matters that amount to a criminal offence in so disclosing, or a breach of legal professional privilege are not qualifying disclosures.[19] The provisions of the Protected Interest Disclosure Act 1998 also do not apply to employment in the Security Service, the SIS or GCHQ, nor to police officers.

5.16 There is a distinction between communicating 'information' and 'making allegations' that do not convey facts. The latter are not protected: *Geduld v Cavendish Munro Professional Risks Management Ltd.*[20] In that case Slade J contrasted the examples of 'health and safety requirements are not being complied with in this hospital', which was not protected, with 'the wards have not been cleaned for two weeks and sharps have been left lying around', which was. There must therefore be a specific factual basis underpinning the disclosure – a mere assertion is not enough. Since the recent amendments to the law it is also necessary for the disclosure to qualify that (1) the discloser believes the information meets the requirements of ERA 1996, s 43B (as outlined above); (2) that that belief is objectively reasonable; and (3) that the disclosure is made in the public interest.

---

[18] ERA 1996 s 43B.
[19] ERA 1995 s 43B(3), (4).
[20] [2010] ICR 325.

5.17 A recent EAT case has given guidance on what is meant by a 'reasonable belief', particularly in the context of what 'objectively reasonable' means. In *Korashi v Abertawe Bro Morgannwg University Local Health Board*,[21] the EAT determined that consideration had to be given to the circumstances of the discloser, and whether that discloser was reasonable to believe that the disclosure met the requirements of s 43B. This familiar subjective gloss on the objectivity test is not unusual and it is respectfully submitted, is a correct and sensible clarification.

5.18 In order for a qualifying disclosure to become a protected disclosure, it must be made to one of the specified categories of persons set out in ERA 1996, s 43C–H. These are:

(a)   the worker's employer;

(b)   a legal adviser in the course of obtaining legal advice;

(c)   to a Minister of the Crown where the employer is appointed under any enactment by a Minister of the Crown;

(d)   a person prescribed in the Public Interest Disclosure (Prescribed Persons) Order 1999[22] (see www.direct.gov.ul/en/employment for a list, effectively of regulators);

(e)   other persons, where in good faith, with a reasonable belief that the information is substantially true, not for personal gain, and it is reasonable to make the disclosure; in circumstances where the discloser reasonably believes that by making a disclosure to any of (a) to (d) above he will suffer a detriment; or there is no prescribed person and there is a reasonable belief that evidence will be concealed or destroyed if disclosure is made to the employer; or a substantially similar disclosure has previously been made to one of the above;

(f)   to any other person in relation to 'exceptionally serious failures'.

5.19 Suffering a detriment as a result of a disclosure results in the right to bring a claim to the Employment Tribunal. For a detriment short of dismissal, an award for injury to feelings will follow the *Vento* guidelines. In *Commissioner of Police for the Metropolis v Shaw*[23] an award of aggravated damages as a subheading to a primary injury to feelings award was endorsed. This is particularly relevant in a social media context. A whistleblower who can establish that they have made a protected disclosure will often complain that they are shunned by fellow employees, particularly where complaint has been made over social media postings. The ostracising of a whistleblowing employee, coupled with pointed tweets, removal from friends or follower lists and an internet impression that the workplace has turned against the whistleblower could in theory amount to an actionable detriment giving rise to liability for the

---

[21]   [2012] IRLR 4.
[22]   SI 1999/401.
[23]   [2012] IRLR 291.

employer. However, as will be seen below, there may be significant difficulties with such an approach to a tribunal by a whistleblowing employee.

5.20   That said, and analogous to the *McKie* decision considered elsewhere in this work, vitriolic or detrimental tweets or other social media posts after an employee has left having blown the whistle might lead to liability. In *Onyango v Berkley (t/a Berkley Solicitors)*,[24] the EAT considered the position where the protected disclosure relied upon was made after the termination of employment, by reference to earlier case-law. Thus, in *Fadipe v Reed Nursing Personnel*,[25] the Court of Appeal had held that post-employment victimisation (in the context of health and safety ERA cases) was not protected. However in *Woodward v Abbey National plc*[26] the line of authority upon which *Fadipe* was decided was not followed. As a result the EAT in *Onyango* held that as a matter of pure construction of the statute, post-termination disclosures and resulting detriments can be relied upon to complete the statutory tort. This is a point worth noting as it may apply to, for example, unfavourable references made following a protected disclosure (in *Onyango*, a letter before claim leading to allegations against him of forgery and dishonesty and a subsequent SRA claim – the EAT did not deal with the factual basis of this claim), or castigation and opprobrium by erstwhile colleagues, where these can directly be attributed to the employer. Social media presents a forum on which employees can vent their feelings and express their views about departed employees. This may particularly be the case where they have been named in, or involved in some way, in the behaviour that led to the whistleblowing in the first case. Mocking, character assassination, exculpatory or justificatory social media posts might well be considered to be a detriment post-dismissal, particularly dependent upon the forum to which such posts are made, and the extent to which they are publicised. Employees will often be connected to their opposite numbers in rival firms. An inappropriate or ill-advised post could scupper the employment prospects of the whistleblowing ex-employee, particularly if the new prospective employer has a social media vetting policy pre-appointment, and could as a result give rise to a significant claim against her ex-employer under the *McKie* doctrine considered elsewhere.

5.21   Having established the potential risks to employers arising out of whistleblowing employees and social media, it is likewise important to consider the potential vicarious liability of an employer for detriments as a result of the reaction of employees. In *NHS Manchester v Fecitt*,[27] the Court of Appeal was asked to determine whether an employer could be vicariously liable for the acts of employees, which themselves were not unlawful, but which amounted to a detriment. The claimants in the case (respondents to the appeal, having succeeded in the EAT) were a group of experienced nurses. One of the nurses discovered that a colleague was significantly overstating his qualifications and experience. She reported this to her line manager, who investigated. It was

---

[24]   [2013] UKEAT/0407/12/ZT.
[25]   [2001] EWCA Civ 1885.
[26]   [2006] EWCA Civ 822.
[27]   [2012] IRLR 64.

accepted that this disclosure, supported by other nurses, amounted to a protected disclosure. After the investigation, the nurse apologised and confirmed that he would not repeat such behaviour. The claimants were not satisfied and sought to take the matter further. After this led to a further investigation, with the same outcome, the nurse lodged a grievance for bullying against the line manager. This led to a further investigation. The line manager then made a formal whistleblowing complaint. She and the other claimants were then treated in a hostile manner by certain other employees, including an anonymous telephone threat to burn down her house. As a result, and following a grievance hearing, certain of the claimants were redeployed or had their management duties downgraded. They claimed that this was a detriment; that the employer had failed to take steps to prevent them from being victimised; and that the employer was vicariously liable for their victimisation.

5.22 The Employment Tribunal found against the employees. It summarised its factual conclusions as follows:

> 'There was, of course, far more evidence given to the Tribunal in relation to the relevant events than can be summarised in these reasons. However, having considered the totality of the evidence presented to it, the Tribunal makes the following findings of fact:

(a) As accepted by the respondent, each of these claimants made protected disclosures during March/April 2008 which related to Mr Swift.

(b) As a direct result of those disclosures, the claimants were subject to unpleasant behaviour on the part of a number of members of staff at the Wythenshawe Walk-In Centre who were supportive of Mr Swift and who felt that the claimants, and in particular Mrs Fecitt, were subjecting Mr Swift to an unwarranted "witch hunt". The Tribunal was satisfied, as indeed were Professor Madhok and Mrs Nixon, that the claimants were justified in raising the issue relating to Mr Swift and to pursue it further when immediate line management decided to take no further action.

(c) Because of the "dysfunctional" (as found by management) situation at the Walk-In Centre which followed the protected disclosures made by the claimants, they were subjected to significant detriment, including in the cases of Mrs Fecitt and Mrs Woodcock, being removed against their wishes from the Wythenshawe Walk-In Centre.

(d) So far as Mrs Hughes is concerned, although there was some confusion as to whether she had herself decided not to work any more shifts or whether they were removed from her, the desire by Mrs Lake to reduce her hours to nil was, at least in part, related to the "dysfunctional" situation that existed at the Centre and which had resulted in Mrs Fecitt and Mrs Woodcock being redeployed.

(e) Management could and should have done more than it did to prevent the claimants from being subjected to the unpleasant and unwarranted behaviour on the part of other members of staff at the Centre who were supportive of Mr Swift.'

5.23 Notwithstanding those findings, the Employment Tribunal went on to hold:

'It is not sufficient, in the Tribunal's judgment, to establish liability on the respondent simply because management either did not do as much as it could have done or was simply unsuccessful in its attempts to resolve matters. However hard management might try, there are sometimes situations that arise in the workforce following a protected disclosure having been made which are extremely difficult to control and prevent. Whilst a reasonable level of proactive engagement with a view to prevent such a situations continuing can be expected, any failings by management in this case to secure the desired result were not sufficient, in the Tribunal's judgment, to amount to a deliberate failure to act.'

5.24   Whilst the conduct complained of in this case did not relate to social media, it is easy to see how in the modern situation it could well have done – and in fact is now likely to do so. Comments on social media are common following factual matrices similar to those above in these times. The views of the Employment Tribunal as to the efforts of management are surely as a result music to the ears of HR practitioners and those who advise them. As will shortly be seen, such representatives can take solace in that an approach.

5.25   However, the EAT upheld the appeal brought by the employees. It found that:

- the Employment Tribunal had failed to identify the appropriate standard of proof for determining whether a protected disclosure had been a reason for the detrimental treatment. The EAT held that the employer was under an obligation to satisfy the tribunal that adverse treatment was 'in no sense whatsoever' on the grounds that a protected disclosure had been made, on the basis that a broad view of the legislation should be taken to afford proper protection to whistleblowers. It also applied the test in *Igen v Wong*[28] that once a prima facie case (of discrimination) had been established, that burden to prove 'in no sense whatsoever' shifted to the employer. Clearly such a stringent test will catch employers whose employees are using social media to 'do down' a leaving fellow employee;

- employers are vicariously liable for acts of victimisation by fellow employees directed at the claimants on the basis that protected disclosures had been made, so long as these acts were in the course of their employment. This was so even though pursuant to the statute the employees were not themselves liable for their acts of victimisation. The EAT followed another EAT decision, *Cumbria County Council v Carlisle-Morgan*,[29] which held that this finding was in accordance with the seminal case of *Majrowski v Guy's and St Thomas' NHS Trust*,[30] which established the 'close connection' test of vicarious liability in substitution for the previous 'frolic of their own' test. An employer will therefore be liable for social media detriments, even if it has no idea that these are going on and has played no part in instigating the same. If there is a close connection (and it appears likely that an employee using social media to

---

[28]   [2005] ICR 931.
[29]   [2007] IRLR 314.
[30]   [2006] UKHL 34.

relate matters that they have learned at work will be found to fall into that category) the ignorant employer will still find itself the respondent in the claim.

The case was appealed by the employer to the Court of Appeal, which dealt with the appeal robustly and in favour of the employer.

5.26 However the points made above are not entirely cured by the judgment: there remains the *McKie*-type tort, which could found liability upon the employer, depending on the circumstances. In relation to the vicarious liability ground in respect purely of the whistleblowing legislation, it was made clear by the Court of Appeal that absent any legal wrong by the employee (such as in respect of any postings to social media made by that employee which themselves are wrongs and which could thus found liability), there is no room within the scope of the whistleblowing legislation for the doctrine of vicarious liability:

'33. Absent any legal wrong by the employee, there is no room for the doctrine to operate. Here, in contrast to the discrimination legislation where individuals may be personally liable for their acts of victimisation taken against those who pursue discrimination claims, there is no provision making it unlawful for workers to victimise whistleblowers. It was solely on the ground of such alleged victimisation that it was sought to make the Employer vicariously liable, and therefore the claim could not succeed. Of course, as Ms Romney, Counsel for the respondents, submits, depending on the nature of the act of victimisation, the employee might be committing other wrongs for which the employer could be vicariously liable. For example, a course of harassment may give rise to liability under the Protection from Harassment Act and any assault would amount to a tort for which an employer might be vicariously liable. But no specific legal wrongs of this nature were either relied upon or established here, and indeed the Employment Tribunal would not have had jurisdiction to deal with them.

34. The *Cumbria* case, which the EAT in this case followed, was wrongly decided. In *Cumbria* the EAT was under the misapprehension that the decision in *Majrowski* meant that the employer could be liable for acts of the employee committed during the course of his employment whether or not those acts constituted an actionable wrong against the complainant employee. That analysis was based on a misconception of what Lord Nicholls was saying in paragraph 14 of the *Majrowski* decision. He was there describing a line of reasoning adopted in a decision of the Australian High Court which, in paragraph 15, he said had now been firmly discarded in English law. He added in that paragraph that the principle that an employer was liable for the wrongs of his employees committed during the course of their employment was now "settled law". The principle underlying the doctrine is that the employee's wrong is imputed to the employer.

35. It follows that, in my judgment, the EAT erred in following the *Cumbria* case and in remitting the issue of vicarious liability to the Employment Tribunal. Accordingly, this ground of appeal succeeds.'

5.27 Thus, unlike in discrimination claims, there was no provision making it unlawful for *workers* to victimise whistleblowers. That was the basis upon which the case was put and, as such, it failed. *Cumbria* was wrongly decided. This part of the decision was clearly of significant benefit to employers who might otherwise have been held to be liable for acts beyond their control. It was also likely that the same principles would apply to employees who victimise whistleblowers, again without more, as the logic of the statutory analysis appears to suggest.

5.28 The decision of the Court of Appeal went on to consider whether the legislation provided a specific protection against harassment or victimisation by fellow-employees or workers. The submission was made that if the employer subjected the employee (presumably either directly or vicariously) to acts undermining the whistleblowing legislation, there should be culpability. The Court of Appeal considered and rejected this argument:

> '56. Mr Allen adopts a more radical position. His analysis is as follows. First, he submits that the purpose behind the whistle blowing legislation, as its title indicates, is to provide protection (and he says full protection) in the public interest for whistleblowers. That requires not only that whistleblowers should be protected from being penalised by the employer for having made the disclosure but also that they should be protected from acts of harassment committed by fellow workers. If that is not done it will undermine the legislation and discourage workers from making disclosures where it is in the public interest that they should do so. He submits that this case provides an instructive example. If these claimants had appreciated how they would be treated as a consequence of making their disclosures, they would never have been willing to speak out. The public interest would have been undermined. He submits that in order to ensure that the proper effect is given to the legislative purpose, words should be added to section 47B so that it reads as follows:
>
>> "A worker has the right not to be subjected to any detriment by any act, or any·deliberate failure to act, by his employer done on the ground that …it undermines the protection to which he or she is entitled by the legislation and must have if the public interest is to be secured."
>
> 57. Applying that principle to this case, he submits that the acts of the Employer so undermined the protection to which the claimants are entitled by the legislation that the acts must be treated as having been on the ground of the protected disclosure.
>
> 58. In my judgment, this goes far beyond the legitimate role of the court in construing legislation. The purpose of a statute has to be gleaned from its language. Parliament has plainly chosen to protect whistleblowers from the acts and deliberate omissions of the employer. If the reason for the adverse treatment is the fact that the employee has made a protected disclosure, that is unlawful. But it is striking that no obligation is imposed on other workers not to take action against the whistleblower in these circumstances, particularly since employees are made so liable with respect to the discrimination legislation.
>
> 59. Mr Allen is asking the court to remedy the lacuna he says exists in the legislation by extending the primary liability of the employer. In my judgment, that involves giving a wholly distorted meaning to the words which Parliament has

employed. I have no doubt that when Parliament used the language "done on the ground that" it was intending that this would involve the consideration of the reason why the employer has taken the action which he has. Mr Allen's analysis gives those words no meaning. The employer will be liable to the employee even where he has acted for reasons wholly unconnected with the protected disclosure if in fact, looking at the matter objectively, the worker would be inadequately protected without imposing liability. The words which Mr Allen would read into the legislation are not there by necessary implication. They involve a wholesale re-writing of the statute. His premise, namely that Parliament must have intended to protect workers from the adverse effects of acts of victimisation by fellow workers, is not in my view sustainable given the language that Parliament has used. Nor does the long title help since it merely says that the Act is to protect whistleblowers; it gives no indication as to how full that protection is intended to be.

60. Furthermore, as Mr Linden pointed out in argument, where the adverse act is dismissal itself then there is only protection where the proscribed reason is the reason or at least the principal reason for the dismissal. That falls short of affording the full and effective protection to the whistleblower which Mr Allen submits we should assume was intended.

61. In my judgment, there is nothing surprising in Parliament considering that the principal protection which needs to be afforded to whistleblowers is from retribution by the employer. It may be that the particular interest groups with an interest in this legislation could agree protection to that extent but no further. This is of course mere speculation but in my view it shows why it would be inappropriate to assume that Parliament intended a fuller protection than naturally arises on the words of the statute. I therefore reject the submission that the Employment Tribunal erred in failing to give this construction to section 47B. I recognise why the claimants feel aggrieved. I accept too that Mr Allen may be right to say that if the Tribunal decision is allowed to stand, it means that on one view of the matter whistleblowers are inadequately protected. If so, for reasons I have given, any remedy must lie with Parliament.'

5.29 The *Fecitt* decision was therefore seen as being of significant benefit to employers. The decision appeared significantly to contrast with the lines of authority considered elsewhere, which act to cast liability upon an employer, often, perhaps, as a matter of public policy, because they are the insured party, in order to afford a financial remedy to the complaint. This will be the case under, for example, the Equality Act 2010 and the Protection from Harassment Act 1997. Employers at the time understandably and with relief considered the decision to be a rare judicial departure from the principle that the entity with the deepest pockets should pay. The decision also provided some welcome relief to employers struggling to control their workers from intemperate postings on social media in light of the decisions being made in other areas of the law rendering them potentially vicariously liable in appropriate circumstances.

5.30 It was also contended in *Fecitt* that the proper test was whether the proscribed reason was the sole or principal reason for the action taken and as a result, even if the EAT burden of proof test was correct, the ET did not err. The Court of Appeal accepted this ground of appeal.

5.31 There are a number of reforms to whistleblowing legislation contained within the Enterprise and Regulatory Reform Act 2013, which have provided limited reforms to the established law in this area. The reforms do not substantially affect the principles set out above, but, notwithstanding their enactment for some time, are worth restating. The reforms in force are as follows:

- The removal of the requirement that, in order to obtain protection under the Employment Rights Act 1996, a protected disclosure must be made in 'good faith' – this is replaced by the 'public interest' test.

- Those claiming protection of the whistleblowing legislation now need to show that they reasonably believed that their disclosure was 'in the public interest'. This reverses the effect of *Parkins v Sodexho* which provided that a disclosure as to a breach of the worker's contract of employment was a qualifying disclosure; we are already seeing the first appellate tribunal cases on this area: *Chesterton Global Ltd v Nurmohamed*.[31] In that case the EAT found that whilst there might be no public interest in the disclosure of an individual's contractual terms, the term of the contract which was the subject of the disclosure was a matter of public interest. In *Chesterton*, the term related to the bonus system the appellants operated and which affected an entire group of people.

- If a disclosure is not made in good faith, compensation can be reduced by 25%.

- In response to *NHS Manchester v Fecitt*, considered above, the House of Lords introduced an amendment in order to render employers vicariously liable for any such treatment by work colleagues, and employees personally liable, unless they are reasonably acting in accordance with employer instructions. Such amendment was inserted into s 47B of the Employment Rights Act 1996 by way of the new subs (1A)–(1E). These provisions hold an employer liable for detriments imposed against whistleblowers by workers in the course of their employment, or by agents acting on the employer's authority. As with the Equality Act 2010 there is a defence available to employers. If the employer is able to show that it took all reasonable steps to prevent the worker accused of imposing the detriment from doing that thing, or from doing anything of that description,[32] he will not be liable. Once again, the need for clear policies, with appropriate cross-references, is illustrated; the social media policy will need to set out in terms that employees are prohibited from retaliating against whistleblowers over social media.

- The inclusion of job applicants into the definition of 'workers'.

5.32 The overturning of *Fecitt* marks the culmination of a complex history of case-law. Statute has now determined that vicarious liability will apply where an employee is subjected to unwanted conduct arising out of whistleblowing.

---

[31]   [2015] UKEAT 0335_14_0804.
[32]   ERA s 47B(1D).

As such the amendment is a matter of policy rather than the culmination of common law consideration, and conforms with the general thrust of legislation in casting liability on the employer.

5.33 It is worth noting that an employer might also be vicariously liable if the acts complained of had been separately categorised in the civil courts as harassment, and could as a result have been held vicariously liable under the Protection from Harassment Act 1997; a consequence directly canvassed by the Court of Appeal.[33] If the actions of an employee causing difficulties for the whistleblower over social media could properly be characterised as harassment for the purposes of the PfHA 1997, it appears clear from *Fecitt* that there would be separate vicarious tortious liability. The consequences of the same are considered elsewhere.

REGULATORY CONSIDERATIONS

5.34 In addition to the general whistleblowing provisions considered above, there are also potential issues for employers arising out of the professional codes of conduct of certain types of employee. If certain professionals become aware of matters that amount to a breach of their code of conduct, it may be a requirement that they make an appropriate report. This will be the case where the employee becomes aware of such matters via social media. Employers need to be aware of the risk to reputation from a report by an employee of a colleague, as well as the risk of retaliation, whether in person or over social media. In addition, professional codes of conduct often impose a duty upon professionals to protect their subordinates from harm following the raising of concerns.

5.35 For example, the Nursing and Midwifery Code of Conduct provides:

> '16 Act without delay if you believe that there is a risk to patient safety or public protection
>
> To achieve this, you must:
>
> 16.1 raise and, if necessary, escalate any concerns you may have about patient or public safety, or the level of care people are receiving in your workplace or any other healthcare setting and use the channels available to you in line with our guidance and your local working practices
>
> 16.2 raise your concerns immediately if you are being asked to practise beyond your role, experience and training
>
> 16.3 tell someone in authority at the first reasonable opportunity if you experience problems that may prevent you working within the Code or other national standards, taking prompt action to tackle the causes of concern if you can

---

[33] See para 33 of the judgment, quoted above.

16.4 acknowledge and act on all concerns raised to you, investigating, escalating or dealing with those concerns where it is appropriate for you to do so

16.5 not obstruct, intimidate, victimise or in any way hinder a colleague, member of staff, person you care for or member of the public who wants to raise a concern, and

16.6 protect anyone you have management responsibility for from any harm, detriment, victimisation or unwarranted treatment after a concern is raised.

The professional duty of candour is about openness and honesty when things go wrong.

> "Every healthcare professional must be open and honest with patients when something goes wrong with their treatment or care which causes, or has the potential to cause, harm or distress."[34]

That said, references to social media usage are confined only to one short passage:

> 'Use all forms of spoken, written and digital communication (including social media and networking sites) responsibly.'[35]

5.36 However the NMC document 'raising concerns' goes on to state, after considering clause 16:

> 'Failure to report concerns may bring your fitness to practise into question and put your registration at risk. If you experience any negative reactions within your workplace after raising a concern appropriately, you should contact your professional body or trade union for support and advice.'

5.37 In addition, the NMC social media guidance states:

> 'Nurses and midwives may put their registration at risk, and students may jeopardise their ability to join our register, if they act in any way that is unprofessional or unlawful on social media including (but not limited to):
>
> • sharing confidential information inappropriately
> • posting pictures of patients and people receiving care without their consent
> • bullying, intimidating or exploiting people
> • building or pursuing relationships with patients or service users
> • stealing personal information or using someone else's identity
> • encouraging violence or self-harm
> • inciting hatred or discrimination
>
> If you are aware that another nurse or midwife has used social media in any of these ways, it might be helpful to refer to our guidance on raising concerns (NMC,

---

[34] Joint statement from the Chief Executives of statutory regulators of healthcare professionals.
[35] Ibid cl 20.10.

2013). This sets out your professional duty to report any concerns you have about the safety of people in your care or the public, and the steps you should take to do this.'

5.38 In a case brought against Allison Hopton in 2013, the Nursing and Midwifery Council considered allegations of inappropriate behaviour by Mrs Hopton, a nurse, arising out of Facebook posts. These posts had been brought to the attention of her employer by an ex-employee. The charges were as follows:

'That you, a registered nurse, whilst employed as a nurse at Tŷ Hafan Children's Hospice ("the Hospice"):

1. Between 8 May 2011 and 2 September 2011 made a series of inappropriate postings on your public Facebook page, more particularly, but not limited to:
    a) "big bollocking shitting bastard work tomorrow";
    b) "Oi Fucknuts";
    c) "been shagged over in work";
    d) "she is only to be known as STUDENT, & has to fetch and carry for everyone and generally be our bitch:) so now she's my bitch";
    e) a photograph of a person sitting on a bed pan in the Hospice;

AND, in light of the above, your fitness to practise is impaired by reason of your misconduct.'

5.39 Mrs Hopton argued that she was merely venting, but accepted that her behaviour was irresponsible. She was suspended, a sanction that was later replaced with striking off.

5.40 A freedom of information request made in September 2013 by a Katie Sutton[36] revealed that nine nurses had been disciplined for misconduct arising out of the use of social media: three were struck off, three suspended, two cautioned and one had a substantive order allowed to expire.

5.41 Similar regulatory issues may arise in respect of numerous professionals. Whilst these issues are likely principally to arise in the public sector, there will be occasions where private sector employees are likewise affected. In either situation the risk of reputational damage and media coverage is significant. In the case of Nicholas Torsney[37] the General Teaching Council of Scotland considered a number of allegations against Mr Torsney, a teacher:

'1. Whilst employed as a registered teacher by West Lothian Council you did:

a. On 22 September 2012 use social media, namely Facebook, to make inappropriate contact with a pupil in that you did send two private messages which stated "Hey man, u looking forward to this ski trip? I'm not ... sorry I've messaged u xx" and "I should not have sent u a message. Sorry xx",

---

[36] https://www.whatdotheyknow.com/request/nurses_suspendedstruck_off_due_t.
[37] February 2015.

and, in doing so you did breach West Lothian Council's Internet, Social Media and Email policy dated 25 June 2012

b.   On 15 June 2013 use social media, namely Facebook, to make inappropriate contact with two female pupils in that you did send them messages which stated "so how was prom then? Xx", and, in doing so you did breach West Lothian Council's Internet, Social Media and Email policy dated 25 June 2012

c.   On 15 June 2013 use social media, namely Facebook, to make inappropriate contact with a male pupil in that you did send him a message which stated 'Hope you enjoyed Prom mate. Me U and Downham need to go and play golf soon', and, in doing so you did breach West Lothian Council's Internet, Social Media and Email policy dated 25 June 2012

And in light of the above it is alleged that your fitness to teach is impaired and you are unfit to teach as a result of breaching Section 1.2, 1.4 and 1.6 of the General Teaching Council for Scotland Code of Professionalism and Conduct 2012.'

5.42   The facts were admitted and as a result found proved. The sending of such messages as private messages via Facebook was a failure to maintain appropriate boundaries and breached the written social media policy, which provided that 'employees must ensure that they do not overstep professional boundaries by communicating with or 'befriending' pupils on social networking sites outwith communications necessary for the purpose of carrying out their professional duties'. Mr Torsney had shown remorse and had closed his social media accounts, and also stated that he believed that when the messages were sent, the relevant recipients had left the school. Whilst the content of the messages had no sinister intent, it was the contact itself that was a breach, and as such fitness to practice was impaired. Mr Torsney received a reprimand. He was not dismissed by the school but was redeployed to another location, and continued to teach.

5.43   It is questionable, absent the professional obligations to which Mr Torsney was subject, whether the mere contacting of pupils, albeit in breach of the social media policy, would have been grounds for dismissal. The authors hazard that, notwithstanding the lack of objective harm (the messages had no sinister intent and were inappropriate solely due to the position of Mr Torsney as a teacher) a dismissal in these circumstances would have been upheld by an Employment Tribunal. Certainly the approach taken by the Regulator was that the behaviour, whilst inappropriate and as a result impairing of Mr Torsney's fitness to practice, should not prevent him from continuing to teach. There is clearly a significant difference between the removal of the ability to practise by a professional regulator and the 'mere' loss of a current employment role. But such communications, in breach of a clear and communicated social media policy, are likely to have allowed the employer to have dismissed.

5.44   A similar approach can be seen in other regulated professions. The well-known case (at least in legal circles) of the prolific tweeter @Geeklawyer (in reality, self-employed intellectual property barrister David Harris), was disbarred for a number of significant breaches of his code of conduct. However of the six counts with which he was charged, only one related to social media use; the first five charges related to far more serious matters, which resulted in his disbarment. The sixth count, relating to a number of inappropriate tweets, resulted only in a fine. That may have been only cold comfort given the sanction arising out of the earlier counts, but given the nature of the tweets, taking place during the course of the trial (his appearance at which led to his disbarment), had Mr Harris been employed it appears likely that as a result of at least some of the tweets a dismissal would have been warranted, though a number appear to be no more than banter:

'1.   I like to think of orders of the court as gentle hints of preferred behaviour. [@HowardMCheng]
2.   Ooooh I kinda misread the claim. That's bad.
3.   IF this settles now I am going to have a frickin' tantrum. [@nipclaw]
4.   *BSkyB v EDS*. Nice to see Herbert Smith win a case for once: http://tinyurl.com/ylavr8v I did them up the arse a while back;)
5.   genius. Have cut n pasted that into the conclusion [@johnhalton]
6.   will staple a couple of £50 notes to skeleton when I hand it up to the judge. [@johnhalton]
7.   bribery. I ask the judge to indict my client for stapling £50 notes to my skeleton when I want looking. Express horror and outrage. [@johnhalton]
8.   then bill client for disbursement to the judge + my uplift [@johnhalton]
9.   Bugger judges chancery division hassling me for my skeleton. Trial is on for monday. damn.
10.   encouraged the other sides expert witness doesnt understand our system: I have have played a part in this. FTW!!!:)
11.   oops. Looks like I admitted something I should have denied. Oh. Dear. Me.:(Gonna catch it in the neck for that)
12.   wondering if I can resile from 'yea we are as guilty as sin, fuck me they are entirely right' [@lilianedwards]
13.   wondering if I can hire a hooker for the judge or rent-boy. Oooh. How do I find out his preference? Could just ask I guess [@Markystewart]
14.   I did my cross examination of expert yesterday. Bugger wouldnt cooperate but I had him. [@Charonqc]
15.   I will try for 'anilingus' as word of the day. Triple word score and a bonus if it's mentioned in the law reports? [@HowardMCheng]
16.   left robes in hotel once, Judge permitted me to appear unwigged, he invited other barrister to appear likewise: prick refused [@nipclaw] (it is notable that opposing Counsel in the case forming counts 1 to 5 had stated in evidence that Mr Harris had forgotten his robes on one occasion)
17.   I was: now far too hungover to tweet. Plus, I need to write closing speech [@CathyGellis]
18.   ooooh, Dont talk to me about breakfast am muchly hungover. That Lex made me drink lots of alcohol, the dirty rat [@_Poots]'

5.45   The distinction between losing a job and losing a profession is important. The tribunals have rightly treated the two as distinct rather than synonymous. Thus, for example, a professional facing allegations that could result in being struck off, rather than simply being dismissed, will ordinarily be afforded the right to representation at disciplinary hearings: *Kulkarni v Milton Keynes*

Hospital NHS Foundation Trust.[38] Dr Kulkarni appealed the decision that he was not entitled to be represented by a legal professional. The Court of Appeal considered that a proper interpretation of his contractual terms gave him such right and further commented on the application of Art 6:

> '65. It appears to me that the distinction which the court was drawing was that, in ordinary disciplinary proceedings, where all that could be at stake was the loss of a specific job, article 6 would not be engaged. However, where the effect of the proceedings could be far more serious and could, as in that case, deprive the employee of the right to practise his or her profession, the article would be engaged.

> 66. The difficulty is to know where to draw the line. Mr Stafford and Miss Lee both submitted that Dr Kulkarni was facing ordinary disciplinary proceedings brought by his employer and the only effect, if the charge were found proved, would be that he would lose his job. Only proceedings before the General Medical Council can deprive a doctor of the right to practise. But, as Mr Hendy pointed out, the National Health Service is, to all intents and purposes, a single employer for the whole country. Indeed, for a trainee doctor, that is literally true as a doctor cannot complete his training in the private sector. If Dr Kulkarni is found guilty on this charge he will be unemployable as a doctor and will never complete his training. If he applies for any other position he will be obliged to declare the finding against him and the fact of his dismissal. Moreover, submitted Mr Hendy, it is highly likely that the system of "alert letters" would be operated in this case if Dr Kulkarni were found guilty. An alert letter is a letter warning other NHS employers not to employ the doctor named, who is regarded as presenting an unacceptable risk to patients. The alert letter procedure is currently governed by the Healthcare Professionals Alert Notice Directions 2006.

> 67. It seems to me that there is force in Mr Hendy's submission and, had it been necessary for me to make a decision on this issue, I would have held that Article 6 is engaged where an NHS doctor faces charges which are of such gravity that, in the event they are found proved, he will be effectively barred from employment in the NHS.'

5.46 Thus, the potential gravity of the situation that Dr Kulkari found himself in was such that it was necessary, to accord with Art 6, that he have appropriate representation at a disciplinary tribunal. Notably however in the paragraph above, it was accepted that the NHS was in effect a single employer. This is unlikely to be the case outside of the professions, and, as is seen in the paragraph below, may well be considerably limited by circumstances.

5.47 In *R (G) v Governors of X School*[39] this dictum was considered in the context of a teacher. Lord Dyson considered the case of a primary school teaching assistant accused of a sexual relationship with a 15-year-old boy, who had undertaken work experience there. He held that it was not (contrary to the

---

[38]   109 BMLR 133, [2009] EWCA Civ 789, [2009] IRLR 829, [2010] ICR 101, (2009) 109 BMLR 133, [2009] LS Law Medical 465.
[39]   [2011] ICR 1033 [2011] UKSC 30.

finding of the Court of Appeal below) a breach of Art 6 not to allow legal representation in a disciplinary context:

> '33. It is common ground that the civil right with which we are concerned is the claimant's right to practise his profession as a teaching assistant and to work with children generally. There is no doubt that this right would be directly determined by a decision of the ISA to include him in the children's barred list. He does not, however, contend that the proceedings before the ISA would violate his article 6(1) rights. His case is that (i) the disciplinary proceedings would have such a powerful influence on the ISA proceedings as to engage article 6(1) in both of them and (ii) the consequences of being placed on the children's barred list by the ISA would be so grave for him that the right to a fair hearing vouchsafed by article 6(1) meant that he was entitled to legal representation in both proceedings.
>
> 34. If there is no connection at all between the disciplinary proceedings and the proceedings before the ISA, it is obvious that article 6 has no role to play in the disciplinary proceedings. Ex hypothesi, they have nothing to do with the civil right in question.
>
> 35. The principal question raised on this appeal is what kind of connection is required between proceedings A (in which an individual's civil rights or obligations are not being explicitly determined) and proceedings B (in which his civil rights or obligations are being explicitly determined) for article 6 to apply in proceedings A as well as proceedings B. Does the connection have to be so strong that the decision in proceedings A in effect determines the outcome of proceedings B (as Mr Bowers QC submits)? Or is it sufficient that the decision in proceedings A has an effect on proceedings B which is more than merely tenuous or remote (as Mr Drabble QC submits)? Or does the connection lie somewhere between these two positions?'

5.48 Lord Dyson accepted the formulation of Laws LJ in the Court of Appeal below and held:

> '69. So where does this leave the test of "substantial influence or effect" proposed by Laws LJ? He was careful to say that an applicant:
>
>> "may (not necessarily will) by force of article 6 enjoy appropriate procedural rights in relation to any of the others [set of proceedings] if the outcome of that other will have a substantial influence or effect on the determination of the civil right or obligation": [2010] 1 WLR 2218, para 37.
>
> In my view, this is a useful formulation. It captures the idea of the outcome of proceedings A being capable of playing a "major part in the civil right's determination" in proceedings B. That is what fairness requires. Anything less would be "excessively formalist" (see para 87 of the Commission's Opinion in *Ruiz-Mateos* 16 EHRR 505) and would give too much weight to the fact that the two sets of proceedings are, as a matter of form, separate. The focus should be on the substance of the matter. The court should always keep in mind the importance of ensuring that the guarantees afforded by article 6(1) are not illusory. It is clearly established that, where a decision in proceedings A is dispositive of proceedings B, article 6(1) applies in proceedings A as well as in proceedings B. That is what the right to a fair hearing in proceedings B requires. Why does fairness not require the

same where the decision in proceedings A, although it is not strictly determinative, is likely to have a major influence on the outcome in proceedings B? As a matter of substance, there is not much difference between (i) an outcome of proceedings A which has a major influence on the result in proceedings B and (ii) an outcome of proceedings A which is dispositive of the result in proceedings B. In each case, the civil right of the person concerned is greatly affected by what occurs in proceedings A. If there is to be a difference in the application of article 6(1) between the two cases, it needs to be justified. There may be policy reasons (such as those referred to in *Fayed* 18 EHRR 393) based on the nature of the body charged with proceedings A which justify a different approach. But absent such policy reasons, it is difficult to see why article 6(1) should not apply in both cases. No such policy reasons have been identified in the present case. I propose, therefore, to consider whether article 6(1) applies in the present case on the basis of the test propounded by Laws LJ.'

5.49   And, in *Mattu v University Hospitals of Coventry and Warwickshire NHS Trust*,[40] the Court of Appeal held that for Art 6 purposes, the right to carry out one's profession was undoubtedly a civil right, and as a result a decision which might lead to the inability to continue within that profession engaged Art 6 of the European Convention on Human Rights. However in the circumstances the employee's contractual provisions were not disapplied by Art 6 in respect of the composition of the disciplinary panel.

5.50   Thus, the availability of Art 6 arguments to professionals will depend on the circumstances. Legal representation at disciplinary hearings is not a given, and should be considered on a case-by-case basis.

CONCLUSION

5.51   Issues arising out of whistleblowing can give rise to significant risks to employers, particularly since the reversal of *Fecitt*, and engenders yet further risk of vicarious liability, arising out of detriments caused by employees to whistleblowers. This is likely particularly to be the case where social media is used to intimidate or denigrate a whistleblowing colleague. Employees who consider blowing the whistle may in addition be aware of the provisions of the PfHA 1997, which may be able to be utilised to bring claims against employers, potentially as an alternative action. Likewise, discriminatory or harassing behaviour under the Equality Act 2010 may give rise to actions against employers. Employers who engage professionals should be aware of their employees' professional codes of conduct, as these may give rise to liabilities or reputational embarrassment in their own right. Employers should also consider carefully any requests for legal representation at disciplinary hearings. Whilst the majority of such requests are likely able to be dismissed, employers need to consider carefully the Art 6 issues that may arise in the minority of cases.

---

[40]   [2012] IRLR 661, CA.

Do	Don't
Consider allegations raised by employees carefully	Dismiss whistleblowers merely as disgruntled employees
Ensure that policies are in place to prevent the risk of unhappy colleagues complaining over social media that a disclosure has been made	Turn a blind eye to such posts. If brought to the attention of the employer, if steps are not taken to prevent the same a claim may be brought
Ensure as far as possible that matters are kept confidential	Allow managers to discuss allegations, as this may give rise to retribution or gossip, particularly over social media
Have in place a policy that prevents employees from discussing their whistleblowing	Assume that a complaint, once made, will stay in-house and will not be discussed or disseminated
Assure whistleblowers that their concerns will be treated in confidence and ensure that this is the case	Allow gossip to spread, particularly over social media
Be aware of employees' regulatory requirements	Allow employees to denigrate an employee for complying with those requirements

CHAPTER 6

ANALYSIS OF THE PROTECTION FROM HARASSMENT ACT 1997 ('PFHA')

INTRODUCTION

6.01 An aspect of social media and other online usage in an employment context that is not commonly recognised to be an issue is the prospect of online actions amounting to harassment in breach of the Protection from Harassment Act 1997 ('PfHA 1997'). Such potential liability applies to usage by employees both at the workplace and potentially in their own time where those employees are linked to an employer. Actions amounting to harassment can involve both criminal and civil liability for an individual, with the attendant risk of damage to his employer's reputation and standing, and, potentially, could involve a tortious claim on a vicarious basis against the employer. The authors consider this to be a potential growth area for claims brought against an employer, who will have insurance or deeper pockets, together with, or instead of, against the employee perpetrator. In addition, a company or a brand (or indeed its employees) may find themselves the subject of unwanted cyber-stalking, bullying or reputational attacks, often from anonymous sources. This chapter will therefore focus on a consideration of the PfHA 1997 and online harassment, together with other areas of law that are potentially relevant. The next chapter will consider from a practical perspective the effects of cyber-harassment and reputational damage and the steps that an employer can take to protect against the same.

WHAT IS ONLINE HARASSMENT?

6.02 The PfHA 1997 is a versatile and wide-ranging statute that has come full circle since its amendment as a result of the coming into force of the Protection of Freedoms Act 2012. The PfHA 1997 was originally envisaged as an Act to prevent stalking and to punish stalkers, following an impassioned campaign by Diane Lamplugh for legislation to protect people from others with an obsessive interest, after the disappearance of her daughter in 1986. However, by omitting reference specifically to 'stalking' and instead focusing on a much broader offence of harassment (undefined, but which 'includes causing alarm or distress'), the PfHA 1997 is of much wider application. Since coming into force on 16 June 1997, it has had its remit expanded significantly by the courts. It is now considered by some to be one of the most widely framed pieces of legislation enacted in recent years and has been given a wide application beyond its original intention of dealing predominantly with the issue of stalking. It is a statute that may now be used to found civil liability on employers for the wrongdoing of their employees, and has particular application to the use of social media to 'troll' or otherwise abuse others.

6.03 However, following lengthy Parliamentary consultation (which the authors were privileged to have been involved in) the PFA 2012 (which received Royal Assent on 1 May 2012) introduced two new specific offences specifically of stalking. The PfHA 1997 remains one of the most flexible pieces of legislation of recent years, though its application to employment relations is relatively under-appreciated.

6.04 Because employees now have instant access to a vast multitude of contacts via the various permutations of social media, the prospects for business are both exciting and alarming. Social media gives companies the ability to interact directly with their customers, often in an informal manner, and to project their products to an extremely wide audience. In addition social media offers a platform to provide efficient customer service, and to build a reputation as a helpful organisation that reaches out to its customers: note the Nationwide policy of making customer services available 24 hours a day, 7 days a week. But social media also has a darker side. Such Twitter-based customer services are often bombarded by abuse, leading many companies to institute the use of algorithms to select those Tweets that merit a swift response, relegating those that are discourteous or abusive for later consideration. A particular employee may find themselves targeted on Twitter and other social media as a result. It is instructive to consider the targeting of the MP Stella Creasy for her support of the campaign by Caroline Criado-Pirez for Jane Austen to feature on the ten pound note, and which led to an 18-week prison sentence for one of her harassers, Peter Nunn. Whilst this harassment was not directed at employees but rather unconnected individuals, it is easy to see how such behaviour could be targeted at an employee.

6.05 Likewise, companies should be aware of the risk of their employees using social media to conduct harassment themselves. This is a particular risk where a corporate social media account is used as the forum for such conduct, but will likewise potentially give rise to liability if a personal account is used, as will be seen later in this chapter.

DEFINITION OF ONLINE HARASSMENT

6.06 The legal concepts of harassment and stalking are fluid and nebulous, deliberately so. In England and Wales neither has a specific legal definition, though following the enactment of the Protection of Freedoms Act 2012, to which the authors contributed, a new offence of stalking was inserted into the PFHA 1997.[1] As noted above, the PfHA 1997 instead provides that harassment

---

[1]   PFHA 1997, s 2A.

'includes alarming a person or causing a person distress'.[2] Whilst it is clear that this legislation, and other statutes, can and do apply to harassment or stalking that is conducted by electronic means, the growth of social media now provides fertile opportunity for online harassment (which may also be anonymous), and the archiving and repetition of distressing material can compound the damage caused to the victim. Online harassment is, in effect, harassment that takes place online. This can include unwanted contact over online media such as social networking sites, email or messaging apps; or more indirect harassment, for example by setting up malicious webpages referring to a person or organisation, which may result in significant reputational damage.

6.07 'Cyberstalking' (and the linked phrases 'cyber-harassment' and 'cyber-bullying') is a term that is becoming increasingly used in both legal parlance and the mainstream media. However there is no strict legal definition of the term in England and Wales. It is often therefore used as a catch-all term for unwanted, distressing or alarming contact by electronic means – in effect, online harassment. The lack of a formal definition in England and Wales contrasts with legislative attempts by other jurisdictions, such as Florida, which seek to define the term as follows: 'communication by means of electronic mail or electronic communication which causes substantial emotional distress & does not serve legitimate purpose'. Cyberstalking as a concept does not however feature in the legislation in England and Wales. Instead, the PfHA 1997 is considered broad enough to encompass the concept.

6.08 The PfHA 1997 does not provide a definition of harassment. Section 1 provides:

1. Prohibition of harassment.

(1) A person must not pursue a course of conduct –

(a)   Which amounts to harassment of another, and
(b)   Which he knows or ought to know amounts to harassment of the other.

(2) For the purposes of this section the person whose course of conduct is in question ought to know that it amounts to harassment of another if a reasonable person in possession of the same information would think the course of conduct amounted to harassment of the other.

(3) Subsection (1) does not apply to a course of conduct if the person who pursued it shows –

(a)   That it was pursued for the purpose of preventing or detecting crime.
(b)   That it was pursued under any enactment or rule of law or to comply with any condition or requirement imposed by any person under any enactment; or

---

[2]   PFHA 1997, s 7.

(c)   That in the particular circumstances the pursuit of the course of conduct was reasonable.

6.09   Section 7 provides:

7. Interpretation of this group of sections.

(1) This section applies for the interpretation of sections 1 to 5.

(2) References to harassing a person include alarming the person or causing the person distress.

(3) A 'course of conduct' must involve conduct on at least two occasions.

(3A) A person's conduct on any occasion shall be taken, if aided, abetted, counselled or procured by another –

(a)   To be conduct on that occasion of the other (as well as conduct of the person whose conduct it is); and
(b)   To be conduct in relation to which the other's knowledge and purpose, and what he ought to have known, are the same as they were in relation to what was contemplated or reasonably foreseeable at the time of the aiding, abetting, counselling or procuring.

(4) 'Conduct' includes speech.

6.10   It can be seen from s 7(2) that harassment has an open definition, which 'includes' alarming or causing distress. This wide clause has ensured that many acts over and above stalking have been brought within its ambit and its application now covers a vast range of activity. It is not enough, however, that an act falls within this broad approach to harassment. The conduct must occur on more than one occasion, or the victim must apprehend a second occurrence. This is because the PfHA 1997 requires a 'course of conduct'. This need not involve two acts directed at the same person. A harassor could, for example, on the first occasion send an abusive email to the victim and on the second post comments about a friend of the harassee on a Facebook page. Provided that it can be demonstrated that this conduct has a common motive, namely the harassment of the victim, then there is nothing, it is submitted, preventing these two acts being deemed a course of conduct. The consideration of a course of conduct is both subjective and objective; it amounts to harassment[3] and the harasser knows or ought to have known.[4] Section 1(2) defines 'ought to have known' by reference to the 'reasonable bystander' test.

6.11   The PfHA 1997 therefore does not require that there is a physical threat or a risk of immediate physical harm to amount to an actionable civil wrong. Further, the mixed criminal and civil aspects of the PfHA 1997 require only a fear of violence to commit an indictable offence. Similarly, conduct amounting

---

3   PfHA 1997, s 1(1)(a).
4   PfHA 1997, s 1(1)(b).

to harassment will also amount to a criminal offence. In both the civil and the criminal aspects therefore, the PfHA 1997 is drawn far wider than laws introduced in various states of the United States, with some states requiring a 'credible threat' of serious physical injury or death. 'Credible threat' is defined for example in Wisconsin as 'a threat made with the intent and apparent ability to carry out the threat'.

6.12 In addition to criminal offences (both summary and either way) the PfHA 1997, unlike other statutes aimed at curbing anti-social behaviour (such as the Family Law Act 1996), allows for the victim to seek compensation from the wrongdoer as well as injunctive relief prohibiting the wrongdoer from continuing with their conduct. Breach of any injunction is a criminal offence. In this sense the wide drafting and even wider application of the PfHA 1997 is well suited to the challenges posed by the internet but may result in its application in the workplace. As the physical posting of a letter containing threats is clearly caught by the PfHA 1997, so would be the emailing of such threats, and, by extension, the creation of tweets, posts, blogs and other social media by employees.

6.13 The new offence of stalking, contained within s 2A of the PfHA 1997, provides as follows:

2A Offence of stalking

(1) A person is guilty of an offence if —

(a) the person pursues a course of conduct in breach of section 1(1), and
(b) the course of conduct amounts to stalking.

(2) For the purposes of subsection (1)(b) (and section 4A(1)(a)) a person's course of conduct amounts to stalking of another person if —

(a) it amounts to harassment of that person,
(b) the acts or omissions involved are ones associated with stalking, and
(c) the person whose course of conduct it is knows or ought to know that the course of conduct amounts to harassment of the other person.

(3) The following are examples of acts or omissions which, in particular circumstances, are ones associated with stalking —

(a) following a person,
(b) contacting, or attempting to contact, a person by any means,
(c) publishing any statement or other material —
    (i)   relating or purporting to relate to a person, or
    (ii) purporting to originate from a person,
(d) monitoring the use by a person of the internet, email or any other form of electronic communication,
(e) loitering in any place (whether public or private),
(f) interfering with any property in the possession of a person,
(g) watching or spying on a person.

6.14 Quite clearly a number of the example circumstances contained within s (3) above are potentially referable to social media and the internet. In particular monitoring internet usage could lead an employee who is tasked with monitoring a competitor in difficulties if that monitoring amounted to harassment.

THE SCOPE OF THE PFHA 1997

6.15 Whilst the courts recognise the flexibility of the PfHA 1997, they at the same time have sought recently to rein in its effect, so as to ensure that it can be invoked only in the most serious incidents of harassment. For example, in the case of *Majrowski v Guys & St Thomas NHS Trust*[5] the House of Lords made it clear that for the PfHA 1997 to apply the standard of conduct attributed to the alleged harasser needed to amount to criminal conduct:

> 'Where ... the quality of the conduct said to constitute harassment is being examined, courts will have in mind that irritations, annoyances, even a measure of upset, arise at times in everybody's day-to-day dealings with other people. Courts are well able to recognise the boundary between conduct which is unattractive, even unreasonable, and conduct which is oppressive and unacceptable. To cross the boundary from the regrettable to the unacceptable the gravity of the misconduct must be of an order that would sustain criminal liability under s 2 [of the Act].'[6]

6.16 This point was re-emphasised by the Court of Appeal in the case of *Conn v Sunderland City Council*.[7] In that case, a line manager confronted three members of staff (including Mr Conn) to determine whether they had left work early. When Mr Conn failed to respond to his satisfaction the line manager shouted, and threatened to smash a window. On another occasion the line manager threatened to hit Mr Conn. This behaviour was not categorised as amounting to harassment under the PfHA 1997 so as to allow the claim to succeed. Therefore it appeared as a result of these decisions that the application of the PfHA 1997 was likely as a result to be limited to such conduct that would sustain criminal liability under its provisions. As Gage LJ stated:

> '11. To this observation I should add a few of my own. As Baroness Hale put it in her speech, harassment is left deliberately wide. Section 7, to which I have referred, points to elements which are included in harassment, namely alarming or causing distress. Speech is also included as conduct which is capable of constituting harassment. The definition of "course of conduct" means that there must be at least two such incidents of harassment to satisfy the requirements of a course of conduct. It is also in my judgment important to note that a civil claim is only available as a remedy for conduct which amounts to a breach of section 1, and so by section 2 constitutes a criminal offence. The mental element in the offence is

---

[5]   [2006] UKHL 34.
[6]   Per Lord Nicholls at [30].
[7]   [2007] EWCA Civ 1492, [2007] 2 All ER (D) 99.

conduct which the alleged offender knows, or ought to know, judging by the standards of what the reasonable person would think, amounts to harassment of another.

12. It seems to me that what, in the words of Lord Nicholls in *Majrowski*, crosses the boundary between unattractive and even unreasonable conduct and conduct which is oppressive and unacceptable, may well depend on the context in which the conduct occurs. What might not be harassment on the factory floor or in the barrack room might well be harassment in the hospital ward and vice versa. In my judgment the touchstone for recognizing what is not harassment for the purposes of sections 1 and 3 will be whether the conduct is of such gravity as to justify the sanctions of the criminal law.'

6.17 Such limitation would likely have removed significant aspects of behaviour from the scope of the PfHA 1997, and in particular workplace-type disputes which, whilst unpleasant (and potentially giving rise to workplace disciplinary proceedings), would often not cross the threshold into criminality. Thus, whilst sending emails that contain untruthful stories about a person via a social networking site to all of their acquaintances may be deeply unpleasant to the maligned person, it is arguable on an analysis of *Conn* that such conduct would not break the law so as to amount to a criminal offence. Such conduct is of course libellous, but as a result of the *Conn* decision might well not have crossed over to an actionable wrong under the PfHA 1997. Such conduct might well fall short of conduct that would sustain criminal liability on the analysis set out in *Conn*.

6.18 However, in late 2009 the Court of Appeal in *Veakins v Kier Islington*[8] considered the not unusual situation of an employee who raised a complaint over the conduct of her line manager. The conduct complained of included an initial dispute over wages, which led to a 'telling off' and the claimant feeling that she was singled out by her line manager and picked on often in front of other employees. The claimant also complained of being told to 'fuck off' by her line manager and that he ripped up a letter of complaint provided to him by her without even reading the same. The claimant sought to claim damages from her employer.

6.19 Mr Recorder Grainger at Brighton county court heard the claim at first instance and focused on the decision of the Court of Appeal in *Conn*. Buxton LJ had there noted that:

'... crucial to [the type of conduct that crosses the line into harassment] is Lord Nicholls' determination [in the House of Lords in *Majrowski v Guy's and St Thomas' NHS Trust* [2006] UKHL 34] "... that the conduct concerned must be of the order that would sustain criminal liability and not merely civil liability on some other register". The recorder went on to note that: "I cannot see that any sensible prosecuting authority would pursue these allegations criminally;

---

8   [2009] EWCA Civ 1288, [2010] IRLR 132, (2010) *The Times*, 13 January.

or, even if a prosecution were somehow brought ... I cannot see that any prosecution would suffer any fate other than to be brought to an early end as an abuse of process."'

Unsurprisingly, based upon his reliance upon the dicta in *Conn*, the Recorder dismissed the claim for damages.

6.20 The claimant appealed this decision and contended that there was no evaluation in the judgment of the Recorder of the behaviour of the line manager beyond the conclusion that it would not justify a criminal prosecution. The claimant argued that while it was correct to keep in mind that the conduct must be 'of an order which would sustain criminal liability' a court must consider what this actually requires when coming to a determination of a case of this sort. Subsequent case-law, it was submitted, had established appropriate considerations for such conduct.

6.21 The court was referred in this context to the passage in para 30 of Lord Nicholls' speech in *Majrowski* cited above. This was however further elaborated upon in *Ferguson v British Gas Trading Ltd*.[9] The conduct complained of in *Ferguson* amounted to the sending of numerous bills and threatening letters relating to Ms Ferguson's gas supply. Jacob LJ referred to three types of threats, being threats to cut off the gas supply, threats to commence legal proceedings and threats to report Ms Ferguson to credit rating agencies. Jacob LJ at para 18 stated: 'I ask myself whether a jury or bench of magistrates could reasonably conclude that the persistent and continued conduct here pleaded was on the wrong side of that line, as amounting to "oppressive and unacceptable conduct".'

6.22 The Court of Appeal considered that the primary focus for a court when faced with a case concerning the application of conduct to a civil claim for damages under the PfHA 1997 is on whether the conduct is oppressive and unacceptable, as opposed to 'merely unattractive, unreasonable or regrettable' albeit that a court must keep in mind that it must be of an order which 'would sustain criminal liability'. The case sets out in clear terms that the 'criminal liability' referred to in earlier case-law amounts in effect to a gloss upon the core test of whether the conduct is oppressive and unreasonable, and as such is not by and of itself the court's primary focus, or determinative of the case. There is no requirement that the civil court must consider that the conduct complained of is in fact criminal in nature before civil liability can be imposed. The appeal was allowed. Jacobs LJ also noted at para 17 of his judgment:

> 'Since *Hatton v Sutherland* [2002] EWCA Civ 76, [2002] ICR 613, it has become more difficult for an employee to succeed in a negligence action based on stress at work. It seems that this may be causing more employees to seek redress by reference to harassment and the statutory tort, although it is doubtful whether the legislature had the workplace in mind when passing an Act that was principally directed at "stalking" and similar cases. Nevertheless, there is nothing in the

---

[9]   [2009] EWCA Civ 46.

language of the Act which excludes workplace harassment. It should not be thought from this unusually one-sided case that stress at work will often give rise to liability for harassment. I have found the conduct in this case to be "oppressive and unacceptable" but I have done so in circumstances where I have also described it as "extraordinary". I do not expect that many workplace cases will give rise to this liability. It is far more likely that, in the great majority of cases, the remedy for high-handed or discriminatory misconduct by or on behalf of an employer will be more fittingly in the Employment Tribunal.'

6.23 The above passage highlights the wide scope of the PfHA 1997. Jacobs LJ took the view that not many workplace cases would give rise to such liability, and that the conduct was both 'oppressive and unacceptable' but also 'extraordinary'. However those advising employers may form the view that, however oppressive, unacceptable and extraordinary the behaviour of the line manager in *Veakins* may have been, such complaints are not particularly unusual.

6.24 It is notable, in the context of the cases cited above, that the criminal courts appear to be taking an increasingly hard line towards social media trolling, which may make reaching the hurdle necessary for a claim under the PfHA 1997 easier to surmount. As noted above, Peter Nunn was imprisoned for his behaviour towards Stella Creasy MP. The messages sent by Mr Nunn included threats to rape Ms Creasy:

'You better watch your back, I'm going to rape your arse at 8pm and put the video all over.

Best way to rape a witch, try and drown her first then just when she's gagging for air that's when you enter.'

6.25 Mr Nunn was charged under s 127 of the Communications Act 2003, though Ms Criado-Perez had stated that in her view the conduct amounted to stalking. Either way, it appears that such a course of conduct by or against an employee could give rise to a civil claim under the PfHA 1997.

6.26 There have been a number of other social media prosecutions. Isabella Sorley was jailed for 12 weeks and John Nimmo for 8 weeks after targeting Ms Criado-Perez arising out of the same background. Tweets included: 'f*** off and die you worthless piece of crap' and 'go kill yourself', 'Rape is the last of your worries', 'shut up bitch', 'Ya not that gd looking to rape u be fine', 'I will find you [smiley face]' and 'rape her nice ass'.

6.27 The CPS issued guidance as to social media prosecutions in June 2013. The guidance includes the following:

'12. Communications sent via social media are capable of amounting to criminal offences and prosecutors should make an initial assessment of the content of the communication and the conduct in question so as to distinguish between:

1.   Communications which may constitute credible threats of violence to the person or damage to property.

2.   Communications which specifically target an individual or individuals and which may constitute harassment or stalking within the meaning of the Protection from Harassment Act 1997.

3.   Communications which may amount to a breach of a court order. This can include offences under the Contempt of Court Act 1981, section 5 of the Sexual Offences (Amendment) Act 1992, breaches of a restraining order or breaches of bail. Cases where there has been an offence alleged to have been committed under the Contempt of Court Act 1981 or section 5 of the Sexual Offences (Amendment) Act 1992 should be referred to the Attorney General and via the Principal Legal Advisor's team where necessary.

4.   Communications which do not fall into any of the categories above and fall to be considered separately (see below): ie those which may be considered grossly offensive, indecent, obscene or false.

13. As a general approach, cases falling within paragraphs 12 (1), (2) or (3) should be prosecuted robustly where they satisfy the test set out in the Code for Crown Prosecutors. On the other hand, cases which fall within paragraph 12(4) will be subject to a high threshold and in many cases a prosecution is unlikely to be in the public interest.'

6.28 It is notable that targeted harassment prosecutions are specifically mentioned. The following paragraphs of the guidance deal with the PfHA 1997:

19. If communication(s) sent via social media target a specific individual or individuals they will fall to be considered under this category if the communication(s) sent fall within the scope of the Protection from Harassment Act 1997 and constitute harassment or stalking.

20. Harassment can include repeated attempts to impose unwanted communications or contact upon an individual in a manner that could be expected to cause distress or fear in any reasonable person. It can include harassment by two or more defendants against an individual or harassment against more than one individual.

21. Stalking is not defined in statute but a list of behaviours which might amount to stalking are contained in section 2A (3) of the Protection from Harassment Act 1997. This list includes contacting, or attempting to contact, a person by any means.

22. When considering an offence under the Protection from Harassment Act 1997, the prosecution will need to prove that the defendant pursued a course of conduct which amounted to harassment or stalking. The Act states that a 'course of conduct' must involve conduct on at least two occasions. Where it forms part of a course of conduct, 'revenge pornography' – where sexually explicit media is publically shared online without the consent of the pictured individual, usually following the breakdown of an intimate relationship – may fall to be considered under this category of cases: see paragraph 42.

23. The conduct in question must form a sequence of events and must not be two distant incidents (*Lau v DPP* (2000), *R v Hills* (2000)). Prosecutors should

consider that a course of conduct may often include a range of unwanted behaviour towards an individual and a communication sent via social media may be just one manifestation of this. Where an individual receives unwanted communications from another person via social media in addition to other unwanted behaviour, all the behaviour should be considered together in the round by the prosecutor when determining whether or not a course of conduct is made out.

24. If there is evidence that an offence of stalking or harassment has been committed and the communication targets an individual or individuals on the 'basis' of their race or religion, prosecutors should consider whether the offence is a racially or religiously aggravated offence. In order to do so, there must first be sufficient evidence that the basic offence has been committed (as set out in sections 29-32 of the Crime and Disorder Act 1998), followed by the aggravating element defined in section 28 of the Crime and Disorder Act 1998. Where there is aggravation related to disability, sexual orientation or transgender identity, prosecutors should have regard to the increase in sentence provisions under section 146 of the Criminal Justice Act 2003.

6.29   These guidelines are likely to be of use when considering a claim brought under the civil jurisdiction of the PfHA 1997 relating to social media. Consistently with the approach of the civil courts, however, offensive or obscene social media posts will not necessarily meet the criminal threshold and thus may well likewise fail on a civil claim.

Course of conduct

6.30   It is also worth noting that the requirement that there be a course of conduct before harassment can be established may equally prevent the PfHA 1997 from applying. Does the sending of one email, with one click of a mouse button, to a thousand recipients amount to one act, or multiple acts? From a straightforward reading of the PfHA 1997 it is submitted that this would likely amount to a single act, even though the impact of that one act would be likely to be more alarming and distressing to a victim than two letters (or emails) being sent by the wrongdoer to separate people at separate times. This is, of course, an extreme example of the application of this provision of the PfHA 1997, but one that illustrates the point in hand. A slightly different example further illuminates this point: in *Law Society v Kordowski*,[10] Tugendhat J accepted submissions that publication on a website of the names of claimants, in the knowledge that publication would inevitably come to their attention on more than one occasion and on each occasion would cause them alarm and distress, constituted harassment. Where publication was on-going on a prominent website, that alarm and distress that would as a result be caused by the publication would also be continuous; and that it was reasonable to infer that the claimants would suffer alarm and distress on at least two occasions.

6.31   The risk to employers is (as will be seen in the next chapter) in respect of claims which may be brought against them on a vicarious basis under the PfHA

---

[10]   [2014] EMLR 2.

1997 as well as to the reputational damage that such a claim would cause, and it is important to note once again that the PfHA 1997, due to its broad scope, has wide application. The watering down of the *Majrowski* and *Conn* criminality element leaves employers potentially more open to claims, as seen in *Ferguson*, if their procedures, or the acts of their employees (or indeed their automated systems) amount to 'oppressive and unacceptable' conduct. This is the case even where such conduct amounts to 'naming and shaming' on the internet, or arguably by the continuation of social media posts that are available to the public.

APPLICATION TO SOCIAL MEDIA IN THE WORKPLACE

6.32 Whilst the erroneous view that there is no law against cyberstalking or cyber-harassment in England and Wales has from time to time been reported by the media, it is clear that this is not the case. Employers who find that they or their employees are facing a campaign of online abuse and harassment, or find themselves the subject of a claim, should be aware of their legal rights, remedies and defences. This section analyses the application of the PfHA to social media in the workplace, with the next chapter going on to consider specific issues and legal developments.

6.33 Cases involving cyber-abuse as considered in the preceding section may often fall within the provisions of PfHA 1997 or, where the parties are associated (broadly speaking, by way of being spouses, cohabitants or relatives, which may be relevant in smaller, family-run businesses) the Family Law Act 1996 (which uses the equally loose term 'molestation' as its touchstone of liability). In addition the criminal law, in appropriate circumstances, may apply (and is considered later on in this book in brief terms). This overlapping of statutory provision has the great advantage of the flexible provisions of those statutes being able to provide proper remedies (by way of prosecution, injunction or damages) where appropriate. This is likely to be more relevant to employers in the sense of having to deal with employees who act in appropriate ways, whether to their colleagues, customers, members of the public, or strangers over social media. The potential for litigation again emphasises the importance of a clear policy in respect of social media usage both from work accounts and equipment and more widely.

6.34 That is not to say that the available remedies are necessarily adequate in all circumstances. What is clear is that cyber stalking/harassment covers a multitude of sins. Clearly, in a more fluid age of communication, it is likely that existing statutory provisions will be engaged, in certain circumstances, by the use of electronic media, such as email, chatrooms, Facebook and Twitter. There will, however, be evidential issues as to who is perpetrating such action, and there are likely to be difficulties in removing hurtful or distressing commentary from the face of the world wide web. The benefit of a law seeking to utilise concepts that were developed prior to the advent of widespread internet access and certainly before the explosion in social media proliferation is flexibility; but this flexibility also causes difficulties where new situations do not fit within its scope.

6.35 However, such behaviour in a social media and online context that could give rise to issues in the workplace, can properly be characterised as simply being delivered by that online medium. The wrongfulness of the behaviour is as apparent as if such conduct were carried out in the 'real world' – social media is merely the delivery system for such behaviour. It should be recognised that the key factor is the weight to be given to the potential for harm, emotional or physical, that such behaviour may entail, particularly as the internet is merely used as a facilitating tool for unacceptable kinetic-world behaviour. It is true that the manner of harm when considering the effect of online harassment may not manifest in the same way as harm in the kinetic-world, but the effect of online harassment may be more pernicious. It is important to recognise that harm can be caused by fear, including anticipation of future physical harm, but also through despair following humiliation, or through financial threats. Examples include the suicide of Tyler Clementi following the posting of a covertly obtained sexual video; but the conduct complained of in *Ferguson* demonstrates that what might be seen as legitimate debt collection can also found liability. The provisions in PfHA 1997 relating to alarm or distress are widely drawn in such a way that they incorporate just such a recognition of the role of fear or emotional distress within the definition of harassment.

Tortious liability: the PfHA 1997

6.36 Over the past two decades, a palpable shift in tortious liability to the party most able to pay has been detectable as an underlying theme in the common law. The clearest and most obvious example of this judicial thinking has been the growth in the scope of vicarious liability of employers for the torts of their employees. It is a well-known principle of the common law that in certain circumstances an employer can be held responsible for the wrongdoings of their employees by way of vicarious liability. Such liability is strict; if the employee is liable then, so long as that employee can be connected to the employer, the employer will become jointly and severally liable. Given that the employer is likely to have deeper pockets than the employee, or be backed by a policy of insurance, this will usually afford a financial remedy to the wronged party. The House of Lords held this doctrine applies to claims brought under the PfHA 1997 in *Majrowski*. Mr Majrowski, after an initial failure at first instance, successfully brought an action against the NHS trust for harassment based on the conduct of fellow employees towards him.

6.37 The scope of vicarious liability has in relatively recent times been greatly expanded and extended in respect of the alteration of the longstanding defence allowing an employer to escape liability if the employee could be shown to be 'on a frolic of his own'. The House of Lords in *Lister v Hesley* Hall[11]

---

[11] [2001] UKHL 22, [2002] 1 AC 215.

disavowed this defence and instead substituted a new test. In that case a caretaker sexually abused boys in a boarding house. It was argued by the boarding house that such abuse clearly was not in the course of employment of the employee, and thus it could not be vicariously liable for those actions. The House of Lords rejected this contention, holding instead that as the employment of the caretaker allowed him into contact with the boys, the relative closeness of his employment and the tort established liability. This far wider test of liability has been applied to found liability where an off-duty policeman carried out a shooting[12] and to a bouncer who, after work, followed and stabbed a customer with whom he had had an argument.[13] Thus for an employer now to be liable for the acts of a tortfeasor employee the act in question must be 'so closely connected' with the work which the employee was employed to do that it is just and equitable to hold the employer responsible. This 'close connection' test has by subsequent cases been refined and extended, but the emphasis is clear: the court will concentrate on the relative closeness of the connection between the nature of the employment and the particular tort and then ask, looking at the matter in the round, whether it is just and reasonable to hold the employers vicariously liable: per Lord Steyn in *Bernard*. The close connection test has been applied widely and catches behaviour which would otherwise have escaped vicarious reference to the employer, as was seen in *Lister* itself, where the employer was held liable for the sexual abuse by the live-in school caretaker of boys, as his access to them was so closely connected with his employment as to found liability.

6.38   The Court of Appeal has revisited the question of vicarious liability in relation to injuries caused to employees as a result of violence towards them by another employee (but, it is submitted, equally applicable in cases involving the PfHA 1997), in the conjoined appeals in *Weddall v Barchester Healthcare Ltd; Wallbank v Wallbank Fox Designs Ltd*.[14] In both cases, at first instance, the trial judge determined that the employer was not liable, as the assaulting employee had been acting outside the scope of his employment. The Court of Appeal took the opportunity to conduct a review of the authorities. One appeal was upheld, the other dismissed, the results turning on the specific facts of each case.

6.39   Mr Weddall was the deputy manager of a care home operated by the defendant in Norwich, which housed people with severe mental health problems. His job description involved him in supporting and caring for residents. Mr Marsh, the tortfeasor, was a senior health assistant and as such was junior to Mr Weddall. Mr Marsh had a previous history of violence, though not towards residents. Mr Weddall and Mr Marsh did not get on. On the evening of 6 September 2006, a nightshift employee called in sick, and Mr Weddall called Mr Marsh at home to offer him the shift. Mr Marsh had had a bad day and was drunk. He did not react well to the call and thought that Mr Weddall was mocking him. He called back and stated that he was resigning;

---

[12]   *Bernard A-G of Jamaica* [2004] UKPC 47.
[13]   *Mattis v Pollock* [2003] 1 WLR 2158.
[14]   [2012] EWCA Civ 25.

then went to the home and assaulted Mr Weddall, unprovoked. He was sentenced to 15 months' imprisonment by the Crown Court. Weddall's claim was dismissed, on the basis that Marsh had committed an independent act, acting personally and for his own reasons, and it would not be fair or just to hold the employer liable.

6.40 In the second case Mr Wallbank was managing director and sole shareholder of Wallbank Fox Designs Limited, who employed him. Mr Brown was employed as a powder coater, spraying metal bed frames. He was 'not a wholly satisfactory employee'. On 16 August 2005 Mr Wallbank criticised him in relation to an aspect of his work. Following on from this Mr Brown threw Mr Wallbank onto a table, fracturing his lower back. Brown was convicted of committing grievous bodily harm. Mr Wallbank was also unsuccessful, as Brown's actions fell outside the close connection required between the tort committed (assault) and the work he was employed to do.

6.41 Both appeals came before the Court of Appeal. In each case it was contended that the assaults had occurred at the workplace, and had been generated by matters relating to employment. Marsh's assault on Weddall was part of a single incident in responding to the call; Brown's assault of Wallbank had also occurred during the course of his employment. It was submitted that the reactions of each tortfeasor was in relation to instructions given as part of the employment, albeit in an inappropriate way: a violent reaction to an instruction is an act in the course of employment.

6.42 Pill LJ analysed in detail the case-law that had developed over the 10 or so years since the decision in *Lister*. He noted that the distinguishing factor in these cases was the violent response to a lawful instruction, and that the claimants' cases amounted to the contention that, since employees must receive instructions and respond to them, an improper form of response, even a violent one, is an act within the course of employment.[15]

6.43 The Court of Appeal dismissed the appeal of Mr Weddall. Pill LJ concluded that the trial judge had reached the right conclusion, for the right reasons. The violence was an independent venture of Mr Marsh, separate and distinct from Marsh's employment. The request was no more than an unconnected pretext for an act of violence. As the violence was far from the modest use of force as a spontaneous reaction, the employer was not vicariously liable.

6.44 However the appeal of Mr Wallbank was upheld. The violence was closely related to the employment in both time and space, and was a spontaneous and almost instantaneous response to an instruction that had been given, and thus the employer was vicariously liable.

---

[15]   [2012] EWCA Civ 25 at 43.

6.45   At first blush the decisions in these conjoined appeals seem to move the law into a different direction to that in which it had been developing. The tenor of a number of the early cases following *Lister* was for a very broad approach to the close connection test. Indeed, Moore-Bick LJ, giving a concurring judgment, noted the introduction of the more flexible principle dependent on the factual circumstances of each given case. However it is that fact-specific approach that distinguished the two cases in this conjoined appeal. As Aikens LJ went on to explain, the intentional tort committed by Mr Marsh, having been at home, off-duty and drunk, and having declined the offer to come in, was obviously not at all connected with his employment: the description by the trial judge of being the 'spontaneous criminal act of a drunken man who was off duty' was 'both graphic and accurate'. However the *Wallbank* appeal was more difficult. The tort flowed directly from the fact that instructions were given in the course of employment and thus was so closely connected with the expectation that Mr Brown would carry out lawfully given instructions, that it would be fair and just to hold the employer liable, applying the formulation of Sir Anthony Clarke MR in *Gravill v Carroll*.[16]

6.46   In *Dowson v Chief Constable of the Northumbria Police*,[17] Mr Dowson, together with five other colleagues, brought a claim under the Protection from Harassment Act 1997. The contention of the claimants, who were all police officers, was that the actions of Detective Chief Inspector Pallas towards them amounted to harassment, for which the chief constable was vicariously liable. Dowson was a detective inspector, and the other claimants were officers in his team. The claim was encapsulated in one sentence by Simon J:

'from the moment he arrived in July 2002, DCI Pallas adopted a hostile and critical attitude, that he harassed each of them on the basis that they were part of Mr Dowson's "team" or "clique" and that this harassment continued until each of them had left CTN [Crime Team North] by July 2003.'

Simon J then summed up the 30 detailed allegations said to amount to harassment as follows:

'Some complaints are about instructions which required them to act contrary to the law or incompatibly with the standards of behaviour expected of a member of the Force. There are other complaints that DCI Pallas covered up his own shortcomings by blaming the claimants for his own failings; and in doing so accused the claimants of lying or failing in their duty. There are also complaints of vulgar abuse, particularly in front of subordinates. There are other complaints of unjustified and otherwise demeaning criticisms made by DCI Pallas which were intended to undermine individual Claimants and which he would have known would be repeated to them. There are further complaints that the claimants suffered further consequences of his harassment in the treatment of their formal complaints of bullying and harassment against him under the Northumbria Force Grievance Procedure. It is also alleged that these complaints were rejected and that

16   [2008] EWCA Civ 689 at [21].
17   [2010] EWHC 2612 (QB).

the claimants were removed from CTN because senior Officers accepted DCI Pallas's untruthful denials of misconduct.'

6.47 Simon J set out the law by reference to all of the major decided cases, noting the development of the law in relation to the inter-relation between criminal and civil liability up to *Ferguson* and *Veakins*. He summarised the necessary findings that had to be made in order to found liability under the PfHA 1997 as follows:

(1) There must be conduct which occurs on at least two occasions,

(2) which is targeted at the claimant,

(3) which is calculated in an objective sense to cause alarm or distress, and

(4) which is objectively judged to be oppressive and unacceptable.

(5) What is oppressive and unacceptable may depend on the social or working context in which the conduct occurs.

(6) A line is to be drawn between conduct which is unattractive and unreasonable, and conduct which has been described in various ways: 'torment' of the victim, 'of an order which would sustain criminal liability'.

6.48 The judgment itself is unsurprisingly lengthy, given the numerous factual allegations. Simon J found that most of the allegations were not proved, and dismissed the claim. However the following paragraphs are worth particular note, to give insight into judicial thinking in the context of such a claim:

'277. For the reasons set out above I have rejected most of the factual allegations and the contention that these amounted to harassment. However, in relation to allegations BD3, BD4 and BD5 I have accepted, at least in part, the factual allegations. These all relate to Mr Dowson; and I can summarise my conclusions by saying that I am satisfied that there were occasions in his dealings with Mr Dowson when DCI Pallas was insensitive, belittling and overbearing. Sometimes this was the way in which he expressed disagreements on matters about which there were respectable views on both sides. During a period between the beginning of October and end of November Mr Dowson's life was made very difficult as a result of DCI Pallas's conduct. Nevertheless, I am satisfied that when he was spoken to about this by D/Supt Vant, DCI Pallas's attitude and conduct towards Mr Dowson improved.

278. The question is whether this conduct constituted harassment. I have concluded that it did not. This was a stressful working environment in which case-hardened officers were dealing with career-hardened criminals. Although this was more than simply a clash of personalities, it was not conduct which was calculated to cause distress and, although it was unacceptable, it was not oppressive in the sense described in the cases. It was not a tormenting by constant interference or intimidation. Rather it was a curt and dismissive attitude which was likely to have the effect, even if unintended, of undermining both Mr Dowson's own self-confidence and the esteem in which he was held by others.

279. In the light of the above and, while keeping in mind that for conduct to amount to the civil tort of harassment it must be of an order which would sustain criminal liability, I have concluded that Mr Dowson's claim fails by a considerable margin.'

6.49   An employee who harasses another, physically or via the internet, may be doing so in circumstances where his employment merely gives him the opportunity to commit the tort (say by posting details about an ex-partner on their Facebook page). However depending on the circumstances it may mean that harassing behaviour were acts done in the course of that employment (for example by posting defamatory comments in respect of a customer on a forum). In such circumstances it is possible that the employer will be liable for any tortious wrong committed, if it is fair and just for the court so to hold them liable. It is therefore feasible that a victim of harassment over social media by an employee could consider bringing a claim against an employer, where the relationship between the perpetrator and the victim was connected to the employment of the former. The reality of modern working environments is that most jobs now require and provide computers and access to the internet. The provision of such access will inevitably result in employers who find their errant employees stalking or harassing others, be they fellow employees, or third parties, being held liable for their actions. The liability of the employer will of course be strict, subject to the close connection defence.

6.50   In addition it may be arguable pursuant to the PfHA 1997 for a harassed victim, in certain circumstances, to be able to seek redress against their employer for harassment caused by third parties, provided that the employer is aware of the harassment taking place. Therefore, if an employee notifies his line manager, or the IT department, that he is the subject of harassing emails from a customer of such a nature that cause him alarm or distress, it is possible that he would be able to succeed in a claim against his employer, provided he could get over the hurdle imposed by *Conn*. These issues will be considered further in the next chapter.

6.51   When considering potential claims arising out of usage of social media, the debate over such legal redress often takes an ideological turn in respect of the question of rights. There is a clear clash between two powerful and important competing rights; the 'right' to privacy (partially embodied in England and Wales by Art 8 of the European Convention on Human Rights as enacted by the Human Rights Act 1998 as 'the right to respect for one's private and family life, his home and his correspondence') and the right to freedom of expression. Both rights, in so far as they derive from the ECHR, are so-called 'qualified' rights, meaning that which prevails depends upon the surrounding circumstances. Such clash goes to the heart of the current debate in the United Kingdom over so-called super-injunctions but is in a very real sense also the key to recognising the difficulties inherent in providing proper satisfaction for victims of cyberstalking. Cases covering such arguments are considered in the following chapters.

6.52 In fact, efforts to apply domestic law to the internet so as to suppress or remove libellous, harassing or damaging statements, photographs or other documentation, can have the opposite result. The so-called Streisand effect has manifested on occasions too often to detail and is a clear risk where an internet community bands together to support the 'right' of the harasser to express himself, to the detriment of the person he is harassing. A further twist on the effect, which illustrates the difficulties that domestic law has in affecting the internet, is the retweeting by multiple users of a tweet made by a young man, Paul Chambers, in frustration at the closure of Robin Hood airport, following his conviction as a result. Using the hashtag #iamspartacus, Twitter users demonstrated their contempt for the application of the criminal law to a comment made via an electronic social medium.

Non-molestation orders

6.53 It is unlikely that the provisions of the Family Law Act 1996 ('FLA 1996') will have much bearing on most workplaces. The provisions may potentially be relevant to family companies, where a husband and wife team are employed, or where numerous members of a family work together. In family-run companies, particularly where there is an acrimonious break up or divorce proceedings, company advisors may therefore wish to familiarise themselves with its provisions and as such the provisions are briefly considered below.

6.54 Part IV of the FLA 1996 contains the familiar provisions allowing for county courts to issue occupation orders and non-molestation orders. In a fashion similar to the PfHA 1997, the FLA 1996 does not seek to give an exhaustive definition of 'molestation', thus allowing the courts to exercise a great deal of flexibility in considering conduct that amounts to molestation.

6.55 Whilst the bulk of cases involving harassment/molestation in the family context will normally be dealt with under the FLA 1996, there are two main important differences between the availability of a remedy under the FLA 1996 and the PfHA 1997. The third difference, that criminal sanctions could be pursued under PfHA 1997 has, since July 2007, fallen away after the introduction of s 42A of the FLA 1996.

6.56 The two differences relate to:

- the scope of the provisions; and
- the remedy that can be afforded.

6.57 FLA 1996 requires, for the court to have jurisdiction to make an order, that the applicant and respondent are 'associated' (s 42(2), unless both are already parties to existing family proceedings). 'Associated' persons are defined in s 62(3):

(3) For the purposes of this Part, a person is associated with another person if —

(a)   they are or have been married to each other;
(aa) they are or have been civil partners of each other;
(b)   they are cohabitants or former cohabitants;
(c)   they live or have lived in the same household, otherwise than merely by reason of one of them being the other's employee, tenant, lodger or boarder;
(d)   they are relatives;
(e)   they have agreed to marry one another (whether or not that agreement has been terminated);
(eza) they have entered into a civil partnership agreement (as defined by section 72 of the Civil Partnership Act 2004) (whether or not that agreement has been terminated);
(ea) they have or have had an intimate personal relationship with each other which is or was of significant duration
(f)   in relation to any child, they are both persons falling within subsection (4); or
(g)   they are parties to the same family proceedings (other than proceedings under this Part).

6.58 It is clear from the definition above that the FLA 1996 is (as its title might suggest) geared towards family members. The definition of 'relatives' is widely drawn:

63(1) 'relative', in relation to a person, means —

(a)   the father, mother, stepfather, stepmother, son, daughter, stepson, stepdaughter, grandmother, grandfather, grandson or granddaughter of that person or of that person's spouse or former spouse, or
(b)   the brother, sister, uncle, aunt, niece nephew or first cousin (whether of the full blood or of the half blood or by affinity) of that person or of that person's spouse or former spouse,

and includes, in relation to a person who is living or has lived with another person as husband and wife, any person who would fall within paragraph (a) or (b) if the parties were married to each other.

Thus it is clear that extended family members (such as in-laws) can be made subject to an NMO.

6.59 The usual form of an NMO also prevents a person from instructing or encouraging any other person to molest, and thus covers situations where third parties are involved on the direction of an associated person.

6.60 The limitation to the FLA 1996 however, in terms of its scope, is that it does not provide protection against molestation by persons who may be close to the parties or either of them, but are not associated. Even if such a person has been so instructed or encouraged (and this can be shown) their actions will not necessarily stop simply because their principal has been made subject of an NMO.

6.61 The other, far starker, difference between the FLA 1996 and the PfHA 1997 is that the latter, in addition to injunctive relief, can result in awards of damages. Whilst such awards are not necessarily huge, the threat of financial penalty can be a significant deterrent, and does provide some redress to the victim.

Family Law Act 1996	Protection from Harassment Act 1997
Prohibition on 'molesting'. 'to cause trouble, to vex, to annoy; to put to inconvenience'	'includes alarming the person or causing them distress'
NMO, breach is a criminal offence	Civil and criminal aspects. Civil injunction and/or damages; either way offence and restraining order
Available in relation to 'associated persons'	Available against anyone
Evidence of molestation need not be shown on more than one occasion, but must demonstrated to be of a type making an order necessary to secure the health, safety and well-being of the applicant	Course of conduct required
Covered by FPR 2010	Covered by CPR 1998
Costs less likely to be recovered, as the default position will be no order as to costs	Costs more likely to be recovered

CONCLUSION

6.62 The PfHA 1997 (and, to a far lesser extent, the FLA 1996) have a potentially significant impact upon companies, particularly with regard to social media usage. There is a real risk that employers may find themselves exposed to liability, whether through an employee who has been harassed by a colleague, or an employee who claims that the employer has not done enough to prevent such harassment; or even, potentially, a third party harasser or harassee. The following chapter will consider the application of the principles considered above.

CHAPTER 7

CYBER-HARASSMENT AND CYBER-BULLYING IN EMPLOYMENT LAW

INTRODUCTION

7.01 The preceding chapter sought to consider from an employer's perspective the legal background to the potential for tortious liability, principally arising under the PfHA 1997. Such potential liability can take numerous forms, such as:

- a claim by a customer who alleges harassment by automated or human processes such as in respect of debt collection (for example in *Ferguson*);
- a claim by an employee who alleges harassment by a colleague (*Dowson*);
- a claim by a customer who alleges harassment;
- a claim by a member of the public who alleges harassment via social media (in which case the close connection test will be relevant);
- a claim by an employee who alleges harassment by a third party.

7.02 In addition such actions could give rise to claims pursuant to the Equality Act 2010 for discrimination and harassment, or could found unfair or constructive unfair dismissal claims. Likewise, employers who seek to discipline or dismiss an employee for harassment should be aware of the potential for claims.

7.03 Social media provides a significant medium through which any of the above allegations could be founded. A claim is time-consuming, expensive and potentially reputationally harmful. However, as noted above, social media is simply a medium by which the course of conduct amounting to harassment manifests. Thus the case-law applicable to harassment without a social media context will be highly relevant. This chapter aims to consider a number of relevant cases and to provide potential defences, tips and ways of avoiding a claim being made.

7.04 Office gossip may give rise to a claim being brought for harassment, whether under the provisions of the Equality Act 2010 or the PfHA 1997. The claim in *Nixon v Ross Coates Solicitors*[1] is an example of the former. It arose out of the pregnancy of Miss Nixon by a colleague in the firm, Mr Perrin, with

---

[1]   [2010] UKEAT/0108/10/ZT.

whom she was in a relationship. The late HHJ McMullen, with typical robustness, noted the 'injudicious behaviour by young professionals at the Christmas party of a solicitor's firm and its consequences for employment relations'. The EAT was considering an appeal by the claimant, Miss Nixon, and a cross-appeal by the respondent, arising out of Miss Nixon's claim for unfair dismissal, sex discrimination and discrimination on the grounds of pregnancy and harassment.

7.05 At the staff Christmas party in 2007 Miss Nixon was, in the words of HHJ McMullen, 'involved flirtatiously [in] kissing the IT manager [Mr Wright]'; the pair later obtained a room and had sex. In the New Year, Miss Nixon informed the principal of the firm of the fact of her pregnancy. However, within an hour the HR manager, Ms Debbie O'Hara, had become aware and had, Miss Nixon alleged, led gossip as to the paternity of the child. The IT manager, Mr Wright, with whom Ms Nixon had had the dalliance, also came to be aware of the pregnancy and, knowing she was in a relationship with Mr Perrin, expressed his alarm over the paternity gossip to Miss Nixon in a series of text messages. Miss Nixon took time off work as a result of her upset at this gossip, and suggested a return to work at a different office, meaning that she would have no contact with Ms O'Hara, who she blamed for the spread of the gossip.

7.06 In February 2008 Miss Nixon entered a grievance on the basis that the respondent had failed to prevent Ms O'Hara from spreading rumours or to chastise her; and that by this stage she had been told that there was 'no room' at the alternative office. On 15 March 2008 Miss Nixon resigned.

7.07 The Employment Tribunal dismissed the harassment and discrimination claims. It found that whilst Ms O'Hara might have been indiscreet in a minor way, there was nothing by her conduct 'which could possibly be regarded as intimidating, hostile, degrading or humiliating'. It also found that the rejection of the suggestion of work at the alternative office was not sex discrimination, as it accepted the evidence of the respondent that this was not appropriate due to the nature of the role of Miss Nixon. However it did find that Miss Nixon had been constructively unfairly dismissed.

7.08 The Employment Appeal Tribunal found that the tribunal had erred in law in relation to its conclusions on harassment and discrimination. The relevant law in relation to sex discrimination and pregnancy as applicable at the relevant time was contained in ss 3A and 4A of the Sex Discrimination Act 1975 (now replaced by the provisions of the Equality Act 2010), was not contentious and was cited by the Tribunal. The EAT also considered arguments in relation to both constructive unfair dismissal and apparent bias, but which are not relevant to the scope of this book.

7.09 The EAT, when considering the appeal of the claimant, accepted her contentions that the gossip about the paternity of the child was connected with pregnancy and that (as the same was unchallenged) the claimant was uncomfortable following the spreading of the gossip. This amounted to a course of unwanted conduct, meeting the definition of harassment. The EAT found, therefore, that the Tribunal was wrong 'not to see this', and that the Tribunal's disapproval of the claimant's conduct 'leaked into its judgment on the law'. Thus, whilst the evidence given by the claimant was unreliable, the 'extrinsic evidence' of Ms O'Hara's conduct (she not having given evidence herself) was available, and 'should have been accepted'. The tribunal thus had made an error of law.

7.10   The EAT further found that the failure to allow the claimant to work at the alternative office did amount to discrimination on the grounds of pregnancy, as it was related. The tribunal was wrong simply to have found that this issue was not related to her sex or pregnancy, as it was related to Ms O'Hara and 'the content of her gossip was unarguably related to pregnancy and pregnancy is related to her sex'. Again, therefore, the tribunal erred in law.

7.11   Whilst the gossip complained of in *Nixon* appears to have been 'watercooler'-type gossip, rather than via social media, the ubiquity of Facebook and Twitter in modern times provide far more risk for employers of such gossip being discovered and documented. The case amounts to a clear reminder of the dangers of allowing office gossip to spread unchecked; and highlights the significant risk that such gossip may take place outside of the control of the workplace. The effect of the transmission of gossip over social media is highlighted in the case of *Teggart v TeleTech UK Ltd*,[2] a case in the Northern Ireland Industrial Tribunal, and an important case for employers who seek to dismiss employees who inappropriately post on social media.

7.12   In *Teggart*, the claimant, in his free time and from his home computer, made scurrilous comments about the sexual promiscuity of a work colleague. That colleague was excluded from the Facebook discussion that then followed, but became aware of it. A complaint by a friend of the colleague who was subject to the Facebook discussion was made to the respondent and led to the suspension of Mr Teggart and subsequently disciplinary proceedings. In the course of the disciplinary meeting the claimant defended himself by asserting amongst other things that his posts were made in his free time and not from work equipment, and he could make such comments as he pleased; he did not mean to offend; and he did not consider the comments to be bullying or harassment. He also denied bringing the company into disrepute.

7.13   Mr Teggart was dismissed, a decision upheld on appeal. At the appeal hearing, Mr Teggart raised further argument, being that his rights under Arts 8, 9 and 10 of the European Convention on Human Rights had been violated. He relied upon Art 8 as the comments had been made in his own time and his rights had been violated by the investigation into his correspondence; Art 9 as he had had his beliefs violated; and Art 10 as he was entitled to freedom of expression.

---

[2]   [2012] NIIT 00704_11IT.

7.14 The tribunal considered the applicable law and referred to the case of *X v Y*,[3] in which Mummery LJ gave guidance as to the applicability of ECHR principles in Employment Tribunal cases. In dealing with the submissions of Mr Teggart, the tribunal made the following findings arising out of the ECHR arguments:

Article 8

(a) When the claimant put his comments on his Facebook pages, to which members of the public could have access, he abandoned any right to consider his comments as being private and therefore he cannot seek to rely on Article 8 to protect his right to make those comments.

Article 9

(b) The tribunal is satisfied that the 'belief' referred to in Article 9 does not extend to a comment about the promiscuity of another person. In the tribunal's view, belief, in keeping with the remainder of Article 9, is intended to refer to a philosophy, set of values, principles, or mores to which an individual gives his intellectual assent or which guides his conduct or behaviour. 'The limits to this concept lie in a requirement of a serious ideology, having some cogency and cohesion, ...' (*Employment Law and Human Rights*, Second Edition, by Robin Allen QC, Rachel Crasnow and Anna Beale).

Article 10

(c) The right to freedom of expression, as set out in Article 10, brings with it the responsibility to exercise that right in a way that is necessary for the protection of the reputation and rights of others. The right of freedom of expression does not entitle the claimant to make comments which damage the reputation or infringe the rights of A. The claimant does not assert that A was promiscuous but states that his comments were a joke or done for fun. A's reputation has been harmed on the basis of a joke or fun. Furthermore she has the right not to suffer harassment.

7.15 These determinations are of significant importance to employers grappling with the social media age. The tribunal determined that because the comments made by Mr Teggart had been put by him into the public domain, he was not able to rely upon a reasonable expectation of privacy within Art 8 of the ECHR. This appears to be the case notwithstanding that the audience able to access those comments was limited. The authors consider that the logic of this conclusion is at best dubious, particularly given the guidance from the Information Commissioners' Office Employment Practices Code, referred to in the first section of this work, that an employee is entitled to have a reasonable expectation that such personal information is private; and caution should be applied to the statement. Once again, the clear relevance of a social media code of conduct is highlighted.

---

[3] [2004] EWCA Civ 662, [2004] IRLR 625.

7.16 There is, however, other judicial support for a narrow interpretation of an Art 8 defence in the context of unfair dismissal claims and personal social media usage. In *Gosden v Lifeline Project Ltd*,[4] a dismissal was upheld where the claimant, Mr Gosden, in his own time and from his home computer, forwarded an email to a work colleague, again to a personal email address. The email contained material of a racist and sexist nature, with the exhortation that the email chain should be forwarded. The colleague complied, and forwarded the email to yet another of their fellow employees, this time to his work email address. Mr Gosden was dismissed on the grounds that his action could have damaged his employer's reputation or integrity. Lifeline was a charity that placed employers within HM Prison Service. The colleague who received the forwarded email did so at his HMPS email address. Notably, following consideration of Art 8 of the ECHR, the tribunal concluded that as the email was a chain email, and as such was intended to be forwarded on, it could not be treated as having been intended to be confidential and Art 8 did not apply. The tribunal expressed the view that, had it been created by Mr Gosden and intended solely to be read by the recipient this conclusion might have been different; however as it was intended to be disseminated, a privacy defence could not be raised and the dismissal fell within the range of reasonable responses. The colleague who had initially received the email and forwarded it was 'allowed to retire'.

7.17 *Teggart* and *Gosden* can be contrasted with the case of *Smith v Trafford Housing Trust*, referred to above. The High Court noted in *Smith* that the Facebook account did not have the necessary work-related context to fall within the prohibition in the code of conduct used by the employer. Further, the offended party had chosen to be friends with Mr Smith on Facebook; the victim of Mr Teggart was not privy to the discussions about her but merely found out about what had been said through a colleague. Those points, it appears, may go some way towards explaining the judicial consideration of the difference between the two situations (though it is also worth noting that *Smith* was not expressly an Art 8 case), and demonstrates a different attitude towards reasonable expectation of privacy between situations where a person who has chosen to 'connect' is offended and where the offence is caused to a non-involved person. It should also be noted that in *Smith* the court found that the comments could not fairly or objectively be described as judgmental, disrespectful or liable to cause discomfort, embarrassment or upset.

7.18 The tribunal's decision in relation to Art 10 is also of interest as it amounts to a potentially powerful defence that could be brought by employees dismissed for social media posts. The courts will give significant weight to Art 10 arguments in claims brought against the media, as can be seen by the case of *Trimingham v Associated Newspapers Ltd*,[5] in which Tugendhat J refused a claim under PfHA 1997. The case provides an important

---

4   ET/2802731/2009.
5   [2012] EWHC 1296.

consideration of Art 10 in the context of the PfHA 1997, but, as should be noted from *Teggart*, those considerations may not apply with such force in the case of individuals.

7.19 Carina Trimingham began an affair with Chris Huhne MP in 2008. The relationship became public and led to the break-up of both Mr Huhne's marriage and Ms Trimingham's civil partnership. Between 20 June 2010 and 1 July 2010 the *Daily Mail* and the *Mail on Sunday* printed a number of articles that, Ms Trimingham claimed, infringed her rights to privacy. She claimed under the Copyright Designs and Patent Act 1988 in respect of two photographs of her; for misuse of private information under the Human Rights Act 1998 and ECHR Art 8; and also claimed under the PfHA 1997. The claim was later amended to include a number of other articles, a total of 65. In addition Ms Trimingham relied on readers' comments published on the *Mail Online* website, in support of her claim of harassment. Ms Trimingham contended that the defendant had pursued a course of conduct that amounted to harassment, including publication of comments about her personal appearance as well as her sexuality, which she found offensive. She also contended that the manner in which the news about her had been gathered amounted to harassment. It was not in issue as to whether there was a course of conduct, nor that the distress caused would amount to harassment, if it could be shown that it was caused by the course of conduct. Ms Trimingham sought damages and an injunction. As the claimed injunction would affect the right to freedom of expression, it was necessary for the court to give consideration to this competing right.

7.20 Tugendhat J summarised the law in respect of the PfHA 1997 and noted that it was one of many laws that give effect to the obligation of the state to prevent interference with the right of individuals to protection of their private lives under Art 8 ECHR. He noted that it was established by the Court of Appeal in *Thomas v News Group Newspaper Ltd*[6] that publication in a newspaper was capable of constituting harassment, but further noted that this was the first trial of a claim in harassment against a newspaper in England, *Thomas* having been a strike-out application which failed. In *Thomas* Lord Phillips had noted that harassment should not be interpreted in such a way that restricted the right of freedom of expression, save so far as is necessary to achieve a legitimate aim. When considering the question of reasonableness of the conduct, the answer did not turn on whether the opinions expressed were reasonably held. Press criticism, even criticism of a robust kind, will not generally constitute unreasonable conduct and thus will not fall within the natural meaning of harassment. In order to establish harassment there must be 'some exceptional circumstance which justifies sanctions and the restriction on the freedom of expression that they involve'.[7] An example was given of articles calculated to incite racial hatred of an individual.

---

[6] [2001] EWCA Civ 1233.
[7] Lord Phillips [2012] EWHC 1296 at[35].

7.21   Tugendhat J considered as a result that, for a court to comply with s 3 of the Human Rights Act 1998, it must hold that a course of conduct in the form of journalistic speech is reasonable under s 1(3)(c) PfHA 1997 unless, 'in the particular circumstances of the case, the course of conduct is so unreasonable that it is necessary (in the sense of a pressing social need) and proportionate to prohibit or sanction the speech in pursuant of ... in particular for the protection of the rights of others under Art 8'.[8] In other words, the rights of the individual will come second to the right of free speech unless it is so unreasonable that the right to private and family life is infringed in such a way as would affect society. It is likely to be extremely difficult to establish this. It is notable, however, that this test is expressly couched as relating to journalistic speech.

7.22   Tugendhat J held that in considering the effect of any such course of conduct, the meaning conveyed by the words used, such as in the *Trimingham* case, 'bisexual', needed to be decided. Ms Trimingham contended that the word was used in a pejorative way towards her by the defendant. Tugendhat J noted that there is no crime or tort of 'insult', save where this could be brought within the ambit of the PfHA 1997, as insults or non-defamatory abuse were not actionable as defamation. He accepted that in principle repeated publication in the media of offensive or insulting words about a person's appearance could amount to harassment; the same applied with much greater force in relation to sexuality. Repeated mocking by a national newspaper of a person by reference to their sexual orientation would 'almost inevitably be so oppressive as to amount to harassment', and likewise in respect of the other protected characteristics set out in the Equality Act 2010. However, the principle that 'harassment must not be given an interpretation which restricts the right to freedom of expression' needed also to be applied when considering what a reasonable person would think would amount to harassment, as well as to reasonableness under s 1(3)(c).

7.23   Tugendhat J determined that Ms Trimingham was not a private individual. He found that none of the witnesses ought to have known what they were writing amounted to harassment, nor that a reasonable person in the possession of the same information as the defendant about the job of Ms Trimingham and her past career as a journalist, that it would amount to harassment. Nor did he find that the distress was caused by the course of conduct – ie the use of the words which had been used in the articles and were said to be pejorative. 'Bisexual' and 'lesbian' would not have been read in a pejorative sense by a reasonable reader of the articles. Discussions or criticisms of sexual relations which arise within a pre-existing professional relationship, or that involve infidelity, are matters a reasonable person would not think were conduct amounting to harassment, and would be reasonable unless other circumstances make it unreasonable. One such circumstance could be interfering with Art 8 rights, but Ms Trimingham's rights were limited by not being a purely private person and that she had been open about her sexuality and relationships. Further, as 'unreasonable' in respect of s 1(3)(c) had to be

---

8   [2012] EWHC 1296 at [53].

read compatibly with the right to freedom of expression, the test for harassment is objective, and the repetition in respect of her sexuality across the numerous articles did not make otherwise 'reasonable' speech cross the line to amount to harassment, because the repetition related principally to articles about Mr Huhne, and not her. The claim did not succeed.

7.24 *Trimingham* demonstrates the high hurdle that a claimant under PfHA 1997 must surmount when bringing a claim arising out of publication. But a claimant seeking to prove a case amounting to harassment is not in the same position as a claimant seeking to contend that a dismissal is unfair. There is a clear relevance for employers whose employees might post remarks on the internet and on social media sites such as Facebook or platforms such as Twitter, and demonstrates the significant weight given to Art 10 (freedom of expression). It is not clear to how great an extent the finding that Ms Trimingham was not a purely private person bore upon the decision; would the balancing act prescribed in *Thomas* between Art 8 and Art 10 have been different if she had been a purely private figure? The phrasing of the decision suggests that it might have been. It may be that the *Teggart* case is on the other side of the 'private person' line from that of *Trimingham*; however, the Tribunal did not appear to engage in a similar consideration of this balance, rather simply determining that the Art 10 right is qualified to protect the reputation and rights of others. *Crisp v Apple Retail (UK) Ltd*,[9] noted above, did not attach weight to an Art 8 argument in circumstances where an employee posted on Facebook, but did reject the argument that the act of posting on Facebook meant the matter was in the public domain for all purposes but did express the view that this would not apply to an employer who had actively sought out the posted information. An employer who does seek to obtain such information, perhaps by creating a false profile so as to be accepted as a connection, may therefore run into Art 8 arguments. As also noted above, an Art 10 argument was dismissed, principally due to the existence of a policy aimed at protecting the reputation of the employer. This demonstrates that the Art 10 balance will likely be affected by express policy provision. A similar argument was upheld in *Preece*.

Harassment by third parties

7.25 It is now established that an employer may be held to be vicariously liable for the actions of their employees following the decision of the House of Lords in *Majrowski v Guy's and St Thomas' NHS Trust*,[10] which held that an employer can be vicariously liable for the harassment of one of his employees by another. The law on vicarious liability and the development of the close connection test has been explored in some detail in the preceding chapter. It is not difficult to envisage the scope for claims of harassment arising out of the employer–employee relationship or complaints made by an employee about another both in the context of the PfHA 1997 and in relation to disciplinary

---

[9]   1500258/2011.
[10]   [2006] UKHL 34.

and dismissal processes. However, it is also important to consider the potential for liability of an employer where allegations of harassment or inappropriate behaviour over social media are raised in the context of third parties.

7.26 In *Burton v De Vere Hotels Ltd*[11] the EAT allowed an appeal by two waitresses against the finding of the Employment Tribunal that they had not been directly discriminated against by their employer when they were subjected to racially offensive remarks by a person working as a comedian at a private function in their employer's hotel, but not employed by the respondent. While the harassment provisions (which were subsequently inserted into the predecessor legislation to the Equality Act 2010) were not in effect at the time, the EAT held that the remarks did amount to direct discrimination against the waitresses. It was therefore the case that an employer could be liable for discriminatory remarks made to employees by a person not employed by him.

7.27 However, in *Pearce v Governing Body of Mayfield Secondary School*[12] the House of Lords stated that *Burton* had been wrongly decided. The law lords opined that to render an employer liable for the direct discrimination claimed, there must be a failure of the employer that must itself be an act of discrimination. So the failure of the employer must subject the employee to less favourable treatment for one of the protected reasons – in *Burton* this was race. This, the law lords found, could not be shown in *Burton*:

> 'The hotel's failure to plan ahead properly [by for example ensuring that the waitresses did not have to work in the room occupied by the private function] may have fallen short of the standards required by good employment practice, but it was not racial discrimination. I consider the case [of *Burton*] was wrongly decided by the Employment Appeal Tribunal ...'[13]

7.28 It must be remembered that *Pearce* is a creature of its time, and must be viewed in context. The law has moved on a great deal in the intervening decade and attitudes both amongst legislators and decision makers have shifted. The ratio of *Pearce* is that the Sex Discrimination Act 1975 applies to sex and not sexuality; the part of the decision concerning harassment was obiter. Further, even if the Act did apply to sexuality the harassment provisions contained in the Sex Discrimination Act 1975 had yet to be brought into effect. Of course the subsequent enactment of reg 5(1) of the Employment Equality (Sexual Orientation) Regulations 2003[14] prohibited harassment on the grounds of sexuality, and sexuality is a relevant protected characteristic for the purposes of harassment under the Equality Act 2010, which has now replaced the previous statutory discrimination provisions. Whilst those statutes were repealed when the Equality Act 2010 came into force on 1 October 2010, the language of the harassment provisions has remained the same and as such earlier case-law will remain relevant.

---

[11] [1997] ICR 1, [1996] IRLR 596.
[12] [2003] UKHL 34, [2004] 1 All ER 339.
[13] Per Lord Nicholls [2003] UKHL 34 at [35].
[14] SI 2003/1139.

7.29   The EAT in *Gravell v London Borough of Bexley*[15] considered afresh the question of third party harassment, and opened up the possibility that an employer can be held liable for the harassment of its employees by third parties. Ms Gravell was employed by the respondents in their housing department. She complained that customers of the respondent used racist language, and that the respondents had a policy of ignoring or not preventing such conduct. At a pre-hearing review in the Ashford Employment Tribunal the claimant's claims in this regard were struck out on the basis of the (obiter) comment expressed by the House of Lords in *Pearce* and cited above. The claimant appealed.

7.30   The matter came before HHJ Peter Clark sitting alone. Referring to his own earlier decision in *Wandsworth Primary Care Trust v Obonyo*[16] he noted that there was no comparative exercise needed when considering s 3A of the Race Relations Act 1976 ('RRA') as opposed to s 1(1)(a) and stated at para 14:

> 14. Thus it seems to me at the strike-out stage that there is considerable scope for argument as to whether the observations of the House of Lords on Burton in Pearce, based on s1(1)(a) RRA, also hold good in a claim of s3A harassment. No decided case on point has been shown to me.

7.31   Seemingly, therefore, to constitute harassment the acts complained of do not themselves need to be discriminatory in as much as they can apply equally to all people (many people would be offended by the use of racist language in their workplace, no matter what racial origin they are themselves, or, for instance, an intimidating, demeaning or humiliating atmosphere can be created for staff of both sexes by the displaying of pornographic material in the workplace). If the harassment provisions of the RRA were in effect at the time of *Burton* it would seem that the claimants may well have been able to succeed in their claim, as the actions of the hotel would not have needed to subject them to less favourable treatment on the basis of their race when compared to a white waitress.

7.32   In *Gravell* the EAT allowed the appeal and pointed out that:

> '18. ... The case which the claimant wishes to advance is that the respondent's policy of not challenging racist behaviour by its clients is capable of itself of having the effect of creating an offensive environment for her. That, if established on the facts, is capable in my judgment of falling within s 3A RRA.

7.33   Therefore there seems to be an argument that the lack of a comparator required in the s 3A exercise means that an employer could be held directly liable for harassment by a third party if the employers' conduct, by failing to address such harassment, can be said to amount to unwanted conduct that has the purpose or effect of violating that other person's dignity or creating a hostile, intimidating, degrading, humiliating or offensive environment.[17]

---

[15]   UKEAT/0587/06/CEA) [2007] All ER (D) 220 (May).
[16]   UKEAT/0237/05/SM.
[17]   EAT in *Conteh v Parking Partners Ltd* [2011] ICR 341.

7.34 If correct, this raises issues as to whether a failure by an employer to put in place an anti-harassment policy can amount to 'unwanted conduct' as required by the harassment provisions of the Equality Act 2010. If an employee has raised the issue of harassment and proposed or asked for a course of action to be undertaken by the employer to reduce this harassment, the failure to consider or implement the proposal may amount to the employer engaging in unwanted conduct (ie intransigence). Of course therefore this would seem to require the employee to put the employer on notice of the harassment.

7.35 It does appear that any assumption that an employer can simply sit back and ignore harassment of which it is aware, on the basis that it will never have any liability, is a dangerous one. Certainly it seems that a policy of simply ignoring racist language, perhaps because this is seen as the easiest thing to do, risks a successful claim. Further such a policy can potentially itself be seen as harassment on racial grounds. Whilst a single, isolated incident is unlikely to found liability, such a policy is now more likely to do so. Employers may be able to better protect themselves by rigorously enforcing a 'zero tolerance' policy and encouraging employees to complain and log incidents, which can then be dealt with.

7.36 Further, the manner in which complaints are dealt with by an employer can also amount to harassment: in *Rose-Brown v Home Office*,[18] a white woman was suspended and, ultimately, given a written warning when she made discriminatory comments about black staff. Ms Rose-Brown, who was herself black, but not directly the target of the other employee's comments, complained about the conduct. When she returned from suspension, the white woman was placed a small distance away from Ms Rose-Brown, who was distressed and felt undermined by this. After she went off work with stress, Occupational Health suggested the Home Office move Ms Rose-Brown to a different office. A tribunal found that by allowing the return to work of the white woman into the same office as the claimant meant the employer was guilty of harassment. Ms Rose-Brown had made it clear that the return to the office of the discriminator was unwanted, and the employer allowing the return to work of the other employee had the effect proscribed by the Equality Act 2010.

7.37 In addition, it may be that the failure of an employer can also amount to a cause of action itself if the employer does not deal with the complaint in as much depth, or with the same degree of procedural rigour, that it would do if the complainant had a different protected characteristic. For instance, the manner in which a gay man's complaint that he had been subject to harassment that related to his sexual orientation was found by a tribunal to amount to direct discrimination in and of itself as, they found, if he had been heterosexual the deficiencies which applied to the investigation into his grievance would not have occurred.[19]

---

[18] (UKBA) No2313044/10.
[19] *Price v Presbyterian Church of Wales* 1603021/07.

7.38 An alternative mechanism by which employers could be held liable for the actions of third party harassers is under the PfHA 1997. What form the harassment takes does not matter, nor the reason for it. Therefore, the PfHA 1997 covers harassment that has been inflicted on grounds other than a protected ground of discrimination. In this respect the scope of the PfHA 1997 is considerably wider than in the employment field. Thus harassment owing to, say, height or hair colour is covered, as is harassment caused to the employee because of who the employer is (for example, an employee is harassed for working for a life sciences company). If a policy of not preventing, or taking any steps to prevent, racist language by third parties can amount to racial harassment under the Equality Act 2010, it is feasible that the continuation of such a working practice by the employer may itself also lead to the possibility of a discrete claim against the employer under the PfHA 1997. Whilst injunctions can be obtained against the harasser in these cases, (see for instance *Huntingdon Life Science Ltd v Stop Huntingdon Animal Cruelty*[20]), there is nothing in theory to prevent an employee seeking an injunction against their employer to compel that employer to take steps to reduce the impact of the harassment, and it is submitted such a course was open to Ms Gravell.

7.39 However, again there needs to be some sort of knowledge by the employer of the conduct of the third party, though again vicarious knowledge may be imparted to the employer where complaints have been raised. In many cases it may be simply the decision of the office manager or similar to adopt a deliberate *laissez-faire* attitude. Even so, the employer itself may be vicariously liable for harassment caused by such a policy. The PfHA requires there to be a course of conduct, namely two or more acts, or at least one act and a perceived second act. Once again, therefore, employers have nothing to fear should there be a single isolated incident. However how they react to any complaint may be relevant to any later claim should further incidents follow.

7.40 A recent example of vicarious liability for social media harassment is the case of *Otomewo v Carphone Warehouse Ltd*.[21] During work hours, two employees accessed, without the consent of Mr Otomewo, his personal Facebook account. Mr Otomewo had recently returned from a suspension imposed for sexual harassment of a female employee at his employer, where he held the post of manager. The employees accessed his account by taking his mobile telephone. Using it, they posted to his Facebook account that he had 'Finally came out of the closet. I am gay and proud.' This was not true and the employees knew that it was not true. Mr Otomewo brought a claim against his employer on the grounds of sexual orientation discrimination. It was accepted by the tribunal that he was embarrassed and distressed that his Facebook status had been updated in this way. This was particularly the case as his account was open, and was capable of being viewed by family and friends. The Tribunal found that his case was made out. The comment related to sexual orientation, and had been unwanted conduct. The purpose or effect of the action was a

---

20   [2003] All ER (D) 280.
21   ET/2330554/2011.

violation of the dignity of Mr Otomewo and/or created an adverse working environment. The tribunal commented that there was no culture of 'office banter' in that workplace. The employees had carried out the action in the course of their employment, and in office time. As a result, Carphone Warehouse was held to be vicariously liable for their conduct.

7.41 This decision can be contrasted, however, with the decision in *Gainford Care Homes Ltd v Kennedy*.[22] The claimant was employed as a senior care assistant. The claimant was a gay woman, and resigned, claiming constructive unfair dismissal, on the basis that she had been sexually harassed by a driver also employed by the respondent. The Employment Tribunal upheld her claim, and found that she had been harassed on the grounds of sexual orientation. The tribunal further found that her employer had not taken sufficient steps to safeguard her or to prevent her harasser from carrying out his actions. The allegations included Mr Tariq, the driver, telling the claimant that she should not be working with old ladies, as she could 'touch them'; that the company did not like gay people; that he made Facebook postings involving the claimant and another woman; that gay people were 'dirty'; and that the claimant was fearful of him. The Employment Tribunal upheld the claim, but interestingly did not make a finding that the employer was vicariously liable for the harassment that took place over social media. It is not clear (as a transcript is not available to the authors) on what basis this was the case, but it is likely that it was on the basis that the posts were not connected to the employment. If this is the case, it is respectfully suggested that such a decision is unsupportable. The basis of the social media postings were connected to Mr Tariq's employment, and it is certainly arguable that posting about matters relating to work could be said to be in the course of employment. However (on this assumption) the decision does demonstrate that not all social media posts will found vicarious liability. The decision was overturned by the EAT, but on grounds that a point upon which the decision was made had not been raised or argued by the parties, which amounted to a serious procedural irregularity.

7.42 As can be seen there is arguably considerable scope for employers to be found liable for harassment caused by the actions of their customers or other third parties. Whilst the discrimination legislation does provide some measure of protection, for existing employees the PfHA allows them to seek injunctions compelling their employers to take steps to protect them, and may be seen as a more constructive remedy than the simple punitive award of compensation that an employment tribunal can award.

7.43 However neither scheme presents a carte blanche for such claims. Employers can take some solace in the fact that they need to have some degree of awareness of the harassment taking place before the employee is likely to be able to succeed in a claim against them. They cannot however simply shut their eyes and pretend that things are not happening. Thus, if there is a problem in the workplace with discriminatory language, or behaviour that results in an

---

[22]   (2014) UKEAT/0155/14/RN.

employee being harassed, and the employer actively encourages and promotes a policy of toleration of such harassment, the likelihood of a successful claim against them is greatly increased.

7.44 Employers should also beware the dissemination of information about ex-employees which may be picked up by future or current employers. In *McKie v Swindon College*,[23] the previous employer was held liable for false information which then led to the ex-employee being sacked from his new employer. Mr McKie had left Swindon's employment in 2002 on good terms, and with a glowing reference from his head of department. The judge found that he was 'an exemplary professional'.[24] In 2008 the head of Swindon College's human resources, upon finding out that Mr McKie's new employment would lead to him potentially carrying out work at the premises of the defendant, sent an email that indicated it had 'very real safeguarding concerns for our students and there were serious staff relationship problems during his employment at this College. No formal action was taken against Mr McKie because he left our employment before this was instigated.' Mr McKie had since leaving Swindon College, worked at Bath College, and the email went on to state that Swindon believed that similar problems had occurred there. These allegations were found to be 'largely fallacious and untrue', but resulted in the dismissal of Mr McKie. He did not have sufficient continuous employment in which to present a claim of unfair dismissal against Bath. Mr McKie brought a claim against Swindon and was successful. The dissemination of the information in the email was not a reference, so the cause of action arising out of false references identified in *Spring v Guardian Assurance plc*[25] did not apply. The judge however found that a tortious duty had been breached, by reference to *Caparo Industries plc v Dickman & Ors*.[26] He found that there was foreseeability of damage; that there existed between the party owing the duty and the party to whom it is owed a relationship characterised by the law as one of 'proximity', and that the situation should be one in which the court considers it fair, just and reasonable that the law should impose a duty of a given scope upon the one party for the benefit of the other. It appears to be arguable that the situation whereby a disgruntled or malicious ex-employee directs social media posts towards an ex-colleague's new employer could potentially give rise to tortious liability, for which the employer is likely to be vicariously liable for as the context would amount to a close connection. There is no reported case to this effect at present, but the authors consider that the logic in *McKie* would apply equally to social media contact as to the email that was sent.

7.45 The following guidance can, we suggest, be drawn from the cases considered above.

---

[23]   [2011] EWHC 469 (QB), [2011] All ER (D) 128 (May).
[24]   [2011] EWHC 469 (QB) at [10].
[25]   [1994] 3 All ER 129, [1994] ICR 596.
[26]   [1990] 2 AC 605, [1990] 1 All ER 568.

(1) Postings on personal social media sites in free time from personal equipment are not generally covered by a reasonable expectation of privacy and Art 8 arguments in this regard will rarely succeed (*Teggart*).

(2) However this will likely apply only where a complaint or a report has been made; a trawl of social media for disciplinary purposes will fall foul of Art 8 unless there is a very clear policy in place. This can be contrasted however with monitoring of workplace accounts and email, if covered by an appropriate and legitimate policy (*Williams v Leeds United*).

(3) Harm and culpability remain relevant, particularly when considering the range of reasonable responses test (*Mason*; *Gosden*).

(4) A failure to bring to the attention of an employer material contained on private social media when a complaint has been made against an employee may well be very dangerous for that employee, although it may make a difference whether the complainant had access to the material, and what the code of conduct covers (*Smith v Trafford Housing*).

(5) Article 10 freedom of expression defences are not likely to succeed when personal comments are made against an individual (*Teggart*); but general expressions of view, however offensive, are likely to be protected to a significant extent (*Smith*).

(6) A company is not likely to be brought into disrepute by personal expressions of view, especially if the audience is small and exclusive.

(7) Claims under the PfHA 1997 will not succeed if they are only offensive: there needs to be something more (CPS guidelines, *Ferguson*).

(8) Companies are responsible for the content of their social media feeds, even where postings are by disgruntled employees (and see, by analogy, *McKie*).

(9) An employer may be vicariously liable for a campaign of harassment (*Otomweyo*, though see also *Gainsford*), even in personal time, if it knows or ought to have known that such campaign is being waged against an employee by a colleague.

Choice of forum

7.46 It is important that employers bear in mind that depending upon the nature of the claim that they are bringing or defending, the forum of litigation will differ. The concepts considered in these chapters straddle the Employment Tribunal and the county and High Courts. Advisors to companies will be familiar with the Employment Tribunal process but not necessarily as much so with the county court system. The following table sets out certain practical differences:

Employment Tribunal	County Court
Starting point is that each party bears their own costs	Save in small claims, loser will ordinarily pay winner's costs

Employment Tribunal	County Court
Relatively informal procedure, governed by the ET Rules	Governed by the CPR. Note far stricter regime for non-compliance with deadlines
Limited to areas falling within its jurisdiction	Wider scope to determine matters
Short limitation periods	Much longer limitation periods – 6 years for harassment and breach of contract claims
Reverse burden of proof may apply in discrimination claims	Burden of proof on the claimant
Limited enforcement powers	Wide enforcement powers
Trial likely necessary	Power to give summary judgment
ACAS gateway	No such gateway

7.47 It is also worth bearing in mind that issues of *res judicata* may arise where claims are brought in one jurisdiction and then proceeded with in another. In *Fraser v HLMAD Ltd*[27] the award for wrongful dismissal of the maximum £25,000 debarred the claimant from then seeking the difference between his actual loss and the statutory cap in the civil courts.

REMEDIES

7.48 Employers facing claims for misuse of social media face, potentially, a wide variety of causes of action and, therefore, differing potential liabilities. This section will consider the consequences of those potential liabilities in brief form.

Introduction

7.49 The House of Lords' well-known decision in *Majrowski v Guy's and St Thomas's NHS Trust*[28] opened up the PfHA 1997 in the field of employment relationships. Albeit somewhat tempered by the Court of Appeal's decision in *Sunderland City Council v Conn*[29] and subsequent authorities thereafter, the PfHA 1997 has potential to impact people in most walks of life, be they employee, neighbour or victim of harassment.

---

[27] (2006) ICR 1395.
[28] [2006] IRLR 695.
[29] [2008] IRLR 325.

7.50 It is well known that victims of harassment can obtain injunctive relief against their harassers pursuant to the Family Law Act 1996, the PfHA 1997 and basic common law principles covering injunctions and torts. However, s 3(2) of PfHA 1997 also allows for the recovery of compensation from the harasser. The section states:

3 Civil Remedy

(2) ... damages may be awarded for (among other things) any anxiety caused by the harassment and any financial loss resulting from the harassment.

7.51 However, despite being some 18 years old there is little case-law on the quantum of damages for claims under the PfHA 1997 and, what law there is, is generally only of first instance authority. Financial compensation is particularly relevant where the conduct complained of has ceased, as in such circumstances an injunction is no longer needed: the employee may have stopped working for the harassing boss, the neighbours may have moved away or the harasser may have been arrested. Indeed, given a 6-year limitation period, there is scope for claims for compensation to be brought some considerable time after the actual harassment has ceased although the measure of damages is to be open to question if the employee who leaves the employer's service waits 6 years before issuing proceedings. Equally, where the harassment is on-going, the risk of paying financial compensation may have the effect of 'focusing the mind' of the harasser and causing him to cease his harassing actions.

7.52 Notwithstanding the importance of its function, s 3(2) of the 1997 Act leaves open the fundamental question: on what basis should such compensation be assessed? In the important case of *Kuwait Airways Corporation v Iraq Airways Co*,[30] a case not involving claims for harassment but of general application to the scope and measure of damages, Lord Nichols of Birkenhead stated:

'71 In most cases, how far the responsibility of the defendant ought fairly to extend evokes an immediate intuitive response. This is informed common sense by another name. Usually, there is no difficulty in selecting, from the sequence of events leading to the plaintiff's loss, the happening which should be regarded as the cause of the loss for the purpose of allocating responsibility. In other cases, when the outcome of the second inquiry is not obvious, it is of crucial importance to identify the purpose of the relevant cause of action and the nature and scope of the defendant's obligation in the particular circumstances. What was the ambit of the defendant's duty? In respect of what risks or damage does the law seek to afford protection by means of the particular tort?'

7.53 Here we seek to consider other areas of law to draw similarities and obtain guidance that usefully can be applied to ascertaining the quantum of damages in harassment cases.

---

[30] [2002] 2 WLR 53.

It seems reasonable to assume that damages for harassment are likely, generally speaking, to be made up in the main of compensation for psychiatric-type harm and injury to feelings. There may also be scope for claims for special damages, for example for torn clothing or broken items after a struggle or caused by running away, are fairly simple to quantify on the basis of actual loss.

7.54 In the traditional arena in which psychiatric injury in recognised, that of personal injury, compensation can be awarded for recognised psychiatric illnesses in accordance with the House of Lords' decision in *McLoughlin v O'Brien*.[31] Lord Bridge in that case stated:

> 'The common law gives no damages for the emotional distress which any normal person experiences when someone he loves is killed or injured. Anxiety and depression are normal human emotions. Yet an anxiety neurosis or reactive depression may be a recognisable psychiatric illness ... So, the first hurdle that the plaintiff must surmount, when claiming damages, is to establish that he is suffering, not merely grief, distress or any other normal emotion, but a positive psychiatric illness.'[32]

7.55 Despite a number of subsequent cases on psychiatric injury, mere anxiety is not enough, without there also being some physical injury, for a successful personal injury claim. There needs to be a recognised psychiatric illness for compensation to be awarded. It would therefore appear that the PfHA 1997 goes further than the common law of personal injury by not actually requiring the victim to suffer such an illness before allowing compensation. If this is so, guidance as to compensation levels drawn from the common law relating to personal injury must be viewed with caution.

7.56 Further guidance in quantifying damages for harassment may be drawn from another scheme that awards damages for anxiety: the Criminal Injuries Compensation Board ('CICB'). The current scheme requires that the illness surpasses a threshold – that the anxiety or illness is 'disabling'. In comparison there is no such threshold for compensation pursuant to PfHA 1997. Indeed, the victim under the PfHA 1997 need not in fact suffer any alarm or distress at all, as the partial definition of harassment contained in s 7(2) states that references to harassment '*include* alarm and distress'. By definition then, 'alarm and distress' are something separate, though contained within the definition of harassment.

7.57 Traditionally also, damages for alarm and distress have been found in contract claims: *Jarvis v Swan Tours Ltd*[33] and *Jackson v Horizon Holidays*[34] being leading examples (dealing with damages for disappointment arising out of holidays that were not what was expected), with low amounts being awarded (£125 and £500 respectively). Whilst the inclusion of the words 'any

---

[31]   [1983] 1 AC 410.
[32]   [1983] 1 AC 410 at 431G.
[33]   [1973] QB 233.
[34]   [1975] 1 WLR 1468.

anxiety caused by the harassment' within s 3(2) of the PfHA 1997 seems to amount to a causative test along the lines of contract law, it is difficult to compare the concept of harassment to damages for distress in relation to breach of contract. Nonetheless the quantum of these awards show in this context that, on their own, alarm and distress do not sound in substantial damages.

7.58 In fact, pursuant to s 3 of the PfHA 1997 harassment amounts to a statutory tort. Rather than a simple causative test, tortious claims import a foreseeability test for recovering damages, with the traditional rules such as the 'egg-shell skull' and 'egg-shell personality' applying. This should be compared with the Court of Appeal's decision in *Essa v Laing Ltd*[35] where it was held that for the purposes of the statutory tort of race discrimination (now a claim under the Equality Act 2010) the victim was to be compensated for the damage that arose as a consequence of and directly from the act, without the need for the traditional concepts of reasonable foreseeability. On balance, however, it seems likely that for harassment damages the traditional tortious rules will apply.

7.59 Some authorities on non-contractual anxiety compensation show an equally low level of compensation to the contractual cases being awarded. In *Westminster Council v Heyward*[36] the Pensions Ombudsman awarded Mr Heyward £1,000 for 'distress and inconvenience in respect of the anxiety which he had suffered' as a result of maladministration. In *Ford v Large*[37] the claimant was awarded £3,000 compensation after a car accident for anxiety whilst driving.

7.60 These low levels of compensation should, however, be compared to the levels of injury to feelings awards recoverable in the Employment Tribunal for successful claims of discrimination. The starting point for the assessment of any such compensation is the well-known guidelines laid down in *Chief Constable of West Yorkshire v Vento*.[38] That case set down three brackets for injury to feelings damages: £500–5,000; £5,000–15,000 and £15,000–25,000. Since the delivery of this judgment, however, the Employment Appeal Tribunal has increased the brackets of awards in *Da'Bell v NSPCC*.[39] *Da'Bell* increased the bands to £6,600, £19,000 and £33,000 respectively. Applying the most recent RPI figures (May 2015) to these figures results in brackets of circa £7,900, £24,000 and £40,000. In addition to this, presently the EAT is handing down differing decisions as to whether these figures are to be uplifted by a further 10% in accordance with *Simmons v Castle*.[40] Can these brackets provide a basis for the quantification of damages under PfHA 1997?

7.61 The civil courts do not award damages to 'injury to feelings' as a separate head of claim in tortious matters and so any sums for anxiety awarded under

---

[35] [2004] ICR 746 (Rix LJ dissenting).
[36] [1997] 3 WLR 641.
[37] [1992] CLY 1563.
[38] [2003] IRLR 102.
[39] [2010] IRLR 19.
[40] [2012] EWCA Civ 1039.

PfHA 1997 are likely to be covered in any award made in a personal injury claim: *Green v DB Group Services (UK) Ltd*,[41] a case that caused many employers to panic when the claimant was awarded over £800,000. However, this was a traditional PI claim brought on the basis of stress at work, with a PfHA 1997 claim bolted on in the alternative. The claimant did not receive any separately quantified compensation for the PfHA 1997 claim. This has led many to feel that claims under PfHA 1997 will not provide much in the way of compensation. This may be correct when compared to psychiatric PI claims where the PfHA 1997 merely comprises an alternative cause of action to such claims (eg where there is a risk that the medical evidence will not show a causative link between the conduct and the illness (a major risk in stress at work claims)).

7.62 However, as in *Vento*, standalone claims under PfHA 1997 may not involve a claimant who has any sort of injury beyond injury to feelings caused by the harassment. Indeed, given the incomplete list of recoverable heads of claim contained in s 3(2) the authors believe that there is at the very least strong scope for arguing for the application of *Vento*-type brackets to claims under PfHA 1997. At the very least the claimant may be able to recover damages for injured feelings under s 3(2). Factors such as the length of time that harassment has taken place, the form it took, and the effect it had all play a part in determining what the level of compensation is to be. Whilst the barrier of the traditional tortious measure of damages would have to be overcome, the fact that the statutory tort created by PfHA 1997 appears to be of a broader nature in terms of recoverability of damages makes it more similar to the *Vento*-type situation than traditional personal injury claims.

7.63 That said, in *S&D Property Investments Ltd v Nisbet*,[42] Nichol J held, in the context of a claim for damages under PfHA 1997 for anxiety:

> '72. Section 3(2) of the 1997 Act says that damages can be awarded for "anxiety" amongst other things. In my judgment, Parliament was here intending to make plain that compensation could be given for the concern that harassment can generate even if it does not give rise to any psychiatric or medical condition. Psychiatric harm is a well recognised form of personal injury. Where a statute creates civil liability it would not be usual for Parliament to specify the particular types of physical harm or personal injury which are compensatable. It would go without saying that psychiatric harm (if proved and if satisfying the other usual conditions such as causation and foreseeability) would be recoverable. The express reference to "anxiety" must be intended to convey something more. In any case, it would be inapt to use this term if it was intended to be limited to a mental state that was so severe as to amount to an illness.
>
> 73. Ms Dainty on behalf of Mr French and S&D appeared to accept that "anxiety" short of psychiatric harm could be the subject of compensation. However, she submitted in her written argument that even in such cases there

---

[41]   [2006] IRLR 764.
[42]   [2009] EWHC 1726 (Ch).

ought to be medical evidence. Otherwise, she argued, the court would not be able to distinguish a groundless from a well-founded claim for damages.

74. I am not sure that she persisted in that position in oral argument. However, in any case, I do not agree with it. If, as I hold, "anxiety" is not limited to conditions which amount to psychiatric harm, medical evidence cannot be the exclusive means of proving the loss. *Martins v Choudhary* [2007] EWCA Civ 1379 does not help. Medical evidence had been available in that discrimination case. But the claimant was there seeking (and was awarded) damages for both psychiatric harm and injury to feelings. That is not the situation in the present case. Evidence of anxiety can instead come from lay witnesses: the victim of the harassment and those around him or her. The court can also take into account what is likely to have been the effect of the harassment in question.'

7.64 It therefore appears clear that damages for harassment are not limited to psychiatric harm. Of more importance to employers facing such claims, and in the context of the application of the *Vento* guidelines, Nichols J stated:

'I accept Ms Dainty's submission that it would be wrong simply to apply the same [*Vento*] bands to harassment cases. Compensation for discrimination necessarily involves an award for the humiliation of being treated differently on an impermissible ground such as race or sex. That is not a necessary feature of a claim under the 1997 Act. On the other hand, it is an essential characteristic of a claim under that Act that there has been a course of conduct. There will not be a case where damages for harassment have to be assessed for an isolated or one off occurrence.'

7.65 *Vento* is therefore not necessarily a clear analogy to PfHA 1997 cases. Each case will turn on its own facts and the evidence promulgated. As a result it is important to procure as much information as possible to rebut claims of loss. If an employee has frequently been on sick leave prior to the alleged behaviour, or has a pre-existing condition, this may be important evidence in respect of quantum. The effect on that particular employee, and the way that he has previously interacted with colleagues, may also be important.

7.66 It must not be forgotten that damages under PfHA 1997, as with damages for discrimination claims, are not limited to psychiatric injury alone. Section 3(2) makes it clear that financial losses resulting from the harassment can also be recovered. The following heads of claim may therefore be recovered as special damages:

- lost salary
- bonuses and other payments/benefits
- pension loss
- any sums the employee has to repay to the employer by way of a loan if the employee leaves employment
- whilst more likely in a neighbour dispute than an employment-based claim, if the victim has had to move home and lost money on the sale of their property then arguably the difference would be claimable ...

- ... this may lead to additional costs of travelling into work.

7.67 However, most reported harassment cases resulted in low damages. The cost, both in terms of legal fees and human time may however be significant. Whilst an employer may not have a significant financial liability for harassment claim, the non-pecuniary effects may nevertheless be substantial.

Practical steps and guidance

7.68 Discrimination claims can be defeated by an employer pleading the 'employer's defence' contained within s 109(4) of the Equality Act 2010, which requires the employer to show that it took all reasonable steps to ensure that discrimination did not take place. It would clearly not be 'reasonable' to expect an employer to have a 'policeman' on every corner; however employers can go a long way to establishing the reasonableness of their conduct by having in place, disseminating and providing, training on policies and procedures. This will include policies relating to social media and harassment.

7.69 It is important when considering issuing a claim for damages under PfHA 1997 that the necessary evidence is assembled to allow any letter before action to schedule the general and special damages claimed. Medical evidence may well be necessary to determine whether a claim can be brought.

Conclusion

7.70 At present the assumption when approaching damages for anxiety and distress for harassment claims under the PfHA 1997 is likely to be that nominal damages only will be awarded. However, in respect of a statutory tort the quantification of damages could arguably be said to be taken out of the general rules applicable to personal injury and is more correctly identified with *Vento*-type bands of awards for injury to feelings in discrimination cases. Indeed, the potential exposure for employers with such claims is considerable and growing with every increase in the retail price index and development in case-law.

CRIMINAL LAW

7.71 The criminal law has, for a number of years, contained a series of offences that protect people from, in effect, being harassed. Whilst employers are unlikely to find themselves in a situation where the criminal law applies to them, it is possible that they may have employees who are subject to criminal sanctions. The Public Order Act 1986 contains various offences protecting individuals from being in situations where they fear for their personal safety (such as affray), from thinking that violence will be used against them,[43] and from being caused harassment, alarm or distress.[44]

7.72 Generally these offences are restricted (at least to some degree) to those offences that occur in a public place, the theory being that protection of the person is safeguarded by the prohibition on offences against the person.

7.73 The PfHA 1997 includes various criminal offences: Harassment:[45] a summary only offence, carrying a maximum of 6 months' imprisonment and/or a level 5 fine; fear of violence:[46] an either way offence, carrying a maximum of 5 years' imprisonment and/or a fine on indictment; breach of a civil injunction:[47] an either way offence, carrying the same penalty as for the s 4 offence; breach of a restraining order;[48] an either way offence, carrying the same penalty as for the s 4 offence; a civil tort of harassment.[49]

7.74 Section 126 of the Serious Organised Crime and Police Act 2005 amended the Criminal Justice and Police Act 2001 and created a new offence of causing harassment, alarm or distress to a person in his or her home. The offence contains four ingredients that need to be proved. A person will commit an offence under s 42A(1) if:

- he or she is present outside or in the vicinity of any premises that are used as a dwelling;
- he or she is there to represent to the resident or another individual or persuade the resident or another individual that he should not do something he is entitled to do; or that he or she should do something he is not under any obligation to do;
- the person intends his presence to amount to the harassment of, or to cause alarm or distress to the resident; or knows or ought to know that his presence is likely to do so; and
- the presence of the defendant amounts to the harassment of, or causes alarm or distress to the resident, a person in the resident's dwelling, or a person in another dwelling in the vicinity of the resident's dwelling; or is likely to result in the harassment of, or cause alarm or distress of any such person.

7.75 The purpose of this offence is to give the police the ability to deal with harassing or intimidating behaviour by individuals towards a person in his home even after an incident has taken place. This means that the police can deal with protestors after the event. This will be useful if, for example, there is evidence of a protest on CCTV but the police were not present, or the police

---

[43] Public Order Act 1986, s 4.
[44] Public Order Act 1986, s 4A.
[45] PfHA 1997, s 2.
[46] PfHA 1997, s 4.
[47] PfHA 1997, s 3(6).
[48] PfHA 1997, s 5(5).
[49] PfHA 1997, s 3.

were present and could identify the protestors but there was some difficulty in enforcing a direction at the scene of the protest.

CONCLUSION

7.76   Employers should be aware of the potential risks that they run arising out of claims against them under the PfHA 1997, whether by employees, against employees or by third parties. In addition, they should be aware of the prospect of significant damages, not necessarily limited to those that an Employment Tribunal might award. The likelihood is that claims for damages under the PfHA 1997 will not be unduly significant, but it is worth noting that, in a deserving case, the court can make significant awards.

CHAPTER 8

INTELLECTUAL PROPERTY RIGHTS IN SOCIAL MEDIA

INTRODUCTION

8.01 There is a Latin quotation (which happens also to be a Metallica lyric), attributed originally to Publius Flavius in *De Re Militari*: '*sic vis pacem, para bellum*', which effectively translates as: 'if you want peace, prepare for war'. Nothing truer has been said with regards to employee relations with their employer. For this reason policies are of critical importance: if an employer is effectively to defend its reasoning before a court or tribunal after it has dismissed an employee, then it will be on firmer ground if it had in place a policy that covered the situation, and it has complied with its policy.

8.02 Many employment contracts, particularly in the private sector, will contain express clauses restricting an employee's right to take with them copyrighted material created by them during their employment, upon their employment ending. This prohibition will usually be designed to protect the intellectual property of the employer. Notwithstanding this well-established practice, there has been a real debate as to whether an employer can prevent Facebook/Twitter/LinkedIn accounts and the like leaving with the employee who was in control of those accounts. Employers are spending considerable capital (both financial and human) to build and develop networks of contacts and customers, often on these three major platforms simultaneously. The loss of such contacts can be a significant blow to the social media profile of the employer, particularly if the account is altered to a personal account or, worse, that of a competitor. Such accounts will also usually double as a database of company contacts, which could be of significant use to any competitor. Whilst the employer will hopefully have retained a database or spreadsheet separate to the social media account, it is the fact that those contacts are made available to a competitor that is likely to give rise to the risk of significant damage.

8.03 By far the most straightforward method to seek to protect the company's social media crown jewels is for those advising employers and those in HR roles to check and ensure there are express terms in the contracts of relevant employees covering the ownership of social media accounts, rather than belatedly to seek to rely on the potentially troublesome implied obligations of fidelity and confidence. However, the ambit of contractual terms, particularly if they are to be held to be enforceable, is likely to be fairly limited, and if an employee is tweeting from a purely personal account with no supervision and without there being an express contractual provision in this regard, then the employer will have little, if any, recourse to claim this account from the departed employee. If, however, the situation were reversed and the employee were tweeting from a corporate branded account about all things corporate then one can see little scope for arguing that the account is the employee's property, particularly where ownership is settled by the terms of the contract and an appropriate policy. A good contract and policy will in any event require an employee to remove any references to their employer even in respect of personal accounts after leaving employment.

8.04 In those Halcyon days prior to the advent of social media, where information was retained solely internally rather than potentially published to the world, the issues considered in this chapter posed little problem. For instance in *Pennwell Publishing (UK) Ltd v Ornstein and others*[1] the seemingly obvious point that the phone number and head office addresses of various contacts, a database of which had been downloaded, were in the public domain and so did not amount to 'confidential information' in the context of restrictive covenants was determined. However, the email addresses and direct dial numbers of contacts were confidential, were created in the course of employment and belonged to the employer. This finding was supported by the fact that the contact details in dispute were retained in the employer's contact management system and backed up to their server. In contrast, with social media the information, in the form of databases of followers, friends and connections, is stored remotely. As a result the logic applicable in *Pennwell* is less stark in the case of social media contacts in the context of confidentiality.

8.05 The defendants in *Pennwell* also sought to argue that the relevant database subject of the claim was a copyright database under the Copyright Designs & Patents Act 1988 ('CDPA') or under the *sui generis* property right created by the Copyright and Rights in Database Regulations 1997. The court dealt with this argument and determined that such a defence was not tenable:

> '107. I can, however, state my conclusions on this topic relatively shortly:
>
> (a) where a database is made by an employee in the course of his employment, his employer is be regarded as the maker of the database subject to any agreement to the contrary (Regulation 14(2));
>
> (b) otherwise, the maker of the database is defined by Regulation 14(1) which provides that 'the person who takes the initiative in obtaining, verifying or presenting the contents of a database and assumes the risk of investing in that obtaining verification or presentation shall be regarded as the maker of, and having made, the database';
>
> (c) thus, if the database was assembled by Mr Isles privately and for his own purposes, he would be treated as the maker of that database under Regulation 14(1) but if it can be said that the database was made in the course of this employment, then ownership will be that of the employer;

---

[1]   [2007] EWHC 1570.

(d)   for a relevant property right in a database to exist, there must be a substantial investment in obtaining, verifying or presenting the contents of the database under Regulation 13;

(e)   if a database constitutes the author's own intellectual creation by reason of the selection or arrangement of its contents, then it may be treated as an original work under Section 3A(2) of the Copyright Designs and Patents Act 1988;

(f)   it is not necessary, in the light of my other findings, for me to reach a conclusion as to whether the database either in its form on the Outlook system or in the form of the JuniorContacts.xls spreadsheet was an original work within the meaning of the Copyright Designs and Patents Act 1988, but it is right to indicate that I was far from persuaded that the exercise of assembling a list of contacts addresses would be sufficient to qualify.'

8.06 As with all things the grey area of mixed use of social media, for both work and personal purposes, presents a challenge. For the purpose of copyright arguments, it seems likely that an employer will be able to argue that a social media account linked to the business amounts to a database, and as such the employer is regarded as the maker of the database. There is, however, scope for argument as to whether a personal social media account that is also used for business purposes from time to time falls within the scope of reg 14(2). The dispute will thus be over whether the database was made in the course of employment. Where the feed is a mixture of personal and professional or if the Twitter handle contains a mixture of personal and professional, this intermingling may be taken to indicate some sort of joint ownership and so creates the potential for conflict when the relationship has ended. LinkedIn itself creates distinct problems: often there may be separate accounts for the company and the employee with their own social media accounts. Nevertheless the employee has the opportunity to gain and share contacts that have been obtained only as a consequence of their employment. Whilst this may in part be an aspect of professional development, and it is unavoidable (and in reality likely to be desirable) that an employee will make contacts during the course of their employment, it is the risk of those contacts being exploited in future that a policy of this nature should be directed towards.

8.07 Further, given the rise of flexible working and working from home particularly in those roles which involve promotion of the employer over social media, it may not be enough to argue that where the account is administered is sufficient to found control of the information. Where the 'workplace' is and how work undertaken can be ascribed to being done on 'work time' is an especially complicated matter. Communications and public relations employees may well be required to carry out work outside of normal working hours, as part of their obligation to respond to matters as they arise, or to exploit opportunities. The prevalence of smart technology and 'bring your own device to work days' muddies the water even further. This is not a problem that affects only the small to medium size business. Indeed, the larger the employer, the more likely it is that its employees will have correspondingly larger followings. In an example of this already mentioned in Chapter 2, when Laura Kuenssberg moved from the BBC to ITV she changed her Twitter handle (a straightforward process) from @CLauraK to @ITVLauraK, taking with her some 60,000 followers. Whilst the BBC did not take legal action against Ms Kuenssberg, the *PhoneDog* case, in which Noah Kravitz changed his handle to @noahKravitz from its previous twitter account name @PhoneDog-Noah, which had attracted 17,000 followers during his time with PhoneDog. PhoneDog commenced proceedings after he resigned. As previously noted, in December 2012 the matter settled with the terms being confidential.

8.08 The question of the ownership of employee LinkedIn contacts came before the High Court in *Whitmar Publications Ltd v Gamage & Ors.*[2] The court granted an interim injunction requiring the ex-employees to facilitate for Whitmar the 'exclusive access, management and control' of the LinkedIn groups they had created during their employment and that operated for Whitmar's benefit and promoted its business. The court summarised the allegations as follows:

'(a)   The taking of impermissible preparatory steps to compete with Whitmar. Mr Gamage and Ms Wright established Earth Island on the 31st August 2012. They were each directors and shareholders of Earth Island, which was established with the intention of competing with Whitmar at a time when they were still employed by Whitmar. In addition, Mr Gamage and Ms Wright identified premises from which to trade in Tunbridge Wells, the very same town as Whitmar has its premises. Furthermore, Mr Gamage registered an internet domain name on the 6th June 2012 for Earth Island's use.

(b)   Mr Gamage sought to solicit at least one other member of Whitmar's staff to Earth Island. He told Whitmar's accounts manager, Jan Hindley, that he would be starting a rival business 18 months before his resignation, and encouraged her to join the new venture. Another of Whitmar's employees, Andy Knaggs, was also solicited to join in 2012.

(c)   Mr Gamage, Ms Wright and Mr Crawley solicited business from Whitmar's clients. In October or November 2012, Mr Gamage and Ms Wright approached one of Whitmar's major customers, and informed him that they would be setting up in competition with Whitmar and sought his support.

(d)   Mr Gamage told Whitmar that he did not intend to publish a print-related title, when he in fact did have that intention.

(e)   Mr Gamage attempted to use the Linked-In groups maintained by Whitmar to further the interests of his new venture. When this was discovered by Whitmar, Mr Gamage was not straightforward about his conduct and in fact continued to attempt to use the Linked-In groups the very next day after his misconduct had been discovered.

(f)   In September 2012, Mr Gamage informed an industry colleague that he would be setting up a competitive business.

(g)   Neither Mr Gamage nor Ms Wright nor Mr Crawley reported their wrongdoing to Whitmar. In particular, Mr Gamage did not inform Whitmar of his intention to leave and form a competing business. As he had a role in Whitmar's corporate decision-making, he was clearly in a position in which he had a conflict of interest. In December 2012, shortly before he resigned, Mr Gamage took part in the decision by Whitmar to close one of its titles.

---

[2]   [2013] EWHC 1881 (Ch).

28. It is also contended on behalf of Whitmar that since Mr Gamage, Ms Wright and Mr Crawley have left Whitmar's employment, they have misappropriated and misused Whitmar's confidential information:

(i) Earth Island has produced a media pack which presents Earth Island as a business with strikingly similar features to Whitmar and boasts circulation figures corresponding to Whitmar's Circulation Database.

(ii) Earth Island is going to produce and market "extra specials" which mirror one of Whitmar's products and a guide to digital presses which mirrors Whitmar's "Printers Guide".

(iii) Ms Wright has not returned to Whitmar confidential information for Whitmar's Printers Guide.

(iv) Ms Wright has refused to provide Whitmar with the user name, password and all other access details for four Linked-In groups managed by her on behalf of Whitmar as part of her employment by Whitmar. Although Ms Wright claims that the Linked-In groups were personal to her and just a hobby, Ms Bone submitted that I should reject that explanation as Ms Wright does not have a computer at home.

(v) the defendants were using the Linked-In groups as their own and for the benefit of Earth Island.

(vi) Mr Gamage removed a large number of Business Cards which he had obtained and collated during the course of his employment by Whitmar.

(vii) Mr Gamage agreed to return the Business Cards to Whitmar, but before doing so and surreptitiously he purchased a programme called "Card Munch" which permitted him to copy and organise the information on the Business Cards.'

8.09 Whilst the case has been lauded as being ground-breaking as far as social media is concerned, in reality it is a more mundane decision concerning implied duties owed by employees to their employers. Further, it must also be borne in mind that the decision was made at an interim stage and was not a decision taken after hearing the evidence. The decision does once again highlight that, as stated throughout this work, social media does not create new wrongs: just new ways of committing those wrongs. Once again the courts have not sought to treat social media as being of a different order or category, or creating new rights or exceptions due to the nature of the platform. Be that as it may, however, the High Court found that the conduct of the ex-employees could be seen as a breach of the implied duty of fidelity which is imposed into all contracts of employment. The LinkedIn groups, whilst maintained by Whitmar, were used by the defendants 'to further the interests of [the] new venture'[3] by inviting members of that group to a bar for drinks, and the employees refused to provide the usernames, password and all other access details for the four groups managed by one of them on behalf of Whitmar. One of the difficulties that Whitmar faced was there were no written contracts of employment between it and the ex-employees and, accordingly, there was nothing into which could be incorporated express post-termination restrictions that would limit the

---

[3]   [2013] EWHC 1881 (Ch) at [27(e)].

ex-employees' activities or that dealt with the ownership of a work-created LinkedIn group. Restrictive covenants in the context of social media are considered later on in this book.

8.10   In a case dating from the same era, *Hays Specialist Recruitment Ltd v Ions, et al*,[4] the court considered the circumstances of a recruitment consultant uploading his employer's database onto LinkedIn for the purpose of starting a rival agency. Mr Ions was an employee of Hays for a period of some 6 years. He then left their employment in order to set up a rival recruitment agency. His employment contract did contain restrictive covenants preventing him from dealing with clients or applicants with whom he had had dealings in the course of his employment with Hays. Hays discovered that Ions had uploaded its internal client database to his LinkedIn profile, and then had used this to solicit clients to connect with him on the social media platform. Hays brought a claim for injunctive relief and for breach of the restrictive covenants. However by the time that the hearing took place Mr Ions had deleted his LinkedIn account. As a result he contended that Hays were simply conducting a fishing expedition and had no evidence upon which they could rely. He also contended that any uploading and soliciting of clients to connect with him was done with the consent and approval of Hays. The High Court found that Hays had reasonably grounds to be contemplating the bringing of a claim for breach of the restrictive covenants, and directed that he provide documentary information.

8.11   In the case of *East England Schools v Palmer*[5] an argument arose as to the enforceability of restrictive covenants in the context of Ms Palmer, a recruitment officer for the claimant. She took a job at an alternative educational recruitment company. She was alleged to be breaching the terms of her restrictive covenants, by soliciting and/or dealing with contacts that she had built up with the claimant. The covenants provided as follows:

15. Restrictions

15.1 In this clause: -

15.1.1 'Candidate' means an applicant for permanent, temporary or contract employment (employment through a service company) who has at any time during the Relevant Period been registered with the Company or any Group Company and with whom the Employee was materially involved or had personal dealings during the Relevant Period;

15.1.2 'Client' means any person, firm, school, nursery, company or entity which has at any time during the Relevant Period been a client of the Company or any Group Company and with whom the Employee was materially involved or had personal dealings during the Relevant Period;

---

[4]   [2008] EWHC 745.
[5]   [2013] EWHC 4138 (QB).

...

15.1.5 'Prospective Candidate' means any person, firm, company or entity who has at any time during the period of six months prior to the Termination Date been in negotiations with the Company or any Group Company about their availability for placement in permanent, temporary or contract employment and with whom during such period the Employee was materially involved or had personal dealings;

15.1.6 'Prospective Client' means any person, firm, school, nursery, company or entity which has at any time during the period of six months prior to the Termination Date been in negotiations with the Company or any Group Company for the supply of services and with whom during such period the Employee was materially involved or had personal dealings;

15.1.7 'Relevant Area' means within 30 miles of any branch of the Company or any Group Company at which the Employee worked in the Relevant Period;

15.1.8 'Relevant Period' means the period of 12 months ending on the Termination Date;

15.1.9 'Services' means services identical or similar to those being supplied by the Company or any Group Company at the Termination Date and with which the Employee was materially involved during the Relevant Period;

15.1.10 'Termination Date' means the date on which the Employee's employment terminates or, if she spends a period on garden leave immediately before the termination of her employment, such earlier date on which such garden leave commences;

15.2 The Employee covenants with the Company that she will not, save with the prior written consent of the Company, directly or indirectly, either alone or with or on behalf of any person, firm, company or entity and whether on her own account or as principal, partner, shareholder, director, employee, consultant or in any other capacity whatsoever:-

15.2.1 for six months following the Termination Date be engaged or concerned in any business supplying Services to schools, nurseries or teachers in the Relevant Area;

15.2.2 for six months following the Termination Date and in competition with the Company or any Group Company canvass or solicit business or custom from any Client or Prospective Client in relation to Services;

15.2.3 for six months following the Termination Date and in competition with the Company or any Group Company be concerned with the supply to any Client or Prospective Client of Services or otherwise deal with any Client or Prospective Client in relation to Services;

...

15.2.6 for six months following the Termination Date canvass or solicit business or custom from any Candidate or Prospective Candidate in relation to Services;

15.2.7 for six months following the Termination Date be concerned with the supply to any Candidate or Prospective Candidate of Services or otherwise deal with any Candidate or Prospective Candidate in relation to Services;

...

15.4 Each of the restrictions contained in this clause is an entirely separate and independent restriction, despite the fact that they may be contained in the same phrase, and if any part is found to be unenforceable the remainder will remain valid and enforceable.

8.12   Ms Palmer contended that the covenants were not enforceable, including because all relevant information was in the public domain, and thus could not be considered to be confidential to any particular agency. This was the case due to the increase in use of social media. All secondary schools publicised the contact details of their recruitment officer, and teachers would publicise themselves on social media in order to maximise their employment prospects. This argument failed and the covenants were upheld. Whilst the judge did not deal specifically with the social media argument in terms, he held that notwithstanding much information was in the public domain:

'Ms Palmer would have acquired other valuable information about schools and candidates in the course of her employment that was not publicly available (or, at least, not so readily available). That would include information about the personalities concerned, about their likes, dislikes and foibles, and about their special requirements. That information, as an aspect of her personal connection with the people concerned, would be of use to Ms Palmer in any attempt that she might make to divert to a new employer the business of those with whom she had dealt while employed by 4myschools.'

8.13   Employers are therefore likely to be able to assert proprietary rights where the information gathered by an employee in the course of her employment is not readily available over social media. It was insufficient for Ms Palmer to assert that the accessibility of contact details, qualifications and employment history could be gleaned from the World Wide Web or by perusing social media. The accessibility of such information by the general public is not in and of itself determinative; rather where information which was not publicly available, or not so readily available, is also obtained by the employee in the course of their employment, the employer is likely to be able to protect its information.

8.14   When considering asserting a right over social media, relevant factors as to the proprietary ownership of an account could include:

•   whether the account was created in the course of employment (in *Whitmar,* one of the ex-employees argued that the LinkedIn group was a hobby of hers; yet she did not have a computer at home);

- where the account was created;
- the purpose for which the account is used;
- whether the account was created prior to employment;
- whether the account identifies the employer, and the extent to which it purports to be a business account;
- the content and nature of the information contained within the social media platform; and
- the contractual relationship between the parties in respect of social media.

8.15 Similar considerations are applied in other jurisdictions. For example in the United States, numerous states have adopted the Uniform Trade Secrets Act. When considering and applying this Act, the courts have examined six factors when considering if information amounts to a trade secret under this Act:

- the extent the information is known outside of the business;
- the extent to which it is known by employees and others involved in the business;
- the extent of measures taken by the employer to protect that information;
- the value of the information to the business and its competitors;
- the amount of effort and money expended by the business in developing the information; and
- the ease by which the information could be properly acquired or duplicated by others.[6]

8.16 However the focus purely on confidentiality or trade secrets is not always wholly apposite in social media cases. Often, as in the *PhoneDog* and *Whitmar* cases, it is the continuing access not just to a database, but to a direct relationship with the connections. Thus it is suggested that seeking to define the ambit of the employer and the employee's respective ownership and control of social media accounts by contractual provisions is likely to assist the employer in asserting such control over access to one of their most important assets: their contacts. As already noted this is considered further in Chapter 10 below.

8.17 It is likely that, in the absence of a clear and enforceable contractual right, disputes over social media accounts and contacts can only be resolved on a case-by-case basis, with consideration of the relevant factual matrix and type of account in the context of the specific employer being undertaken in each case, applying the considerations suggested above. Does a LinkedIn connection have more of a 'quality of confidence' for the purposes of the employer's rights, than, say, a Facebook friend or Twitter follower? Applying those factors outlined above may give the likely answer.

---

[6] See, for further information, the Restatement of Torts (First) §757, vmt. B (1939) cited from JD McNealey, PhD, 'Who Owns your Friends?': *Phonedog v Kravitz* and business claims of trade secret social media information', Rutgers University Computer and Technology Law Journal 39: 30.

8.18   Who owns a mixture of public and private information may also depend on what platform the information is stored on: if it is contained in a closed networked system (such as an employer's internal computer network) then it is more likely to be owned by the employer, whilst publicly advertised connections are less likely to be the confidential property of the employer, absent a policy setting out contrary provisions.

8.19   Therefore, a social media policy is a useful starting point. Strong consideration should be given to requiring a total separation between work and personal social media accounts. If this is adopted then steps should be put in place to ensure 'social media-succession' when the present incumbent social media tsar moves on. The delivery of all passwords and usernames etc (as ordered in *Whitmar*) is the obvious answer (although careful reading of the terms of use between the platform and the employee who created the page will be important to ensure there is not breach of these terms). In situations where there is a division between personal and work social media usage then the policy needs to be expressly clear as to what happens to the information on the personal page that has only been created during the employment of the employee. In addition, the policy should also be bolstered by a contractual term requiring the removal by the employee upon termination of all such work-related information from the personal site. This will be further supported by post-termination restrictions on solicitation and dealing.

8.20   However, whilst this separation of the personal and the work-based may be practical for Twitter or Facebook, which are not likely to be primarily work focused (although of course accounts solely for the purpose of the work of the employer may be controlled by the departing employee, as considered above), it is more difficult in the context of a LinkedIn account, which is likely to attract connections to a pre-existing account on the basis of the employee's employment. It is far harder at first glance to see how a platform that is essentially an online CV could be separated out. For this reason, it may be that the employer will wish to consider covenants not just in respect of non-solicitation and non-dealing but also a contractual requirement to delete connections acquired arising out of the employment. This may lead to difficulties however, as, as already noted, in many cases it will be part of normal career progression for employees to make connections with contacts that already exist within his employer. It is for this reason that non-solicitation and non-dealing clauses, alongside or instead of such requirements, may in appropriate cases need to be deployed.

8.21   Whilst passwords and usernames are likely to be covered by the implied obligations of confidentiality, it is always best to have express terms covering these, which should be simple to draft and relatively easy to incorporate into a contract of employment. However, as noted above the real value in LinkedIn/Twitter/Facebook for a company are the actual contacts/followers/friends. There does not as yet appear to have been a decision directly on point in terms of ownership of such contacts. *Whitmar* seems to have been decided under the principles of confidentiality, as opposed to determining whether contacts/followers/friends can amount to a database either under the Copyright, Designs and Patents Act 1988 or under the Copyright and Rights in Database Regulations 1997.[7] One approach is to require the departing employee to delete and remove all such contacts that they have obtained during their employment with the employer. A useful, and probably unobjectionable, step here would be to require the individual employee who develops the lead to update the employer's central database, which would ensure the employer has the correct information stored on its systems and not remotely.

8.22 A distinctly less appealing option when an employee is leaving the company is for the outgoing employee to close or abandon the work-related social media account. This is distinctly less attractive than ensuring succession in the role as the contacts developed and the following nurtured over the years will be lost. However, it may be the only option for an unfortunate employer who has not safeguarded their position in advance. If the employer has not obtained the usernames and passwords for all platforms before terminating the employee, and has no contractual right to do so, it is likely to be difficult for the employer to take control of the account. It is submitted that it is unlikely to be reasonable to seek to oppose or realistically object in any way to a term in the contract of employment requiring the storing of all usernames and passwords by the employee in a fixed place. This can be bolstered by terms requiring the provision of all these details upon termination of the employment relationship.

8.23 The theft of sensitive information by employees, be it to pass onto competitors, or to provide the miscreant employee with an advantage when setting up a rival business, is and always has been a concern for employers and those advising them. Most contracts should contain clauses addressing the obtaining and use made of confidential information by employees. More detailed considerations of restrictive covenants are considered in the next chapter.

8.24 Employers should also beware the risks of giving away their intellectual property by posting on social media platforms. The Facebook terms and conditions provide as follows:

Sharing Your Content and Information

You own all of the content and information you post on Facebook, and you can control how it is shared through your privacy and application settings. In addition:

1. For content that is covered by intellectual property rights, like photos and videos (IP content), you specifically give us the following permission, subject to your privacy and application settings: you grant us a non-exclusive, transferable, sub-licensable, royalty-free, worldwide license to use any IP content that you post

---

[7]   SI 1997/3032.

on or in connection with Facebook (IP License). This IP License ends when you delete your IP content or your account unless your content has been shared with others, and they have not deleted it.

2. When you delete IP content, it is deleted in a manner similar to emptying the recycle bin on a computer. However, you understand that removed content may persist in backup copies for a reasonable period of time (but will not be available to others).

3. When you use an application, the application may ask for your permission to access your content and information as well as content and information that others have shared with you. We require applications to respect your privacy, and your agreement with that application will control how the application can use, store, and transfer that content and information. (To learn more about Platform, including how you can control what information other people may share with applications, read our Data Policy and Platform Page.)

4. When you publish content or information using the Public setting, it means that you are allowing everyone, including people off of Facebook, to access and use that information, and to associate it with you (i.e., your name and profile picture).

8.25 Likewise, Twitter provides:

5. Your Rights

You retain your rights to any Content you submit, post or display on or through the Services. By submitting, posting or displaying Content on or through the Services, you grant us a worldwide, non-exclusive, royalty-free license (with the right to sublicense) to use, copy, reproduce, process, adapt, modify, publish, transmit, display and distribute such Content in any and all media or distribution methods (now known or later developed).

Tip: This license is you authorizing us to make your Tweets on the Twitter Services available to the rest of the world and to let others do the same.

You agree that this license includes the right for Twitter to provide, promote, and improve the Services and to make Content submitted to or through the Services available to other companies, organizations or individuals who partner with Twitter for the syndication, broadcast, distribution or publication of such Content on other media and services, subject to our terms and conditions for such Content use.

8.26 Such terms and conditions are common to most other social media platforms. As such it is essential that companies are aware of the significant rights assigned to social media platforms when posts are made. When content is posted to such social media sites, a licence is granted (usually for the duration that the content is available) for the social media platform to use that content in any manner that it chooses, without any financial benefit to the user. This has led to unfortunate difficulties. In 2009, an American man, Peter Smith, was innocently perusing the internet, and was browsing Facebook. An advert popped up, offering Mr Smith the chance to meet single women on an online dating site. Unfortunately the photograph used by the advertiser to promote the site was that of Mr Smith's wife, Cheryl. It transpired that Facebook had sold on an image from a blog posted by Mrs Smith to the third party advertiser. Facebook subsequently blamed the 'rogue' third party, and modified its privacy settings. However as an example of the vulnerability of users' intellectual property, the case of Mr Smith is hard to beat.

8.27   The policies cited above lead to an interesting theoretical consideration: if the social media platforms obtain a licence to the content posted, which, even if deleted may remain available if it has been shared (perhaps involuntarily) what control, if any, does an employer actually have over the material posted, or over the account itself? However the material issue is not often likely to be as between the social media platform and the employer, but rather between the employer and the employee. This issue will ordinarily be controlled by the contract of employment and the attendant policies of the employer. The fact that content posted is automatically licensed should, however, worry employers; as the *Smith* case above shows, the harvesting of that licensed material could result in significant reputational damage.

8.28   Employers should therefore also ensure that social media policies and guidance make clear to employees that they should be careful what they post. A photograph by a tired secretary of the mess on her desk may inadvertently reveal confidential or proprietary information, which is then licensed to be distributed. Likewise, if employees are regularly posting on social media, they need to be careful not to infringe trademark or copyright. An employer could find itself liable or subject to a 'cease and desist' letter if employees are marketing the business using photographs taken from Google Images or Instagram, or infringe trademarks. Further, company slogans should be trademarked as necessary to avoid their infringement.

CONCLUSION

8.29   Employers should take steps to protect themselves and their intellectual property, both in the form of social media accounts and more generally. Once again it is worth stressing the need for a good and comprehensive policy that sets out in clear and unambiguous terms the rights respectively of the employer and the employee to social media accounts. Any account that is directly relevant to the business of the employer should be expressly stated to be the property of the employer, with provision for access details to be handed over on the termination of employment. Separation between work-related and personal social media accounts should be encouraged. Policies should make clear who has a right to contacts garnered in the course of employment. Likewise employers should take steps to ensure that their employees are not disclosing confidential or sensitive information during the course of their employment on social media, and should ensure that their monitoring policy stretches at least to the regular checking of company-operated social media accounts.

CHAPTER 9

CONTROLS AND CHECKS ON SOCIAL MEDIA PRESENCE

9.01 The preceding chapters have focused primarily upon the employer–employee relationship, and issues that can arise out of that relationship in the context of employment law and the law of harassment. The purpose of this chapter is to consider more broadly other legal matters that may cause concern for employers. This chapter will therefore consider the application of restrictive covenants to protect employers; the risks of defamation claims arising out of social media, and the right to be forgotten, together with further steps that employers may wish to take to protect themselves from liability.

POST-TERMINATION RESTRICTIONS

9.02 Contractual obligations that govern the employment relationship can either be express or implied. Implied into every contract of employment is the duty of fidelity that, essentially, means an employee should act honestly towards their employer, not make a secret profit from that relationship and should not compete with the employer; further, the employee should disclose to its employer all relevant information the employee gains during the course of their employment. Misuse of social media, as with any other sort of misconduct, can offend these duties. However if an employee leaves the employer's employment and merely takes the contents of their LinkedIn profile with them this is unlikely to fall within the scope of this general duty, as it will come to an end with the termination of the contract of employment. Yet businesses today spend an inordinate amount of money and time (both employee and management) in nurturing relationships. The loss of a robust social media presence can result in the loss of months, if not years, of marketing and development. With the ubiquity of portable handheld computers in the form of internet-enabled smartphones, and the rise in homeworking where the employee has remote access to the employer's networked system the potential for misuse is immense. Reliance upon a mere implied term does not carry with it any disincentive against misconduct, because an implied term is, by its very nature, not spelled out in the contract and so the employee may be blissfully and understandably ignorant of its existence.

9.03 Accordingly, it is suggested that it is sensible practice to ensure that there are express terms incorporated into every contract of employment regulating the use of social media during employment and the effect of the ending of employment on the social media profile of the employee. For instance as to the question of legal ownership of a social media account and its followers (which was considered in Chapters 2 and 8), there is, at present, no specific determination in English law that resolves this question. However this issue will only arise where the question is left undecided by the contract between employer and employee, including the former's policies in this regard. Whilst the terms of that contract will ordinarily only apply during the course of the employment relationship it may be that employers will wish to consider including social media restrictive covenant provisions as a standard term, in order to ensure that an employee remains bound by particular duties and obligations even after the termination of their employment.

9.04 The impact of express terms in the contractual arrangement between employer and employee cannot be overemphasised: express terms in this area are vital because as the implied duty of fidelity owed by an employee to his employer comes to an end upon termination of employment,[1] it is necessary for such a covenant to be inserted into the contract of employment for the employer to be able to enforce any desired rights and obligations against an employee once they have departed. On a more human level, however, the clear language that should be contained within a contract of employment should, it is hoped, deter an employee who is considering moving employment from committing acts of misconduct, or from being less than open with their employer: such terms and conditions, coupled with effective policies, should have at least some deterrent effect.

9.05 Unfortunately the area of restrictive covenant law is notoriously complex, and the complexity is compounded as irreparable damage can be inflicted upon the ex-employer within a dramatically short period of time: if an employee walks out of work with the employer's customer lists (metaphorically) under their arm, every day the employee has access to this information is a day the ex-employer stands to lose sales, contacts and the benefit of the time it has dedicated to developing its market position.

9.06 Issues arising out of such covenants are becoming increasingly common as more and more employers seek to protect themselves and their businesses, and to protect their customer bases by seeking to impose post-termination restrictive covenants, particularly in the field of social media. Yet again it is worth noting that social media does not create in and of itself a new field of jurisprudence; it merely changes the form and manner in which the threat to the employer of an employee using its information for his own purposes, or acting carelessly or foolishly, is realised.

9.07 However the very real and very damaging threat does not mean an employer will find courts willing to uphold all and any covenants after termination. Such terms are, as a starting point, considered to be void as illegal restraints of trade and an affront to public policy and as such unenforceable

---

[1]   *J A Mont (UK) v Mills* [1993] IRLR 172.

unless they can be shown to amount to a reasonable restriction. As with all such factually sensitive matters each case gives rise to its own unique set of factors: what is reasonable in one situation will not be reasonable in another and so restrictive covenants, unless carefully and properly drafted, can be a minefield for both employers and employees. The simple adoption or copying and pasting of covenants from one contract to another, or taken from the internet or bland precedent, will often not result in a covenant which a court is prepared to enforce. For instance a 'blanket' restrictive covenant will not normally be upheld by the courts. In order for a restrictive covenant to have any prospect of being able to be enforced, it must merely afford reasonable protection of legitimate business interests. Thus a blanket non-competition covenant will generally be void for illegality (eg 'You will not compete with the employer for a period of 2 years after the termination of your employment'). Such a clause is likely to fail on numerous grounds: the period for which it applies; the lack of any geographic limitation, and the lack of any apparent need for such a restriction (eg why limit a cleaner from cleaning for another).

9.08 Against this, however, must be weighed the right of an employer to seek to protect customer connections or goodwill, including the risk of reputational damage; connections with suppliers; and trade secrets and confidential information.[2]

9.09 However, the covenant must extend only so far as is reasonably necessary to protect the legitimate interests of the employer. Thus it is usual when considering valid restrictive covenants to find provisions preventing an ex-employee:

- competing within a certain area;
- soliciting or dealing with customers or suppliers of the employer;
- enticing away former colleagues from the employer;
- using or disclosing trade secrets and confidential information.

9.10 Covenants that are unreasonable or wider than necessary to protect legitimate business interests will likely therefore not be enforceable and the court has no power to rewrite the covenant so as to make it reasonable and, therefore, enforceable: see for instance the recent case of *Prophet v Huggett*,[3] where the contract of the employee contained a restrictive covenant that prevented him from working 'in any area and in connection with any products in which he was involved whilst employed'. He worked on a software product called PR3. This was a unique product to Prophet. Huggett left and injunction proceedings ensued. The High Court noted that the clause gave no protection to Prophet, as only they used PR3, so the judge concluded that it was appropriate to rewrite the clause to include the words 'or similar thereto' at the end. The Court of Appeal overturned the decision below. It agreed that the

---

[2] *Stenhouse Australia Ltd v Phillips* [1974] 1 All ER 117; *Herbert Morris Ltd v Saxelby* [1916] AC 688.
[3] [2014] IRLR 797 CA.

clause gave no protection to Prophet but the language used was unambiguous, and there was no basis for the court to recast the term.

9.11   Thus, simply providing that an employee cannot deal, solicit or work in 'any industry that competes with the employer' or similar is likely to be unenforceable, especially in the age of multi-service companies. An employee employed in an arm of a company that deals with aerospace, is unlikely lawfully to be prevented from working for a business that provides contract cleaning services, simply because a branch of his ex-employer undertook such work.

9.12   An employer cannot enhance the possibility of enforceability by including within their contracts a term that states that the employee agrees the restriction is reasonable: the expressed views of the parties to the contract are not of assistance when assessing the adequacy of the protection: *Ashcourt Rowan Financial Planning Ltd v Hall*[4] in which the High Court stated that it gave 'little weight' to clauses in the contract where the parties stated that the covenants were 'fair and reasonable in the circumstances', as the covenants were matters of public policy that parties were not permitted to prevent or limit a court from enquiring into.

9.13   The net effect of the above case-law and the 'all or nothing' nature of restrictive covenant litigation (in most cases, either the covenant applies or it does not) means that care needs to be taken to ensure as far as is possible that the covenant will be enforceable, not just at the outset of the employment but frequently and regularly whilst employees remain employed. The reasonableness of the covenant is assessed at the date that the contract was entered into, so employees who move (be it to different roles, or up the hierarchy), may be covered by wholly inappropriate terms which, as a result will not be enforceable. It is therefore important to ensure that upon such a move, fresh contractual terms are agreed and any restrictive covenants are appropriately updated. It is likely in traditional situations to be the case that the more senior the employee, the broader the terms of the covenant. However with social media, young and junior employees may be far more likely to be given the responsibility of creating and/or maintaining a social media presence. As a result, care needs to be taken in crafting appropriately the terms of restrictive covenants to cover the risks perceived in respect of such junior employees, without drawing the same so widely as to make them unenforceable.

9.14   Accordingly, a considerable amount of care and attention needs to be spent when drafting such contractual terms. And dealing with each of the bullet points above is not just a simple tick box exercise: eg merely because the term prevents competition in a certain defined area does not mean it will be enforceable, as everything will depend on the facts. Equally the nature of the information to be protected is of key importance, as is the location where it is

---

4   [2013] IRLR 637.

stored: in *Pennwell Publishing v Ornstein and others*[5] information such as addresses and mainline phone numbers were not held to be confidential as such information could easily be obtained from public sources yet the direct dial numbers could be the subject of protection. It is worth noting however, and is a factor considered below, that the details in that case were maintained on the employer's networked computer system and, in particular, in Outlook.

9.15 In the High Court's judgment it highlighted the seminal definition of trade secrets:

> 'It is clear from the decision in the Court of Appeal in *Faccenda Chicken Ltd v Fowler* ([1987] 1 CH 117) that an employee cannot be restrained from using information obtained during his employment after that employment has come to an end unless it falls within the category of specific trade secrets. That applies even where the employee has gained knowledge of a large range of useful commercial information such as names of customers and how to contact them. Thus, although an employee will be restrained from using that information during his employment, he is not restricted from using it afterwards unless it falls into the restricted category. The Court of Appeal concluded that in order to assess whether particular information is protected it is necessary to consider all the circumstances of the case and they set out the following as matters to which attention must be paid: -
>
> "(a) The nature of the employment. Thus employment in a capacity where 'confidential' material is habitually handled may impose a high obligation of confidentiality because the employee can be expected to realise its sensitive nature to a greater extent than if you were employed in the capacity where such material reaches him only occasionally or incidentally.
>
> (b) The nature of the information itself. In our judgment the information will only be protected if it can properly be classed as a trade secret or as material which, while not properly to be described as a trade secret, is in all the circumstances of such a highly confidential nature as to require the same protection as a trade secret *eo nomine*. The restrictive covenant cases demonstrate that a covenant will not be upheld on the basis of the status of the information which might be disclosed by the former employee if he is not restrained, unless it can be regarded as a trade secret or the equivalent of a trade secret."'

9.16 It is plain from this decision that individual addresses and contact details were not in themselves sufficiently confidential to amount to a trade secret. Many of them would fall into the first category identified by the court in *Faccenda Chicken*, namely material easily available and in the public domain, although certain items, such as direct telephone numbers and private email addresses, would not fall into that category.

---

5   [2007] EWHC 1570 (QB).

9.17 The situation is much less certain where the information is not stored on the employer's network, eg on LinkedIn, as it will be harder to establish a proprietary right for such information that has never been in the physical possession of the employer.

9.18 At a general level, therefore, what can an employer do to protect their interests when drafting such covenants? As stated above, every case is fact sensitive and a boiler-plate approach to covenants is unlikely to result in enforceable restrictions. However, some factors do appear to be of such key importance that they should be actively considered. It goes without saying that such contractual terms should be bolstered by a robust and well-disseminated social media policy. Further, in the precedents section of this work, the authors have suggested the type of covenant which we consider would need to be in place in a case such as *Whitmar* to protect not just access to the LinkedIn groups but also to the accounts and information themselves. As is noted in this chapter, it is unlikely that simply applying a template covenant to a contract will be sufficient to render that covenant enforceable, but the precedents we have provided should be capable of thoughtful adaptation to particular circumstances.

9.19 It is important to consider the express terms that should be contained in contracts. Firstly, there is nothing inappropriate or unlawful in a contract of employment vesting the ownership of any social media profile with the employer, be it work related or a personal profile, if that is a contractual term to which the employee has signed up. A personal profile created for non-work purposes and that is not used for work purposes will, however, likely not be amenable to such a term, but an account run by an employee from which work-related material is published, or which identifies with the employer, may well be able so to be controlled. Whilst it is possible that an employer could succeed in requiring an employee to hand over a work-related profile without such an express term, such an argument would be difficult to make out as being covered by implied contractual terms, and undoubtedly would be bitterly fought. Requiring an ex-employee to hand over a personal profile to an employer is likely to be highly controversial and so, the authors believe, would require a clear express contractual term setting out this obligation in unequivocal terms.

9.20 An employer can take various steps to enhance its prospects in compelling the delivery-up of social media assets from departing employees. For instance, it can require the alignment of the social media profile with its business: Twitter handles can be required to indicate the name of the business, whilst dedicated LinkedIn profiles can be imposed. This would, of course, remove the argument that could otherwise be raised by the employee that they came to the role with the contacts already in place. Of course, such measures bring with them the potential for credibility damage if the employee tweets derogatory things from an account expressly linked to the business.

9.21 Other overt relevant steps to align the profile and the business could include, for instance, the inclusion of the business logo and links to the businesses website. Less overt methods could include the use of a dedicated LinkedIn profile that can only be accessed or edited via the computer system/technology provided by the employer.

9.22 The above considerations highlight that if employers are to require their employees to use social media, they should ensure that they are contractually protected, so far as is possible, against risk. It cannot be stated strongly enough that whilst contractual clauses requiring the alignment of the social media asset to the business are a vital first step to protecting the employer, they are not enough alone fully to protect it. Such clauses should also be bolstered with non-compete and non-solicitation clauses, so as to prevent the employee upon his departure from immediately approaching the customers over whom they had influence. Such clauses clearly offend the public interest of freedom to work and so there are important factors that will weigh upon any judicial consideration of their enforceability when assessing whether to uphold them. Basic points to be considered include that the business of the employer should be clearly identified and identifiable, as should the geographic or sectorial area in which the employer conducts its business.

9.23 Another relevant consideration is the influence the employee has over customers and other members of staff (a more senior employee is likely to have more influence than a more junior one); closely aligned factors are the impact such covenants are likely to have on an employee (eg a 2-mile exclusion for a banker in the city of London is likely to have more of an impact than a 2-mile exclusion for a hairdresser, owing to the concentration of bankers in the city) and the duration of any restriction. The longer the restriction the harder it is to justify its legitimacy: in a market where customers only buy their products annually (eg insurance) it is likely to be harder to justify any exclusion for more than this period,[6] and it will likely be harder still to justify the prohibition in cases where the employee has no contact with the restricted customer.

9.24 It should not, however, be thought that there is anything to prevent an employer effectively using an express term to bolster the implied duty of fidelity and require that the employee only use professional networking to advance the employer's business. It is simply necessary to ensure that any such requirement is tightly, appropriately and proportionately drawn to protect the employer's legitimate business interests.

9.25 A further potential protection which could be deployed is for the employer to require its employees to duplicate all contacts they have and which they obtain in the course of their employment on the employer's computer network or master database, thus effectively duplicating the *Pennwell* position where contacts were stored on the employer's network. In doing so the employer may be able to argue that all such contacts were obtained in the

---

[6]   *Romero Insurance Brokers v Templeton and another* [2013] EWHC 1198.

course of employment and were compiled as part of its master database. As such, the employee is not entitled to retain such data or contacts.

9.26 It should be usual for employers to include provisions in their contracts of employment requiring the surrender of passwords to the relevant social media profiles controlled by their employees for the purposes of work upon the termination of employment. The authors suggest that such a term is the most efficacious provision to retain control at least of company social media accounts or those which have been set up under the aegis of the employer. An alternative is a term requiring the deletion of social media profiles upon the ending of employment. However such terms could very well have the effect of depriving the employer of the material that is contained within the profile (which might from the perspective of the employer mean that it loses important contacts, as well as any evidence of wrongdoing by the employee.

9.27 Many employees may be working under contracts that pre-date the advent of the world wide web or of the prevalence of social media. Employers may wish to consider whether it is as a result appropriate to consider the provision of new contractual terms. It is important to note that the mere imposition of new contractual terms containing appropriate restrictive covenants may give rise to difficulties, particularly due to the requirement for consideration supporting any such provision in order for an enforceable contractual term to arise. There must be some consideration to support the restraint, which must be more than merely a promise to perform an existing contract.[7] Where there is no express benefit of payment associated with a variation of contract, such a covenant will be unenforceable.[8] That case also made clear that continued employment in the absence of a dismissal or other sanction for a failure to accept the variation does not amount to good consideration. There are conflicting authorities as to whether the courts will consider the adequacy of the consideration when considering enforceability; as a result employers seeking to insert covenants of the sort considered here by way of variation would be well-advised to ensure that they can demonstrate that the restriction is supported by consideration.

9.28 Whilst any covenants contained in a contract of employment should be restated in any settlement agreement that is agreed between the employer and departing employee, there is nothing inappropriate in the ex-employer seeking to introduce such terms into a settlement agreement for the first time. Of course, the willingness of the employee to agree to such terms will obviously depend on the limit that these new terms are likely to have upon the employee and their future employability: for instance, if the employee was not required to have a dedicated Twitter account for their business tweets during their employment and so used a personal account to tweet business news they are less likely to be willing to surrender this account or its password as part of the settlement agreement. However in the absence of contractual provisions in the

---

7   *WRN Ltd v Ayris* [2008] EWHC 1080 (QB).
8   See, eg, *Reuse Collections Ltd v Sendall* [2015] IRLR 226.

terms of employment or any incorporated social media policy, such negotiation may be a way in which employers can seek to protect themselves.

9.29   It is submitted that the biggest challenge employers face in respect of retaining social media accounts used for business purposes is that of the mixed social media profiles, where an account is used for both business and personal usage by the employee. Such mixed accounts pose very real issues for employers and potentially insurmountable problems for the court when it is being asked to uphold covenants limiting an ex-employee's use of such profiles. However, an employer who has appropriately drafted covenants is likely to succeed in any action based on the conduct of an employee who, upon moving from Employer A to Employer B tweets using their mixed-Twitter account that includes numerous customers of Employer A that they have moved employers and that they can be reached at their new employer's offices. Even if this tweet was sent with the intention of informing their friends and family, such a tweet is likely to offend any non-solicitation and/or non-dealing clause in their contract of employment as it will be seen as a communication to a work contact informing that contact of the move of the employee. The work-centric nature of the tweet is likely to be seen as an attempt to have that follower have their custom move to the new employer.

9.30   This situation is more involved, and potentially more troublesome, for the employer, where the employee joins them (Employer B) from Employer A and brings with them a following of 200 customers on their Twitter feed. By requiring the employee to enter any new followers they obtain during their employment with Employer B onto a database owned and administered by Employer B during their employment with Employer B, both parties are likely to be protected. However, when the employee moves to Employer C, Employer B is likely not be able to prevent the employee taking the original 200 contacts with them, as they were (after all) contacts originating with the employee to begin with. Employer B meanwhile will have gained rights over those new contacts subsequent to the move, who have been logged into its database. In this situation it is likely that Employer B will not be able to require the deletion of the employee's Twitter account in its entirety as that would thwart the employee's rights to his original 200 contacts. However, with an appropriately drafted clause in the contract, Employer B will be able to require the deletion of those followers obtained during the employment period with it, and the database will provide a good starting point to identifying who those followers are.

9.31   A 'deletion of contacts upon ending of employment' clause will have to be bolstered, however, by clauses preventing 'dealing' (that is, in the broadest sense, having contact with) and solicitation (that is, contacting for the purposes of obtaining work) clauses as otherwise the utility of the deletion clause is undermined. If, on their first day with Employer C, the employee is able to contact the customers he has only just deleted, perhaps by keeping a separate record, the purpose of such a deletion clause is obviated. This is another example of just how much social media is embedded into business and modern industry, yet many employers are not protecting what is probably their biggest asset: their contacts book.

9.32 What this section has sought to highlight therefore is the need for all employers and those advising them to revisit the whole suite of post-termination restrictions to ensure that they are fit for purpose and are adequate to protect the interests of the employer, whilst allowing the employee access to their own personal experience and contacts. Cases such as *Whitmar Publications Ltd v Gamage & Ors*[9] are rare: the wrongdoing of the employees was so pronounced and obvious that the court was able to uphold the claim for injunctive relief on the basis of breaches of the implied duty of fidelity where there were no written contracts of employment in place between the ex-employer and its ex-employees who left to compete with the employer. Ordinarily it is likely that the factual matrix in that case will not be replicated. As a result employers should sensibly ensure that their restrictive covenants are fit for purpose in the new connected world.

Do	Don't
Ensure that a covenant is drafted so as to cover only the legitimate business needs of the employer	Use blanket terms: these will often be construed as too wide
Make sure that employees are required to give up work-related social media accounts and passwords	Allow employees sole control of workplace feeds
Consider imposing restrictive covenants for existing employees	Forget to ensure that there is appropriate consideration
Update covenants to take account of changing aspects of social media platforms	Assume that terms will apply to all future developments
Be aware of what social media usage from a workplace perspective is taking place	Leave social media to the young
Consider the risk to the business of social media contacts falling into the hands of a rival employer once an employee leaves	Assume that social media contacts have no value

---

[9]   [2013] EWHC 1881 (Ch).

Do	Don't
Consider limiting reference to work only to professional social media accounts	Run the risk of mixed use work and personal accounts

Defamation

9.33 It is only relatively recently that issues relating to online defamation and harassment have really come to the fore. This is, perhaps, surprising given the size of the internet and the ability of anyone with even vague technical ability to create a website but it may also represent a shift away from the informality of electronic communication as a medium and recognition by business that their reputations can severely be damaged by defamation on the internet. There is also the potential for liability if corporate social media feeds are used in a defamatory manner.

9.34 A powerful weapon available to a victim of malicious statements on the internet is the law of defamation. This was loosely defined by Halberstam in an article in 2008 entitled 'Defamation and the Internet' as 'the publication of a statement which tends to lower a person in the estimation of right-thinking members of society generally'. Such remedy may be available both to a company subject to a campaign against it or an individual seeking redress Where the creator of a malicious website or creators of defamatory statements, emails or postings can be identified, it is usually fairly straightforward for a claim for compensation to be brought against that person, provided, of course, that they are of sufficient financial substance for this to be worthwhile. Together with such a claim, or as a standalone remedy, an application for an injunction requiring the removal of such information is likely to be an effective remedy.

9.35 Such claims can result in significant financial compensation as well as ruinous costs. In around 2007 an award in the region of £100,000 was made against John Finn, who had anonymously created a website known as 'Dads Place', which was the conduit for various seriously defamatory allegations on what was described as 'a seriously defamatory, abusive and scurrilous anonymous website'. Whilst the defamation in question was directed in that case to an individual, it could just as easily have been directed against an employer or business. Other high profile UK cases include the Gina Ford action against the Mumsnet website and the action brought by advertising agency WPP against Fullsix Spa.

9.36 It is clear that defamation claims in the context of social media are on the rise. In October 2014, *The Guardian* reported that claims had risen 23%. Cases brought by individuals relating to social media, text message and other online forums quadrupled, albeit from a low base of six cases to 26 cases. 31 claims were brought by businesses, a number of those cases resulting from matters taking place over social media. It may be that the reforms to English law brought in by the enactment of the Defamation Act 2013, which requires proof of 'serious harm', which in the context of a company is likely to require significant financial damage, will alter this trend, but this is not yet borne out by the statistics. A high profile case in 2013 was the action brought against Sally Bercow by Lord McAlpine,[10] following comments which she had made on Twitter. Lord McAlpine also brought claims against numerous other Twitter users. In that case, Tugendhat J found that the tweet was libellous. Damages were later agreed at £15,000. Tugendhat J made clear that, when applying the 'reasonableness' test in terms of meanings and inferences, the hypothetical reader must be taken to be a reasonable representative of followers:

> '57. The legal principles to be applied when determining the question of meaning are in part derived from the *Rubber Improvements* case. They were summarised by Sir Anthony Clarke MR in *Jeynes v News Magazines Ltd* [2008] EWCA Civ 130 at [14]-[15] (where "he" means "he or she"):
>
>> "The legal principles relevant to meaning have been summarised many times and are not in dispute ... They may be summarised in this way: (1) The governing principle is reasonableness. (2) The hypothetical reasonable reader is not naïve but he is not unduly suspicious. He can read between the lines. He can read in an implication more readily than a lawyer and may indulge in a certain amount of loose thinking but he must be treated as being a man who is not avid for scandal and someone who does not, and should not, select one bad meaning where other non-defamatory meanings are available. (3) Over-elaborate analysis is best avoided. (4) The intention of the publisher is irrelevant. (5) The article must be read as a whole, and any 'bane and antidote' taken together. (6) The hypothetical reader is taken to be representative of those who would read the publication in question."
>
> 58. It is important in this case to stress point (6). The Tweet was not a publication to the world at large, such as a daily newspaper or broadcast. It was a publication on Twitter. The hypothetical reader must be taken to be a reasonable representative of users of Twitter who follow the defendant. What the characteristics of such people might be is in part agreed, and in part for submissions by the parties as to what I should infer from what is agreed.'

9.37 This is clearly relevant when considering the risk of libel proceedings against an employer for a tweet or (possibly) a retweet: what are the natures of the followers? It is likely that a business's followers will be drawn from a somewhat narrow pool – customers, employees, and the like. As such there is potentially more of a risk that, particularly if a defamatory tweet relates to a competitor, they will be found to be able reasonably to draw an inference as to meaning, even if the tweet is relatively oblique. In respect of Sally Bercow, Tugendhat J concluded that her followers were likely to be people sharing her interest in politics and current affairs. A company's followers are likely to be deemed to share its interest in whatever field it is involved in. In similar fashion, an individual defaming a company may well have a follower profile that results in an oblique meaning being clear to them.

---

[10] *McAlpine v Bercow* [2013] EWHC 1342 (QB).

9.38 Nor will a small number of followers or a limited period of time necessarily mean that damages awarded will necessarily be nominal. Lord McAlpine did not pursue Twitter users who had commented or retweeted where they had a small number of followers, instead requiring them to make a donation to charity. It is, though, clear that posting on social media does not give rise to a presumption in law that a substantial publication has occurred, as Eady J made clear in *Carrie v Tolkien*[11] in the context of a post that remained live for a little over 4 hours:

'17. It would appear to be established that there is no presumption in law to the effect that placing material on the Internet leads automatically to a substantial publication: see eg Al *Amoudi v Brisard* [2001] 1 WLR 113. It is necessary to plead and establish any publication relied upon. There must be some evidence on which an inference can be drawn in relation to that very short period of time.

18. It will not suffice merely to plead that the posting has been accessed "by a large but unquantifiable number of readers". There must be some solid basis for the inference. That form of pleading is no more than bare assertion.

19. It may very well be that the claimant could gain access to the records of visitors to his website. Be that as it may, he has not done so. Without evidence of substantial publication it is submitted that there is no basis for concluding that there was, over the short period in question, the commission of a real and substantial tort such as to justify the deployment of the court's resources. I have already referred to the case of *Jameel*, although it is fair to point out that this jurisdiction will only be exercised in relatively rare cases: see eg *Steinberg v Pritchard Englefield* [2005] EWCA Civ 288. Nevertheless, this would appear to be a suitable case to classify the claim as an abuse of process, in accordance with the *Jameel* doctrine, because of the minimal (if any) level of publication.

20. Sometimes it may be necessary to pursue a claim, notwithstanding the evidence of substantial publication, in order to obtain an injunction and silence the defendant from continuing to defame the claimant. There is no reason in this case to suppose that the defendant is likely to publish any allegations of a similar nature in the future. It may be that others have made such allegations on the Internet, but that would not justify proceeding against this Defendant. It goes without saying that an injunction against him would have no effect upon others.'

9.39 It is therefore necessary in a libel claim to establish publication by evidence. The mere fact that a post has been made does not automatically mean that publication has been established. Instead a potential claimant must establish that the post has been read or downloaded before proceeding with a claim. This may well be relevant where a post has been swiftly deleted and has not been retweeted or otherwise replicated, and demonstrates the importance of management monitoring Twitter, LinkedIn and other social media corporate feeds. This is particularly the case where the alleged defamer has a limited number of followers.

---

[11] [2009] EWHC 29 (QB).

9.40 Such issues were considered in a social media context in the case of *Cairns v Modi*,[12] in which the former chairman of the Indian Premier League tweeted in respect of the well-known New Zealand cricketer that: 'Chris Cairns removed from the IPL auction list due to his past record in match fixing. This was done by the Governing Council today.' In response to a query from the cricketing magazine *Cricinfo*, Mr Modi further stated: 'We have removed him from the list for alleged allegations [sic] as we have zero tolerance of this kind of stuff. The Governing Council has decided against keeping him on the list.' Mr Modi was not able to prove his allegation and as a result damages were awarded. Bean J stated:

> 'The original Tweet was received by only a limited number of followers within England and Wales. One expert calculated that they numbered 95, the other 35. The parties have sensibly agreed that I should take the figure of 65. The second publication, to *Cricinfo* was on their website only for period of hours. The expert's figures for numbers of readers of this publication are respectively 450 and 1500. I shall proceed on the basis that about 1000 people read the second publication, which I have found carried the less grave but nonetheless serious meaning that there were strong grounds for suspecting that the claimant had been involved in match fixing. In respect of the second publication I also bear in mind that *Cricinfo* have settled with the claimant, paying him £7,000 damages and a further sum for costs.'

9.41 But although publication was limited, that does not mean that damages should be reduced to trivial amounts. In 1935, long before the internet was thought of, Lord Atkin said *in Ley v Hamilton:*[13]

> 'It is precisely because the "real" damage cannot be ascertained and established that the damages are at large. It is impossible to track the scandal, to know what quarters the poison may reach ...'

This remains true in the 21st century, except that nowadays the poison tends to spread far more rapidly.

9.42 Damages of £90,000 were thus awarded by Bean J, notwithstanding that relatively few people in England and Wales had seen the tweet and the *Cricinfo* article. Interestingly, £15,000 of this sum amounted to aggravated damages due to the conduct of counsel on behalf of Mr Modi. The quantum of damages was however subject to an appeal to the Court of Appeal.[14] An extremely powerful tribunal comprising the Lord Chief Justice, Lord Neuberger and Eady J delivered a combined judgment. In an unusual grasp of social media terminology, the court noted:

> '27. Mr Caldecott QC contended that with allegations of this scandalous nature it is likely nowadays that word will "percolate" by way of the Internet, and particularly in this case among those interested in cricket – not least because of the

---

[12]   [2012] EWHC 756 (QB).
[13]   153 LT 384, cited by Lord Reid *in Broome v Cassell* [1972] AC 1027 at 1092G.
[14]   [2013] 1 WLR 1015, [2012] EWCA Civ 1382, [2012] WLR(D) 302, [2013] EMLR 8.

responsible position held by Mr Modi and the apparent authority of his words. Dealing with it generally, we recognise that as a consequence of modern technology and communication systems any such stories will have the capacity to "go viral" more widely and more quickly than ever before. Indeed it is obvious that today, with the ready availability of the world wide web and of social networking sites, the scale of this problem has been immeasurably enhanced, especially for libel claimants who are already, for whatever reason, in the public eye. In our judgment, in agreement with the judge, this percolation phenomenon is a legitimate factor to be taken into account in the assessment of damages.'

Notably, the court rejected the submission that the analysis of damages under *Vento* should apply by analogy. The appeal was dismissed.

9.43 In *Bryce v Barber*,[15] the defendant posted an indecent image of children on the claimant's Facebook page, with the comment: 'Ray, you like kids and you are gay so I bet you love this picture, Ha ha.' He had manipulated the photograph to include an image of Mr Bryce. The image was tagged with the name of Mr Bryce, together with a number of other people. As a result the potential to view the post numbered in the thousands, as the fact of 'tagging' allows the image to be accessible far beyond the followers of the original poster. This is because Facebook uses an algorithm to allow tags automatically to be more widely disseminated. Tugendhat J found that a large number of people could have viewed the post, (there had been 11 links to it, two comments, and potential exposure to 800 users) and awarded damages of £10,000. And, in *Applause Store Productions Ltd & Firscht v Raphael*,[16] a Facebook profile was created in the name of Mathew Firscht. It contained private information. The following afternoon, a Facebook group was set up, linked to the profile, which was called 'Has Mathew Firscht lied to you?'. It contained material that was admitted to be defamatory of Mr Firscht and of Applause Store. Neither the profile nor the group was set up by the claimant. Both were set up using a computer with the IP address of the defendant. The false profile contained information relating to the claimant's sexual orientation, relationship status, his birthday, and his political and religious views. Not all this information was accurate, and was conceded to be information in respect of which the claimant had a legitimate expectation of privacy. The matters subject to the claim related to the sexuality of the claimant, as well as the comments about the claimant lying. The case is of interest particularly because significant steps were taken to prove that the defendant had created the false profile. These included the obtaining from Facebook of its activity log, together with a witness statement from a senior executive. £15,000 damages were awarded to Mr Firscht, with £5,000 to his company. And in *Horne v Dempster*,[17] which related to a Facebook page set up by two business partners to publicise a pub, £9,000 of damages was awarded after a campaign of serious abuse on the page when the pair fell out.

---

[15] Unreported, 2010.
[16] [2008] EWHC 1781 (QB).
[17] Unreported, 2013.

9.44 As alluded to above, the changes to the English law of defamation as a result of the Defamation Act 2013 have made some significant alterations to its applicability. It is now necessary for the claimant to demonstrate that the words complained of have caused or are likely to cause 'serious harm' to the reputation of the claimant. This is defined in respect of profit-making organisations as not being such unless it has caused or is likely to cause the body serious financial loss[18] and which, in the case of an individual, is to be given its ordinary English meaning.[19] Thus, serious distress or injury to feelings is no longer sufficient. This may mean that companies are less at risk of such claims for alleged defamatory statements made by employees over social media, but each case will be analysed on its own facts. Notably, the existence of a prompt and well-publicised apology may well obviate serious harm. Bean J stated in *Cooke*:

> '43. I do not accept that in every case evidence will be required to satisfy the serious harm test. Some statements are so obviously likely to cause serious harm to a person's reputation that this likelihood can be inferred. If a national newspaper with a large circulation wrongly accuses someone of being a terrorist or a paedophile, then in either case (putting to one side for the moment the question of a prompt and prominent apology) the likelihood of serious harm to reputation is plain, even if the individual's family and friends knew the allegation to be untrue. In such a case the matter would be taken no further by requiring the claimant to incur the expense of commissioning an opinion poll survey, or to produce a selection of comments from the blogosphere which might in any event be unrepresentative of the population of "right thinking people" generally. But I do not consider that the Article in the present case, with the meaning relating to the claimants which I have held it to have, comes anywhere near that type of case.
>
> 44. In assessing the likelihood of serious harm being caused to the claimants' reputation in the present case I attach significance to the apology. I have already held that the apology was sufficient to eradicate or at least minimise any unfavourable impression created by the original article in the mind of the hypothetical reasonable reader who read both. That leaves a residual class of readers of the original article who did not read the apology. As for them, it is important to note that the apology is now far more accessible on internet searches than the original article. Mr Price observes, and I agree, that "only somebody actively trying to find the unamended Article may come across it, if they try hard enough. But there is no reason for anyone to do so other than for the purposes of this claim."'

9.45 A number of the cases cited in this chapter might well satisfy the 'serious harm' test, particularly those such as *Reachlocal*, which is considered in greater detail below. In addition, thought may need to be given as to whether a company launching a defamation action should also include as a co-claimant a director or employee who has been personally defamed, as an insurance policy against a finding that serious financial harm has not been proved.

---

[18]   Defamation Act 2013, s 1(2).
[19]   *Cooke v MGM Ltd* [2015] WLR 895, [2014] WLR(D) 379, [2015] 2 All ER 622, [2014] EWHC 2831 (QB), [2015] 1 WLR 895, [2014] EMLR 31.

9.46 The Defamation Act 2013 contains a power to order removal of material. Section 13 gives the court the power to make orders against an intermediary (such as a social media site), even where no liability or claim exists against that intermediary. The court therefore can order that:

- the operator of a website on which the defamatory statement is posted must remove the statement, or
- any person who was not the author, editor or publisher of the defamatory statement must stop distributing, selling or exhibiting material containing the statement.

9.47 This is a potentially significant remedy for a successful claimant, as, particularly combined with a request that offending material be taken down, it goes some way to ensuring that an award of damages is more than simply a Pyrrhic victory where the content still remains accessible.

9.48 In an American case, *Gordon & Holmes v Love*,[20] the first libel case in that jurisdiction dealing with Twitter (and as a result immediately dubbed the 'Twibel' case), the defendant, the singer Courtney Love, had tweeted: 'I was fucking devestated when Rhonda J Holmes Esq of san diego was purchased off @FairNewsSpears maybe you can get a quote' (sic). This related to the refusal of her previous lawyer to be re-engaged on a case for Love. The jury decided that this tweet was not libellous. Love's defence included contending that she had intended to send the tweet as a Direct Message. The plaintiff's lawyer summed up the risks of libel via Twitter as follows:

> 'Once this kind of charge is made on the Internet, you never know who read it. You never know where it went. Just because you don't have a list of everyone who saw it doesn't mean it's not a problem. You never know where it's sitting as a ticking time bomb waiting to come out.'

9.49 The jurors decided that Love did not know that the information was not true and, as a result, she won the case. It is interesting to note that a member of the jury was discharged for expressing the view that the case was ludicrous, principally for the reason that a tweet should not be capable of libel; the First Amendment applied. It is unlikely that a similar result would have been reached in this jurisdiction.

9.50 The *McAlpine* case also highlights another danger for employers with an online social media presence: the concept of 'repetition'. As Tugendhat J explained:

> '44. One of these is known as the repetition rule. Under that rule a defendant who repeats a defamatory allegation made by another is treated as if he had made the allegation himself, even if he attempts to distance himself from the allegation: *Flood v Times Newspapers Ltd* [2012] UKSC 11; [2012] 2 AC 273 para [5] and *Gatley on Libel and Slander* 11th ed (2008) para 11.4.

---

[20]   No BC462438 (2014).

45. The harshness of that rule is tempered by another rule, known as reportage. As Lord Phillips explained in *Flood* at para [34] a defence known as Reynolds privilege could be made out:

> "in respect of a report in a newspaper of defamatory allegations made in the course of an ongoing political debate, notwithstanding that the publishers had made no attempt to verify the allegations. The newspaper had not adopted or endorsed these allegations. … [in] circumstances where both sides to a political dispute were being reported 'fully, fairly and disinterestedly' and where the public was entitled to be informed of the dispute. In such circumstances there was no need for the newspaper to concern itself with whether the allegations reported were true or false. The public interest that justified publication was in knowing that the allegations had been made, it did not turn on the content or the truth of those allegations. A publication that attracts Reynolds privilege in such circumstances has been described as 'reportage'. In a case of reportage qualified privilege enables the defendant to avoid the consequences of the repetition rule.'"

9.51 It appears therefore that an employer could find itself liable for a retweeted defamatory tweet, even if the original tweet was not created by it (or on its behalf). The introduction of the single publication rule[21] does not appear to assist in this regard. Section 8 provides that the 1-year limitation period runs from the time of the first post, unless the manner of any subsequent post is materially different from the manner of the first post, in which case the section is disapplied. It certainly appears arguable however that a retweet by another person will amount to a fresh publication (thus potentially founding liability upon them), and, dependent upon its manner, could arguably be a materially different publication, thus potentially extending the limitation period. At this stage it is too early to know how the jurisprudence in this regard will develop, but employers should adopt a protective course of action. Reportage is unlikely to assist most employers.

9.52 The *Cairns* and *McAlpine* judgments are not limited to Twitter. Both make clear that established defamation principles will apply to social media. In the case of *Walder v Smith*[22] the defendant posted a message on Facebook, which was untrue. She had privacy settings engaged, meaning that only her contacts could see the message. She suggested, as in the *Love* case, that she had intended that the post be seen only by one person, but had accidentally posted it so that all of her friends could see it. Her sister then reposted it. Around 950 people were therefore able to see the message (Ms Smith's 300 friends and her sister's 650). A claim was brought, but was not defended in time, resulting in a procedural judgment.

9.53 In *Dabrowski v Greeuw*,[23] a decision of the Western Australia District Court, the defendant, who was the estranged wife of the plaintiff, posted on her Facebook page: 'separated from Miro Dabrowski after 18 years of suffering

---

[21] Defamation Act 2013, s 8.
[22] Unreported.
[23] [2014] WADC 175.

domestic violence and abuse. Now fighting the system to keep my children safe.' Ms Greeuw ran an argument that her computer had been accessed and her husband's name had been added in by a third party to the printed-out post that was relied upon. The court did not accept this. Ms Greeuw was unable to evidence the defence of justification as her evidence was found to lack credibility. Once again, the court commented on the 'percolation phenomenon' coined by Andrew Caldicott QC in *Cairns*, though referring to it instead as the 'grapevine effect':

> '264 Similarly the mode, medium and manner of publication are relevant to an assessment of damages. The nature of the internet is such that it records what might once have been transient and ill-considered statement said in the heat of the moment: *Boyd v The State of Western Australia* [2012] WASC 388 [22] (Hall J).
>
> 265 Defamatory publications on social media spread easily by the simple manipulation of computers. A public Facebook page is able to be viewed worldwide by whoever clicks on that page and the grapevine effect stemming from the use of this type of medium must be considered: *Mickle v Farley* [2013] NSWDC 295. However it must also be recognised that Facebook is a source other than a mainstream news or information provider.
>
> …
>
> 267 That is not to say the defamation was trivial but the fact it was on Facebook and made by the estranged spouse is part of the relevant context. The doubts about the character of Mr Dabrowski would still exist but they would not be as grave as if the defamatory post had been published in a reputable newspaper.
>
> 268 However the grapevine effect could mean that the defamatory imputations are repeated without revealing that the source was a Facebook post made by an estranged wife and this must not be overlooked when assessing damages.'

Damages of Aus$12,500 were awarded.

9.54 Companies can also use defamation law when outside parties conduct a campaign against them on social media. In *Reachlocal UK Ltd & Anr v Bennett & Ors*,[24] the claimant company carried out search engine optimisation (SEO) services. The defendants, Your Online Digital Agency Limited, its directors and other involved parties, were in direct competition. The claimants' case was that the defendants had, since early 2014, carried on a sustained campaign of denigration of them, principally directed at the claimants' customers. This was done by emailed material followed up by telephone calls, which led the claimants to believe that the defendants were in possession of a list of their customers. The emails contained an attachment in PDF format, setting out specific allegations to the effect that the claimants were conducting a scam in respect of how they made their money from their customers. A later email contained the following passage:

---

[24] [2014] EWHC 3405 (QB).

'Did you know ReachLocal can take upto [sic] 50 per cent of your Campaign Media Budget as an Optimisation Management Fee. Half of your marketing budget could be wasted by being disguised as an Optimisation Marketing Fee without you even knowing. That is one shocking and expensive marketing service!'

Numerous other emails were sent, and the allegations were repeated in telephone calls. In addition, the defendants used a website and a press release to further publicise their claims, together with a Twitter account. In respect of this last, the judge noted:

'It is Mr Bray's evidence that the fifth defendant has published a series of tweets on its Twitter page, to the effect that ReachLocal is engaged in dishonest and deceptive practices and is scamming its customers. The audience for these tweets will include all the followers of the fifth defendant's Twitter page, which amounts to 3,780 Twitter users. It seems unlikely, perhaps, that many people would follow the Twitter page of the fifth defendant unless they were professionally engaged in, or interested in, digital marketing. According to Mr Bray, the fifth defendant has also sent tweets about the claimants to other Twitter accounts, including two controlled by ReachLocal (@ReachLocalUK and @ReachLocal), which have some 7,300 followers. One account to which the fifth defendant has sent its tweets is that of one Ian Puddick, who has 90,000 followers. It also "retweets" and "favourites" material published on its own Twitter page. Similarly, according to Mr Bray, it has attracted attention to material on its Twitter page by the use of hashtags, and in particular #SearchWars, which is a topic with a very large readership concerned with broader issues of competition between search engines. The use of that hashtag will bring more readers to the fifth defendant's website. Similarly, the fifth defendant has used its Facebook page and its LinkedIn page to publish material identical or similar to that complained of.'

The above passage reflects a growing awareness amongst the defamation judiciary of the effect that social media can have. Total damages of around £450,000 were awarded. It is notable that the defendants did not engage in the court process, but it is clear that significant awards can be recovered where an employer can demonstrate that business has been lost as a result of a malicious social media campaign.

9.55 Thus, whilst the advent of the Defamation Act 2013 appears to have removed the title previously 'enjoyed' by England and Wales as the libel capital of the world, it is clear that in appropriate cases claims will still be able to be brought and won as a result of online behaviour and social media posts. The requirement to show serious harm may also lead to a rise in dual claims, where the employer seeks to demonstrate serious harm, which requires financial loss, whilst an executive who has been personally defamed also brings a claim, demonstrating the effect upon his reputation. It remains to be seen whether the upward trend of social media defamation cases will go into reverse; however, the ubiquity of social media and the clear reputational damage that can be caused via such an instantaneous medium may mean that employers continue to seek to litigate.

RIGHT TO BE FORGOTTEN

9.56 In *Google Spain SL and Google Inc v Agencia Española de Protección de Datos (AEPD) and Mario Costeja González*,[25] the CJEU established the existence of what has been termed the 'right to be forgotten': that personal data could be required to be removed from the internet. Search engines deal with data in a manner falling within the definition of 'processing personal data' within Directive 95/46/EC, which requires that member states ensure that personal data are processed 'fairly and lawfully' (and hence the Data Protection Act 1998). 'Processing' is defined as:

> 'any operation or set of operations which is performed upon personal data, whether or not by automatic means, such as collection, recording, organisation, storage, adaptation or alteration, retrieval, consultation, use, disclosure by transmission, dissemination or otherwise making available, alignment or combination, blocking, erasure or destruction.'

9.57 The 'data controller' is 'the natural or legal person, public authority, agency or any other body which alone or jointly with others determines the purposes and means of the processing of personal data'. 'Data subjects' are granted the right to require a data controller to erase or rectify personal data. Google was found by the CJEU to be data controller,

> 'as it enables any internet user to obtain through the list of results a structured overview of the information relating to that individual that can be found on the internet — information which potentially concerns a vast number of aspects of his private life and which, without the search engine, could not have been interconnected or could have been only with great difficulty — and thereby to establish a more or less detailed profile of him.'

There is a presumption, the CJEU concluded, that personal rights override, as a rule, not only the economic interest of the operator of the search engine but also the interest of the general public in having access to that information upon a search relating to the data subject's name. That presumption is rebuttable only where it appeared, for particular reasons that the interference with the fundamental rights of the subject is justified by the preponderant interest of the general public in having, on account of its inclusion in the list of results, access to the information in question. An example might be the role played by the data subject in public life. Google has received around 100,000 requests for information to be removed as a result. It is important to note that, as the ruling applies to search engines, it does not involve the take-down of data, but rather the removal of links to it.

9.58 It is important to note that the right to be forgotten applies to individual data subjects only – it does not apply to companies, as Art 12 of the Directive 95/46/EC gives the legal basis to individuals only. Thus, a company may be able to request an employee (or, possibly, compel him, should an express contractual

---

[25] Case C-131/12, 13 May 2014.

term exist, which was not held to be unlawful) to utilise the right to be forgotten to remove information about that employee that was damaging to the company. If damaging material was identified by the company, which the employee had not already taken steps to request links to it be deleted, it is certainly arguable that failure to comply with a lawful and reasonable instruction by the employer to make a request to be 'forgotten' would amount to a disciplinary offence. The reasonableness of any sanction will likely depend upon there being a clear and well-known policy in place to cover such eventuality. Thus, where damaging information in the public domain relating to employees exists, companies may be able to utilise the right to be forgotten. However they are unable to make requests in their own right (though an individual running a business in his own right is able to make a request about himself qua individual).

9.59 Another possibility open to a company seeking to limit damage through internet or social media publications directed at it or its employees relates to civil injunctive relief. In the case of *ETK v News Group Newspapers Ltd*,[26] the court considered an appeal relating to an order preventing publication of revelations relating to a man working in the entertainment industry, in the context of the risk of harm that could be caused to the applicant's wife (who opposed publication) and to their children. Ward LJ said:

> '22. In my judgment the benefits to be achieved by publication in the interests of free speech are wholly outweighed by the harm that would be done through the interference with the rights to privacy of all those affected, especially where the rights of the children are in play.'

9.60 There are other methods of seeking to control commentary on social media sites. It has been suggested that direct approaches to the abuse and security departments of various social media platforms, highlighting violations of the user agreement, may result in resolution by way of the removal of the offending information. However such approaches are unlikely, on their own, to resolve the issue. There is increasing pressure on service providers to self-regulate. In the United Kingdom the storm caused by the recent disclosure by an anonymous Twitter account of the alleged holders of various super-injunctions (so called because they prevent not just disclosure of the identity of the holder of the injunction, but the existence of the injunction itself) has led to renewed calls for a rebalancing away from the right to absolute freedom of expression and towards the imposition of a statutory right to privacy. Such legislation, if implemented, would, in order to be effective, have to impose curbs on the freedoms of the facilitators of the provision of information (such as social media sites, web hosts and ISPs), by way of sanction. If the political will to challenge the insouciant repetition of injuncted details does arise, such facilitators may then find themselves subjected to strict and onerous screening requirements.

---

[26]   [2011] EWCA Civ 439 (19 April 2011).

9.61 Such facilitators are appearing instead to take the initiative by seeking to resolve matters via their own policies. There has also been a suggestion that such organisations may seek to agree a common set of principles and procedures by which any aggrieved person could seek an adjudication on whether a particular post, web page or email address was being used in such a way that the harm that it caused that individual outweighed any right to free expression or obligation to facilitate. Such a move towards a voluntary but industry-wide code of practice would chime with the current mood of corporate social responsibility and the concern amongst many that the internet and its dominant players are not prepared to contribute towards a safe and unintimidating online environment.

9.62 Thus, and to take an example, the Twitter terms of service provide as follows:

> 'All Content, whether publicly posted or privately transmitted, is the sole responsibility of the person who originated such Content. We may not monitor or control the Content posted via the Services and, we cannot take responsibility for such Content. Any use or reliance on any Content or materials posted via the Services or obtained by you through the Services is at your own risk.
>
> We do not endorse, support, represent or guarantee the completeness, truthfulness, accuracy, or reliability of any Content or communications posted via the Services or endorse any opinions expressed via the Services. You understand that by using the Services, you may be exposed to Content that might be offensive, harmful, inaccurate or otherwise inappropriate, or in some cases, postings that have been mislabelled or are otherwise deceptive. Under no circumstances will Twitter be liable in any way for any Content, including, but not limited to, any errors or omissions in any Content, or any loss or damage of any kind incurred as a result of the use of any Content posted, emailed, transmitted or otherwise made available via the Services or broadcast elsewhere.
>
> ...
>
> Please review the Twitter Rules (which are part of these Terms) to better understand what is prohibited on the Twitter Services. We reserve the right at all times (but will not have an obligation) to remove or refuse to distribute any Content on the Services, to suspend or terminate users, and to reclaim usernames without liability to you. We also reserve the right to access, read, preserve, and disclose any information as we reasonably believe is necessary to (i) satisfy any applicable law, regulation, legal process or governmental request, (ii) enforce the Terms, including investigation of potential violations hereof, (iii) detect, prevent, or otherwise address fraud, security or technical issues, (iv) respond to user support requests, or (v) protect the rights, property or safety of Twitter, its users and the public.'

9.63 In other words, according to its terms of service, no responsibility for facilitating harmful content can attach to Twitter, and whilst the right is reserved to remove content, there is no obligation for Twitter to do so.

However, Art 14 of the Electronic Commerce Directive[27] does provide some redress. In order for content providers to retain limitations to their liability for content that is, for example, defamatory, they are required to respond promptly to take down requests.

9.64 Twitter also has policies in place to comply with requests for information, to found evidence in civil or criminal litigation, but only on the basis that a court order is obtained.

9.65 Such types of terms of service are not uncommon. However some social media have taken further steps towards regulating their content. Facebook, for example, whose terms of service do outlaw bullying behaviour (as do Twitter's), has publicised its 'hate and harassment team' which seeks to provide some regulation of its pages, albeit highly subjective. Whilst such schemes (which are, in effect, logical progressions of the original regulator, the forum moderator) are laudable, in the view of the authors they do not go far enough, and are likely to lead to complaints from those who believe that the world wide web is an environment of pure entitlement to freedom of speech that a company is not the correct arbiter of what is and is not appropriate. Where Facebook determines that its policy is not breached (such as in relation to a public figure) it will not remove a page.

9.66 The recent issues relating to the website Reddit.com highlight this debate. Reddit is in effect an evolution of an internet bulletin board. Registered users are able to post content, news and other material. Users also vote up or down submissions, to increase or decrease their prominence. It is divided into various forums ('subreddits'), each with their own posted and voted-upon content.

9.67 Reddit is policed principally internally, with various 'subredditors' responsible for dealing with inappropriate content. In addition, it banned the use of information that could identify 'redditors' (ie contributors) after a spate of incidents whereby such personal information was used to contact individuals in the kinetic world. In May 2015, Reddit announced a change to its policies, and updated these in June 2015, apparently as a result of concerns over, amongst other things, harassment of individuals. In its post announcing the improvement of its policies so as to prevent harassment, on 14 May 2015, Reddit defined harassment as being:

> 'Systematic and/or continued actions to torment or demean someone in a way that would make a reasonable person (1) conclude that Reddit is not a safe platform to express their ideas or participate in the conversation, or (2) fear for their safety or the safety of those around them.'

9.68 The above definition is significantly narrower than the PfHA 1997 provisions whereby a course of conduct which causes alarm or distress is covered by the Act. By 14 June 2015 Reddit had acted to close a number of inappropriate subreddits, including /r/fatpeoplehate, which had around

---

[27]   00/31/EC.

150,000 members. The reaction to the policy has been mixed, with significant debate between those who believe that free speech should be allowed to flourish unchecked and those who consider that the risk of harassment is significant. Employers need to be aware of sites such as Reddit and numerous imitators, for all of the reasons considered above.

CONCLUSION

9.69 The right to be forgotten is a powerful tool, but applies only to individuals. Its title is a misnomer – the data will remain available, but the links to it will be removed. At present, Europe is seeking to force the various content providers to extend the right worldwide, thus creating an even more powerful reputation management tool. Companies cannot avail themselves of the right, but might want to consider whether they should include in policies and contracts a right to require an employee to take such steps as are reasonable to protect the reputation of the company by exercising their individual right.

CHAPTER 10

SOCIAL MEDIA AND COMPARATIVE LAW

10.01 As is to be expected, issues relating to social media in the workplace have arisen in most legal jurisdictions. Whilst the courts of England and Wales have, for the most part, declined to give specific guidance as to the impact of social media specifically on workplace relations, preferring instead to apply well-established legal principles arising out of employment law and the PfHA 1997 and any extant IT or social media policies, it is instructive to consider how the courts of other jurisdictions have dealt with its increasing influence. This is of particular use given that the issue of social media within the workplace remains relatively new. Thus, a comparative approach may give rise to issues that have not yet troubled the courts of England and Wales, or where the judicial thinking is more advanced due to a greater volume of cases. In fact, an analysis of a number of examples of common law jurisdiction cases demonstrates a similar approach to that of England and Wales. Unsurprisingly, the same issues arise, given the ubiquity of social media: inappropriate posts and disciplinary and dismissal issues; harassment; and discrimination. This section will therefore consider the application of employment law to issues raised by social media in jurisdictions including Canada and Australia, both major developed common law jurisdictions, and the United States, the home of many of the major social media platforms. In addition this chapter contains a short consideration of the approach taken by European jurisdictions.

CANADA

10.02 Canadian jurisprudence has grappled with a number of cases arising out of social media. In *Re Lougheed Importers Ltd*,[1] a case before the British Columbia Labour Relations Board (the Canadian equivalent of the Employment Tribunal), the Board considered the dismissal of two employees, who had claimed that their dismissal was in breach of the Labour Relations Code. Their claim was brought by their union. It related to posts made on Facebook.

10.03 Given the nature of the Facebook postings in question, the Board decided to refer to the witnesses it heard from only by their initials. FY was a manager. JT reported to him. AP also took direction from him but had a different line manager. All three were Facebook friends.

---

[1] BCLRB No B190/2010.

10.04   FY came across a post by JT in August 2010:

> 'Sometimes ya have good smooth days, when nobodys fucking with your ability to earn a living ... and sometimes accidents DO happen, its unfortunate, but thats why there called accidents right?'

10.05   FY reported this to his manager. Part of the dispute before the Board was the reason for this report. JT was a key figure in the union, and it was alleged on his behalf that this was the real reason that the report was made. FY's evidence was that he was concerned, as JT had previously been confrontational with him, and that there was no union-related animus. Had any other employee posted in the same way, they would have been treated similarly.

10.06   Other posts made by JT were also reported by FY in due course, as follows:

> 'When a labour relations lawyer calls ya at 7PM and ya fax him 25 task sheets, ya gotta wonder??? Unfair labour practices, coupled with workplace harassment ... C'mon Guys??? At least read up on the laws before ya throw the first punch ... because that second punch can by a DOOZY ...'

> If somebody mentally attacks you, and you stab him in the face 14 or 16 times ... that constitutes self defence doesn't it????

> ... Works been a shit-storm lately, our shop is a certified union now, so been stressed rt out (Management needs somebody to blame & Im that guy) ... so yeah if you see summa my ANGRY statuses lately, that's why ...'

10.07   Further down in the postings, JT stated his status as 'stress relief anyone' and then posted the top five kills from *Dexter*, a television show concerning a vigilante killer. Whilst this post did not directly reference his employer, it was argued that the intention behind the posting was clear – to intimidate, based upon the previous postings.

10.08   A previous employee then informed FY that he was no longer a 'friend' of JT on Facebook. That employee however allowed a more senior manager, to whom FY had reported his concerns, to use his account to view that of JT, and to print out any concerning comments, including those referenced above.

10.09   JT then intervened in an unrelated meeting held at work by bursting into it and seeking to become involved, again citing his capacity as union representative, and was subsequently 'written up' for his behaviour. The Facebook posts were not mentioned in this process. As a result of this disciplinary action, JT made further Facebook posts. On 23 September 2010, JT posted as his status update:

'Completely Exploded & SNAPPED on the Fixed Ops/Head Prick at work today … He sent me Home (With Pay) and wrote me up (Strike 1) … although the FUKN gloves are off now,,,I gotta control my temper. One strike in 4 years aint bad, I guess.'

On 24 September2010, JT posted:

'Hhhmmmm??? According to this reprimand at work, Im confrontational & disruptive to the WHOLE shop … AND … My outburst yesterday was threatening and didn't allow The WestCoastAutoGroup to conduct regular business … well????All I Gotta say is they pissed off the WRONG GUY … big time.'

10.10 The senior manager was made aware of both of these posts. He was concerned, due in particular to the reference to the whole of the group, rather than the specific employer, and the aggressive questioning of the reprimand. The 'Head Prick' reference to the senior manager likely did not assist in alleviating these concerns. On 27 September 2010, JT wrote another post. He stated:

'Is wondering if his 2 supervisors at work, go to the bathroom together?? And who holds who's penis while pissing??'

10.11 Management had by this stage become increasingly alarmed by the personal nature and aggressive tone of the posts. It appeared that JT had ceased to have any respect for his workplace or managers, and was willing to post potentially damaging material. Over the next few days the comments on Facebook by JT continued:

'Was asked for my opinions at a morning safety meeting… I replied 'No comment' … Seems my Boss, whos owned the business 25 yrs & is fixed operations director of 2 dealerships as well … couldnt comprehend my reply?? So its confirmed … HE'S A COMPLETE JACK-ASS … not just Half-a Tard.'

The next day the other employee who was a complainant in the claim eventually brought, AP, interjected, again on Facebook:

'west coast detail and accessory is a fuckin joke … dont spend your money there as they are fuckin crooks and are out to hose you … there a bunch of greedy cocksucin low life scumbags … wanna know how I really feel??????'

It is clear that such a post amounted to a direct attack on the product of his employer. JT then posted in response:

'I heard that Marco and [FY] were seen fondling each others nut sack in the shop bathroom?? Any truth to that? That shop ripped off a bunch ppl I know. All in humour,, however,, none of the stereo shit I bought there works, at all … Deck only plays store bought discs and subs are blown and amp is fried, again. The alpine stuff I bought from A&B works awesome tho.'

AP responded:

'I dont think theres enough room on Facebook to type all the bullshit out ... gloves are off now ...its game time'

AP's girlfriend then became involved, seeking to calm matters:

'Somethings just shouldn't be broadcasted on facebook, especially when you still work there.'

AP appears to have posted back:

'That's the whole point honey'

10.12 Managers were made aware of these more recent posts by an ex-employee, who was worried about what was being said on social media. Concerns were understandably raised in the minds of management in respect both of the tone used and the deprecation of the employer's products, together with a direct recommendation made by JT to use the products of a competitor (the reference to A&B in the post cited above). Investigatory meetings were instituted as a result. The employees were ultimately dismissed for making disrespectful and derogatory comments and bringing the reputation of the employer into disrepute.

10.13 The employer did not have a specific social media policy in place. Instead it relied upon existing Canadian case-law. This case-law was set out by the Board in the course of its judgment:

'61 The Employer submits that there does not have to be a workplace rule prohibiting putting inappropriate postings on Facebook. It relies on *Chatham-Kent (Municipality)*, 159 L.A.C. (4th) 321, paras 21 and 22 ("Chatham-Kent") for the principle that there does not have to be a specific rule prohibiting such conduct as insubordination. In particular, at para 7:3660 in Brown and Beatty, *Canadian Labour Arbitration* (4th ed), it stated:

"Conduct that is threatening, insolent, or contemptuous of management may be found to be insubordinate, even if there is no explicit refusal to comply with a directive where such behaviour involves a resistance to or defiance of the employer's authority."

62 In *Chatham-Kent*, the arbitrator upheld the termination of an employee for posting comments about work on her personal blog on the internet. The arbitrator found, at para 25, that the comments put on the internet were insolent, disrespectful and contemptuous of management and were an attempt to undermine the reputation of management and undermine their authority. The arbitrator concluded this was insubordinate behaviour.

63 In *Alberta v Alberta Union of Provincial Employees*, 174 L.A.C. (4th), 371 ("Alberta"), the arbitrator upheld the termination of an employee's employment for posting comments on her personal blog site on the internet concerning her co-workers and management. At para 97, the arbitrator concluded:

"While the Grievor has a right to create personal blogs and is entitled to her opinions about the people with whom she works, publicly displaying those opinions may have consequences within an employment relationship. The Board is satisfied that the Grievor, in expressing contempt for her managers, ridiculing her coworkers, and denigrating administrative processes engaged in serious misconduct that irreparably severed the employment relationship, justifying discharge."'

10.14   The dismissal was upheld. The Board found that:

'98 The comments also included very offensive, insulting and disrespectful comments about supervisors or managers. As the Facebook comments were also made to other employees and former employees that were friends with J.T. and A.P. on Facebook, I accept the Employer's assertion that these comments are akin to comments made on the shop floor. The comments about the supervisors amount to insubordination within the meaning of BCFP as they are "used as a verbal weapon to degrade a Supervisor in front of others". J.T. also made comments that clearly identified and referenced discipline he had received at work. He also identified the manager and called him derogatory and insulting names. I therefore find the Facebook 2010 postings are not similar conduct to the inappropriate comments made on the shop floor on a regular basis.'

10.15   The approach of the Board in this case is very similar to that taken by the English courts in the cases of both *Preece* and *Weeks*, considered above, and underlines the application of an approach based on existing employment law principles to social media. It is notable that there was an absence of a policy in the case, which allowed the union to seek to raise arguments in this regard. The lack of a policy was not however determinative, as it was likewise not in the *Williams* case, but the arguments raised would likely not have been open to the union at all had a clear policy been in place.

10.16   Once again, as has been established through the case-law of England and Wales, the argument that the absence of a specific social media policy meant that a dismissal for its usage was unfair did not find favour where the behaviour complained of was egregious and which would, in the view of the ordinary person, constitute behaviour which amounted to gross misconduct. This is in effect the application of a common sense principle – if behaviour is clearly unacceptable, the absence of a policy will not render that behaviour acceptable – rather, where a line has clearly been crossed, an employer will be entitled to dismiss It is those cases in which behaviour may or may not be so categorised that a social media policy will provide protection to an employer making a decision within the range of reasonable responses.

10.17   It is also of note that the Facebook postings were not necessarily public; whilst fellow employees were aware of them, management did not have access to them without the assistance of other employees. Whilst, as Canada is not a signatory of the same, the particular arguments surrounding the specific provisions of the European Convention of Human Rights do not apply, it is of interest that, as in England and Wales, a private posting, or posting outside of work hours and without a specific link to the employer, will not necessarily provide a blanket defence.

10.18   A further example from the same jurisdiction highlights these points, and provides further extra-jurisdictional common law support to the English decisions which relate to social media privacy and posts made outside of working hours on a personal basis. In *Canada Post Corp v Canadian Union of Postal Workers*[2] a postal clerk was sacked after Facebook posts came to light, in which she mocked her supervisors and her employer. The employer argued that the posts were grossly insubordinate and had the potential to damage the employer. The employee contended that the workplace environment justified the posts. She also argued that she had thought that they were private. This was not as a matter of fact the case – the account was fully public. Again, the risk to reputation on the basis of social media postings was emphasised by the employer:

> '82 The Employer suggested that there is a fundamental difference between "bar talk" and social media: social media is accessible for months or years; it has a huge potential audience; the contents are discoverable through key word searches; and the contents are easily copied and forwarded to others. For those reasons, the Employer argued, arbitration awards dealing with Facebook, blogs, email, and other social media cases had universally concluded that employees cannot shield themselves from the consequences of inappropriate postings by claiming an expectation of privacy. The Employer cited *Naylor Publications Co and Media Union of Manitoba* (2003) CLB 13386 (Peltz); *Chatham-Kent and CAW, Local 127* (2007) 159 LAC (4th) 321 (Williamson); *Government of Alberta and Alberta Union of Provincial Employees* (2008) 174 LAC (4th) 371 (Ponak); *Wasaya Airways and Air Line Pilots Association, International* (2010) 195 LAC (4th) 1 (Marcotte); and *Lougheed Imports v UFCW Local 1518* (2010) CLB 26395 (BCLRB).'

10.19   The above passage is instructive. The contended difference between the venting by an employee of issues and grievances whilst with colleagues in the pub or around the water cooler on the one hand, with on the other hand the effects of such venting on social media, is starkly contrasted. The accessibility, and potential as a result of harm to the employer, of those posts, featured strongly in the arguments put forward by the employer, as did the potentially perpetual nature of social media commentary, contrasted with the transitory nature of comments made in the spur of the moment.

10.20   The union relied on two major arguments: the lack of a communicated social media policy, and the fact that the posts were not likely to be widely disseminated:

> '90 The Union acknowledged that the Grievor's inappropriate Facebook postings justified discipline but argued that discharge was excessive in the circumstances. The Employer's social media policy had not been communicated to employees and

---

[2]   (2012), 216 LAC (4th) 207 (Calgary, Aberta).

the Employer had relied on grounds, such as the Grievor's use of her cell phone at work, that were not part of the letter of discharge and therefore could not be used to justify discipline (*Canada Post Corporation and Canadian Union of Postal Workers* [Jeworski] (1984) Unreported (Norman)). It was submitted that the Grievor had no intention of making her Facebook postings public and was simply venting to her friends and co-workers. She had assumed her privacy settings had been enabled, a mistake easily made, according to the Union, due to the multiple steps involved in enabling the settings. The Grievor had been genuinely shocked and upset when she had learned that her Facebook postings were publicly available and had been seen by management. In the Union's submission, that was never the Grievor's intention.

91 The Union argued that while in theory the Grievor's postings were available to any of the millions of people with Facebook accounts, there was no evidence of actual widespread access or any harm to the Corporation. Canada Post was not expressly named in any of the postings until after the Grievor's Facebook site had been discovered by management. It would have been difficult, in the Union's submission, to identify where and for whom the Grievor worked. The last names of the supervisor and the superintendent were not mentioned in any of the postings.'

10.21 Once again, familiar arguments, tried and tested in the courts of England and Wales as to the scope of dissemination of the policy and the belief that social media is private, were raised. The arguments raised as to actual as opposed to potential harm and the fact that the employer was not specifically named are also factors considered in the English cases cited herein. The argument run involved a confusion over privacy settings; no evidence of widespread access or harm; difficulty in identifying the place of employment; and a lack of full identification of the people who were targets of the posts.

10.22 The analysis of the arbitrator is of significant relevance. A focus on harm caused, together with the nature of the content posted, was applied in this case to come to a robust conclusion:

'101 To determine whether the Grievor's misconduct was sufficiently serious to warrant discharge, I begin by examining her Facebook postings, the contents of which have been set out earlier in the award. The material postings began on October 10, 2010 and continued until shortly after their discovery by management on November 19, 2010. In this period, the Grievor made 26 postings on 14 separate dates about her workplace and supervisors. Five of the postings were made via cell phone while the Grievor was at work. The postings are universally nasty in tone and content, with the majority aimed at Superintendent D. She is frequently referred to in vulgar and contemptuous terms, including, "bitch", "c_nt", "wicked witch", "evil hag" and "devil", sometimes capitalized for emphasis. The postings contain threats, most notably "die bitch die", "run you over" and 'missing permanently'. While the Grievor explained that in some postings she was only referring to a voodoo doll of the superintendent, not the real superintendent, it is a distinction without a difference. The Grievor's sentiments were clear – her words, whether aimed at a voodoo doll or directly at Superintendent D, are offensive and frightening. Is the superintendent supposed to feel better because the Grievor only expressed an interest on running over and killing a voodoo doll of the superintendent? The answer is obvious.

102 In addition to the abusive and intimidating language, the postings are mocking to the point of bullying with many of the more offensive comments accompanied by "lol" which stands for "laugh out loud". The postings invite others to join in and indeed others do offer their own mocking comments from time to time. A set of postings on October 21 & 22 contained a photo of the Halloween skeleton hung in the Midtown lunchroom with comments like 'she's lost some weight' and "go back to hell, they miss you", that unquestionably referred to the superintendent. In a later posting about the skeleton, the Grievor wrote, with what can only be described as glee ("lol"), that 'if she thinks it looks like her, I am not going to disagree". A non-employee chipped into the general ganging up on the superintendent by calling her "the hag" and "wicked witch". After human resources and the union arranged a meeting to address employee–management friction in Midtown, the Grievor referred to these efforts as Superintendent D's "pity party". Another posting belittled the fact that Superintendent D wore a coat at work and then mocked the coat itself. Other postings boast how the Grievor and co-workers had tricked Superintendent D into calling in extra staff after they had misled her about whether they would be reporting to work (October 13). A second posting jokes (with multiple "lolol") that the superintendent must be afraid of staff since Employee K 'phoned the police on her'.

103 A co-worker posted that the superintendent had "mean employees", which pretty much sums up the attacks. The postings are mean, nasty, and highly personal. They go well beyond general criticism of management and essentially target one person with a degree of venom that is unmatched in other social media cases. In *Government of Alberta* the criticisms of management only infrequently take on a personal tone, with most of the offensive comments directed at co-workers in a misguided attempt at humour. Management as a whole is targeted in Naylor Publications and Lougheed Imports, rather than a specific individual. *Chatham-Kent* involves general criticism of management and the denigration of a client. The current case is unprecedented in the repeated mockery, the threatening language, the vile insults, and the debasement of an identifiable manager. Nor are the postings a momentary lapse, perhaps carried out in a short-lived fit of rage. They take place over more than a month on multiple days.

104 Given the vitriolic nature of the postings, it is unsurprising that their discovery harmed the targeted managers. Both Superintendent D and Supervisor M were extremely shaken by what they read and they had every right to be upset – the postings making chilling reading. Both needed substantial time off work for emotional distress and Superintendent D required medical care. Neither manager returned to Midtown and Supervisor D has not returned to an operational position with direct supervisory functions. The evidence of actual damage caused by the postings is uncontradicted.'

10.23   Once again, it appears likely that the decision made related to the nature of the postings made. That the postings made 'chilling reading' for the specific supervisor makes it likely that had such behaviour taken place outwith a social media forum, it would have amounted to gross misconduct. The lack of a disseminated social media policy again did not matter, pace *Williams*, because the behaviour established was so outrageous. The prospect of harm to the company, combined with the fundamental actual harm to the employee who eventually saw the posts, appears to have given rise to significant moral condemnation. The behaviour of the errant employee was culpable; the 'venom' was unmatched in other social media cases. Such behaviour should not be required to be tolerated; that it was over social media merely exacerbated the harm caused or potentially caused.

10.24 In addition, it is notable that the material posted was in fact publicly available. As seen in the English jurisprudence, this is potentially a significant distinguishing factor (see eg *Smith v Trafford Homes*). This again highlights the 'harm' aspect of social media disciplinary proceedings: what harm has, or has potentially, been caused? The decision went on to consider the contention that the employee had believed that her posts were private:

> '108 The fact that the Grievor was under a misapprehension about who could access her Facebook site, however, does not relieve her from the responsibility for what she wrote. The Grievor demonstrated a degree of recklessness in not even considering how easily her postings could be spread, even if restricted to just her Facebook friends (see, *EV Logistics*, para 60 and *Wasaya Airlines*, page 63). There is nothing, for example, to prevent friends from forwarding a posting to other friends. It is difficult to believe that the Grievor would have been completely oblivious to the growing controversy over Facebook privacy, widely reported in the media (Statement of Agreed Facts, paragraph 42) and the subject of a commentary in the local union newsletter that warned that "you never know who sees your comments" (Exhibit 24). The Grievor greatly increased the likelihood that her postings would be eventually discovered by management by having current and former postal workers among her friends. This brought her Facebook postings directly into the workplace, undermining any claim her site was intended as a private, non-work, forum.'

10.25 It is well worth noting that, regardless of whether the posts were private or not (which in this matter they were not) the Canadian court considered that the risk of them becoming public should be taken into account. The reference to the 'degree of recklessness' in not even considering the risk of dissemination, appears to have been an aggravating factor. The reasoning noted that friends could forward comments (see *Celestine*, above, for similar reasoning by an Employment Tribunal) and as such any supposed privacy settings could be bypassed in any event. This is a highly relevant consideration. The existence of privacy settings has been argued as a mitigating factor in numerous cases; that the Canadian court was aware that regardless of the same, a post could be replicated on an unprotected account is worth noting. As in *Celestine*, such an argument has far less force in the increasingly social-media-savvy field of employment law.

10.26 In another Canadian case, *Credit Valley Hospital v Canadian Union of Public Employees, Local 3252 (Brathwaite Grievance)*,[3] an employee was dismissed after posting to Facebook after he had finished his work photographs that he had taken of a hospital patient who had jumped to his death.

---

[3]   (2012), 214 LAC (4th) 227.

Notwithstanding that the photographs were posted out of working time and to a personal account, the dismissal was upheld. The employee was engaged as a part-time environmental service representative, and had been involved in cleaning up the scene. The employer again did not have a specific social media policy, but did have a code of conduct, which dealt amongst other things with patient confidentiality.

10.27 Mr Braithwaite, the employee in question, originally admitted one posting to Facebook, which he subsequently deleted. He subsequently admitted a second. It was common ground that the posts were made whilst he was on a rest break. The comment under the first picture posted appeared sympathetic, though wildly inappropriate: 'Mother pleads with kid not to jump off PRCC side of the parking lot but did anyways poor thing.' In any event the text of the caption was disputed by witnesses. The second picture he posted, however, was far less so: 'This is what I have to clean up.'

10.28 The court was unimpressed with the evidence of Mr Braithwaite, finding that he had breached the confidentiality policy. Even on his version of events, the first post identified the location; the fact that the deceased was a child; and the involvement of the mother. Nor did his argument that his posts had been spur of the moment avail him:

> '20 Mr Brathwaite said that he was all emotional, and that he got caught up in the moment, when he uploaded and posted the pictures on his Facebook page. Viewed objectively in their entirety, Mr Braithwaite's actions cannot be properly characterized as being a momentary aberration, or being spur of the moment. While his actions had some element of being spur of the moment, they were mainly premeditated. In that regard, the first picture ostensibly appeared to be spur of the moment. However, the second picture was premeditated, given the passage of time between when the two pictures were taken. Further, Mr Braithwaite's posting of the pictures with captions on his Facebook page had the hallmarks of premeditation, given the passage of time between when the pictures were taken and when they were posted, and the fact that Mr Brathwaite posted them while he was on break. Given the foregoing time-line and chronology, Mr Brathwaite had sufficient time for reflection before taking his second picture, and before posting both pictures on his Facebook page with comments. By his actions of taking the pictures and posting them on his Facebook page with comments that others viewed, Mr Brathwaite without any justification has put his own self-interest and feelings ahead of the well-known, the well-understood and the all-encompassing fundamental obligation on employees to maintain the confidentiality of patient information. Consequently, I do not find Mr Brathwaite's ostensible spur of the moment decision to take the first picture to be a sufficiently compelling factor to form part of a principled basis to mitigate the penalty.'

10.29 As such, this judgment amounts to a salutary warning to employees. The nature of much of social media is transitory and spur of the moment. A post can be made within seconds from a mobile phone. Even if that was what Mr Braithwaite had done, in the circumstances of this case, where confidentiality of patient information was fundamental, and where he had signed a policy confirming that he understood it, his behaviour did not amount to mitigation. Query whether the same conclusion would have been reached where the 'all-encompassing fundamental obligation' of patient confidentiality had not applied. In other circumstances, the existence of a clear policy might well have been important.

AUSTRALIA

10.30 It may not be entirely surprising, given the robust approach to the development of the common law taken by the courts of that jurisdiction, that Australian jurisprudence has provided a number of noteworthy cases of social media employment issues. Once again the general principles developed by the jurisprudence of England and Wales have been applied to Australian law, and, once again, Australian legal thinking in this area may come to play an important part in the continuing development of our precedential law.

10.31 Thus, in *Mr Damien O'Keefe v Williams Muir's Pty Ltd T/A Troy Williams The Good Guys*,[4] a case heard in Australia's Fair Work Act tribunal, Mr O'Keefe claimed that he had been unfairly dismissed. He had posted rather charmingly on Facebook:

'Damien O'Keefe wonders how the fuck work can be so fucking useless and mess up my pay again. C..ts are going down tomorrow.'

Management became aware of the post, and considered that it was both abusive, and, in respect to the latter part, a threat. Mr O'Keefe did not deny posting the message, which related to a failure to get his pay right, but argued instead that his privacy settings were at the maximum possible; only 70 people could have seen them, and that, of these, 11 were co-workers. As such, he contended, the limited effect of the post did not entitle his employer to dismiss him.

10.32 There was in place at the workplace no specific social media policy. However the general disciplinary policy did make clear that offensive language and personal abuse would not be tolerated. The tribunal found that:

'Even in the absence of the respondent's Handbook warning employees of the respondent's views on matters such as this, common sense would dictate that one could not write and therefore publish insulting and threatening comments about another employee in the manner in which this occurred.'

Further, the fact that the comments were made on the applicant's home computer, out of work hours, did not make any difference:

---

[4] [2011] FWA 5311.

'The comments were read by work colleagues and it was not long before Ms Taylor was advised of what had occurred. The respondent has rightfully submitted, in my view, that the separation between home and work is now less pronounced than it once used to be.'

10.33 The dismissal was upheld. The last sentence cited above is of interest. It is certainly true that the workplace and the home environment have merged to a certain extent. Once again, the shift from venting with colleagues at the local hostelry and posting ill-advised comments on social media is starkly highlighted. Rather than moaning and banter with a select group of trusted employees in the tacit knowledge that all will be forgotten or forgiven the following morning, an ill-judged social media post, tweet or update done at home, on a personal account, without necessarily a link to the workplace, may now result in dismissal across the common law jurisdictions. Were an English Employment Tribunal to accept that the post in this case was threatening and abusive, a dismissal would likely be found to be within the range of reasonable responses.

10.34 The cases considered above appear to deprecate the need for a social media policy as, consistently, employees have been found to be fairly dismissed (or the equivalent) in the absence of the same. Such decisions appear at least at first blush to go against the English jurisprudence and the recommendations set out in the earlier chapters of this work. However as has been clearly seen from the English decisions considered above (such as *Williams*) the absence of a social media policy in cases where the conduct should self-evidently be considered to be a breach of the employment relationship will frequently be considered to be within the range of reasonable responses (or equivalent extra-national common law tests). It is those cases where the misconduct is not so clear in which the need for a policy becomes clearer.

10.35 Thus, *in Glen Stutsel v Linfox Australia Pty Ltd*[5] the Commissioner for Fair Work Australia found that the dismissal of an employee was not fair. The grounds for dismissal were as follows:

'1. on your Facebook profile page, which was open to the public, you made a number of statements about one of your managers, Mick Assaf, that amounted to racially derogatory remarks;

2. on your Facebook profile page, which was open to the public, you made a statement about one of your managers, Ms Nina Russell, which amounted to sexual discrimination and harassment; and

3. you made extremely derogatory comments about your managers, Mr Assaf and Ms Russell.'

10.36 Mr Stutsel contended that his account was private, and that the comments he had posted were not derogatory. It was found that he had around

---

[5] (U2011/8497) [2011] FWA 8444.

170 'friends' on Facebook, a significant number of whom were colleagues. The Commissioner did not consider that the posts were as serious as the employer had considered. From an evidential perspective he stated:

'[81] I note that none of Mr Stutsel's Facebook friends posted any comment objecting to any of the above material (or indeed to any of the material complained of) and apparently found it unexceptionable. That does not totally excuse it but rather, indicates the nature of the milieu in which the remarks were made. When the Facebook comments are read in sequence and as a whole, the nature of them becomes clearer. In context, there are several participants in each thread of discussion, all of whom appear well versed in what the discussion involves and the personalities involved. The chains of comments have very much the f[l]avour of a group of friends letting off steam and trying to outdo one another in being outrageous. Indeed it has much of the f[l]avour of a conversation in a pub or cafe, although conducted in an electronic format. Any external reader not familiar with either Linfox or particularly the NDC, would have considerable difficulty in making out what was going on in several instances and would have some difficulty in determining about whom some of the remarks were made.'

10.37 This view is of interest, as it demonstrates the importance of context. It is of significant interest that the court compared the discussion, read as a whole, as requiring to be put into context and being of the flavour of friends in a pub letting off steam. This appears to contrast initially with those cases where conversations have been carried out on private accounts, as in the Canadian cases referred to above, but culpability has nevertheless been found. However the contrast appears here to be in the nature of the posts. Again, harm seems to be the determinative factor. External readers would not have been able to discern the identity of the subjects of the posts; whilst the Commissioner did not expressly say so, it appears likely that individuals were not identifiable. As such, the case is clearly distinguishable from the 'harm' cases considered above and those in the English jurisprudence; here, specific harm was not caused, and although the employees were behaving badly, there was no identifiable risk of such harm. Again, comment was not made as to the risk of reposting outside of the private network of friends; but where the context of those posts was not harmful, it appears to be likely that the risk of harm from such reposts was minimal.

10.38 Another familiar factor was considered: the lack of a specific social media policy. The need for such policy has been stressed repeatedly; however, it has also been clearly seen that in egregious cases the absence of such a policy will not save the errant employee. In *Stutsel*, having already concluded that the posts did not cause harm, the Commissioner also noted:

'[87] At the time of Mr Stutsel's dismissal, Linfox did not have any policy relating to the use of social media by its employees. Indeed, even by the time of the hearing, it still did not have such a policy. The Company relies on its induction training and relevant handbook (see paragraphs 28 and 29 above) to ground its action against Mr Stutsel. In the current electronic age, this is not sufficient and many large companies have published detailed social media policies and taken pains to acquaint their employees with those policies. Linfox did not.'

10.39   As a result of all of the above considerations, the dismissal was found to be harsh, unjust and unreasonable. The lack of harm, coupled with the lack of a policy (which could potentially have made a difference, at least in the English jurisprudence, by setting out a clear and narrow definition of harm) was fatal to the case. As such the dismissal was unfair.

10.40   The decision was appealed by the employer, who was vexed with the outcome.[6] The employer was not successful. The Full Panel noted that:

> '[26] In the present case, the series of Facebook conversations in which the comments were made were described by the Commissioner as having the flavour of a conversation in a pub or cafe, although conducted in electronic form. We do not agree altogether with this characterisation of the comments. The fact that the conversations were conducted in electronic form and on Facebook gave the comments a different characteristic and a potentially wider circulation than a pub discussion. Even if the comments were only accessible by the 170 Facebook "friends" of the Applicant, this was a wide audience and one which included employees of the Company. Further the nature of Facebook (and other such electronic communication on the internet) means that the comments might easily be forwarded on to others, widening the audience for their publication. Unlike conversations in a pub or cafe, the Facebook conversations leave a permanent written record of statements and comments made by the participants, which can be read at any time into the future until they are taken down by the page owner. Employees should therefore exercise considerable care in using social networking sites in making comments or conducting conversations about their managers and fellow employees.'

10.41   It is notable that the Full Panel were less comfortable with the conclusions below. They did not appear to accept entirely that the characterisation of the Facebook discussion as being akin to a pub discussion where employees were simply letting off steam was wholly accurate. Of perhaps more importance is the recognition of potential harm from the potential of the forwarding of messages, widening the audience for the comments. However, notwithstanding these words of concern, the Full Panel declined to overturn the decision, again, it appears, on a harm-based analysis, coupled with the lack of a policy: 'having regard in particular to the nature of the comments made, the limited understanding of the employee as to the privacy of Facebook communications and the *employee's long and satisfactory employment record*' the appeal was dismissed. A Review was brought before the Full Federal Court, who again upheld the first instance decision.

10.42   Codes of conduct clearly can matter in Australia. In *Banerji v Bowles*,[7] a case involving an application for an interim injunction preventing dismissal, the Federal Circuit Court of Australia considered a case involving a public employee, employed in the public relations department of the Department for Immigration and Citizenship, tweeting in a manner critical of the Minister for Immigration and Government policy. Miss Banerji had made, or shared, regular

---

6   [2012] FWAFB 7097.
7   [2013] FCCA 1052.

comments (sometimes mocking, sometimes critical) on, for example, (a) the practices and policies of the company that provides security services at Commonwealth immigration detention centres, (b) the immigration policies of the Australian Government, (c) information and comment by the Opposition spokesman on immigration (Mr Morrison), (d) the Minister for Foreign Affairs (Senator Carr), (e) the (then) Prime Minister, (f) the Leader of the Opposition, and (g) employees of the Department. Her comments were posted from an account that did not identify her or her employer and which had around 700 followers.

10.43 The employer relied upon its social media policy in opposing the application for an injunction. It had published a document entitled 'Guidelines on Use of Social Media by DIAC Employees'. These Guidelines were reinforced by a 'fact sheet' which it also published, entitled 'What is Public Comment? Workplace Relations Conduct Section Fact Sheet.' Miss Banerji contended that her right to freedom of political expression prevented her dismissal in the circumstances. Whilst the Australian constitution does not explicitly protect such expression, there have been a number of decisions of the Australian High Court suggesting that an implied right of this type may exist, albeit not by way of a personal right. Justice Neville rejected this contention in the circumstances of Miss Banerji's conduct:

> '... the unfettered right asserted by the Applicant does not exist. In the circumstances outlined in the current matter, and certainly only in the context of an interlocutory Application, I do not see that Ms Banerji's political comments, 'tweeted' while she remains (a) employed by the Department, (b) under a contract of employment, (c) formally constrained by the APS Code of Conduct, and (d) subject to departmental social media guidelines, are constitutionally protected. Further, it makes no difference, and actually strengthens the case against granting the relief she seeks, that her 'tweets' occurred (in part or in full) while she was also professionally retained or engaged in employment outside her duties with the Department, and in relation to which she has/had no formal permission from the Department to be so employed.'

10.44 The explicit references to the contract of employment, the code of conduct and the social media guidelines in the passage above once again demonstrate the importance and relevance that will be attached to such policies in workplace disputes. There is also commentary in respect of the contention that Miss Banerji was, whilst employed, also carrying out work for a third party employer, with some of the tweets occurring whilst engaged in this other employment. It appears that the view of the court, consistently with much of the jurisprudence of England and Wales, was that the fact that the conduct complained of took place outside of the workplace did not matter. This point was further developed in *Pearson v Linfox Australia Pty Ltd*.[8]

10.45 In *Pearson*, the Fair Work Commission considered a complaint for dismissal based upon allegations that an employee had, inter alia, disregarded

---

[8] [2014] FWC 446 (17 January 2014).

the social media policy put in place. It is worth noting the identity of the respondent, in the context of the criticisms made in *Stutsel*, above, as to a lack of a policy – which was commented upon in the reasons given:

> '[46] Secondly, Linfox's desire to have a policy in place about the use of social media by employees can be understood. The evidence indicated it had been criticised in other proceedings for not having done so. Further, in an employment context the establishment of a social media policy is clearly a legitimate exercise in acting to protect the reputation and security of a business. It also serves a useful purpose by making clear to employees what is expected of them. Gone is the time (if it ever existed) where an employee might claim posts on social media are intended to be for private consumption only. An employer is also entitled to have a policy in place making clear excessive use of social media at work may have consequences for employees.'

10.46   The penultimate sentence of the quotation above is stark, and consistent with the development of common law jurisprudence in the field of social media: the intention or belief of privacy will likely not trump the harm caused or likely to be caused by the post.

10.47   Mr Pearson refused to sign the policy. He was particularly exorcised by the fact that the social media policy was intended to apply outside of working hours. He felt that 'Linfox do not pay me or control my life outside of my working hours, they cannot tell me what to do or say outside of work, that is basic human rights on freedom of speech ...' He was disciplined as a result of this, and a number of other policy breaches.

10.48   Importantly, the court said this in respect of the scope of the policy:

> 'However, it is difficult to see how a social media policy designed to protect an employer's reputation and the security of the business could operate in an "at work" context only. I accept that there are many situations in which an employer has no right to seek to restrict or regulate an employee's activities away from work. However, in the context of the use of social media, and a policy intended to protect the reputation and security of a business, it is difficult to see how such a policy could operate in this constrained way. Is it suggested that an employer can have a policy in place that seeks to prevent employees from damaging the business's reputation or stopping them from releasing confidential information while at work, but leaving them free to pursue these activities outside of working hours? This would be an impractical approach and clearly there are some obligations employees accept as part of their employment relationship that have application whether they are at work or involved in activities outside of working hours.'

10.49   The above dictum encapsulates and summarises the current judicial position in respect of the ambit of social media usage. It is legitimate for an employer to seek to prevent harm by careless or malicious social media interaction. Given the permeation of social media, it must also be the case that the desire of the employer to protect itself can stretch into personal usage outside of working hours.

10.50   There are however limits to which a policy can be used to justify a harsh decision. In *Wilkinson-Reed v Launtoy Pty Ltd*,[9] the court found that the dismissal of a manager, who had sent a private Facebook message to the estranged wife of her boss, had not breached the policy when the boss logged into his wife's account and saw it:

> 'I do not think discovery by a manager that an employee holds a low opinion of him is sufficient reason to terminate the employment of a long serving employee with an impeccable employment record. In my view more is required, particularly some evidence that the employee's opinion is having a deleterious effect on the workplace, its employees or the business of the employer.'

10.51   The passage above appears to lend support to the harm theory – that the conduct of an employee over social media must be sufficient to cause actual harm. Merely expressing dislike or a low opinion will probably not be sufficient. There needs to be something more. In a number of the cases cited above, there have been explicit or implicit threats; or abuse of a character significantly worse than intemperate non-specific language. There is a fine line between robust expressions of discontent and trolling; in some cases, *Wilkinson-Reed* being one, the employer can find itself on the wrong side of that line. It remains important in England and Wales for employers to consider whether their response is reasonable, and the existence of a policy specifying examples of misconduct is likely to assist. But the courts are likely to remain slow to endorse dismissal without harm.

10.52   Further commentary was given in *Wilkinson-Reed* in respect of what the court perceived as potential limiting effects on a social media policy:

> 'I do not accept that the applicant breached the respondent's social media policy. While the Facebook conversation may have been conducted by means of social media it was in the manner of a private email. It is unlikely that a policy that was an attempt by an employer to control the contents of private emails between their employees [and] third parties, written in their own time and using their own equipment would be found to have the requisite connection to the employment relationship such that an employee could be terminated for a breach.'

10.53   With respect, this paragraph appears somewhat sweeping and ill-thought-out. Many of the cases considered above, as already noted, focus on the risk of a social media post, even to a private account, being reposted or retweeted. The same risk applies to an email sent from a private account – it can easily be forwarded. Indeed, this is precisely what occurred in *Gosden v Lifeline Project Ltd*,[10] considered above. It appears to the authors that there is no good reason why a social media policy cannot encompass the use of private email, within limits. If the reasoning behind the above quotation is that it would not be right to allow an employer to seek to control what is said privately, purely by way of a conversation conducted over personal email,

---

[9]   [2014] FWC 644 (24 January 2014).
[10]   ET/2802731/2009.

outside of working hours, that proposition is self-evidently correct. However, the consequences for an employee who causes harm by such a method after that private email is deliberately released into the public sphere and who has the intention that it be so released, or where such an email is brought to the attention of an employer by a third party, can, and should, be spelled out in a social media policy. There is a distinction between private communications between individuals and information that is intended to be put into the public sphere. In *Gosden*, the email was a chain email, intended to be forwarded. The tribunal expressed the view that if it had been a purely private communication, the position might well have been different, and Art 8 considerations might well have applied. In such a case, where an employer becomes aware of the contents of an email intended at all times to be private, that intention of the employee that the email should be private will be a factor in considering fairness in the circumstances pursuant to s 98(4) of the Employment Rights Act 1996, but will not in all situations amount to a defence. As always, each case will be fact sensitive, and notwithstanding the obiter observation in *Gosden* that a purely private email might be protected by Art 8 rights, this will depend on the particular circumstances of each case It is perhaps initially surprising that the Fair Work Commission equated a Facebook interaction with private email, but it is notable that rather than a post, the message was a private message, not easily able to be disseminated. Given that this was the case, and harm was only potentially able to be caused by the act of accessing the account (which in itself is a breach of Facebook policy) the comparison seems apt, and in line with the expression of view of the Tribunal in *Gosden*. However a social media policy should still seek to cover the circumstances of a private email coming to the attention of the employer.

UNITED STATES

10.54 The National Labour Relations Board, the Federal Agency established to enforce the National Labour Relations Act 1935, has produced various reports into the use of social media by employees and consequent actions by employers. Such claims first came to its attention in 2010 and between 2010 and 2012 the Board issued three separate memoranda relating to social media policies in the workplace. The first decision of the Board relating to a dismissal was issued in September 2012.

10.55 In *Karl Knauz Motors, Inc. d/b/a Knauz BMW and Robert Becker*,[11] a car salesman was dismissed as, the employer contended, he was in breach of its general policy (rather than any specific social media policy). The particular passage of the policy in question was as follows:

'(b) Courtesy: Courtesy is the responsibility of every employee. Everyone is expected to be courteous, polite and friendly to our customers, vendors and

---

[11] Case 13–CA–046452.

suppliers, as well as to their fellow employees. No one should be disrespectful or use profanity or any other language which injures the image or reputation of the Dealership.'

10.56   The Board found that the policy violated Federal law, due to its breadth, but upheld the dismissal, as certain Facebook posts that formed the basis of the decision to dismiss were not protected.

10.57   The dismissal was based in part on posts that were derogatory of the employer's efforts at the launch of a new vehicle:

> 'I was happy to see that Knauz went "All Out" for the most important launch of a new BMW in years... the new 5 series. A car that will generate tens in millions of dollars in revenues for Knauz over the next few years. The small 8 oz bags of chips, and the $2.00 cookie plate from Sam's Club, and the semi fresh apples and oranges were such a nice touch... but to top it all off... the Hot Dog Cart. Where our clients could attain a over cooked wiener and a stale bunn [sic].'

And:

> 'No, that's not champagne or wine, it's 8 oz. water. Pop or soda would be out of the question. In this 'photo, Fadwa is seen coveting the rare vintages of water that were available for our guests.'

10.58   There were a number of additional comments and responses to the comments of others, along the same lines. These posts were found to be protected as concerted activities, on the basis that what was being raised was a protest against working conditions. These were not, however, the only posts that Mr Becker had made. A few days later, he became aware of an incident at the Land Rover dealership also operated by his employer. A saleswoman had allowed the 13-year-old son of her customer to get into the driver's seat of the vehicle. She was in the front passenger seat, with the door open. The boy hit the accelerator; ran over his father's foot, and drove into a pond. In this respect, the judge below recorded:

> 'On June 14, Becker also posted the pictures of the Land Rover accident, as well as comments, on his Facebook page. The caption is "This is your car: This is your car on drugs." The first picture shows the car, the front part of which was in the pond, with the salesperson with a blanket around her sitting next to a woman, and a young boy holding his head. Becker wrote: This is what happens when a sales Person sitting in the front passenger seat (Former Sales Person, actually) allows a 13-year-old boy to get behind the wheel of a 6000 lb. truck built and designed to pretty much drive over anything. The kid drives over his father's foot and into the pond in all about 4 seconds and destroys a $50,000 truck. OOOPS!'

10.59   In evidence, the employer contended that it was this post, and not the previous Facebook posts complaining about the food, that was the reason for dismissal. The judge agreed (and the Board upheld his decision). This post was not protected, as it was neither a protected nor a concerted activity. The judge accepted that harm and embarrassment had been caused and, as such, dismissal was appropriate in the circumstances.

10.60 The case provides an interesting insight as to how the American employment jurisprudence differs from its common law cousin. Significant protection is afforded to employees acting in concert to protest their working conditions. The Facebook criticisms of the employer as to its launch party could conceivably have led to a fair dismissal (or the equivalent) in common law jurisdictions; the sarcastic tone could arguably rise beyond banter or jest and amount to an undermining of the employer. However s 7 of the National Labour Relations Act provides:

Rights of employees

Sec. 7. [§ 157.] Employees shall have the right to self-organization, to form, join, or assist labor organizations, to bargain collectively through representatives of their own choosing, and to engage in other concerted activities for the purpose of collective bargaining or other mutual aid or protection, and shall also have the right to refrain from any or all such activities except to the extent that such right may be affected by an agreement requiring membership in a labor organization as a condition of employment as authorized in section 8(a)(3).

Pursuant to section 8 of the Act, it is unlawful for an employer to seek to restrain the same. In Meyers Industries, 268 NLRB 493 (1983) (Meyers I), the Board held that the discipline or discharge of an employee violates Section 8(a)(1) if the following four elements are established:

(1)   the activity engaged in by the employee was 'concerted' within the meaning of Section 7 of the Act;
(2)   the employer knew of the concerted nature of the employee's activity;
(3)   the concerted activity was protected by the Act; and
(4)   the discipline or discharge was motivated by the employee's protected, concerted activity.

10.61 In *Meyers I*, the Board defined concerted activity as activity that is 'engaged in with or on the authority of other employees, and not solely by and on behalf of the employee himself'. In *Meyers II*,[12] the Board expanded this definition to include those 'circumstances where individual employees seek to initiate or to induce or to prepare for group action, as well as individual employees bringing truly group complaints to the attention of management'.

10.62 This is clearly a very wide definition, and may have significant impact in respect of social media cases. Thus, in *Hispanics United of Buffalo, Inc. and Carlos Ortiz*,[13] the dismissal of five employees for Facebook comments following a criticism of them by another employee was found to be an unlawful

---

[12]   281 NLRB.
[13]   Case 03–CA–027872 (2012).

breach of s 8. After discovering that that employee wished to raise concerns about the help provided to clients, Ms Cole-Rivera posted on Facebook:

> 'Lydia Cruz, a coworker feels that we don't help our clients enough at [Respondent]. I about had it! My fellow coworkers how do u feel?'

10.63 A number of responses were posted. Ms Cruz also responded, expressing a desire that the 'lies' stop. She also complained to the employer, who dismissed Ms Cole-Rivera and four colleagues who had responded, for breach of the bullying and harassment policy. The Board agreed with the judge below that the dismissal was unlawful:

> 'As set forth in her initial Facebook post, Cole-Rivera alerted fellow employees of another employee's complaint that they "don't help our clients enough," stated that she "about had it" with the complaints, and solicited her coworkers' views about this criticism. By responding to this solicitation with comments of protest, Cole-Rivera's four coworkers made common cause with her, and, together, their actions were concerted within the definition of *Meyers I*, because they were undertaken "with ... other employees." 268 NLRB at 497. The actions of the five employees were also concerted under the expanded definition of *Meyers II*, because, as the judge found, they "were taking a first step towards taking group action to defend themselves against the accusations they could reasonably believe Cruz-Moore was going to make to management."

10.64 As a result, the actions on Facebook were protected. Again, it is unlikely that a similar result would have found to be outside the range of reasonable responses in the tribunals of England and Wales, but the significant protection of s 7 of concerted activity appears to trump bullying and harassing behaviour, though it is arguable that, on the facts of this case, the mere posting of messages expressing discontent would not amount to such behaviour.

10.65 The NLRB gives the following guidance on its website to employees in respect of social media use:

> 'Even if you are not represented by a union, federal law gives you the right to band together with coworkers to improve your lives at work – including joining together in cyberspace, such as on Facebook.
>
> Using social media can be a form of "protected concerted" activity. You have the right to address work-related issues and share information about pay, benefits, and working conditions with coworkers on Facebook, YouTube, and other social media. But just individually griping about some aspect of work is not "concerted activity": what you say must have some relation to group action, or seek to initiate, induce, or prepare for group action, or bring a group complaint to the attention of management.'

10.66 Section 7 also provides a headache for employers in the United States in respect of social media policies. The Board has repeatedly declared unlawful provisions in social media policies which have the effect of violating s 8(a)(1). Thus to give a number of examples:

- a social media rule requiring employees to identify themselves when posting comments about the respondent, the respondent's business, or a policy issue was overly broad, as employees would reasonably construe it to cover comments about their terms and conditions of employment, and the self-identification requirement would reasonably interfere with their protected activity in various social media outlets;[14]

- a provision that employees may not 'release confidential guest, team member or company information' would reasonably be interpreted as prohibiting employees from discussing and disclosing information regarding their own conditions of employment, as well as the conditions of employment of employees other than themselves, which activities are protected by s 7;[15]

- a requirement that employees be sure that their posts are 'completely accurate and not misleading and that they do not reveal non-public information on any public site.' is unlawful. The term 'completely accurate and not misleading' is overbroad because it would reasonably be interpreted to apply to discussions about, or criticism of the employer's labour policies and its treatment of employees that would be protected by the Act so long as they are not maliciously false. Moreover, the policy does not provide any guidance as to the meaning of this term by specific examples or limit the term in any way that would exclude s 7 activity;[16]

- a provision that 'Employees are prohibited from posting information regarding [Employer] on any social networking sites (including, but not limited to, Yahoo finance, Google finance, Facebook, Twitter, LinkedIn, MySpace, LifeJournal and YouTube), in any personal or group blog, or in any online bulletin boards, chat rooms, forum, or blogs (collectively, 'Personal Electronic Communications'), that could be deemed material non-public information or any information that is considered confidential or proprietary. Such information includes, but is not limited to, company performance, contracts, customer wins or losses, customer plans, maintenance, shutdowns, work stoppages, cost increases, customer news or business related travel plans or schedules. Employees should avoid harming the image and integrity of the company and any harassment, bullying, discrimination, or retaliation that would not be permissible in the workplace is not permissible between co-workers online, even if it is done after hours, from home and on home computers ...' was unlawful save in respect of the harassment and bullying provisions (ibid).

10.67 Such reasoning is alien to common law jurisdictions, which focus more on general provisions of fairness and contractual agreement. For those companies trading and employing in multiple jurisdictions including America therefore, a blanket policy is unlikely to be of assistance; a tailored policy taking into account the powerful protections conferred by s 7 will be required.

---

[14] *Boch Imports, Inc. d/b/a Boch Honda and International Association of Machinists & Aerospace Workers, District Lodge 15, Local Lodge 447*, Case 01–CA–083551, 2015.
[15] MEMORANDUM OM 12-59 30 May 2012.
[16] OM 12-59, ibid.

10.68 That is not to say that 'Facebook firings' – as dismissals for inappropriate social media posts have inevitably been dubbed – are unknown in the United States. In fact, quite the contrary. There is a significant body of case-law considering the interaction of social media posts, dismissals and First Amendment rights. The First Amendment provides:

> 'First Amendment – Religion and Expression. Congress shall make no law respecting an establishment of religion, or prohibiting the free exercise thereof; or abridging the freedom of speech, or of the press; or the right of the people peaceably to assemble, and to petition the Government for a redress of grievances.'

10.69 Unsurprisingly, First Amendment arguments have been deployed in defence of employees dismissed for social media posts. In *the matter of the tenure hearing of Jennifer O'Brien*,[17] the court considered and upheld the dismissal of a schoolteacher. She taught 6-year-olds, and was unexpectedly transferred to a school where her class comprised exclusively of students of Latino or African-American heritage. After about 6 months, Ms O'Brien made two relevant posts on her personal Facebook page. The first post was 'I'm not a teacher I'm a warden for future criminals!' and the second, 'They had a scared straight program in school why couldn't [I] bring [first] graders?' Her previous head teacher contacted her school, expressing his concern and stating that he was 'appalled'. Ms O'Brien was suspended.

10.70 The comments quickly went viral. Parents complained almost immediately, threatening to remove their children; the next day, television crews arrived. Ms O'Brien subsequently gave evidence to the Office of Administrative Law, contending that she had around 300 Facebook friends, who were friends, or friends of friends. She had not posted the first comment through any reason of race or ethnicity, but because of the behaviour of her students. She had posted out of frustration, and had not in any way intended to be racist. She contended that her posts were protected by the First Amendment.

10.71 This argument was rejected. The remarks were not related to matters of public concern, but were a personal expression of dissatisfaction with her job, and as a result were not protected. Even had they been related to matters of public concern, they were outweighed by the need for schools to be run efficiently. The Administrative Law Judge stated:

> 'An internet social-networking site such as Facebook is a questionable place to begin an earnest conversation about an important school issue such as classroom discipline. More to the point, a description of first-grade children as criminals with their teacher as their warden is intemperate and vituperative. It becomes impossible for parents to cooperate with or have faith in a teacher who insults their children and trivializes legitimate educational concerns on the internet.'

10.72 Further, while First Amendment protections do not generally turn on the public reactions to a person's statements, 'in a public school setting thoughtless

---

[17] (2013). Docket No A-2452-11T4 (Sup Ct NJ).

words can destroy the partnership between home and school that is essential to the mission of the schools'. As such a balance very similar to that struck by the courts when considering Art 10 freedom of expression qualified rights appears to have been carried out; weighing up on the one hand the protections afforded to free speech but on the other the harm caused.

10.73 In considering the appeal, the Superior Court of New Jersey carried out a review of precisely that balancing exercise. In order:

> '... to determine whether a public employee's statements are protected by the First Amendment, we balance the employee's interest "as a citizen, in commenting upon matters of public concern and the interest of the State, as an employer, in promoting the efficiency of the public services it performs through its employees." *Karins v City of Atlantic City*, 152 N.J. 532, 549 (1998) (quoting *Pickering v Bd. of ed*, 391 US 563, 568, 88 S. Ct. 1731, 1734-35, 20 L. ed2d 811, 817 (1968)).
>
> Here, O'Brien claimed that her statements were addressed to a matter of genuine public concern, specifically student behavior in the classroom. The ALJ and Commissioner found, however, that O'Brien was not endeavoring to comment on a matter of public interest, that is, the behavior of students in school but was making a personal statement, driven by her dissatisfaction with her job and conduct of some of her students. The ALJ and Acting Commissioner further found that, even if O'Brien's comments were on a matter of public concern, her right to express those comments was outweighed by the district's interest in the efficient operation of its schools. There is sufficient credible evidence in the record to support these findings. Therefore, O'Brien failed to establish that her Facebook postings were protected speech under the Pickering balancing test.'

10.74 Notwithstanding the differing constitutional and statutory protections for freedom of speech, it is clear that across numerous jurisdictions a balancing test based around harm will be carried out when considering social media behaviour. Privacy settings will likewise not necessarily assist in the United States, as in the common law jurisdictions. In *Payne v Barrow County School District*,[18] a complaint from a parent as to postings relating to visiting an Irish pub whilst on holiday and the use of the word 'bitch' led to an ultimatum of 'resign or be sacked'.

EUROPE

10.75 Things are done somewhat differently in Europe, too, though many of the base principles are in common with the approach of the UK jurisprudence as a result of EU legislation. There are cases from the Netherlands, Spain and Germany where social media posts have led to dismissals, with similar considerations of what falls into public and private communication; the extent to which the risk of posts on private networks being made private by reposting affects this consideration; and the distinction between griping and something more serious, with very similar conclusions to the common law jurisdictions.

---

[18]   (2009). Civil Case No 09CV-3038-X (Super Ct Ga).

However, other aspects of European legislation appear more unusual. France banned references to Facebook and Twitter on television in 2011, save in respect of stories particularly about the social media platforms, on the basis that this amounted to surreptitious advertising detrimental to other social media sites, in violation of a 1992 law. The irony of social media barely existing when that law was passed appears to have been largely overlooked by legislators. Posts on public forums are not deemed private and thus can constitute grounds for dismissal for misconduct, but apparently not for gross misconduct.[19] In Germany an employer's ability to use employee data obtained from social media depends upon its social media or internet policy: see the Bundesdatenschutzgesetz (Federal Data Protection Act 1990, as amended). This derives from the same EU Directive as the UK Data Protection Act and the principles to be applied are broadly the same. However, what is clear is that social media use is an issue across the continent and a potential headache for employers around the world.

EXTRA-TERRITORIALITY

10.76   Some of the issues considered earlier in this work may give rise to issues relating to extra-territoriality: actions that have an effect across national borders. Since the enactment of the Private International Law (Miscellaneous Provisions) Act 1995, the general rule is that the applicable law is the law of the country in which the events constituting the tort in question occur. Section 11(2) then adds qualifications to this principle with regards personal injury and damage to property. However, the entirety of s 11 can be displaced when it would appear to be substantially more appropriate that the governing law be that of another country altogether. As a result difficulties may be caused in seeking remedy where harassing or other behaviour originates from abroad. However a consideration of the conflict of laws is outside the scope of this work.

CONCLUSION

10.77   Common law jurisdictions and European jurisdictions (the former due to our shared legal heritage, the latter principally due to the effect of EU law) appear to be developing broadly similar jurisprudential approaches to the particular issues caused by the application of social media to the workplace. A common sense approach to behaviour that does, or has the potential, to cause harm to the employer or specific employees appears increasingly to be taken so as to justify disciplinary or dismissal action. A growing awareness of the open-ended nature of social media communications and the risk of private postings being made public is a common facet, as is the belief that purely private communications from the employee's own equipment, in a manner never intended to become public (such as email or private or direct messages) should not ordinarily be taken into account when considering the behaviour of

---

[19]   *Dupre v SAS Contact FM*, Court of Appeal of Douai, 16 December 2011.

an employee. The clear dangers to employers of disgruntled or loose-tongued employees appears clearly to be recognised by the various court and tribunal systems. It is likely that the jurisprudence in this field will continue to develop and, as with, for example, tort law in the 1990s, it may be that the English courts will find themselves increasingly referred to decisions of common law jurisdictions when developing further the jurisprudence in this country.

CHAPTER 11

FUTURE DEVELOPMENTS

11.01 It is all but certain that the use of IT and social media in a workplace context will continue to grow. In its 2013–14 survey, 'Social Media In the Workplace Around the World 3.0',[1] Proskaur Rose LLP analysed the impact of this growth. The survey notes that at the time of its first survey, carried out in 2011, the use of social media from a business perspective appeared to be a novelty. However by the time of the third survey (2013–14), some 90% of businesses by that stage used social media for business purposes. The amalgamation of social media and marketing is thus nearly complete. This interrelationship clearly therefore gives rise to risks, particularly from the perspectives of reputation and brand control.

11.02 Whilst the sample used for the Proskaur survey is relatively small, with 110 self-selecting respondents, some of its findings were highly notable:

- More than 70% of employers reported having to take disciplinary action against employees for misuse of social media.
- 80% of respondents had implemented some form of social media policy.
- Only 13% of employers had taken steps to avoid misuse of social media by ex-employees.

The survey does not set out what the steps taken by that small minority of employers entail, but it is likely that they will include restrictive covenants as considered above.

11.03 It is, we hazard, abundantly clear that the rise of social media and internet interconnectivity is not likely to abate. Whilst there has been some decline in usage of the more mainstream social media sites over new, emerging sites, the statistics are stark. The 2014 Ofcom report noted that Facebook remains the default social media site for UK adults – 96% of those who use social media are members of Facebook. Twitter considers that one-quarter of UK internet users are members – some 9.5m people. LinkedIn has 15m UK members. That said, Facebook, YouTube and LinkedIn are all seeing UK declines in their membership bases. Numerous new sites and platforms are springing up constantly, many trading on their commitment to privacy, such as Ello, EveryMe and Path. Different media, such as Snapchat, allow for the

---

[1] http://www.proskauer.com/files/uploads/social-media-in-the-workplace-2014.pdf (retrieved 31 May 2015).

short-term transmission of information, which is wiped after a short period of time, but still allows screenshots to be taken and then reposted on 'traditional' social media. All of these pose potential risks for employers and, as technology develops, further platforms will emerge, each of which may give rise to risk.

11.04 The rise of social media is both an opportunity and a headache for employers. The current generation have grown up more connected and more internet-aware than ever before. Those aged from around 20 and under have always had the internet, and have spent their formative years immersed in social media. The next generations will continue to adopt and to adapt to the ever-increasing innovations, centred on the smartphone. Within 20 years the Internet of Things is estimated to have transformed human interaction. Recent newspaper reports suggest a decline in teenage drinking, drug use and pregnancy, as this generation's youth spend their time interacting online rather in the old-fashioned face-to-face manner. As result, the business of the future will increasingly be conducted online. Reputation, advertising and marketing has already shifted to online platforms, at the expense of traditional marketing media. Facebook, Google, LinkedIn, Twitter and every other social media platform is monetising its membership through advertising. Companies that do not adapt to this new opportunity will not thrive and may not survive. Therefore, harnessing the power of social media is very much in the interests of companies, to reach out to their markets, and their younger employees will consider it a matter of course that interactions are carried out on this basis. But the ubiquity and vast reach of social media carries the concomitant risk of instant reputational damage.

11.05 Most mainstream large workplaces now have dedicated employees manning their Twitter feeds. Train companies, banks, mobile telephone businesses and numerous others will scan social media and respond pre-emptively to concerns, complaints or reputational issues. Famously, when McDonalds instigated the #McDstories Twitter hashtag, it received responses relating to people hospitalised for eating its food and becoming vegetarian. When the music retailer HMV went bust employees tweeted overheard conversations by the managing director such as 'how do I shut down Twitter' and 'live tweeting' the HR sacking of 'loyal employees'. Control over social media output is essential, particularly when something goes wrong, and senior management need to know how to take charge of the social media output whenever there is a crisis. A failure to do so is likely to be increasingly damaging as more and more customers rely on social media rather than traditional marketing campaigns for their choices of retailer.

11.06 It is impossible to predict how social media and the internet will develop over the next 1, 5 or 10 years. What is near certain, however, is that the current trend will only accelerate. Companies will rely more and more on their online presence, and customers will rely more and more on what they read online. Scandals such as the periodic allegations that reviews on sites such as Tripadvisor are faked or paid for already can cause huge reputational damage. The ease with which customers can castigate service, or name particular employees who have been 'difficult' to deal with, raises real risks. Employers might well find themselves the subject of claims if their employees are being attacked over social media by reason of a protected characteristic unless they take steps to prevent this from happening. Senior management can no longer consider that social media is something with which they need not concern themselves.

11.07 In addition the blending of both the real and kinetic worlds and the melding of work and personal time is likely to lead to a rise in potential claims against employers. There already exists a trend in English law towards a transference of liability from individual tortfeasors to those with deeper pockets or insurance policies – employers. The expansion of the scope of vicarious liability and third party harassment raises the alarming spectre from employers of liability for actions by their employees where the tort bears a 'close connection' to their employment. A Twitter-trolling exercise by a rogue employee using a company account or a sustained email campaign of harassment against a customer, ex-employee or competitor, however well-intentioned, could well give rise to an actionable wrong which could sound in significant damages, if this amounts to harassment, defamation or discriminatory commentary. It is essential that employers take steps to ensure as far as possible that the actions of their employees are properly regulated.

11.08 Increasingly, employers are likely to want to vet their employees or prospective employees based upon their social media footprint. It is likely that younger employees will feel more and more defined by their online presence. There is, however, a perversity in the combination of an 'over-sharing' generation, who also consider privacy to be paramount. Employers will need to tackle this impossible contrast and train staff to realise and understand that the needs of the business and their personal actions may not always be symbiotic.

11.09 From a legal perspective, it is likely to be increasingly necessary that the rights and obligations of employees are clearly spelled out in policies, and that sufficient and significant training is provided to employees based around the vanishing distinction between the public and the private; the professional and the personal. Huge numbers of employees now feel that there is no reason why they should not share with the world at large how awful their manager has been, or how rude the customer was, heedless of the fact that their social media profile clearly identifies their employer. In order for employee discipline appropriately to be managed employees need to have made clear to them, in a detailed and readily understandable manner, what is and is not acceptable. If a company fails to do this, and to keep its social media policy constantly up to date, it runs the risk of significant reputational damage and potentially third party liability, without being able to manage, discipline or dismiss an employee who has given rise to the problem.

11.10 Whilst an attempt to forecast legal developments is a notoriously difficult and often embarrassing task, doubly so in an area of law involving fast-changing technological mediums, the authors respectfully suggest that the following issues and matters will potentially be developed further by the appellate courts:

- Guidance may be promulgated by the higher courts as to the contents of social media policies. It is notable that, unlike in the United States, there is no body similar to the National Labour Relations Board that can scrutinise and strike down policies or particular provisions as being in breach of s 7. However the tribunals do have the power pursuant to s 124(2)(c) in discrimination cases to make recommendations. It is possible that in an appropriate case the effect of a social media policy could be found to be discriminatory, thus allowing recommendations as to that policy to be made by a tribunal.

- Perhaps more likely, the same power may be used in relation to a complaint of discrimination in respect of a social media vetting policy, either at the stage of engagement or during the course of employment. The risks of discrimination arising out of social media vetting have been considered above, and are highlighted by ACAS as a particular risk. It is not hard to imagine recommendations as to an extant policy being made in an appropriate case.

- Almost certainly, consideration of the application of restrictive covenants to social media accounts, together with further dispute over the 'ownership' of such accounts and their contacts. This issue has not been determined substantively, as the case-law that we do have relates only to interim applications. At some point this question will need to be resolved, and the existence of restrictive covenants is likely to be a significant factor in such determination.

- Possibly, further consideration of the application of the range of reasonable responses test in the context of employers that (a) do and (b) do not have social media policies. It is clear from the commonwealth jurisprudence that the existence of a policy is likely to be a factor to be taken into account where the behaviour is not so outrageous as to be obviously dismissible (such as in *Williams*). However as noted previously, the trend of appellate courts simply applying existing principles and not treating social media cases as in a separate legal class is continuing: *The British Waterways Board (t/a Scottish Canals) v Smith (Unfair Dismissal: Reasonableness of dismissal)* [2015] UKEAT 0004_15_0308 (3 August 2015).

- Less likely, some guideline principles from the higher courts as to the type of behaviour that will or will not ordinarily justify disciplinary or dismissal in social media cases. It is likely that the issues will remain case and fact sensitive so as to preclude the issuance of such guidance.

- An increased emphasis on staff training and awareness of policies. The case-law in this regard is mixed. If an employer wishes to take a hard line on a breach of a social media policy that does not cause significant harm, staff awareness may be a key factor.

- Perhaps most importantly, a consideration at Court of Appeal level of the interaction between Art 8 privacy rights, Art 10 freedom of expression rights, and the legitimate needs of an employer to protect its reputation and interests. The case-law in this regard is at present somewhat muddled. Much is likely to turn on the distinction between misuse and harm postulated by the authors herein; but the commonwealth jurisprudence in particular certainly appears to consider the risk, rather than the actuality, of harm: consideration of reposts of material notwithstanding privacy settings being engaged, can be seen from a number of the decisions. In England and Wales there is an apparent contrast between a number of the social media employment tribunal cases and the decision of the High Court in *Smith v Trafford Homes*. It may be that much will depend on context: is the post an expression of view, even an offensive one, or is it more properly characterised as abusive? The cases that consider the risk of promulgation rather than such actually having occurred tend to involve abusive and harmful posts, rather than the expression of views that happen to be offensive. The question of privacy vs policy is however an area in which guidance is likely to be both helpful and forthcoming.

- A linked issue may be the extent to which an employer can seek to 'control' an employee's purely private conversations. As already noted, in *Gosden* the tribunal considered that purely private emails always intended as such might have given rise to a different result. However it appears to the authors that should a purely private email be made public, there is no reason in principle why an employer could not properly consider that the fact of the email and that it has been made public amounts to misconduct such that it would be fair in the circumstances to discipline or dismiss, particularly where the contents of that email once it has been made public have caused actual harm. That said, there is the clear potential for a public policy argument that private communications, intended always to be kept that way, should not, simply because they come to light (even by legitimate means) be able to be relied upon by an employer. A consideration of the application of Art 8 in such circumstances may be instructive. Notably, even absent Art 8, the court in *Wilkinson-Reed* opined that a policy designed to control such private communications was unlikely to justify a dismissal.

11.11 All of the above duly said, the courts have appeared content thus far to apply existing common law principles and established lines of authority. Whether this can continue as social media develops and embeds yet further into employment relationships remains to be seen. The authors look forward to revising and revisiting these predictions, it is hoped, in future editions of this work.

CHAPTER 12

CONCLUSION

12.01 There are numerous potential consequences to the employer-employee relationship arising out of the ubiquity of the internet and social media. Whilst some of the potential heads of liability considered in the preceding chapters may appear on a first consideration to be unlikely to apply, the case-law considered in this book demonstrates that such claims can and do arise, in numerous situations. What is also abundantly clear is that an employer that does not take basic steps to protect itself, by implementing an appropriate policy and providing its staff with the information necessary to understand the ambit of that policy (whether by training or otherwise) leaves itself open to numerous potential difficulties. It is also likely that the types of claims considered above will only manifest more frequently, given the embedding of social media into more and more workplaces. In addition, the latest generation of employees, having grown up with social media as an integral part of their social scene, are increasingly unlikely to respect the previously established delineation between that which is acceptable at work and that which is acceptable in personal time, given the informality of approach and ease of accessibility that social media engenders.

12.02 The embedded nature of social media into popular culture, both amongst customers and employees, means that businesses must reconcile themselves to the concomitant risks that this brings. Where once a cross word or an inappropriate comment in the workplace could be glossed over by a swift apology and perhaps a bunch of flowers, or by an informal or formal disciplinary process, an ill-advised or inappropriate angry tweet has the potential to be seen by significant numbers of people within an extremely short period of time. This is a real change for companies: where once an employee would vent to a select group of supporters within the office, an isolated tweet can be spread by numerous followers with no connection or loyalty to the employer. A dismissed employee can set out their position in an instant, and their post can be seen by a potentially huge number of strangers. A disgruntled employee can cause significant damage to a company extremely swiftly and to a much wider audience than was ever before possible. Discrimination claims can be generated by an informal Google search into the background of a prospective employee, which many members of recruitment panels may informally carry out as a matter of course, absent a policy to control such steps. Competitors are able to identify customer bases by trawling social media feeds. Employees who take social media accounts with them when they leave their employment are potentially handing a vast resource to their new employer. For all of these reasons it is essential that employers catch up and take practical steps to protect themselves.

12.03 According to a survey for thedrum.com, 56% of the Millennial Generation constantly check their social media due to 'FOMO' (Fear Of Missing Out). The new generation of workers are constantly plugged in and are not afraid of expressing their views. This can give rise to significant concerns for employers where those views can be attributed to the corporate brand.

12.04 As such, the risks to employers of social media and the emerging concept of 'Web 2.0', the name coined in 2004 for the interactive social media-type sites, rather than the passive accessing of web pages, are increasing exponentially. As has been noted, the law at present treats social media and the internet simply as another medium over which misconduct or tortious behaviour can be carried out. This is likely to continue. However, as social media and online connectivity continues to advance, numerous unforeseen examples of risk to employers are likely to present themselves. Business is adaptable. The melding of computing power and biology is in its infancy, but will likely continue to develop apace. Groups such as the Swedish BioNyfiken seek to connect themselves physically to the internet. It is now possible for an implanted microchip to be used wirelessly to transfer an electronic business card: contact details, Twitter and other social media accounts being transmitted without technology straight to another's mobile telephone. If such details can be sent so easily, so can confidential electronic information, contacts and connections fundamentally useful to a competitor. It is essential for employers to recognise that information once held on an internal server (and prior to that, in ledgers and paper diaries) can now be transmitted at the literal press of a button.

12.05 The so-called 'Internet of Things' is often touted as the next big advance. It is predicted that global spending on such technology will reach £500 billion by 2020, up from a current £20 billion (2012). It is already the case that business can receive instant feedback from its customers. Many large service organisations have invested heavily in their Twitter teams (train companies and mobile telephone providers being at the forefront of such development). This often leads to customers expressing strongly-held views, which are usually not limited in accessibility to the company. The current thinking of such organisations is that a friendly and prompt response amounts to good customer service. When customers are able to feed back swiftly and efficiently, companies can adapt to their needs. But human nature will almost certainly mean that such constant interactions, particularly with difficult or disinhibited customers using an informal medium rather than interacting face to face or through another more formal medium, allows far more scope for misunderstanding, complaints, grievances and disciplinary issues. In addition, the more connected the workforce becomes, the more the line blurs between personal and private use. As seen in the case-law cited in this work, this is sometimes a distinction without difference; but so the more important becomes a good and up-to-date social media policy.

12.06 As will have become abundantly apparent, the starting point is to implement a policy, tailored to the workplace and cross-referencing existing policies such as the whistleblowing policy. The implementation of a policy will afford the employer some protection and will also act to establish workplace societal norms as to the usage of social media. A template basic policy appears in the next chapter, together with a commentary. A policy is obviously not a complete cure. But as can be seen from the cases analysed in the preceding chapters, the existence of, and the employee's knowledge of, a comprehensive policy may make the difference between a dismissal being fair and it being unlawful or wrongful. It is therefore also important to ensure that employees are made aware of the policy, not solely in the abstract but in respect of its particular terms and requirements. It is likely that regular staff training on such policies will be desirable to maximise the chances of its terms being upheld in any claim. It will also be important to keep the policy up to date, and Human Resources departments should schedule regular assessments of the policy and its fitness for purpose. Likewise, a policy will assist where employees raise grievances or bring claims for harassment, and may go some way towards providing some exculpatory cover if a claim is made against the employer on a vicarious basis. There are a number of cases in which the existence or otherwise of a policy has not affected the outcome of a claim, which have been considered in earlier chapters. Where misconduct is stark, or the employee should reasonably have known that their actions were inappropriate or wrong judged by objective standards, a tribunal will not interfere with a dismissal that is within the band of reasonable responses. However, likewise, a number of cases have been considered where tribunals have found that, absent a clear policy, a dismissal is unfair. If employers want to be as sure as they can be that internet misconduct will be a dismissible offence, even if, outwith the terms of the social media policy, the behaviour in question would not lead to a dismissal, they need to spell this out clearly in the policy and provide appropriate training to their employees as to the scope, nature and effect of that policy. This is particularly the case given that the development of the jurisprudence surrounding particular social media elements is in its infancy. As a result, anything that can assist the employer, the employee and, ultimately, a tribunal, to consider what is reasonable in the particular circumstances of the case is likely to be of assistance to the employer.

12.07 As well as a general social media policy, employers are well advised to consider inserting appropriate contractual provisions into their employee contracts. To avoid a defecting employee from taking social media accounts with them, contractual terms that require them to transfer, surrender or delete such accounts can go a long way towards preventing significant damage. The modern employer will do business across the spectrum of the internet and social media. A key employee, conversant with the customer base and who is connected to major customers, or who has built the company reputation through social media, can potentially take the entirety of the customer base with them when they move, absent clear guidelines and contractual terms as to what they are permitted to do. Restrictive covenants have historically been important for senior management; increasingly they may be relevant to the ambitious school-leaver tasked with building a social media presence but whom bosses may erroneously consider to be unimportant to the needs of the business.

12.08   Employers also need to be aware of the risks to them of defamation claims where employees are operating corporate social media accounts. Such activities should always be monitored, to ensure that such accounts are not being used to engage in 'Twitter wars' or postings that could found liability. There are numerous examples of everyday postings that are intemperate or abusive. Employees may not even consider that their posts are inappropriate, but rather are genuinely held views. But if they are defamatory or harassing, a claim can and may be brought.

12.09   It is important to bear in mind that social media magnifies the risks to employers of claims against them or reputational damage, but fundamentally it does not change the employer–employee relationship. Harassment on Twitter is fundamentally no different to a drunken encounter at the company's work do. Taking Facebook contacts and the account is no different to the employee who walked out with a photocopy of the company's contact book. There are many more cases of defamation and third party harassment that do not involve social media than those that do. Forwarding a smutty email is little different in principle than displaying pornographic magazines in the work cubicle. Where social media has come into its own, however, rather than simply being yet another platform that can found legal liability for employers, is its speed, reach and spontaneity. Employers need to adapt to these changing times. Social media is here to stay. The courts will always apply the law to novel situations. The key for employers is to be aware of the changing landscape and to make sure that they are aware of the risks. Ensuring policies are in place, training staff, monitoring official accounts, and ensuring that new developments are catered for will ensure as far as possible that the employer does not find itself losing in a tribunal or court.

12.10   Are employers getting it? The case-law considered in this book suggests that some do; some have made an effort; and some simply do not. Recent surveys suggest that anything from 35% to 60% of employers do not have a written social media policy. Those that do often are unsure what it covers. By contrast, the majority of employers have a social media presence, usually split over a number of platforms, with Twitter, LinkedIn and Facebook remaining the most consistently popular. But few employers appear properly to be aware of the multitude of potential risks that they face. It is clear that the courts and tribunals largely appear to be coming to decisions that conform with the view expressed by the authors: that social media is merely another platform over which actionable wrongs can be caused. Social media can convey bullying, harassment, discriminatory language or general misconduct. However the potential audience is dramatically expanded, at least potentially, from colleagues at the pub or around the water cooler to the world at large. Thus, the prospect for harm and humiliation is magnified exponentially. Employers must get a grip upon social media usage at work, to protect themselves both in respect of internal disciplinary procedures and from reputational damage or third party liability. A robust, well-considered and frequently updated policy, combined with appropriate training, is an essential first step. But employers should also go further, and insulate themselves as far as possible from any of the various consequences considered herein. Social media is not going away. It will become more embedded in the workplace every day. As with all other legal and technological advances, employers will adapt and embrace its opportunities; but must be wise to the consequences that will inevitably ensue.

CHAPTER 13

PRECEDENTS, FLOWCHARTS AND TEMPLATES

13.01 Throughout this book we have made clear our view that it is crucial to have a policy in place covering social media use by employees. Notwithstanding that a dismissal may be fair without such a policy in place, particularly where the actions of the employee are self-evidently misconduct such that it is reasonable for an employer to dismiss, that will not always be the case. Further, the principal purpose of such a policy is to regulate the behaviour of employees and to set out clear guidelines so that employees are aware of what social media and internet behaviour is and is not acceptable to their employer. Whilst there is no 'one-size-fits-all' policy capable of application in all industries, what follows later is a precedent policy that is intended to be adaptable to the needs of particular employers.

13.02 Before introducing a policy into the workplace various considerations need to be addressed in order to ensure that the policy is fit for purpose and that it provides the maximum protection for the employee and workplace.

DO YOU NEED A POLICY?

13.03 The short answer, in the authors' view is: yes you do. Whether or not the workplace has a social media profile itself and whether or not it embraces mass communications as part of its primary business functions, it is overwhelmingly likely that the internet and social media will have an impact. Different workplaces will have different approaches to online use. At one end of the spectrum are those workplaces that are heavily invested in technology, or that permit every member of staff access to social media and the internet on a 'trust' basis, only seeking to limit the types of site accessed from work as opposed to the amount of time that is spent on a site. At the other end of the spectrum are the workplaces where access online is limited or non-existent for a variety of reasons (be it security or cost). Other workplaces may take a middle ground by restricting access from work terminals but provide standalone computers that can be used to access the internet during break times. Each of these workplaces will need a policy: those workplaces that eschew social media are fooling themselves if they think they could not be the victims of reputational harm from employees using their own online profiles to discuss workplace matters. In any event, given the advent of significant computing power in the form of smartphones, which are likely to be with employees throughout their working day, together with the unrestricted ability of employees to use their own devices outside the workplace, the ubiquity of the online world is inescapable.

13.04 A good policy will fulfil a number of important roles. It will be instructional in that it should aim to inform the behaviour of individuals and so, hopefully, reduce risk and exposure to litigation. It will be directive, in that it sets out what is and is not acceptable. It will be disciplinary, in that it will make clear the consequences of failing to act in accordance with the policy. And it will be protective, in that it should ensure in so far as is possible that the employer is insulated from the consequences of a breach of the policy. The introduction and highlighting of such a policy also insulates the employer from internal drains on resources as well: with the implementation of a clear policy that is in tune with the corporate culture of the workplace productivity can be maintained and management time is ideally not spent investigating and disciplining staff for transgressions. Should it be necessary to carry out such processes, this will be able to be achieved within the bounds of that policy, providing guidance and clarity for all parties involved.

FORMULATING THE POLICY

13.05 Before putting pen to paper and drafting a policy, certain theoretical matters will need to be borne in mind. If the policy is to be effective it needs to aim to reflect the social media culture of the workplace. If the policy is to be effective and upheld then it needs to set out in clear terms the workplace's values whilst also bearing in mind the provisions permitting whistleblowing and which grant employees protective rights.

13.06 A study conducted on behalf of ACAS[1] suggested adopting a 'common sense' approach when using social media and ideally carrying out research to find out the extent of social media use within the workplace by employees before developing a policy so as to be able to understand prior to implementation the purpose to which the policy is directed.

13.07 Once the culture of the workplace has been identified, the risks posed to that workplace need to be considered and recorded: is there a reputational risk; is there a security risk; are there any particular confidentiality risks posed in this particular workplace sector? The identification of risks and the corporate culture is a multi-disciplinary enterprise with involvement likely to be necessary from human resources, lawyers and senior management and other involvement highly encouraged, especially any employee representatives or trade unions.

---

[1]   *Workplaces and Social Networking: The Implications for Employment Relations* (2010).

CONSIDERATIONS FOR THE POLICY

13.08 Once the culture of the workplace and the potential risks have been identified the drawing up of a policy should be relatively painless, even more so if there are existing policies in place that can be cross-referred to. The most obvious examples are the IT policy, the whistleblowing policy, the disciplinary policy and the equality and diversity policies. There should also be cross-references back from those policies to the social media policy. It may also be necessary to consider the terms of employees' contracts, particularly if there is a need to consider restrictive covenants or contractual confidentiality provisions, together with the ownership and control of social media accounts.

13.09 The policy should also not be just a negative, proscriptive document informing employees of what they cannot do in broad terms. It should also set out what employees can do when they consider there has been a breach of the policy by another employee. It is here that express reference to the whistleblowing policy is vital.

13.10 In order to enhance the effect of the policy and, hopefully, the prospects of it being adhered to by staff, simply setting out a list of 'do's and don'ts' is unlikely to be sufficient. There should be a section addressing 'why': why the policy is needed, why social media pose which risks to employees and the employer and why the employee needs to think about what they are posting/typing. By giving examples of the risks posed and the need for the policy the reasonableness of the policy is enhanced as it has a solid foundation of necessity from a business perspective, backed up with sanctions imposed for breaching the policy which are more likely to be seen as understandable and within the band of reasonable responses if they are based in fact. Such a policy also has the benefit of flexibility, rather than rigidly setting out lists of what is and is not acceptable. The reader should also be aware of what the policy covers: both in terms of the platforms or types of platform the policy applies to as well as the timing of the use of those platforms. This necessarily requires the policy to be continually reviewed and updated to reflect the development of technology. That said, new forms of social media are developing constantly and electronic information is becoming ever more embedded into our culture. A policy that sets out its purpose and aims is more likely to be able easily to be adapted or applied to novel situations by analogy, even if those new risks have not been specifically identified.

13.11 Other considerations include the extent of the policy. If personal use of the internet or of social media is to be permitted, then: is it unrestricted, in the sense that employees have only the loosest limitations imposed upon them, such as certain types of sites being blocked? If an employer is seeking to limit usage, in terms of scope, time, nature of device, or content, and to back up that limitation with disciplinary consequences, it is important, as stated earlier in this book, to ensure that the limits are set out in objectively determinable terms: if the workplace has defined lunch breaks for its staff, when social media usage is permitted, then this can be stated in the policy. Otherwise restricting use to 'when not busy' or similar terminology leaves too much open to interpretation and may be difficult to justify when imposing a sanction, or defending a dismissal in an employment tribunal. If limitations are to be imposed on personal usage then these need to be spelt out with absolute clarity as the limitations are impinging on personal time and the employee has a right to know where the limits are and where the boundaries are imposed.

IMPLEMENTING THE POLICY

13.12   Merely having a policy is not, however, the end of the process; the policy needs to be disseminated and the workforce made aware of its existence and effect. As with all polices and procedures consultation with the workforce prior to its introduction will assist with the successful implementation of the policy as its legitimacy will be increased. In its guide on *Social Media: How to Develop Policy Guidance*, ACAS recommend consultation with employees to determine what is to be included in the policy; they further recommend that the dissemination of the policy should be conducted by various means, including social media itself and when 'settling in new staff' at an induction day. Records of training received should be obtained and retained. Again, the level and content of such training will necessarily be dependent on the level and range of perceived threats posed to the workplace which have been identified and covered by the policy along with the size and resources of the organisation.

13.13   Implementing the policy is a process that extends beyond merely handing out copies of the policy or highlighting its existence to staff members. Training of management staff is also necessary; albeit that it is likely to dovetail substantially with any training provided on disciplinary and conduct issues.

13.14   As with all policies it is useful to have an identified point of contact who has responsibility to deal with questions from staff about the policy and its application. This can either be an identified role, or a generic role such as 'line manager'. Imposing that obligation on a manager necessitates, however, that they receive training that is kept up to date, particularly if the policy is intended to develop in line with new methods of online interaction.

13.15   There now follows two sample social media policy templates, one a general policy and one relating to pre-employment vetting. These templates are deliberately basic, and do not cover by any means everything that a good policy should. Social media policies need to be tailored to the circumstances of individual employers, and need to interact and cross-reference with other existing policies. What follows should therefore be treated as basic building blocks – the fundamentals but not necessarily suitable in all circumstances, and certainly not comprehensive 'cut and paste' policies. If in doubt, the best advice is always to seek specialist input from outside advisors.

SAMPLE SOCIAL MEDIA POLICY

13.16

Social media policy

1. Introduction

1.1 The company provides its employees with access to the internet at work and allows reasonable use of personal devices so long as such work does not interfere with your responsibilities.

2. The Risks

2.1 Social media is a prevalent part of today's methods of communication and [the Company] do not seek to limit this. However, there are risks which mass communication poses which the COMPANY wish to minimise for the benefit of its employees as well as itself, this can include liability for downloading obscene, illegal or offensive images,

2.2 With these risks in mind the policy has been developed to maximise the safety of the COMPANY and its workers.

2.2.1 All social media interactions can be adduced in evidence in legal proceedings.

2.3 This policy is part of a set of policies implemented by [COMPANY] to which your attention is drawn. Full copies of all of these polices can be obtained from [LOCATION: eg HR or file on intranet].

3. Statement of Policy

3.1 The purpose of this policy is to provide guidance for employees of [   ] ('[   ]') in relation to the use of social media. 'Social media' refers to but is not limited to media such as blogs; wikis; Twitter; Facebook; LinkedIn; podcasts; message boards; and other forums and comments on web pages. These examples are not exhaustive and this policy will apply to all other forms of social media.

3.2 This policy contains an outline of the standards that [   ] expects of all its employees irrespective of role, grade or status in relation to social media to observe, the circumstances in which [   ] may monitor the use by employees of social media and the steps that [   ] will take where this policy is breached.

3.3 This policy does not form part of the contract of employment of employees of [   ], and may be amended without notice at any time on which occasion a copy of the amended policy will be provided to employees.

3.4 This policy is intended to apply to all individuals employed by [   ].

3.5 All employees are expected to comply with the provisions of this policy at all times. The provisions of this policy are intended to protect the privacy, confidentiality, reputation and interests of [   ] and its members and those of

[   ]' employees, clients, partners and competitors. Breach of this policy may be dealt with under the provisions of the Disciplinary Policy which can result in revocation of access to internet facilities, warnings and, for serious or repeated breaches may constitute gross misconduct with the consequence of summary dismissal. The full range of sanctions permissible is contained within the disciplinary Policy, and your attention is directed to that policy.

3.6 The COMPANY also reserves the right to report any illegal activities to the relevant authorities [think, does your business have any regulatory overseer's who may require reports to be sent to them?].

4. Implementation of Policy

4.1 The ('[WHO IS IN CONTROL]') has overall responsibility for the implementation of this policy and for its reviewing, monitoring and shall periodically report to the [WHO IS IN CONTROL] in this regard.

4.2 All employees are personally responsible for their own compliance with this policy and its application. All staff should ensure that they are familiar with the terms of this policy and such familiarity will be assumed following its circulation. You are also expected to exercise your good judgement and common sense when using social media and, if you have any doubts about what you are doing, you should ask {WHO IS IN CONTROL].

4.3 Any breaches of this policy should be reported in confidence to the [WHO IS IN CONTROL].

4.4 Although the intention is that this policy is easy to understand and apply if you have any questions relating to this policy, its implementation, application or effect, these should be directed to the [WHO IS IN CONTROL].

4.5 Again, if you have any doubt as to what you are about to do on social media you should ask before you do it!

5. Use of Work-Related Social Media

5.1 [   ] recognises the importance of the internet and social media in promoting [   ], its members and its services to a wide audience of potential and existing clients.

5.2 [   ] operates across various social media and internet platforms, including but not limited to the [   ] website, LinkedIn and Twitter.

5.3 The [WHO IS IN CONTROL] is responsible for promoting [   ]' profile across all social media platforms but may authorise specified employees to carry out this role.

5.4 Only persons authorised by the [WHO IS IN CONTROL] from time to time are permitted to post material on the internet or on social media platforms on behalf of [   ]. Any breach of this restriction will amount to gross misconduct.

5.5 Employees authorised to do so are encouraged to utilise social media platforms to promote the interests and activities of [   ] and may refer to [   ] or to specific members of [   ] in doing so. However any such utilisation of social media must be professional, courteous, appropriate, non-defamatory and relevant. The use of work-related social media platforms for personal promotion or gain or any posting that brings or may bring the reputation of [   ] or of a member of [   ] into disrepute will amount to gross misconduct. This includes but is not limited to the use of work-related social media to advance a personal interest, cause or argument; the posting on work-related social media of personal or inappropriate information or comment; the uploading of inappropriate photographs or other media; and the re-tweeting or re-posting of inappropriate comment.

5.6 The use of [COMPANY'S] social media platforms shall not be used for purposes detrimental to your role within the workplace and your responsibilities; this includes acting for personal gain or acting in a way that breaches any of the [COMPAY'S] policies and procedures.

5.7 Before using work-related social media you must have read and understood this policy and indicated the same as a result of which you will receive written authorisation from a member of the [WHO IS IN CONTROL].

5.8 [   ] retains the ownership and control of any accounts set up in its name or purporting to engage on its behalf and upon the ending of the employment relationship with any employee in control of any such social media account, control of that account, any passwords or other account information and any connections, followers or other links shall remain the property of [   ] and shall forthwith be provided to the [WHO IS IN CONTROL].

5.9 Usage of the social media platform is subject to scrutiny by the COMPANY. You should be aware that the COMPANY'S network creates a record of all communications and such material can and will be forwarded to the relevant and appropriate authorities as indicated above.

6. Personal Use of Social Media

6.1 During working hours [   ] permits the incidental use of personal social media, personal telephone conversations and personal emails on a limited basis and subject to conditions as a privilege and not a right. This privilege may be withdrawn indefinitely or for a specified period of time from any employee at the entire discretion of [   ].

6.2 Such permission is subject to the following conditions:

6.2.1 use must be minimal and must take place during [authorised breaks], and [outside of normal working hours];

6.2.2 Such use must not be in breach of the rules for social media use set out below;

6.2.3 such use must not interfere with work-related commitments;

6.2.4 Such use must comply with [   ]' policies including but not limited to the [   ] Equal Opportunities Policy.

6.2.5 Such use is not for personal gain;

6.2.6 Such use does not damage or in any way reflect detrimentally upon the COMPANY.

6.3 The following rules will apply to the use of social media both during working hours and outside working hours:

6.3.1 Personal social media profiles should not identify [   ] or any members thereof or where they do must include a disclaimer substantially in the form: 'any views expressed are my own views and do not necessarily reflect the views of my employer';

6.3.2 Postings, Tweets or other interaction should not identify [   ] or any members thereof or where they do must include a disclaimer substantially in the form: 'any views expressed are my own views and do not necessarily reflect the views of my employer';

6.3.3 it is forbidden to upload, post, link to, retweet or otherwise promote any obscene, abusive, discriminatory, defamatory, harassing, derogatory or inappropriate content;

6.3.4 it is forbidden to upload, post, link to, retweet or otherwise promote any material or content that may be damaging to [   ], its reputation or any member, other employee or their reputations;

6.3.5 it is forbidden to disclose any details of [   ]' work, clients, cases or any other commercially sensitive, anti-competitive, private or confidential information;

6.3.6 should any employee feel that they have been harassed or bullied by a colleague or member via social media or have been offended by material or comment made by a colleague or member they shall immediately inform the [   ] in writing of the same;

6.3.7 it is forbidden to upload, post or forward any information or content belonging to a third party without their consent;

6.3.8 you must have read, understood and at all times comply with the terms and conditions of any social media platform that you use;

6.3.9 If you notice content posted on social media whether by an employee or a third party that is or is potentially in breach of this policy or refers to [   ] whether complimentary or derogatory, you shall report this to the [WHO IS IN CONTROL].

7. [   ]' Monitoring of Social Media

7.1 Any use of social media platforms, whether or not accessed for work purposes and whether or not accessed during working hours may be monitored by [   ] and any breaches of this policy whether in or out of working hours may lead to disciplinary action being taken.

7.2 [   ] reserves the right to restrict or prevent access to certain social media websites if we consider personal use to be excessive. Any monitoring carried out by [ ] is carried out only to the extent permitted or required by law and as necessary and justifiable in the interests of [ ]' business.

7.3 Misuse of social media websites may lead to criminal or civil liability to third parties both of employees and of [ ]. In such circumstances it is the policy of [ ] to seek an indemnity against any liability from the offending employee.

7.4 The following non-exhaustive list of actions whether from a work or personal account and whether in a personal or professional capacity either in or out of ordinary working hours will constitute gross misconduct and will lead to the activation of the disciplinary policy with the potential sanction of summary dismissal:

7.4.1 the uploading, posting, linking to or forwarding of pornographic material;

7.4.2 false or defamatory statements against any person or organisation;

7.4.3 offensive, obscene, defamatory, discriminatory, criminal, derogatory or embarrassing material;

7.4.4 Uploading, posting, linking or forwarding any material which could bring the COMPANY into disrepute or damage the relationships the COMPANY has with others, or its standing or perceived standing.

7.4.5 confidential information relating to [ ], its members or its clients;

7.4.6 disclosure of proprietary information, which includes: [any relevant information which may, or may not also be confidential];

7.4.7 any other statement likely to create criminal or civil liability;

7.4.8 Information or material that is in breach of copyright, intellectual property rights or in breach of privacy.

7.5 Evidence of a breach of this policy may result in an investigation including requests for disclosure of social media account details (including private, locked or other confidential accounts) and postings.

7.6 Any breach of this policy should be reported to the [WHO IS IN CONTROL].

SAMPLE PRE-EMPLOYMENT VETTING ONLINE POLICY

13.17

Pre-employment vetting online policy

Introduction

1. This policy sets out the basis upon which [THE COMPANY] may undertake vetting of prospective employees through a consideration of information publicly available through social media and the internet.

2. [THE COMPANY] will restrict any such vetting to that which is reasonably necessary to pursue the legitimate and proportionate aims of [THE COMPANY]. This may include the potential for reputational damage to [THE COMPANY] arising out of the social media usage of prospective employees.

3. It is important that applicants are aware that [THE COMPANY] is seeking to protect its legitimate interests in considering the social media profile of prospective employees. This does not mean that [THE COMPANY] will take into account personal posts, tweets or comments outside the context of work unless such information is of a significantly offensive or inappropriate nature. [THE COMPANY] is not seeking to have regard to ordinary social interaction which it recognises may be informal and inappropriate in a workplace context but which is not carried out in such context.

Scope

4. [THE COMPANY] may undertake a search of publicly available social media profiles, including but not limited to LinkedIn and information available through searches conducted via search engine such as Google or Yahoo [AND IN APPROPRIATE CASES, DEPENDING ON THE ROLE Twitter, Facebook, Instagram and other publicly accessible social media platforms.] [THE COMPANY] has carried out an impact assessment, a copy of which will be provided on request, to determine the extent to which such searches are legitimate and proportionate to the needs of its business and to the particular role for which recruitment is sought.

5. Such search will be carried out at [STAGE OF PROCESS – AS LATE AS POSSIBLE].

6. The impact assessment sets out in detail the purposes behind the vetting in the context of the particular needs of [THE COMPANY] and the benefits it is likely to deliver. [THE COMPANY] recognises that it is essential to respect the privacy of its potential employees and to balance that privacy against the needs of its business and as a result has determined that it is appropriate to carry out searches in respect of recruitment to this role limited to [   ] / [those set out in the impact assessment], for the reasons also set out therein.

7. The purpose of such search is to enable [THE COMPANY] to consider whether there are reasons for which it may be legitimately, reasonably and proportionately concerned as to information publicly available and which may give rise to a risk to or conflict with the interests of [THE COMPANY]. However it is important to make clear that [THE COMPANY] is specifically searching for information which may pose a risk to its reputation and the beneficial functioning of the workplace environment and the suitability of the candidate to the role and is not conducting a generalised search into the background of the candidate.

8. The core aims of [THE COMPANY] in carrying out pre-employment social media vetting are as follows:

- To protect [THE COMPANY];
- To protect clients and customers;

- To be fair to all candidates;
- To ensure non-discrimination and compliance with data protection law;
- To rely on fact, not opinion;
- To validate information to be relied on;
- To ensure relevance to the post to be filled;
- To see the candidate in the round;
- To be transparent and open to candidates about the vetting process.

9. In particular [THE COMPANY] will relate any internet or social media search to the particular skills, education and experience of the candidate and will not take account of purely personal information. The purpose of [THE COMPANY] carrying out social media checks is principally to determine whether the candidate has previously misused social media in a way which would or might impact upon [THE COMPANY].

10. [THE COMPANY] will not seek and will not ask you to disclose, personal log-in details, and will not access or seek to access social media profiles which are secured by privacy settings. [save in respect of certain high profile roles, where it may be legitimate to require you to disclose such information prior to the appointment process in which case this is identified in the impact assessment for the purpose of enabling [THE COMPANY] to ensure that private use of social media will not adversely impact upon the needs of [THE COMPANY]]. [THE COMPANY] will carry out only a proportionate search of the internet and social media with the object of considering only that information which is directly identifiable as being created by or relating to the candidate and will not seek to establish through more detailed searches social media accounts not obviously linked to the candidate. The purposes for which [THE COMPANY] will carry out social media and internet searches are set out in the impact assessment. [IN CERTAIN CASES [THE COMPANY] may if justified by the impact assessment ask you to disclose the user names, handles or other identifiers by which the candidate utilises social media].

11. [THE COMPANY] will not collect more information than is necessary, and will not collect or rely upon information which is irrelevant or excessive.

12. [THE COMPANY] in choosing to carry out any such search will not take into account in any employment decision the age, sex, sexual orientation, race, gender, disability, gender reassignment, marital or civil partnership status or religion or belief, or any other characteristic deemed from time to time by operation of law to be a protected characteristic of any prospective candidate which may be disclosed by any search of the internet or social media that is carried out.

13. [THE COMPANY] will prior to the making of any decision raise with you any information that it has obtained from the searches covered by this policy in order to provide you with an opportunity to comment upon the same and will make no decision prior to allowing you the opportunity to make such comment that you wish.

14. [THE COMPANY] recognises that many prospective employees will not engage with social media and may not have an online profile as a result. [THE COMPANY] will take no regard of the lack of a visible social media or internet presence.

15. [THE COMPANY] will keep a record of the searches that it carries out over social media and search engine profiles which will be made available to candidates upon request.

16. [THE COMPANY] will retain the record of searches and the information retrieved only for such period as is proportionate. Where a candidate is successful [THE COMPANY] will ordinarily delete such information as it has gathered within a period of [NO MORE THAN TWO YEARS]. Where information is gathered on a candidate who accepts an offer of employment, the information will be retained for such period as [THE COMPANY] considers to be necessary and proportionate.

17. All information gathered by [THE COMPANY] shall be done so anonymously and all such information will be stored securely during its period of retention.

18. For the avoidance of doubt, any employee or agent of [THE COMPANY] carrying out a search of social media and the internet will not form part of the interview or decision-making panel.

[THE COMPANY] seeks your informed consent to carry out such searches. Please therefore sign and date this policy to confirm your consent.

SAMPLE RESTRICTIVE COVENANT TEMPLATE

13.18 As previously noted, it is important for an employer to seek to protect itself from the loss of proprietary information when an employee leaves. We have set out in some detail the need for employers to consider in appropriate cases the inclusion of specific restrictive covenants supplemented by a social media policy. It is important to stress that, in order to be effective, a restrictive covenant must be tailored to the particular circumstances of the employee and the business – it cannot simply be cut and pasted and automatically enforceable. As such, the provision of a template covenant is perhaps not necessarily that useful. However, the authors have endeavoured to consider the terms of an appropriate restrictive covenant in the circumstances prevailing in the case of *Whitmar Publications Ltd v Gamage & Ors*.[2] It will be recalled that in *Whitmar*, there were no contracts of employment, and thus no restrictive covenants to be enforced. However, the authors have sought to imagine model restrictive covenants to govern the situation therein, adapted from the covenant contained within the *Palmer* contract. It is, of course, important to bear in mind that the simple reproduction of a template may well give rise to enforceability issues. Restrictive covenants need to be tailored to the specific circumstances of

---

[2]   [2013] EWHC 1881 (Ch).

the employer and the specific employee. The authors do not make any warranty as to the enforceability of what follows.

13.19

Restrictive covenant template

Restrictions

In this clause:-

a. 'contact' means any person, business, organisation, company or other entity who has at any time during the Relevant Period been registered with the Company or any Group Company and with whom the Employee was materially involved or had personal dealings during the Relevant Period;

b. 'client' means any person, business, organisation, company or other entity which has at any time during the Relevant Period been a client of the Company or any Group Company and with whom the Employee was materially involved or had personal dealings during the Relevant Period;

c. 'prospective client' means any person, business, organisation, company or entity who has at any time during the period of [X] months prior to the Termination Date been in negotiations with the Company or any Group Company with regard to entering into business with for the supply of services or seeking to connect with the Company or any Group Company with whom during such period the Employee was materially involved or had personal dealings;

d. 'Relevant Area' means within [X] miles of any branch of the Company or any Group Company at which the Employee worked in the Relevant Period;

e. 'Relevant Period' means the period of [X] months ending on the Termination Date;

f. 'Services' means services identical or similar to those being supplied by the Company or any Group Company at the Termination Date and with which the Employee was materially involved during the Relevant Period;

g. 'Termination Date' means the date on which the Employee's employment terminates or, if he spends a period on garden leave immediately before the termination of his employment, such earlier date on which such garden leave commences;

h. 'Social Media Platform' means any online or electronic media through which the Employee has interacted with contacts, clients or prospective clients of the Company or any Group Companies and includes in particular any such media through which the Employee has connected with, linked to, followed or been followed by, any such contacts, clients or prospective clients.

The Employee covenants with the Company that he will not, save with the prior written consent of the Company, directly or indirectly, either alone or with or on behalf of any person, firm, company or entity and whether on her own account or as principal, partner, director, employee, consultant or contactor:

a. for [X] months following the Termination Date be engaged or concerned in any business supplying [the services] within the Relevant Area;

b. for [X] months following the Termination Date and in competition with the Company or any Group Company canvass or solicit business or custom from any Client or Prospective Client in relation to Services including via any Social Media Platform;

c. for [X] months following the Termination Date and in competition with the Company or any Group Company be directly involved in the supply to any Client or Prospective Client of Services or otherwise deal with any Client or Prospective Client in relation to Services including via any Social Media Platform;

d. for [X] months following the Termination Date canvass or solicit business or custom from any contact, client or prospective client in relation to Services including via any Social Media Platform;

e. for [X] months following the Termination Date be directly involved in the supply to any contact of Services or otherwise deal with any contact, client or prospective client in relation to Services including via any Social Media Platform;

f. immediately prior to the Termination Date to tender up to the Company:

   i)   the user names, login details, passwords and security details of all Social Media Platforms operated by The Employee on behalf of the Company whether authorised or not for the purpose of the transfer absolutely of the same to the Company such accounts and their users, contacts, followings or any other connections howsoever described remaining the absolute property of the Employer;

   ii) the user names, login details, passwords and security details of all Social Media Platforms operated by The Employee making express reference to the Company whether authorised or not for the purpose of the transfer absolutely of the same to the Company such accounts and their users, contacts, followings or any other connections howsoever described remaining the absolute property of the Employer;

   iii) To delete from any personal Social Media Platforms the users, contacts, followings or any other connection howsoever described of any clients, contacts or prospective clients gained during the course of employment.

Each of the restrictions contained in this clause is an entirely separate and independent restriction, despite the fact that they may be contained in the same phrase, and if any part is found to be unenforceable the remainder will remain valid and enforceable.

FLOWCHARTS

13.20

1. Social media implementation

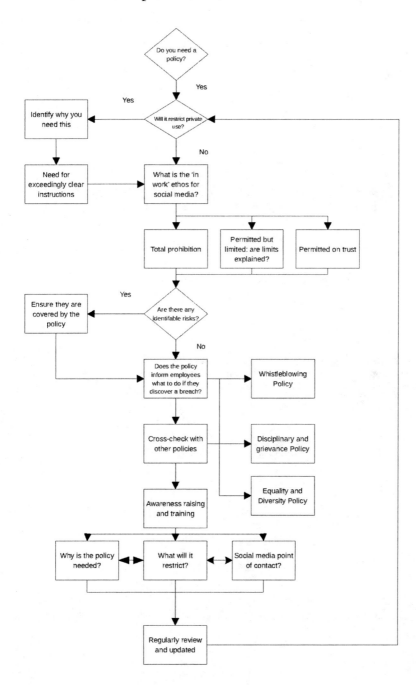

13.21

2.   Consultation on policy

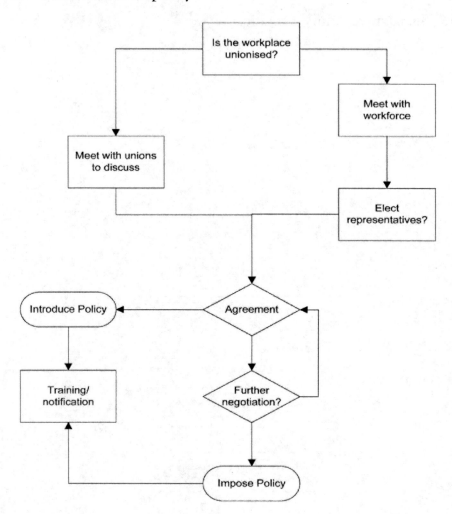

13.22

3.   Social media misconduct

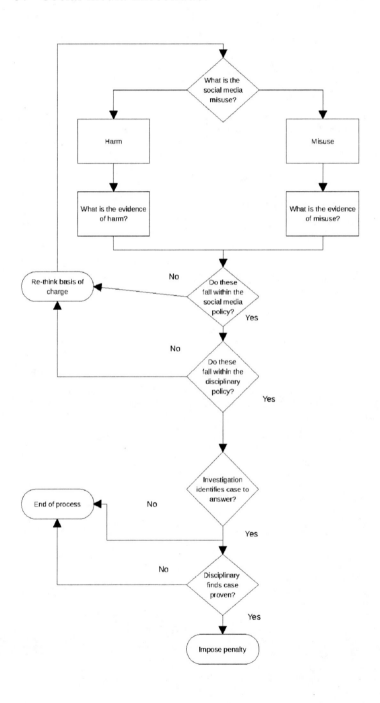

13.23

4.   Types of claim

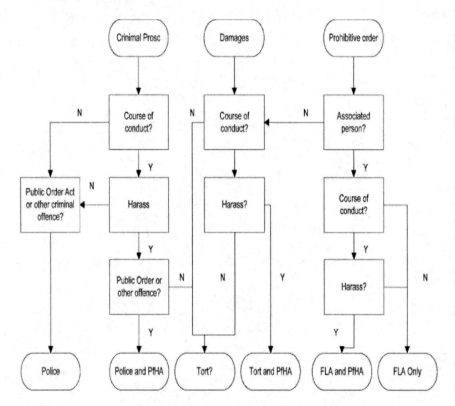

13.24

5.   Contractual terms

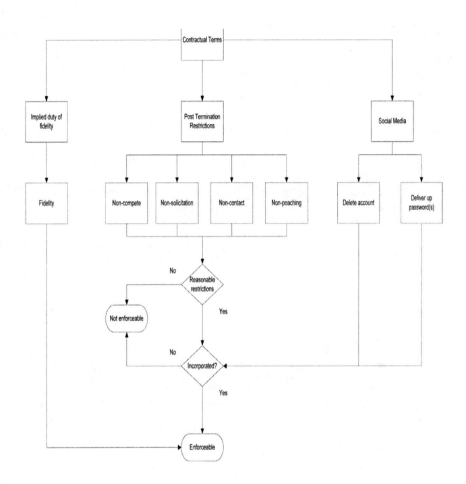

CHAPTER 14

CASE STUDY

14.01 The following case study has been created by the authors to illustrate some of the issues considered in this work. Whilst an academic analysis of the legal aspects of employment and workplace law is doubtless of benefit to practitioners and those entrusted by their employers to manage such issues, the application of such analysis in practice may not always be as readily apparent and thus as useful. The authors recognise that employers will not always find themselves involved in proceedings having had the luxury of detailed and specific legal advice, and this case study is therefore designed to afford a practical example of a case arising out of social media issues. It should not be considered to be a template for best practice (and in fact is deliberately anything but); rather, it is designed to be treated as a vehicle for the practical application of a number of the principles set out herein.

14.02 The factual matrix of the scenario is relatively simple. Following Facebook posts that could be taken to be deriding their core product and drawn to the attention of the employer and, after a disciplinary process, the employee is told to cease posting or face dismissal. The posts were made using private equipment, though the employee was provided with a smartphone manufactured by his employer, and about which his complaints related. He resigns, and claims constructive unfair dismissal. On the facts of the case, the tribunal finds for him.

14.03 The case study comprises a number of elements, as follows:

- policies (which, as will be seen, are far from model policies);
- the relevant posts;
- correspondence arising out of the ensuing disciplinary process and the minutes;
- the resignation letter;
- the ET1 and particulars of complaint;
- the ET3 and grounds of resistance;
- witness statements for the parties; and
- judgment.

14.04 As such, the case study considers from genesis to resolution the type of scenario which could arise in numerous workplaces. A commentary to each section of the documents gives an analysis of the case on an evolving basis and seeks to set out problems and pitfalls, with suggestions as to what else could have been done to prevent the result. Of course, each case will be different; and in considering this case study, it will become apparent that the outcome could well have been different even on the facts and papers herein presented. The scenario is however designed to allow the authors to make practical suggestions as to the failings on the part of the employer, with a view to enabling readers to apply the analyses of the case-law and principles contained in preceding chapters to a set of circumstances. For the avoidance of any doubt the parties, witnesses and facts are entirely fictional.

14.05

PART 1: POLICIES
IT rules
Introduction

Techno Co is at the heart of the digital world, and we actively encourage the use of the Company's computer system, including the email system and the internet, to enhance the reputation of the company and its brand, which we aim to make the premier aspirational technology product line available.

Misuse and negative publicity can cause problems including claims against the company and potentially prosecution against an individual.

In order to seek to strike a balance Techno Co has this policy. Failure to comply may lead to disciplinary action including, in serious cases, dismissal.

Use of Equipment

Computers and related equipment are provided for business use only. They are not to be used for any personal matter, the watching of videos, the playing of games or for personal correspondence.

The networked system has been set up and developed for business use and must not be adapted to the implementation of personal settings or preferences. In particular, personalised desktops and setting are not permitted.

Email, internet and social media

As stated above the use of the Company's networked computer systems is restricted to business use only. Similar restrictions are placed on the communication systems operated by the Company including the email system and any internet based forms of communication. Any such system should only be used for matters directly concerned with the business of the Company.

As a market leading Technology Company, the Company encourages its employees to embrace developments in technology. One key aspect of this is social media engagement. However, the company reminds its employees of the high value it places in the positive and aspirational image it promotes for its products.

Employees using email, the internet and social media should remember that the following points apply:

1. The content of an email message must be consistent with the standards, business aims and objectives that this Company expects from written communications – that is positive and with an aim to promote the company's image;

2. Messages should only be sent to those employees for whom they are particularly relevant.

3. The appropriateness of email. Email should not be used as a substitute for face-to-face communication.

4. if you need to think about whether you should send the email or make the post, you probably should not.

5. email and social media posts are not private and permanent records are made of them. Merely deleting them from your system or timeline will not remove them from all systems, and people forwarding the message/tweet will bypass any limits you thought you had placed on the circulation of the message.

Unauthorised Use

Any use of the email system or internet which is not related to the business is contrary to the Company's rules

Commentary

There are numerous difficulties and issues with this policy. For a market-leading technology company, it is remarkably out of date. It lacks specifics and fails to set out properly the circumstances that may lead to dismissal. A simple policy of this sort, which seeks to use blanket terms and fails to cross-reference to other policies, is likely to run into significant difficulties where an employee alleges that their dismissal was unfair and that dismissal arises out of the existence of the policy. Specific points include:

- the fact that this policy clearly appears to be an existing IT policy that has clumsily been updated to take into account social media (which is specifically referenced) but appears to have been built on a foundation of a much earlier policy, designed perhaps to encompass early internet use. It does make reference to other devices (as would be expected given the nature of the company) but does not appear to differentiate between internet use generally and the specific issues raised by social media. All in all, it has the flavour of a policy that has been bolted together and not a policy to which specific thought has been given as to the risks particularly of social media and the harm that can be caused by misuse;

- no examples are given of the sort of breaches that might lead to dismissal. The disciplinary and dismissal policy follows on from this section, but there is no cross-reference whatsoever. The only →

guidance that an employee reading this policy can obtain is that a breach may result in disciplinary procedures and potentially dismissal. However the policy does not set out what may lead to disciplinary procedures and certainly does not make clear what might amount to misconduct leading to dismissal. There is an understandable temptation to keep social media or IT policies vague given the developing technology and the myriad circumstances in which social media may impact upon the workplace. However a policy that does not make clear the consequences of particular categories of breach is likely to be impugned as being far too vague;

- the policy rightly notes that employees are encouraged to use social media but that it places a premium on its positive image. Any employer operating in the field of social media would be well-advised to spell out what it expects and hopes to gain from such interactions, and which employees should be expected to be using social media for employer purposes, in order to underpin the necessity of positive rather than negative coverage. However in this policy these objectives are not as clearly spelled out as would be hoped;

- the policy attempts to conflate personal and private use, and, whilst setting out in some detail the expectations of the company in respect of devices and connections maintained by it, is then ambiguous as to its terms relating to own devices and own accounts. The lack of a distinction between such things and in particular the fact that the policy appears to be directed principally to employer-controlled connections causes difficulty in applying the policy to social media posts outside of working hours, or, in particular, through personal accounts or devices. Whilst the paragraph relating to the fact that social media posts are not necessarily capable of permanent deletion may lend some support to the ambit of the policy, the provisions are vague, ill-defined and not properly thought out;

- the 'standards, business aims and objectives' of the company are not defined and are not cross-referenced to another policy or the employee handbook. As such, the employer may struggle to justify a dismissal for a breach of these standards where the same are not defined, save in egregious situations;

- the 'unauthorised use' section is particularly useless. It does not make clear to what this applies; appears to conflate numerous issues, and arguably only applies in respect of the stated aim of the policy, which appears to be the use/misuse of the company's IT system;

- no consideration is given as to what is and is not misuse; what is and is not harm; how such information can be gathered; or when it is appropriate for the company to take disciplinary measures.

As has been made abundantly clear, a good, up-to-date, specific, detailed and promulgated social media policy is of critical importance to employers. Whilst clear breaches of appropriate standards of behaviour ➙

(such as in *Williams*) will support a dismissal regardless of the existence of a policy, it is likely that the harm caused by employees over social media will often be of the misguided or inappropriate variety, rather than the forwarding of pornographic emails that the High Court made clear should plainly be treated as a breach of the employment relationship. If an employer is to seek to justify a dismissal as being fair in the circumstances, absent such a breach, part of the consideration carried out by the tribunal will inevitably be of the terms of the social media or IT policy. If that policy does not deal with such circumstances, it will be less likely that the tribunal will find that the dismissal fell within the range of reasonable responses. An employer might well reasonably wish to dismiss an employee who has embarrassed it or caused it harm over social media; but if a seemingly minor post is not backed up by policy terms, the tribunal is more likely to feel sympathy for the dismissed employee. Employers may be able to save themselves by reliance on their general disciplinary policy, but as will be seen in the next section, such policies will often be drawn widely and non-specifically, and thus will be of limited assistance.

Disciplinary Procedure

1.   The following is the Company's disciplinary policy. Its aim is to ensure that every employee is given a fair chance to explain the situation that has developed. The Company will comply with the relevant ACAS code of practice.

2.   Matters covered by this disciplinary policy include any breach of the company's terms and conditions of employment, any relevant policy or procedure as well as conduct outside working hours which, in the opinion of the Company, affects the performance of your duties or may bring the Company into disrepute or adversely affect it.

      ...

5.   This will be initiated by the Company in the case of any matter that is considered sufficiently serious.

      ...

10.   You will not normally be dismissed unless it is of a serious nature. Examples of serious misconduct which are likely to lead to your contract being terminated are:
      • violence or verbal abuse towards fellow employees
      • giving information about the Company to third parties without permission or otherwise disclosing or assisting in the disclosure of information gained or overheard in the course of your employment where the information is likely to harm the interests of the Company
      • theft or fraud
      • serious insubordination
      • physical violence or bullying
      • deliberate and serious damage to property
      • serious misuse of an organisation's property or name

- deliberately accessing internet sites containing pornographic, offensive or obscene material
- unlawful discrimination or harassment
- bringing the organisation into serious disrepute
- serious incapability at work brought on by alcohol or illegal drugs
- causing loss, damage or injury through serious negligence
- a serious breach of health and safety rules
- a serious breach of confidence
- sexual, racial, religious harassment, or harassment based on sexual orientation or other harassment
- criminal conduct in relation to the Company, including driving Company vehicles whilst using a mobile telephone
- conduct likely to bring the Company into disrepute;
- dishonesty.

It must be stressed that this is not an exhaustive list and summary dismissal may follow where the gravity of the offence is considered to warrant this sanction.

Commentary

Again, this policy is not well drafted. It adopts a similar broad-brush approach to the IT policy, but at least has the redeeming feature that it sets out examples of serious misconduct and notes that they are not exhaustive. It is based on a template commonly available, but that does not in the view of the authors provide anything like the necessary protection to the company. It also fails to cross-refer even by implication to the IT policy, and fails as a result to give any specific examples relating to social media use. The following particular criticisms can be made:

- Paragraph 2 of the policy is clearly intended to incorporate policies issued from time to time by the company. However given the specific and particular terms of any given social media or IT policy and the particular aims to which such a policy is directed, it is unlikely that such tangential reference will be sufficient to persuade a tribunal that the policy has properly been incorporated within the disciplinary policy.
- Paragraph 5 of the policy is ambiguous and does not set out any criteria for the company to consider what is sufficiently serious.
- The examples of circumstances in which dismissal may be appropriate do not pertain in any way to IT or social media circumstances. The examples are all highly general, and open to interpretation and challenge. There is a real risk with such generalisations that a specific allegation arising out of social media usage will not fit into any such categorisation. The difficulty with seeking to import into terms such as 'serious misuse of an organisation's property or name'; 'bringing the organisation into serious disrepute' 'a serious breach of confidence' or 'conduct likely →

to bring the Company into disrepute' is that they all amount to extremely vague abjurations. In order to bring within the scope posts on social media, particularly those that may appear at first blush innocuous but that may in fact cause the company real or potential harm, it may well be necessary for more specific examples of misconduct to be particularised, ideally in the social media policy with appropriate cross-references to the disciplinary policy. A vague reference to 'misconduct' in a policy is unlikely to stand up to scrutiny in those cases where a dismissal may be warranted by the particular behaviour of the employee but may nevertheless not amount to significant misconduct;

- The policy sets out a list of fairly significant examples of harm. A social media posting could potentially not 'tick' any of those boxes and yet cause harm. It is essential that employers tailor their policies to include specific examples of social media harm rather than relying on generic policy terms, to ensure that disciplinary and dismissal procedures can be applied to particular situations;

- This is not to say that generic 'cover alls' should not be included in a social media policy: they should. It is important for employers to seek to cover themselves against all eventualities as far as is possible; but a balance needs to be struck. Generic terminology may be out of date in a matter of months; what is important is that the goals, aims and objectives of the policy are clearly communicated, and that staff are made aware of the same.

14.06

PART 2: THE OFFENDING POSTS

On 14 December 2014 at 14:00 SmiffMeister1 wrote:

'Hi both, looking forward to seeing you later for the Xmas Blow out! ☺. Stupid wonderbox™ is not working, so cannot text, call or email better use FB to arrange!..so glad I got it free from work, would hate to pay for this trash! Would happily injure the tech-geeks who made this waste of silicon! Laterz!'

On 14 December 2014 at 14:30 SmiffMeister1 wrote:

'Sounds good to me, bloody thing still not working, reckon retailers should sell it with a mallet as it's the only way it will work. The bloody thing reckons I am in Tokyo! Heaven forbid anyone realises these things don't work! Lol!'

On 15 December 2014 at 03:20 SmiffMeister1 wrote:

'Great night guys. Wonderbox™ now confined to the toilet where it belongs! Whoever buys this rubbish should be tested as they clearly are a moron! I want to hit whoever made it with a bloody big stick!'

Commentary

The posts complained of by the company are set out above. There are a number of factors to note in respect of their content, as follows:

- The first post indicates that it is not intended to be for public consumption: it is addressed 'hi both'. The intended audience for the post is therefore confined to two people. As has been made clear from case-law considered elsewhere, intention or a belief that a message is private will not in and of itself provide protection for the employee from disciplinary proceedings, but may be a factor in considering fairness in the circumstances.
- The first post is also significantly disparaging of the Wonderbox, describing it as 'trash'. In addition there appears what potentially could be taken to be an intimation of violence towards the 'tech-geeks' who made the device.
- The second post makes further significantly disparaging comments, including a particularly potentially damaging comment, relating to consumers realising that the device does not work.
- The third post repeats similar disparaging comments about the quality of the device and a further potentially violent comment. →

It is however notable that there is no positive element that identifies the posts with the claimant, or in particular that he is an employee of the respondent. Whilst the first post refers to his getting the device 'free from work' his workplace is not identified, although the product clearly is. His user name likewise does not disclose a link. However it is likely that the friends to whom he is directing his posts do know where he works.

14.07

PART 3: DISCIPLINARY PROCEEDINGS

Techno Co Ltd
24 Soldier Place
London
NW1 6EX

John Smith
12 Smith Street
London
SE5 2EZ

16 December 2014

Dear John,

An allegation has been made against you which, if true, means you are in breach of the Code of Conduct by breaching the confidentiality obligations imposed on you by your contract of employment with the result that the reputation of Techno Co Ltd could have been brought into disrepute.

I am told that your posts on Facebook are inappropriate.

If this allegation is found to be correct it is a serious one and we will need to consider your continued employment with us.

Accordingly we have arranged for a disciplinary hearing to be held on 21 December 2014 at 10am.

Yours sincerely

Brenda Marshall

Accounts Manager

Commentary

> This is not a well-considered letter. It is deficient in a number of important respects:
>
> - No details of the allegation that has been made is given.
> - The charge itself is badly framed. The reference to the code of conduct is unspecific and does not identify with any particularity the breach alleged or the provision said to have been breached. ➙

- The reference to confidentiality, and that the company's reputation 'could' have been brought into disrepute is not well-phrased and is a hostage to fortune.
- Where any detail is in fact provided, being that the Facebook posts are 'inappropriate', no particularity is given and the posts are not identified.
- The potential sanction is not clear.
- No investigatory meeting is scheduled.
- The right to be accompanied to the meeting is not referenced.

It is of significant importance that an employer seeking to deal with an alleged breach of the social media policy or general misconduct taking place on social media especially in the absence of any policy sets out in significant detail the case to be answered. Whilst this is always desirable, it is of particular importance in relation to social media misconduct, given the considerations set out in the various cases considered above. This is of particular importance where no social media policy is in place, especially where the conduct complained of takes place outside of working hours and using personal equipment and accounts that do not reference the employer. In such circumstances the employer may well wish to set out at an early stage, such as the investigatory or disciplinary letter:

- the specific allegations to be answered, enclosing copies of the posts in question and, potentially, the method by which the employer came to have them;
- where there is a social media policy, specific reference to particular provisions. Where there is no such policy, details of why this behaviour is considered to be unacceptable, with reasons why such conduct is considered to be a disciplinary matter despite when and how it occurred;
- a copy of the social media or other policy, or reference to where it is available;
- details of the harm said to be caused or potentially caused; and
- details of the potential sanctions that may be considered.

Notes of Disciplinary Hearing

Date: 21 December 2014

Present: Brenda Marshall (BM), John Smith (JSm),

Start: 10:00

End: 10:30

JSm attended the office to answer allegations as set out in letter. JSm confirmed he had had an opportunity to read the disciplinary policy that was provided to him today.

I asked if there any mitigation JSm wanted to put forward.

Throughout the hearing JSm pretended to be confused about the allegations, claiming he did not understand the breach of confidence allegation. he asked for a break to consider this.

JSM agreed he had received a copy of the IT Policy.

JSm admitted to posting the comments on Facebook, he stated that he was annoyed as he was arranging to meet friends for their Christmas party but his phone was not working. he stated that he only has a few Facebook friends and so did not believe anyone, apart from them, could read his comments. His friends know he gets frustrated and doesn't mean anything by what he says. In fact they know he loves having a Wonderbox and he has posted to this effect before.

JSm stated that as soon as he received the letter of 16 December 2014 he removed the comments from Facebook, he was very sorry for the comments, but felt frustrated as he did not want to miss meeting his friends. It was banter and he certainly was not making threats.

JSm understood and fully appreciated that the image of TCC and the Wonderbox were vital to the company's survival. His profile does not refer to TCC and he has never mentioned where he works. His friends do know where he works.

JSm stated he wanted to keep his job.

Commentary

Again, the employer has certainly not followed best practice in carrying out this meeting. It would have been sensible for a note-taker to be present, and the notes are clearly not a verbatim record of the meeting. →

Policies were only provided at the meeting, and the approach appears to have been one of seeking to consider mitigation rather than a full consideration of the circumstances. No real mention is made of the policy. This case study is not however principally concerned with general employment law failings but rather those that pertain particularly to social media. As such, the following specific comments are made:

- The allegation of social media misconduct needs to be properly particularised and considered. In this scenario it is treated as a breach of confidence. It is not surprising that the claimant was confused as to this allegation. From his perspective he has used intemperate and foolhardy language, but he has not breached any confidence. Characterising the misconduct in that manner appears to suggest that there is an element of truth in what he has disclosed!

- The claimant makes a number of potentially important points that should form part of the consideration of a reasonable employer when considering sanction. These include the fact that he has only a few Facebook friends and that he believed that the messages were private. His friends apparently also do not take seriously what he says, and will be aware that he has previously been positive about the Wonderbox. These assertions appear to be accepted without further investigation. How many Facebook friends does he actually have? What other posts has he made? What privacy settings did he in fact have? These sort of considerations should inform an employer in considering what harm has been caused or could have been caused by social media misconduct.

- The posts were taken down after a short period of time. No consideration appears to have been given to whether it was possible to consider how many views (or comments) had been made in response to the posts. This is clearly a potentially relevant factor when considering harm, particularly in the absence of a clear and targeted social media policy.

- The potentially serious allegation in respect of the two prospective threats that were made in the posts, relating to physical harm, albeit to unnamed stereotypes, is not really considered at all. That violence was not intended is recorded almost as an afterthought. Again, a proper assessment of harm both to reputation to the world at large but also the prospective effect of the potential threat, appears to have been entirely glossed over, and the disciplinary process does not appear to be addressed in any meaningful way towards this aspect of the posts.

- Some consideration does appear to have been given to the link between the profile and the employer. However the relevance of this does not seem to be explored at all.

Techno Co Ltd
24 Soldier Place
London
NW1 6EX

John Smith
234 Smith Street
London
SE5 2EZ

22 December 2014

Dear John,

This is to confirm the outcome of the disciplinary hearing held on 21 December 2014.

I fully considered all the material and the points you put forward at the hearing.

I have concluded that the complaint is made out and that some sort of disciplinary action is appropriate. In view of the serious nature of the allegations and the damage to the reputation of Techno Co Ltd I have concluded that you should be dismissed if you do not agree to not use Facebook again. If you do agree to this reasonable request then the appropriate penalty, we feel, will be a Final Written Warning which will remain on your personnel file for 12 months.

We will permit you one week to decide what you want to do. If we do not hear from you by 29 December 2014 we will proceed to dismiss you.

You have the right to appeal against this outcome. Normally we would require any appeal to be notified to us within five working days. However, in light of the above we will extend this period to Friday 8 January 2015.

Yours sincerely

Brenda Marshall

Accounts Manager

Commentary

The result of the disciplinary process is an ultimatum. Such ultimata are thought by the authors not to be uncommon in social media cases, though that contained in this letter is particularly Draconian. In effect the employer is seeking to require the claimant not to use a particular social media site, notwithstanding that his posts related to a profile unconnected ➡

with work, and in his own time. However the authors are aware of cases where employers have sought to limit the use of social media in a private capacity. Such ultimata are unlikely to be considered lawful. It is clearly inappropriate for an employer to require an employee not to use a particular social media site at all. A requirement that an employee not use social media to reference his workplace or his employer's products might be more justifiable, particularly if backed up by a clear policy, but a blanket denial of access for personal use to a social media account is unlikely ever to be considered appropriate or a reasonable request.

In reality, an employer is always likely to be in a difficult position when seeking to control *access* (as opposed to *content*) in respect of social media sites outside of the workplace arena. A ban on accessing social media from workplace equipment, or during working hours, or from work-provided devices, will often be justifiable (so long as a policy in this regard is in place) but save in exceptional circumstances (such as national security, or possibly the use of rival social media platforms by an employee working for one) an attempt to prevent an employee from general personal access to a social media platform, regardless of the misconduct over that site, is unlikely to be upheld. An agreement that the social media account may be monitored by human resources could potentially be acceptable; a requirement that the employee not reference the employer or its products likewise; or a 'zero tolerance' final warning. Alternatively, a dismissal, if a reasonable response, would also be lawful.

In this scenario, unless the claimant agrees not to use social media again (or, specifically, Facebook), he is told that he will be dismissed. If he agrees to this 'reasonable request', he will receive a final written warning. None of the caveats referred to above are considered, but rather, a stark ultimatum is proffered. The company also fails to detail in any way the basis upon which the complaint is made out, or the harm relied upon, beyond an assertion that the reputation of the company has been damaged. This in itself is an unexplained progression from the original allegation of the potential damage to reputation.

What Mr Smith does next is therefore perhaps not that surprising.

John Smith
12 Smith Street
London
SE5 2EZ

Mrs Marshall
Techno Co Ltd
24 Soldier Place
London
NW1 6EX

Dear Mrs Marshall,

I am writing to complain about the disgusting treatment I received by you, which after taking advice I have been informed was totally inappropriate and unfair and I feel that the position I have been put in has totally undermined my confidence in you and any trust I had.

I have worked for Techno Co Ltd for a long period of time and was treated awfully because of some comments that were directed at only a few friends and were borne out of frustration and anger.

I look forward to you arranging for this injustice to be rectified within seven days.

Kind regards

John Smith

Techno Co Ltd
24 Soldier Place
London
NW1 6EX

John Smith
234 Smith Street
London
SE5 2EZ

11 January 2015

Dear John

Thank you for your undated letter which I received on Thursday 7 January 2015. I shall treat this as an appeal against the disciplinary findings and outcome.

I am very happy to meet with you, and have arranged the meeting for 14 January 2015 at 2pm.

I look forward to seeing you there.

Yours sincerely

Jayne Cutter

Managing Director

Notes of Appeal Meeting

Date: 14 January 2015

Present: Jayne Cutter (JC), John Smith (JS)

Start: 1400

End: 1450

JS attended to have his appeal heard.

Throughout the appeal JS answered no comment to questions that were asked of him. I wanted to see whether there was any understanding by JS about the damage his comments could cause.

Despite his refusal to engage in the process JS did reiterate his gripe arguing that these were private messages that should not have been read by his employer but in any event were borne out of a sense of frustration in the product that was likely to spoil his Christmas party plans.

I stated he had given me little new material to work with. I would reply to him in the next few days.

Commentary

Once again, this book is not a general employment law textbook, so the deficiencies of these notes are not its subject matter. It is clear, however, that the minute-taking is little short of appalling. Once again, the minutes clearly do not reflect the breadth of discussion. Further, the employer should have been on notice from the fact of the appeal letter that Mr Smith was unhappy with his treatment, thus giving rise to the risk of a claim. As such the appeal hearing was a clear opportunity to remedy defects in the earlier procedure. That Mr Smith was likely to bring a claim can also be inferred from his language in the appeal letter; he references taking advice and alludes to a breach of the implied term of trust and confidence. Alarm bells should certainly have been sounding on its receipt, which makes the failure properly to minute the appeal meeting doubly poor.

In addition, the claimant makes clear that he is asserting that the messages were private; that appears to have been treated as new information. Further details of this assertion should certainly have been minuted, and if not given, they should have been sought.

Further, the minutes, in considering harm, revert to damage that 'could have [been] cause[d]', rather than any consideration of actual harm, that being the point referenced in the disciplinary outcome letter. This illustrates a failure by the company to consider appropriately the distinction between actual and apparent harm, which clearly has a bearing when considering what is and is not a reasonable response.

Techno Co Ltd
24 Soldier Place
London
NW1 6EX

John Smith
234 Smith Street
London
SE5 2EZ

17 January 2015

Dear John,

This is to confirm the outcome of the meeting.

I fully considered all the material and the points you put forward at the meeting.

I was disappointed you chose not to answer my questions. However, I believe that there is no excuse for your conduct and so the disciplinary outcome still stands. I would ask you to reconsider your resignation as you are a good worker.

If you choose not to come back to work I wish you well in the future.

Yours sincerely

Jayne Cutter

Managing Director

14.08

PART 4: PLEADINGS

Fees and Remissions

Although this form is not part of the ET1 it **must** be returned with the claim form if you are making your claim by post. This will assist our staff in confirming that the correct fee has been paid.

What type of claim are you making?	☑ a single claim
	☐ a claim on behalf of more than one person
If more than one claimant, how many are there?	
After reading the fees and remissions guidance booklet, do you intend to make an application for remission?	☐ Yes ☑ No
If Yes, how many claimants are applying for remission?	

Does your claim relate to any of the following?

☐ Not applicable	☐ Prevent unauthorised deductions
☑ Pay	☐ Antenatal care
☐ Terms and Conditions	☐ Public duties
☐ Redundancy	☐ Failure to allow time off for trade union activities/safety rep duties

Is your claim related to an application or failure by the Secretary of State?	☐ Yes ☑ No

Is your claim related to an appeal against or a notice issued by:

☑ Not applicable	☐ Environmental Agency
☐ Her Majesty's Revenue and Customs (HMRC)	☐ Equality and Human Rights Commission
☐ Environmental Health	☐ Health and Safety Executive
☐ Working Time Regulations or an Industrial Training Board Levy Assessment	

Or another type of claim	☐
I agree to the payment of this fee	☑

Fees

In order to submit a claim to the employment tribunal a fee will need to be paid.

If you are not entitled to claim remission you will need to make payment of the fee in full before you can submit your claim.

There are two fee levels:

For a single claimant

Type A – £160.00

Type B – £250.00

For group claimants different amounts apply depending on the number of claimants in the group. As a guide the **minimum** payments for each level would be:

Type A – £320.00

Type B – £500.00

The level of fee due will depend on the type of claim you are making. Based on the information you supply, we will inform you if you have paid an incorrect fee.

Remissions

If you meet certain criteria, you may be able to apply for remission for some, or all, of the fee due.

There are two levels of remission:

Remission 1
If you are in receipt of specified benefits

Remission 2
If you and your partner's gross income is below a certain amount

Please see the fees and remissions guidance documents for full details.

Employment Tribunal

Claim form

Official Use Only			
Tribunal office			
Case number		Date received	

You must complete all questions marked with an '*'

1 Your details

1.1	Title	☑ Mr	☐ Mrs	☐ Miss	☐ Ms	

1.2* First name (or names)   John

1.3* Surname or family name   Smith

1.4 Date of birth   4 / 06 /   Are you? ☑ Male ☐ Female

1.5* Address

     Number or name   12

     Street   Smith Street

     Town/City   London

     County

     Postcode

1.6 Phone number
Where we can contact you during the day   020 7123 6788

1.7 Mobile number (if different)

1.8 How would you prefer us to contact you?
(Please tick only one box)   ☑ Email ☐ Post ☐ Fax   Whatever your preference please note that some documents cannot be sent electronically

1.9 Email address

1.10 Fax number

2 Respondent's details (that is the employer, person or organisation against whom you are making a claim)

2.1* Give the name of your employer or the person or organisation you are claiming against (If you need to you can add more respondents at 2.4)   Techno Co Ltd

2.2* Address

     Number or name   24

     Street   Soldier Place

     Town/City   London

     County

     Postcode

     Phone number

ET1 - Claim form (05.14)   © Crown copyright 2014

2.3* Do you have an Acas early conciliation certificate number?

☑ Yes ☐ No

Nearly everyone should have this number before they fill in a claim form. You can find it on your Acas certificate. For help and advice, call Acas on 0300 123 1100 or visit www.acas.org.uk

If Yes, please give the Acas early conciliation certificate number.

EC 345739845

If No, why don't you have this number?

☐ Another person I'm making the claim with has an Acas early conciliation certificate number

☐ Acas doesn't have the power to conciliate on some or all of my claim

☐ My employer has already been in touch with Acas

☐ My claim contains an application for interim relief (See guidance)

☐ My claim is against the Security Service, Secret Intelligence Service or GCHQ

2.4 If you worked at a different address from the one you have given at 2.2 please give the full address

Address

Number or name

Street

Town/City

County

Postcode | | | | | | | | |

Phone number

2.5 If there are other respondents please tick this box and put their names and addresses here. ☐

(If there is not enough room here for the names of all the additional respondents then you can add any others at Section 13.)

Respondent 2

Name

Address

Number or name

Street

Town/City

County

Postcode | | | | | | | | |

Phone number

2.6 Do you have an Acas early conciliation certificate number?

☐ Yes ☐ No

Nearly everyone should have this number before they fill in a claim form. You can find it on your Acas certificate. For help and advice, call Acas on 0300 123 1100 or visit www.acas.org.uk

If Yes, please give the Acas early conciliation certificate number.

[   ]

If No, why don't you have this number?

☐ Another person I'm making the claim with has an Acas early conciliation certificate number

☐ Acas doesn't have the power to conciliate on some or all of my claim

☐ My employer has already been in touch with Acas

☐ My claim contains an application for interim relief (See guidance)

☐ My claim is against the Security Service, Secret Intelligence Service or GCHQ

Respondent 3

2.7 Name

[   ]

Address

Number or name [   ]

Street [   ]

Town/City [   ]

County [   ]

Postcode [| | | | | | |]

Phone number [   ]

2.8 Do you have an Acas early conciliation certificate number?

☐ Yes ☐ No

Nearly everyone should have this number before they fill in a claim form. You can find it on your Acas certificate. For help and advice, call Acas on 0300 123 1100 or visit www.acas.org.uk

If Yes, please give the Acas early conciliation certificate number

[   ]

If No, why don't you have this number?

☐ Another person I'm making the claim with has an Acas early conciliation certificate number

☐ Acas doesn't have the power to conciliate on some or all of my claim

☐ My employer has already been in touch with Acas

☐ My claim contains an application for interim relief (See guidance)

☐ My claim is against the Security Service, Secret Intelligence Service or GCHQ

3   Multiple cases

3.1   Are you aware that your claim is one of a number of claims against the same employer arising from the same, or similar, circumstances?   ☐ Yes   ☑ No

If Yes, and you know the names of any other claimants, add them here. This will allow us to link your claim to other related claims.

4   Cases where the respondent was not your employer

4.1   If you were not employed by any of the respondents you have named but are making a claim for some reason connected to employment (for example, relating to a job application which you made or against a trade union, qualifying body or the like) please state the type of claim you are making here. (You will get the chance to provide details later):

Now go to Section 8

5   Employment details

If you are or were employed please give the following information, if possible.

5.1   When did your employment start? | 16 February 2000 |

Is your employment continuing?   ☐ Yes   ☑ No

If your employment has ended, when did it end? | 21 December 2014 |

If your employment has not ended, are you in a period of notice and, if so, when will that end? | |

5.2   Please say what job you do or did. | Account Administrator |

6   Earnings and benefits

6.1   How many hours on average do, or did you work
each week in the job this claim is about?   `35`   hours each week

6.2   How much are, or were you paid?

Pay before tax   £ `35,000`   ☐ Weekly   ☐ Monthly

Normal take-home pay   £   ☐ Weekly   ☐ Monthly
(incl. overtime, commission, bonuses etc.)

6.3   If your employment has ended, did you work
(or were you paid for) a period of notice?   ☐ Yes   ☐ No

If Yes, how many weeks, or months' notice did   ☐ weeks   ☐ months
you work, or were you paid for?

6.4   Were you in your employer's pension scheme?   ☐ Yes   ☐ No

6.5   If you received any other benefits, e.g. company
car, medical insurance, etc, from your employer,
please give details.

7   If your employment with the respondent has ended, what has happened since?

7.1   Have you got another job?   ☐ Yes   ☑ No

If No, please **go to section 8**

7.2   Please say when you started (or will start) work.

7.3   Please say how much you are now earning
(or will earn).   £

8 Type and details of claim

8.1* Please indicate the type of claim you are making by ticking one or more of the boxes below.

☑ I was unfairly dismissed (including constructive dismissal)

☐ I was discriminated against on the grounds of:

☐ age   ☐ race

☐ gender reassignment   ☐ disability

☐ pregnancy or maternity   ☐ marriage or civil partnership

☐ sexual orientation   ☐ sex (including equal pay)

☐ religion or belief

☐ I am claiming a redundancy payment

☐ I am owed

☐ notice pay

☐ holiday pay

☐ arrears of pay

☐ other payments

☐ I am making another type of claim which the Employment Tribunal can deal with.
(Please state the nature of the claim. Examples are provided in the Guidance.)

> I was an Account Administrator for Techno Co Ltd. Techno Co Ltd are producers of the Wonderbox Smart Phone, the worlds most desired mobile telephone.
>
> I was off work for a week on leave and my Wonderbox did not work, this was very annoying for me as i was trying to arrange to see some friends, so i posted on FaceBook that my phone was not working so my friends could meet me.
>
> When i returned to work i was told i had breached the company's confidentiality agreement. i was called to a disciplinary hearing and was told either i would be dismissed or, if i agreed never to use FaceBook again i would get a final written warning. I quit
>
> The two people who were involved in the process were women and i know they would not have told a female that she could not use facebook.
>
> I was fortunate enough to be offered an interview with another mobile phone provider. however when i asked for a reference Techno Co Ltd refused to provide me with one and called the other provider and bad-mouthed me!

8.2*   Please set out the background and details of your claim in the space below.

The details of your claim should include **the date(s) when the event(s) you are complaining about happened.** Please use the blank sheet at the end of the form if needed.

9   What do you want if your claim is successful?

9.1   Please tick the relevant box(es) to say what you
want if your claim is successful:

- ☐   If claiming unfair dismissal, to get your old job back and compensation (reinstatement)
- ☐   If claiming unfair dismissal, to get another job with the same employer or associated employer and compensation (re-engagement)
- ☑   Compensation only
- ☐   If claiming discrimination, a recommendation (see Guidance).

9.2   What compensation or remedy are you seeking?

If you are claiming financial compensation please give as much detail as you can about how much you are claiming and how you have calculated this sum. (Please note any figure stated below will be viewed as helpful information but it will not restrict what you can claim and you will be permitted to revise the sum claimed later. See the Guidance for further information about how you can calculate compensation). **If you are seeking any other remedy from the Tribunal which you have not already identified please also state this below.**

My lost salary

10 Information to regulators in protected disclosure cases

10.1 If your claim consists of, or includes, a claim that you are making a protected disclosure under the Employment Rights Act 1996 (otherwise known as a 'whistleblowing' claim), please tick the box if you want a copy of this form, or information from it, to be forwarded on your behalf to a relevant regulator (known as a 'prescribed person' under the relevant legislation) by tribunal staff. (See Guidance). ☐

11 Your representative

If someone has agreed to represent you, please fill in the following. We will in future only contact your representative and not you.

11.1	Name of representative	Sarah Davies
11.2	Name of organisation	Bloggins & Co
11.3	Address Number or name	67
	Street	Acre Street
	Town/City	London
	County	
	Postcode	
11.4	DX number (If known)	1234 ACRE
11.5	Phone number	020 7567 7643
11.6	Mobile number (if different)	
11.7	Their reference for correspondence	
11.8	Email address	
11.9	How would you prefer us to communicate with them? (Please tick only one box)	☑ Email ☐ Post ☐ Fax
11.10	Fax number	

12 Disability

12.1 Do you have a disability?   ☐ Yes   ☑ No

If Yes, it would help us if you could say what this disability is and tell us what assistance, if any, you will need as your claim progresses through the system, including for any hearings that may be held at tribunal premises.

13 **Details of additional respondents**

Section 2.4 allows you to list up to three respondents. If there are any more respondents please provide their details here

Respondent 4

Name

Address

Number or name

Street

Town/City

County

Postcode

Phone number

Do you have an Acas early conciliation certificate number?

☐ Yes   ☐ No

Nearly everyone should have this number before they fill in a claim form. You can find it on your Acas certificate. For help and advice, call Acas on 0300 123 1100 or visit www.acas.org.uk

If Yes, please give the Acas early conciliation certificate number.

If No, why don't you have this number?

☐ Another person I'm making the claim with has an Acas early conciliation certificate number

☐ Acas doesn't have the power to conciliate on some or all of my claim

☐ My employer has already been in touch with Acas

☐ My claim contains an application for interim relief (See guidance)

☐ My claim is against the Security Service, Secret Intelligence Service or GCHQ

Respondent 5

Name

Address

Number or name

Street

Town/City

County

Postcode

Phone number

Do you have an Acas early conciliation certificate number?

☐ Yes   ☐ No

Nearly everyone should have this number before they fill in a claim form. You can find it on your Acas certificate. For help and advice, call Acas on 0300 123 1100 or visit www.acas.org.uk

If Yes, please give the Acas early conciliation certificate number.

If No, why don't you have this number?

☐ Another person I'm making the claim with has an Acas early conciliation certificate number

☐ Acas doesn't have the power to conciliate on some or all of my claim

☐ My employer has already been in touch with Acas

☐ My claim contains an application for interim relief (See guidance)

☐ My claim is against the Security Service, Secret Intelligence Service or GCHQ

14 Fee

Please re-read the form and check you have entered all the relevant information. Once you are satisfied, please tick this box. ☐

For those submitting their claim by post

☑ I enclose the appropriate fee

OR

☐ I enclose an application for remission of the fee

If you fail to do so your claim form will be returned to you and you will be told it has been rejected. This means that any time limit which applies to your claim will still be running and the claim form will have to be re-submitted within that time limit.

Data Protection Act 1998.

We will send a copy of this form to the respondent and Acas. We will put the information you give us on this form onto a computer. This helps us to monitor progress and produce statistics. Information provided on this form is passed to the Department for Business, Innovation and Skills to assist research into the use and effectiveness of employment tribunals. (URN 05/874)

15 **Additional information**

You can provide additional information about your claim in this section.

If you're part of a group claim, give the Acas early conciliation certificate numbers for other people in your group. If they don't have numbers, tell us why.

HM Courts & Tribunals Service

Diversity Monitoring Questionnaire

It is important to us that everyone who has contact with HM Courts & Tribunals Service, receives equal treatment. We need to find out whether our policies are effective and to take steps to ensure the impact of future policies can be fully assessed to try to avoid any adverse impacts on any particular groups of people. That is why we are asking you to complete the following questionnaire, which will be used to provide us with the relevant statistical information. **Your answers will be treated in strict confidence.**

Thank you in advance for your co-operation.

Claim type

Please confirm the type of claim that you are bringing to the employment tribunal. This will help us in analysing the other information provided in this form.

(a) ☑ Unfair dismissal or constructive dismissal

(b) ☐ Discrimination

(c) ☐ Redundancy payment

(d) ☐ Other payments you are owed

(e) ☐ Other complaints

Sex

What is your sex?

(a) ☐ Female

(b) ☑ Male

(c) ☐ Prefer not to say

Age group

Which age group are you in?

(a) ☐ Under 25

(b) ☐ 25-34

(c) ☑ 35-44

(d) ☐ 45-54

(e) ☐ 55-64

(f) ☐ 65 and over

(g) ☐ Prefer not to say

Ethnicity

What is your ethnic group?

White

(a) ☑ English / Welsh / Scottish / Northern Irish / British

(b) ☐ Irish

(c) ☐ Gypsy or Irish Traveller

(d) ☐ Any other White background

Mixed / multiple ethnic groups

(e) ☑ White and Black Caribbean

(f) ☐ White and Black African

(g) ☐ White and Asian

(h) ☐ Any other Mixed / multiple ethnic background

Asian / Asian British

(i) ☐ Indian

(j) ☐ Pakistani

(k) ☐ Bangladeshi

(l) ☐ Chinese

(m) ☐ Any other Asian background

Black / African / Caribbean / Black British

(n) ☐ African

(o) ☐ Caribbean

(p) ☐ Any other Black / African / Caribbean background

Other ethnic group

(q) ☐ Arab

(r) ☐ Any other ethnic group

(s) ☐ Prefer not to say

Disability

The Equality Act 2010 defines a disabled person as 'Someone who has a physical or mental impairment and the impairment has a substantial and long-term adverse effect on his or her ability to carry out normal day-to-day activities'.

Conditions covered may include, for example, severe depression, dyslexia, epilepsy and arthritis.

Do you have any physical or mental health conditions or illnesses lasting or expected to last for 12 months or more?

- (a) ☐ Yes
- (b) ☑ No
- (c) ☐ Prefer not to say

Marriage and Civil Partnership

Are you?

- (a) ☑ Single, that is, never married and never registered in a same-sex civil partnership
- (b) ☐ Married
- (c) ☐ Separated, but still legally married
- (d) ☐ Divorced
- (e) ☐ Widowed
- (f) ☐ In a registered same-sex civil partnership
- (g) ☐ Separated, but still legally in a same-sex civil partnership
- (h) ☐ Formerly in a same-sex civil partnership which is now legally dissolved
- (I) ☐ Surviving partner from a same-sex civil partnership
- (J) ☐ Prefer not to say

Religion and belief

What is your religion?

- (a) ☑ No religion
- (b) ☐ Christian (including Church of England, Catholic, Protestant and all other Christian denominations)
- (c) ☐ Buddhist
- (d) ☐ Hindu
- (e) ☐ Jewish
- (f) ☐ Muslim
- (g) ☐ Sikh
- (h) ☐ Any other religion (please describe)

[   ]

- (I) ☐ Prefer not to say

Caring responsibilites

Do you have any caring responsibilities, (for example; children, elderly relatives, partners etc.)?

- (a) ☐ Yes
- (b) ☑ No
- (c) ☐ Prefer not to say

Sexual identity

Which of the options below best describes how you think of yourself?

- (a) ☑ Heterosexual/Straight
- (b) ☐ Gay /Lesbian
- (c) ☐ Bisexual
- (d) ☐ Other
- (e) ☐ Prefer not to say

Gender identity

Please describe your gender identity?

- (a) ☑ Male (including female-to-male trans men)
- (b) ☐ Female (including male-to-female trans women)
- (c) ☐ Prefer not to say

Is your gender identity different to the sex you were assumed to be at birth?

- (f) ☐ Yes
- (g) ☑ No
- (h) ☐ Prefer not to say

Pregnancy and maternity

Were you pregnant when the issue you are making a claim about took place?

- (a) ☐ Yes
- (b) ☑ No
- (c) ☐ Prefer not to say

Thank you for taking the time to complete this questionnaire.

Employment Tribunals check list and cover sheet

Please check the following:

1. Read the form to make sure the information given is correct and truthful, and that you have not left out any information which you feel may be relevant to you or your client.
2. Do not attach a covering letter to your form. If you have any further relevant information please enter it in the 'Additional Information' space provided in the form.
3. Send the completed form to the relevant office address.
4. Keep a copy of your form posted to us.

If your claim has been submitted on-line or posted in with the appropriate fee you should receive confirmation of receipt from the office dealing with your claim within five working days. If you have not heard from them within five days, please contact that office directly. If the deadline for submitting the claim is closer than five days you should check that it has been received before the time limit expires. Claims which include an application for a full or partial remission of the fee may take a little longer to deal with.

You have opted to print and post your form. We would like to remind you that forms submitted on-line are processed much faster than ones posted to us. If you want to submit on-line please go back to the form and click the submit button, otherwise follow the check list before you post the completed form to the relevant office address.

A list of our office's contact details can be found at the hearing centre page of our website at – www.justice.gov.uk/tribunals/employment/venues; if you are still unsure about which office to contact please call our Public Enquiry Line England & Wales: 0300 123 1024   Scotland: 0141 354 8574 (Mon – Fri, 8.30am – 5pm) or Textphone: 01509 221564; they can also provide general procedural information about the Employment Tribunals.

IN THE EMPLOYMENT TRIBUNALS

CASE NO:

LONDON CENTRAL

BETWEEN:

JOHN SMITH

Claimant

-and-

TECHNO CO LTD

Respondent

PARTICULARS OF COMPLAINT

1.   I was employed by the respondent as an account's administrator.

2.   I had been employed since 16 February 2000.

3.   Techno Co Ltd develops and sells the Wonderbox, a smartphone and all members of staff are given preferential prices (essentially a nominal price) if they wish to buy a Wonderbox. I bought one as soon as it came out.

4.   However, the Wonderbox was plagued with technical issues and I lost my temper when I was trying to arrange a meet up with my friends just before Christmas 2014. My phone kept crashing and did not allow me to arrange the time or the place of the meeting.

5.   As such I was angry as I haven't seen my friends for a while and so I expressed my dismay on Facebook. These posts were not defamatory or untrue, they merely expressed my frustration. My Facebook settings are such that only people who are my friends can see my posts. I haven't been on Facebook for very long, and only have about 45 friends on the site. They are all social friends of mine who know me and what I'm like. I don't refer to my work on my profile and haven't ever said on it where I work. The posts I made were made in anger but were also just banter and no-one would ever take what I said seriously. I'm known as a bit of a rogue and a joker.

6.   I was shocked, therefore, to receive a letter calling me to attend a disciplinary hearing as a result of these posts.

7.   I immediately took the posts down.

8.   Despite this, and my exemplary disciplinary record with Techno Co I was told that if I agreed to stop using Facebook I would receive a Final Written Warning, but if I continued to use Facebook I would be dismissed. I appealed this, but my appeal was dismissed.

9.   I could not understand what I did wrong, so I quit. I had no alternative but to resign. I told them this at the appeal meeting.

10.   The Company's conduct was wholly unjustified and unreasonable, and has destroyed the relationship of trust and confidence between Techno Co and me.

11.   I was constructively dismissed and that the dismissal was, in all the circumstances, unfair.

Employment Tribunal

Response form

Case number [   ]

You must complete all questions marked with an "*"

1 Claimant's name

1.1 Claimant's name   John SMith

2 Respondent's details

2.1* Name of individual, company or organisation   Techno Co Ltd

2.2 Name of contact   Kevin Morrow

2.3* Address

Number or name 24

Street Soldier Place

Town/City

County

Postcode [| | | | | |]

DX number (If known)

2.4 Phone number
Where we can contact you during the day

Mobile number (If different)

2.5 How would you prefer us to contact you?
(Please tick only one box)   ☑ Email   ☐ Post   ☐ Fax   Whatever your preference please note that some documents cannot be sent electronically

2.6 Email address

Fax number

2.7 How many people does this organisation employ in Great Britain?   2000

2.8 Does this organisation have more than one site in Great Britain?   ☑ Yes   ☐ No

2.9 If Yes, how many people are employed at the place where the claimant worked?   100

3   **Acas Early Conciliation details**

3.1   Do you agree with the details given by the claimant about early conciliation with Acas?   ☑ Yes   ☐ No

If No, please explain why, for example, has the claimant given the correct Acas early conciliation certificate number or do you disagree that the claimant is exempt from early conciliation, if so why?

4   **Employment details**

4.1   Are the dates of employment given by the claimant correct?   ☑ Yes   ☐ No

If Yes, please **go to question 4.2**

If No, please give the dates and say why you disagree with the dates given by the claimant

When their employment started

When their employment ended or will end

I disagree with the dates for the following reasons

4.2   Is their employment continuing?   ☐ Yes   ☑ No

4.3   Is the claimant's description of their job or job title correct?   ☑ Yes   ☐ No

If Yes, please **go to Section 5**

If No, please give the details you believe to be correct

5 Earnings and benefits

5.1 Are the claimant's hours of work correct? ☑ Yes ☐ No

If No, please enter the details you
believe to be correct.

[   ] hours each week

5.2 Are the earnings details given by the
claimant correct? ☐ Yes ☑ No

If Yes, please **go to question 5.3**

If No, please give the details you believe to
be correct below

Pay before tax
(incl. overtime, commission, bonuses etc.) £ 18000 ☐ Weekly ☐ Monthly

Normal take-home pay
(incl. overtime, commission, bonuses etc.) £ 14723 ☐ Weekly ☐ Monthly

5.3 Is the information given by the claimant
correct about being paid for, or working a
period of notice? ☑ Yes ☐ No

If Yes, please **go to question 5.4**

If No, please give the details you believe to
be correct below. If you gave them no
notice or didn't pay them instead of letting
them work their notice, please explain what
happened and why.

5.4 Are the details about pension and other
benefits e.g. company car, medical
insurance, etc. given by the claimant correct? ☑ Yes ☐ No

If Yes, please **go to Section 6**

If No, please give the details you believe to
be correct.

6 **Response**

6.1* Do you defend the claim?   ☑ Yes   ☐ No

If No, please **go to Section 7**

If Yes, please set out the facts which you rely on to defend the claim.
(See Guidance - If needed, please use the blank sheet at the end of this form.)

Please see attached

7 Employer's Contract Claim

7.1 Only available in limited circumstances where the claimant has made a contract claim. (See Guidance)

7.2 If you wish to make an Employer's Contract Claim in response to the claimant's claim, please tick this box and complete question 7.3 ☐

7.3 Please set out the background and details of your claim below, which should include all important dates
(see Guidance for more information on what details should be included)

8 Your representative

If someone has agreed to represent you, please fill in the following. We will in future only contact your representative and not you.

8.1 Name of representative

> Boris Wolton

8.2 Name of organisation

> Text

8.3 Address

Number or name | 34
Street | Beaminster Rd
Town/City | London
County |
Postcode | | | | | | | | | |

8.4 DX number (If known)

8.5 Phone number

8.6 Mobile phone

8.7 Their reference for correspondence

8.8 How would you prefer us to communicate with them? (Please tick only one box) ☐ Email ☑ Post ☐ Fax

8.9 Email address

8.10 Fax number

9 Disability

9.1 Do you have a disability? ☐ Yes ☑ No

If Yes, it would help us if you could say what this disability is and tell us what assistance, if any, you will need as the claim progresses through the system, including for any hearings that maybe held at tribunal premises.

Please re-read the form and check you have entered all the relevant information. Once you are satisfied, please tick this box. ☑

Data Protection Act 1998.

We will send a copy of this form to the claimant and Acas. We will put the information you give us on this form onto a computer. This helps us to monitor progress and produce statistics. Information provided on this form is passed to the Department for Business, Innovation and Skills to assist research into the use and effectiveness of employment tribunals. (URN 05/874)

Employment Tribunals check list and cover sheet

Please check the following:

1. Read the form to make sure the information given is correct and truthful, and that you have not left out any information which you feel may be relevant to you or your client.
2. Do not attach a covering letter to your form. If you have any further relevant information please enter it in the 'Additional Information' space provided in the form.
3. Send the completed form to the relevant office address.
4. Keep a copy of your form posted to us.

Once your response has been received, you should receive confirmation from the office dealing with the claim within five working days. If you have not heard from them within five days, please contact that office directly. If the deadline for submitting the response is closer than five days you should check that it has been received before the time limit expires.

You have opted to print and post your form. We would like to remind you that forms submitted on-line are processed much faster than ones posted to us. If you want to submit on-line please go back to the form and click the submit button, otherwise follow the check list before you post the completed form to the relevant office address.

A list of our office's contact details can be found at the hearing centre page of our website at – www.justice.gov.uk/tribunals/employment/venues; if you are still unsure about which office to contact please call our Public Enquiry Line England & Wales: 0300 123 1024   Scotland: 0141 354 8574 (Mon – Fri, 8.30am – 5pm) or Textphone: 01509 221564; they can also provide general procedural information about the Employment Tribunals.

Continuation sheet

IN THE EMPLOYMENT TRIBUNAL

CASE NO:

LONDON CENTRAL

BETWEEN

JOHN SMITH

-and-

TECHNO CO LTD

GROUNDS OF RESISTANCE

The Parties

1. It is admitted that at all material times the claimant was employed by the respondent as an Accounts Administrator from 16 February 2000 until their resignation, with effect from 21 December 2014.

2. At all material times the respondent is the producer of the Wonderbox Smartphone.

Background

3. Owing to the nature of its business and the highly competitive business in which it operates the respondent is very concerned about the maintenance of confidentiality and image of its products.

4. On 14 December 2014 the claimant posted highly critical comments on Facebook concerning the claimant's Wonderbox phone. Such comments were likely to damage the respondent's reputation with its exclusive UK retailer M0bilePh0nes.co.uk

Alleged constructive dismissal

5. The claimant was not dismissed after a disciplinary process had been conducted into his Facebook posts. He was given reasonable options. He did not select an option but instead resigned.

6. In the circumstances, it is averred that the respondent had acted reasonably in all the circumstances.

7. If, which is denied the respondent did constructively dismiss the claimant then, it is contended, the respondent would have fairly dismissed the claimant in the circumstances of this matter. Accordingly any constructive dismissal was a fair dismissal.

Alleged losses

8. The claimant is put to strict proof of all his alleged losses. Further and in any event, it is not admitted that the claimant has taken reasonable steps to mitigate his losses.

Conclusion

9. Save where specifically denied, not admitted or admitted, each and every allegation made against the respondent is denied as though the same were individually set out herein and traversed. In the circumstances and for the reasons set out above, the claimant is not entitled to the relief claimed against the respondent or to any other relief, and it is denied that the respondent is in any way liable to the claimant.

Commentary

These are not intended to be model pleadings. They are far from it. Rather, they illustrate the fact that, particularly with smaller companies, pleadings may not be as detailed and thought-through as they could be. However the ET3 and Grounds of Resistance in particular are a huge opportunity for advantage to be seized by the employer. The following general points are proffered:

- The principle role of the respondent, its HR department or its legal team, is to respond to the claim as presented. This often can lead to a judgment call as to whether the claim contains a particular complaint or not, or a particular factual allegation or not. If in doubt, plead to it. Control the narrative and guide the case in the direction that the respondent wishes it to go. In this scenario, dealing with the issues relating to reputational damage in some detail, the nature of the posts, the risks identified and the reason that they were taken as seriously as they were is of crucial importance.
- It is rarely helpful simply to issue a blanket denial of allegations; explain why they are denied: is it because the act complained of never happened, is it denied because the act complained of is not unreasonable (so here, explain the reasoning of the disciplinary and appeal conductors), or is it denied because the particular response was appropriate, fair and justified (and again, make clear the rationale with reference to policies and harm)? Spell this out: ensure that allegations are properly grappled with, and drive the narrative: explain why a particular course of action was adopted and justified.
- Deal with people, not titles: failing to do so may render grounds of resistance confusing and of little use, as well as irritating the tribunal. Names are constant; use them. ➥

- Do not be afraid to accept assertions: it is not beneficial to leave the tribunal guessing if the claimant was an employee – it is far more helpful to set out the boundaries of the dispute early and make clear to the tribunal the crux of the case in the first paragraph. It is hugely helpful to a tribunal for the response to set out in one or two lines at the very outset of the grounds of resistance what, in a nutshell, are the main points to be considered, which again helps to drive the narrative. Thus, in this scenario, the response might open with 'the respondent denies that the claimant was constructively unfairly dismissed as alleged or at all. The claimant resigned in response to a lawful and appropriate determination by the respondent in the circumstances that his use of Facebook was inappropriate. The respondent presented the claimant with legitimate and reasonable options to enable him to continue his employment but the claimant refused properly or at all to consider the same and instead resigned. In the circumstances the claimant's claim is without merit.' After reading this one line the employment judge will know the basis of the argument and what is not necessary to consider.

- In an ideal world the particulars of complaint would be clear, logical and concise. Often they will not be, as in this scenario. However this should not be taken to mean an arms race has commenced whereby the response has to be longer than the claim. Again, control the narrative rather than focusing on following the potentially nebulous structure put forward by the claimant.

- Focus when considering the drafting of the response not just upon the initial task at hand but also consider other tactical steps in the process: in pleadings settled by the authors we will often set out any applications we intend to make at the outset of the pleading in one of the first three or four paragraphs. This gives the employment judge who is tasked with considering the papers an early indication of what is wanted and why. If sensible and logical an application for the claim to be rejected on the initial consideration would (hopefully) strike a chord with the employment judge who has just read the particulars of complaint. In appropriate cases it will be also helpful to suggest a time-estimate for a preliminary hearing to consider such matters. In a case such as this, the need for further and better particulars appears fairly stark, and the nature of those further and better particulars can be controlled to a significant extent by the nature of the details in the response.

- Alternatively, whilst the employment judge may not sift the claim at such an early stage, by flagging relevant issues they may well accede to an application for a preliminary hearing to consider case management of the claim.

Similarly, some general points can be made in respect of particulars of complaint: ➙

- Too often, after reading an extremely lengthy particulars of complaint that does not identify much in the way of actionable wrong, a general line is added at the very end that says: 'For the reasons given above the claimant was [insert complaint here]' this does not assist, especially in claims that are quite technical: eg constructive dismissal and whistleblowing. In this case, very limited details are given, though the facts are set out. However a good particulars of complaint will set out the various stages required to establish a complaint of constructive unfair dismissal; where, as here, this is not done, the respondent has a superb opportunity to set out in detail why the grounds for a constructive unfair dismissal claim is not made out. Where the narrative is lost, control passes. This is a real shame and a real opportunity to take the initiative has been lost by the claimant as a claim that is unable to be clearly set out in the key document is, more often than not, likely to be unclear when it is presented at final hearing or preliminary hearing.

- Employment lawyers are exceedingly fortunate that most of the causes of action that arise are set out in statute in terms. As such, there is a clear and eminently pleadable structure inherent in many causes of action and, very often, by reading that structure in reverse, it is straightforward for practitioners to derive the methodology for any pleading. For example, a claim of unfair dismissal of an employee would require a pleading that shows:
  (1) the claimant was an employee;
  (2) the claimant was dismissed;
  (3) that dismissal was unfair;
  (4) the particular aspects of unfairness.

- Bearing in mind the likely 'initial consideration' by the tribunal (pursuant to rules 26 and 27) a pleading may begin with what effectively amounts to a tick-box formulation for the employment judge conducting the initial consideration: in an unfair dismissal case this may simply be: 'I was an employee of the respondent until I was dismissed for no potentially fair reason.' This simple formulation is the equivalent of the 'setting the scene' paragraph in the context of responses, above;

- Again, it is important to use facts rather than emotions/feelings. The tribunal will be looking to see what it can find on the facts of the matter, and assertions of emotions will, more often than not, simply result in an application for further and better particulars and the loss of narrative control.

These suggested guidelines have been largely ignored by the parties in this scenario. The particulars of complaint lack detail and fail to set out the case; but the respondent fails entirely to take advantage and control the narrative. It might be expected that the various issues raised by the documentation would be explored in the response; the thought-process (going to the reasonableness of the sanction) should be clearly set out; and →

in general a far clearer and more detailed response to the allegation should have been entered. Instead the option to seize the initiate is squandered, and the tribunal is presented with unhelpful pleadings from both parties. As such, the evidence given to the tribunal (and the inevitable hostage to fortune that that presents) will be the sole determinative factor.

14.09

PART 5: WITNESS EVIDENCE

IN THE EMPLOYMENT TRIBUNAL

CASE NO:

LONDON CENTRAL

BETWEEN:

JOHN SMITH

Claimant

-and-

TECHNO CO LTD

Respondent

WITNESS STATEMENT OF

THE CLAIMANT

1. I am the claimant in this matter. I have always loved IT and wanted to start my career working for a company with a unique and recognisable brand image in this field.

2. I was employed by the respondent in 2000. When I joined the company was not half as successful as it is now. I started as a 'Customer Experience Maker'. I worked on the shop floor of its one London Shop.

3. I remember that when I joined there was some training. It took the form of a half day talk by the senior Experience Maker in the shop. I don't really recall what it was about. Some policies were mentioned but we never got a copy.

4. Over time I was able to develop my expertise and this was recognised when the respondent asked me to become an account manager responsible for, effectively, the wholesale side of the business in London. I dealt with the sale of the respondent's products to businesses which may provide the phones and computers to their staff, as well as other shops who may sell them to the public.

5. I have never had any disciplinary findings against me.

6. This is a very responsible position that requires a deep knowledge of the products, of IT and the ability to relate to people.

7.   As like many people I maintain a Facebook page, and Twitter account. I am however, very selective in who I let have access to my Facebook page and who I accept as a follower. I am a fairly late adopter to social media, as I have never really seen its point. At the time I made the posts in question, I had 32 friends. None of them are colleagues, and I have always been careful not to mention my employer. I have looked back over my previous posts and have never given any clue that I work for the respondent.

8.   Every year since leaving school my closest friends and I have met up for a Christmas party. Over time some of them have moved away from the area or have stopped attending owing to family commitments.

9.   Last year there were three of us who were planning on meeting up. They both live out of London so were travelling into town especially for the event. I had arranged to be off work on the 13th until 16 December in order that I could do my Christmas shopping and enjoy meeting my friends.

10. Just before Christmas though my phone was playing up. I have the respondent's Wonderbox mobile phone, the sales of which have propelled the respondent into the upper tier of IT companies. It got so bad that not only could I not call people or regularly use the internet that when I was able to do so it kept telling me I was in Japan, that it had deleted my contacts and that I did not have any email accounts set up on it. Needless to say I was not happy with that!

11. I had raised the issues with the respondent's customer helpline. They just told me to turn the phone off and turn it back on again. This didn't resolve the issue.

12. I decided that rather than miss meeting my two friends at Christmas I decided I would use my Facebook page to communicate with them. These were only my fifth, sixth and seventh posts I posted on 14 December the items you can see in the bundle. I was really frustrated by my phone's technical problems.

13. After I returned home in the early hours of 15 December I posted the final post. I had been drinking.

14. It was a total shock therefore when I received the letter from Ms Marshall dated 16 December 2014. It was emailed to me and was in my inbox when I turned on my computer around noon on the 16th.

15. My Facebook settings were, I thought, private. I was confused therefore about the accusation that the reputation of the respondent had been damaged as I didn't think any other people could read my posts. Literally as soon as I read the letter I took the posts down off Facebook as I knew my employer was unhappy.

16. I attended the meeting on 21 December 2014. Ms Marshall handed me a copy of the disciplinary policy. The meeting was just me and Ms Marshall. Although it lasted about half an hour I asked for a break as I did not understand what the allegation she focused on was, that I had breached

confidence. The break lasted about 10 minutes as I was so worried. It was clear nothing I said was making any difference to her and that she had made her mind up.

17. She never explained the breach of confidence allegation to me at any point.

18. It was no surprise to me that I was threatened with dismissal on 22 December. I knew they were out to get me. I was shocked to see that it was said that there was damage to the reputation of the respondent. This was never raised in the meeting at all. The only way I could keep my job seemed to be that I could never use Facebook again. Whilst as I have said I don't particularly enjoy social media, the fact that the respondent was trying to control what I did in my personal time made it a point of principle as this was so unfair.

19. I immediately appealed, however the letter was not acknowledged until after the New Year when I received the letter from Ms Cutter, the MD of the respondent.

20. I attended the meeting with Ms Cutter. I did not think I needed to say anything as my appeal was clear and, besides, I was very upset at the ultimatum so I decided to resign.

21. I received the letter of 17 January 2015 dismissing my appeal.

IN THE EMPLOYMENT TRIBUNAL

CASE NO:

LONDON CENTRAL

BETWEEN:

JOHN SMITH

Claimant

-and-

TECHNO CO LIMITED

Respondent

WITNESS STATEMENT OF

BRENDA MARSHALL

1. I am the respondent's Accounts Manager. I have occupied this role for a number of years.

2. I have received training in the Company's disciplinary policies and on how to conduct disciplinary hearings. Over the last few years I estimate I have conducted about a dozen disciplinary hearings.

3. I have known John for five or so years since he became an accounts executive for the respondent. I know him because he is one of the executives who reports to me. I have overall responsibility for the South of England. John oversees our accounts in London.

4. Techno Co Ltd produces the world's leading smartphone: the Wonderbox. It is a unique piece of equipment and we are extremely proactive in protecting our patents and interests in this item. We view it as an item that enriches the lives of people who use it.

5. We also view our brand as a key component to maintain our position in the competitive world of telecommunications and IT. We are seen as a luxury item which is easily affordable by many people, accordingly we have mass appeal and yet retain an air of exclusivity.

6. Needless to say our items are in great demand.

7. Being at the forefront of this developing marketplace we are keen to ensure that we embrace all types of media. We have a dedicated team of staff who focus on online branding and marketing. This includes social media and viral marketing.

8. Our staff are well aware of the importance we place on brand retention.

9. I was stunned therefore to be told on 16 December that John had posted on Facebook comments that were highly critical of the product and our customers and creators. I immediately spoke to HR and afterwards wrote to John calling him to a disciplinary hearing. I sent this to him by email.

10. When he arrived at the meeting he pretended not to understand the allegations against him. However they were perfectly clear.

11. I did consider everything that John had said to me during the hearing however, it was perfectly clear to me there was no mitigation that could possibly have reduced the severity of what he had done. I decided therefore that the claimant should be given a choice: either be dismissed or have a final written warning placed on their record with the condition that he does not use Facebook again.

12. Our exclusive retailer M0bilePh0nes.co.uk would have been mortified to have read the comments by one of our senior employees. I would estimate that the Wonderbox accounts for about 45–50 per cent of their retail business. Any lack of public confidence in the phone caused by the comments could result in a massive loss of income for them, and therefore us, if customers were to turn their back on our product and instead go to one of our competitors.

IN THE EMPLOYMENT TRIBUNAL

CASE NO:

LONDON CENTRAL

BETWEEN:

JOHN SMITH

Claimant

-and-

TECHNO CO Ltd

Respondent

WITNESS STATEMENT OF

JAYNE CUTTER

1. I am the respondent's Managing Director.
2. I have been the MD for the respondent for a number of years as a result of being one of the first employees when the holding company decided it wanted to open operations here in the UK.
3. The respondent is a wholly owned subsidiary of the US company Techno Corp.
4. I have known John for a long time. He was one of the company's success stories and was a rising star having worked his way up from the shop floor and into a senior position. His enthusiasm for the products we sell and the lifestyle image they carry was infectious.
5. He knows full well that the company is very protective of its image and takes a robust approach to anyone who tries to imitate or damage the product or its image.
6. It was therefore stunning that he did something as stupid as post critical comments about the Wonderbox on Facebook.
7. I was asked to hear the appeal in this matter. I had no hesitation in deciding I was the appropriate person to do this as I wanted to give him a full opportunity to justify his acts. It was a real disappointment therefore when he refused to answer any of the questions I asked him during the meeting. It was exceedingly frustrating for me to sit there asking him questions to hear him answer 'no comment' to them.
8. In the circumstances I had no option but to entirely endorse the decision of Brenda for such a reckless act which put the company's reputation and image at stake.

Commentary

As is often the case, the final opportunity for the respondent to set out in detail its case, to anticipate the arguments that are likely to be raised, and to present its factual assertions in order to counteract those arguments, has not been taken in the statements above. Together with the pleadings, it is likely that these are the primary documents that will be read by the tribunal at an early stage, and thus afford an important opportunity for the parties to present their spin on the facts. In this scenario, the factual matrix is in large part not contentious, and as such there is no real need to spell out differing interpretations of events. However it is plain from the particulars of complaint the basis upon which the claimant seeks to bring his case; the witness statements of the respondent are an important chance for it to make its case in response.

In particular, there is no explanation in either of the witness statements submitted on behalf of the respondent of the harm caused. Whilst there is a reference in the last paragraph of the witness statement of Ms Marshall to the risk to the respondent had the largest supplier learned of the posts, there is no evidence that it did in fact do so. There is no consideration or detail of the discussions had at the disciplinary meeting, and there is certainly no illumination as to the reasons behind the ultimatum given to the claimant or the reasoning behind such a proposed sanction. Where a company wishes to take any step that relates to individual and personal use of a social media platform, its reasons for seeking to do so will need to be explored in detail, ideally by reference also to the appropriate policy, in order to demonstrate that the response was reasonable. Failing to do so will doubtless give rise to detailed cross-examination and questions from the tribunal.

Employers seeking to defend a claim of this sort should consider including passages on the following matters in their witness evidence:

- the policies that they have in place, the reasons for those policies and how the conduct complained of is said to have been in breach;
- details of the investigation, the risks identified by the offending posts, and an explanation of why personal posts fall within the scope of the policy;
- the considerations applied when coming to the sanction decision: harm, actual or potential; the nature of the comments; the risks of the comments becoming more wide-spread; and the audience for those comments. Identifying details connecting the employee with the employer may also be important;
- the rationale behind the sanction: what is the purpose of an action short of dismissal, particularly when this has a bearing on an employee's right to a private life and freedom of expression; how is the sanction addressed to the harm sought to be prevented or mitigated; why was it reasonable to impose it? ➜

As tribunals are called upon to tackle more and more cases involving social media, the above considerations are likely to form a significant part of the judicial consideration of fairness in the circumstances and, if a cogent and reasoned explanation is contained within the respondent's witness evidence, the tribunal is more likely to be well-disposed to upholding a dismissal as reasonable.

14.10

PART 6: JUDGMENT

IN THE EMPLOYMENT TRIBUNALS

CASE NO:

LONDON CENTRAL

BETWEEN:

JOHN SMITH

Claimant

-and-

TECHNO CO LIMITED

Respondent

Judgment

It is the judgment of the tribunal that the claimant's claim that he was constructively dismissed is well-founded and accordingly succeeds.

Reasons

Introduction

1.   These are the reasons of the tribunal after hearing evidence from the parties over one day.

Background

The claimant's case as formulated in his ET1

2.   The claimant's complaint, as formulated in his Form ET1, runs to some 11 paragraphs. His claim is that he was constructively dismissed owing to the conduct of the respondent.

The respondent's response

3.   In its Form ET3, the respondent denied that the claimant was constructively dismissed. They allege the claimant simply resigned.

4.   As is becoming increasingly frequent in matters heard by the tribunal, the factual matrix in this case involves the use of social media by the claimant in a manner which the respondent contends was inappropriate and entitled it to commence disciplinary proceedings. The tribunal is aware that there is a growing body of case-law in this area, as will be considered in more detail below.

The hearing

5.   The matter came before the tribunal today for a final hearing of this claim. As is increasingly common in this jurisdiction both parties were unrepresented, though it is clear that both parties had some awareness of the legal issues pertinent to this type of case.

The claims and issues

6.   At the outset of the hearing the tribunal identified with the claimant the claims he had presented. The claimant confirmed that his claim was one of constructive dismissal arising out of the manner in which he was dealt with by the respondent when it conducted a disciplinary process in relation to his use of Facebook.

7.   The tribunal as a precursor to hearing the oral evidence of the parties took the opportunity to discuss with the parties the issues to be determined at the commencement of the hearing. The respondent confirmed that it admitted that the claimant was an employee and that, at the time his employment ended, he had sufficient continuous employment to present a claim of unfair dismissal. The respondent also accepted that the claimant had satisfied the conditions of ACAS early conciliation and that he had presented his claim within the relevant time period. The respondent does not allege that the claimant delayed in resigning, so waiver is not an issue for the tribunal to determine. Finally, the respondent does not allege that the claimant had any other reason for resigning: accordingly causation is not in issue here. The respondent does allege that it would have had a fair reason to dismiss the claimant in the circumstances of this case: namely his conduct.

8.   The parties agreed that this left the issues for the tribunal to determine as being:

    a.   Whether the claimant was constructively dismissed in accordance with the provisions of section 95(1)(c) of the Employment Rights Act 1996; namely was there conduct by the respondent that amounted to a fundamental breach of contract.

    b.   The claimant relies principally on the requirement by the respondent that he refrain from using Facebook, including outside of working hours and from his own personal equipment, if he wanted to remain in its employment.

    c.   The claimant alleges that this condition of his continued employment amounts to breaches of the implied duty of trust and confidence

d. The respondent denies these occurred as alleged by the claimant, and if they did the respondent denies these amount to a clear breach of the implied duty of trust and confidence.

Is the breach sufficiently serious to allow the employee to resign?

e. Has the claimant showed that objectively considered the actions of the respondent amounted to repudiatory breaches of contract?

Quality of the act

f. Did the employer have reasonable and proper cause for that conduct?

Would any actual dismissal have been fair?

g. If it is found that the claimant's resignation did fall within the provisions of section 95(1)(c) ERA, entitling him to resign, and that his resignation amounted to a dismissal, whether any constructive dismissal was also an unfair dismissal having regard to the provisions of section 98 of the Employment Rights Act 1996, namely the consideration that the claimant was being put through a disciplinary procedure because of his conduct.

Documents and evidence

General

9. At the outset of the hearing today it was agreed that evidence would initially be limited to issues of liability. Further evidence on remedy including in respect of *Polkey*, contributory conduct and consideration of any financial penalties pursuant to section 12 of the Employment Tribunals Act 1996 was to be called, if necessary, after judgment on liability.

Witness evidence

10. The tribunal heard evidence from the claimant himself.

11. The tribunal also heard evidence from the following witnesses called on behalf of the respondent. Again, each of them gave evidence by means of a written witness statement: Brenda Marshall, who heard the disciplinary hearing, and Jayne Cutter, who chaired the appeal meeting.

12. All three witness statements were read by the tribunal in advance of the hearing.

Bundle

13. To assist in determining the issues identified above there was before the tribunal a small agreed bundle of documents. The tribunal's attention was taken to a number of these documents as part of receiving evidence and, as

discussed with the parties, the tribunal has not considered any document to which its attention was not drawn.

The material facts

14. From the evidence and submissions the tribunal made the following findings of fact. In this decision the tribunal does not address every episode covered by that evidence, even where it is disputed. Rather, it has set out the findings that it considers to be necessary in order fairly to determine the claims and the issues before the tribunal today.

15. Somewhat unusually, in this case many of the key facts were agreed between the parties. The real issue for the tribunal rather than untangling factual disputes is as a result the application of the law to those facts and as a result the conclusions it draws from those facts.

16. The respondent is a technology company, world famous for its WonderBox smart phone. Whilst the tribunal did not hear evidence as to the functions and features of the WonderBox, it is entitled to take, and does take, judicial notice of the fact that this device is well-known and apparently popular. The claimant does not dispute in any event that the WonderBox is a popular device.

17. The claimant was an employee of the respondent and, at the time his employment ended, was employed as an Account Administrator. This, it was agreed by the parties, was a senior executive position, with the claimant responsible in a sales capacity for the London-based accounts of his employer.

18. The claimant owned a WonderBox, which he was given by the respondent as part of his role for a nominal sum. He told the tribunal in evidence that he used the WonderBox as his primary communications device and does not have another smartphone. He also confirmed, in response to questions from the tribunal, that he has used the WonderBox throughout his employment with the respondent. He also possesses a desktop PC at home, though he was not able to recall the brand, and a laptop computer. Both of these were purchased by him and he uses them from time to time for personal and work purposes.

19. The claimant had a social media presence, though, perhaps surprisingly for his generation, was not a particularly heavy or sophisticated user of any social media site. He had an account on Twitter and a Facebook page. It is the latter of these two sites that the tribunal is concerned with. Facebook is a social media website that enables messages and other media to be placed online ('posted') and for others to view and comment on those posts. There are various levels of protection afforded to the posts placed on Facebook. These levels of protection are referred to as 'privacy settings'. A user has the ability to restrict their posts to those who are their Facebook 'friends' (that is, other users with whom the Facebook user has agreed to connect with) or to arrange their profile settings so that the posts can be seen by the world at large if the page is public.

20. Users of Facebook will often include within their profile various biographical details. The profile can contain photographs and other images, contact information, biographical details and details of employment, amongst other things. The profile will also include a 'feed', comprising status updates and other posts made by the user and by his connections (known as a 'wall', and akin to a sophisticated bulletin board). The user name and any profile photograph can be seen by all, but the various privacy settings referred to above allow the other biographical details to be disclosed only to particular connections.

21. Facebook also has a private messaging function, akin to an email, which only the recipient can view.

22. Connections can select a button to indicate approval for posts, known as 'liking'.

23. The evidence of the claimant was that he was not a heavy social media user. At the time he made the posts in question, he tells us that he had no more than 32 'friends' on Facebook, none of whom were connected with his work. Whilst we have not seen a precisely contemporaneous copy of the claimant's Facebook page, we have seen one printed shortly after his resignation, which appears to corroborate this. Again, the claimant stated in his evidence that there are no identifying characteristics relating to either him or more particularly to his employment, and that he has never before the incident in question referred to his employment or the fact that he had a WonderBox. The tribunal has not seen definitive evidence in this regard, but the same was not challenged by the respondent.

24. The claimant, he told us, would often use his WonderBox to arrange social gatherings and in particular annual Christmas meetings with friends of his. It was in mid-December 2014 that the claimant was seeking to arrange that years' Christmas meeting and, according to him (again without challenge from the respondent) his WonderBox was not working correctly. He told the tribunal that he was frustrated by this, and so turned to Facebook to contact his friends to make the arrangements to meet. He posted three posts within a short period of time between the afternoon of 14 December and the early hours of 15 December 2014. It is unnecessary to set these posts out in this judgment as all parties agree they were made and are set out in the bundle. The claimant told the tribunal that he made these posts from his personal equipment, at home, though he could not recollect whether he used his PC or his laptop.

25. The tribunal finds that the relevant posts were critical of the WonderBox and, in the view of the claimant, its failings. The language used is intemperate and inappropriately derogatory, particularly as the claimant now accepts that the difficulties he was experiencing related to a software update at or around that time, rather than any inherent fault with the WonderBox himself. He stated when questioned in this regard that he was aware that this upgrade was taking place, but that it had slipped his mind. The tribunal finds this an implausible excuse, given the level of seniority of the claimant. The tribunal notes with surprise however that this was not

put to the claimant either at the disciplinary or appeal stages by the respondent, and that no reference is made to it in the witness evidence of the respondent.

26. When questioned as to the tone of the first and third posts, both of which, it was put, showed violent intent, the claimant insisted that he was merely engaging in 'banter' with his friends, and that anyone who knew him and read the messages would have known that he was not serious. He described himself as a 'bit of a Tech-Geek', and that his reference to the designers of the WonderBox using this derogatory terminology was an in-joke.

27. When questioned over the various seriously disparaging comments that he made as to the fundamental quality of the WonderBox, he again stated that he did not mean them, and that his friends would have known that he was simply frustrated. He went further, stating that he was often teased by his friends for singing the praises of his WonderBox and his loyalty to the brand. The tribunal however has no objective evidence in this regard.

28. The claimant accepted that the comments were potentially damaging, and that this was particularly the case if it were to be known that a senior executive of the company manufacturing the WonderBox had made such comments. He pointed to three things in this regard: that the number of people who could have seen the post was extremely low, that no-one other than the two friends with whom he was making arrangements had made any comment on his posts (and even then had refrained from commenting in any way in respect of the parts of the posts relating to the WonderBox) and that he had deleted the posts as soon as the respondent had written to him.

29. The claimant in any event says that his posts are private, and that as a result they should not be held against him. The tribunal accepts that the posts are private to a degree: it may well have been that this was what the claimant thought, and it is common ground that he had activated privacy settings. However, the nature of the internet and in particular social media is that nothing is ever really transient or private, as even when access to messages is restricted to a small group, posts can be commented upon, reposted or printed. The messages sent were not of the nature of private emails, but rather were posted to the social media website. Indeed, despite not being a 'friend' of the claimant on Facebook the respondent became aware of his posts and so wrote to him on 16 December 2014 inviting him to a disciplinary meeting.

30. The respondent does not, surprisingly, have a social media policy in place at all. The tribunal considers this to be somewhat strange given the nature of its business and the evidence of its witnesses that much of its marketing is carried out over social media. It has employees whose job description is principally to build the reputation of the WonderBox over social media. Instead the respondent relied on its IT policy and disciplinary policy and, in particular, the clause that treats as gross misconduct actions which bring the company into serious disrepute. A copy of the policies was not

provided to the claimant with the letter that called him to the disciplinary meeting but was provided on the morning of the meeting itself.

31. As noted above, as soon as the claimant received the letter calling him to the disciplinary hearing he immediately took the posts off his Facebook page.

32. The disciplinary hearing took place on 21 December and lasted for about 30 minutes. Despite the letter calling the claimant to a meeting to discuss the allegation of bringing the respondent into disrepute, the meeting progressed by way of an allegation that the claimant had breached confidentiality. The claimant was surprised by this change of approach by Ms Marshall and sought time to consider his response. Therefore there was a 10-minute break during the meeting to allow him to do so. This break is included within the 30-minute duration of the meeting. At the outset of the meeting Ms Marshall asked the claimant whether there was any mitigation he wished to put before her.

33. The next day the claimant received a letter from Ms Marshall concerning the meeting on 21 December. This letter addresses the allegation that the claimant had damaged the reputation of the respondent. Ms Marshall found this accusation proven and therefore offered the claimant a choice: if he were to agree not to use Facebook again he would receive a final written warning; however, if he did not do so he would be dismissed.

34. The claimant appealed this outcome, and his appeal was heard by Jayne Cutter, the respondent's Managing Director. During this appeal hearing it is accepted that the claimant told Ms Cutter that he quit. This is not recorded in the minutes of the meeting but is referred to in Ms Cutter's appeal outcome letter. This letter ultimately upholds the respondent's disciplinary sanction.

The law

35. The right to claim constructive unfair dismissal is contained within section 95(1)(c) of the Employment Rights Act 1996. The Court of Appeal in *Western Excavating v Sharpe* [1978] ICR 221 elucidated the test a tribunal should apply in cases of constructive dismissal:

> if the employer is guilty of conduct that is a significant breach going to the root of the contract of employment, or which shows that the employer no longer intends to be bound by one or more of the essential terms of the contract, then the employee is entitled to treat himself as discharged from any further performance. If he does so, then he terminates the contract of employment by reason of the employer's conduct. He is constructively dismissed.

Contract of employment

36. The EAT in *Courtaulds Northern Textiles Ltd v Andrew* [1979] IRLR 84 held that there was an implied term in every contract of employment that

an employer will not, without reasonable or proper cause, conduct themselves in a manner calculated or likely to destroy or seriously damage the relationship of trust and confidence.

37. Browne-Wilkinson J in *Woods v WM Car Services* [1981] ICR 666 described how a breach of this term may arise:

> to constitute a breach of this implied term it is not necessary to show that the employer intended any repudiation of the contract: the tribunal's function is to look at the employer's conduct as a whole and determine whether it is such that its effect, judged reasonably and sensibly, is such that the employee cannot be expected to put up with it.

38. In *Malik v Bank of Credit and Commerce International SA* [1997] IRLR 462, Lord Steyn stated that, in assessing whether or not there has been a breach of the implied obligation of mutual trust and confidence, it is the impact of the employer's behaviour on the employee that is significant – not the intention of the employer. Moreover, the impact on the employee must be assessed objectively. Furthermore, their Lordships decided that the breach occurs at the time of the employer's conduct not at the time the employee becomes aware of that conduct.

39. There is no need for the acts of the employer to be 'arbitrary or capricious'; it is sufficient if the employer acted in a way that was incompetent or insensitive: *Sheridan v British Telecommunications plc* EAT 76/88.

40. The tribunal is required to decide whether a breach is repudiatory by objectively assessing the effect of the breach on the contractual relationship of the parties: it is possible for there to be a breach of a term of the contract of employment without it being a fundamental breach of contract: *Conlon v Buckinghamshire County Council* EAT 630/88.

41. As the question of breach is objectively assessed, the motive of the party said to be in breach is irrelevant: *Malik v BCCI*, ibid. Any breach of the implied term of trust and confidence is a repudiatory breach: *Morrow v Safeway Stores* [2002] IRLR 9.

42. If the tribunal finds that an employee was constructively dismissed it can, if the respondent raises it as an issue, go on to investigate whether the conduct that led to the constructive dismissal could have lead to a fair dismissal. In this case the respondent was undertaking a disciplinary process in relation to the claimant and so argues that it would have fairly dismissed the claimant.

43. By reference to section 98 of the Employment Rights Act 1996 it is for the employer to show a genuinely held reason for the dismissal and that it is a reason which is characterised by sub-sections 98(1) and (2) of the ERA 1996 as a potentially fair reason. There are five potentially fair reasons for dismissal under section 98 ERA 1996: conduct, capability, redundancy, breach of statutory restriction and 'some other substantial reason of a kind as to justify the dismissal of an employee holding the position which the employee held'.

44. If the respondent does show that that reason is one of the potentially fair reasons specified in that section it is then for the tribunal to determine the matter on the basis of the legal principles contained within *British Home Stores v Burchell* [1980] ICR 303. Thus, in so far as may be relevant, the Tribunal may need to consider whether the employer conducted a reasonably sufficient investigation and whether it had reasonable grounds for forming its belief on the evidence before it. The tribunal should not substitute its own view for that of the employer but should consider whether the employer's handling of the disciplinary process, and the application of dismissal as a sanction for the conduct found, were within the band of reasonable responses open to it.

45. Further guidance is to be found in the ACAS Code on Disciplinary and Grievance Procedures of 2009, as recently amended; and the Tribunal is required to take account of any provision of that Code which appears to it to be relevant to any issue before it.

Conclusions on the issues

46. Having made the findings of fact set out above, the tribunal returned to the agreed issues in this case in order to make these conclusions applying the law to the facts found in relation to the issues identified above.

Issue 7(a): The claimant relies on the respondent requiring him to refrain from using Facebook if he wanted to remain in its employment

47. It is agreed that this occurred.

Issue 7(b): The claimant alleges that this amounts to breaches of the implied duty of trust and confidence

48. All parties accept, as does the tribunal, that social media has significantly blurred the line between work and home. This is particularly in cases where work equipment is used in private time on private matters, but is also relevant when personal equipment is used to make posts which are relevant to work or to the workplace environment. Whilst the tribunal finds that it can be legitimate for an employer to impose limits on an employee's conduct and behaviour outside of work and/or when using both work and personal equipment, such limits must, necessarily, be clearly spelt out in an appropriate policy if they are to be enforceable as being reasonable, owing to the obvious impact such restrictions will have on the employee.

49. In this case the respondent had no policy in place which addressed the usage of social media at all, let alone one which addressed standards of behaviour outside of work. The absence of a policy will not render clear acts of misconduct unobjectionable, as there is a large measure of common sense that employees must apply to their behaviour outside of work: see for example *Williams v Leeds United Football Club* [2015] EWHC

376 (QB). However, where an employer wishes to regulate the comments of its employees over social media in circumstances where, but for the employment relationship, there would be nothing objectionable about the conduct, and that conduct does not directly affect the ability of the employee to undertake their role, then clear policies and procedures are much more likely to be required: see for example *Alan Blue v Food Standards Agency* and *Lake v Amey Services Ltd Sheffield* ET 1807678/2013. Whilst both of these decisions are first instance tribunal decisions, the tribunal finds that they indicate a need for employers to have in place a clear policy when seeking to control social media posts outside of the workplace. The tribunal finds that the consequences of such conduct should therefore have been spelt out in a clear policy. This is particularly so for a company such as the respondent which bills itself as being familiar with social media and indeed markets itself significantly over such media.

50. The tribunal was especially troubled by the approach taken by the respondent. There appears to have been little consideration of the actual effect of the actions of the claimant in making his posts. There appears to have been little or no consideration of the fact that the posts were swiftly deleted. Whilst not directly analogous to the facts of the instant case, the tribunal notes the decision of the High Court in *Mason v Huddersfield Giants* [2013] EWHC 2869 (QB), a claim arising out of what was said to be a wrongful dismissal. The claimant herein deleted the posts as soon as he was made aware that that the respondent was unhappy. But this appears to have played no part in the decision-making process, a step which, in the absence of a policy, the tribunal considers to be of central importance.

51. The tribunal is also particularly concerned with the proposal of the respondent that the claimant cease from ever using Facebook again. The proposal was not limited to inappropriate use, whether in respect of matters generally or the WonderBox in particular. The tribunal in the course of submissions raised with the parties the applicability or otherwise of Articles 8 and 10 of the European Convention on Human Rights, incorporated into domestic law by the Human Rights Act 1998. In particular the tribunal was concerned that a blanket prohibition on the use of a social media platform could be seen to be a breach of Article 10. In the course of preparing this judgment, the tribunal has considered the decision of the court of Northern Ireland in *Teggart v TeleTech UK Ltd* [2012] NIIT 00704_11IT and notes that the court in that case considered that the posting of material on Facebook meant that Article 8 rights were not engaged; and that Article 10 did not give a licence to make disparaging comments. However it seems to this tribunal that a prohibition on any posts at all might well be a breach of Article 10. However as neither party chose to address the tribunal on these issues, we do not take this point further, as, as will be seen below, it is unnecessary for us to do so.

52. The tribunal notes that the evidence of the claimant, which was not challenged, was that the posts to Facebook were not made using his

WonderBox but rather by the use of a home PC or laptop. In any event the respondent had no policy which the tribunal has been shown that addresses the use of work-supplied equipment. Had the respondent sought to limit its sanction as to the use of social media via the WonderBox, or to prevent social media posts about the WonderBox, the decision of this tribunal could perhaps have been different. However that is not the case, and as such, no relevant findings are made in this regard.

53. It is the view of this tribunal that the actions of the respondent, by not having an appropriate policy in place, by failing to address this with the claimant in the meetings or in advance of the meetings, and in circumstances where the allegations the claimant faced seemed to differ at various stages (of which see below) the tribunal finds that the conduct of the respondent did amount to a breach of the implied duty of trust and confidence when it sought to prevent the claimant's private usage of Facebook. Even had appropriate policies been in place and the matters referred to above had been properly addressed, this tribunal considers that it is highly unlikely, absent any specific and detailed concerns, such as national security, for it ever to be appropriate for an employer to seek to prevent the use by the employee of either specific or general social media websites.

Issue 7(c): The respondent denies these occurred as alleged by the claimant, and if they did the respondent denies these amount to breaches of the implied duty of trust and confidence; issue 7(d) Has the claimant showed that objectively considered these were repudiatory breaches of contract and issue 7(e) is the breach sufficiently serious to allow the employee to resign.

54. These three issues can, the tribunal thinks, be dealt with as one. In line with *Morrow* referred to above, any breach of the implied duty of trust and confidence is repudiatory. It was therefore sufficient to permit the claimant to accept the respondent's breach of contract and resign.

Issue 7(f): Did the employer have reasonable and proper cause for that conduct?

55. This aspect of the claim has presented the tribunal with considerable difficulty in deciding. Clearly, as both parties accept, the respondent is very protective of its image and brand. The tribunal can well understand its point on this and the tribunal accepts this is a legitimate aim of any business. However, in seeking to limit the conduct of an employee outside of work in circumstances, as we say above, where the commentary was lawful, does require clearly defined limits and an awareness of the employee that their lawful conduct will be measured and weighed against this standard. In any event, as we have also already stated, the ambit of the proposed restriction went too far. Had the claimant been told that he was not to post to social media any reference to his employer or to the WonderBox, or that he must not make derogatory or disparaging comments, the situation might well be different (particularly where a

policy existed) but the Draconian nature of what was here proposed went too far to be able to be considered either reasonable or proper.

56. Here, there are no such policy restrictions imposed by the respondent generally, and for that reason no reason for the claimant to be aware that his conduct outside of work online could be used as a reason to impose disciplinary sanctions upon him.

57. On balance therefore the tribunal finds that whilst there may have been proper cause for commencing the disciplinary procedure against the claimant the manner in which it was conducted and the result of the process cannot be said to have been reasonable in the circumstances of this case: for instance, as we have said before, the claimant had no notice that his conduct in his personal time and from an account that did not identify him or his employer, could be considered from a disciplinary perspective; the misconduct he is alleged to have committed differs in the letter calling him to the meeting from that which is raised at the disciplinary hearing; and in any event there was no consideration whatsoever of the extent to which the posts were seen. Any restriction by an employer on an employee's private life and behaviour must be clearly defined and circumscribed. The sanction of 'be dismissed or don't use Facebook again' is not so circumscribed, even if such a sanction could ever be considered reasonable.

58. Accordingly, the respondent fails in its argument that it has reasonable and proper cause for the conduct.

Issue 7(g): Would any actual dismissal have been fair?

59. The respondent says that if it had dismissed the claimant then its dismissal of him would have been fair. This is an argument that is open to the respondent, as a constructively dismissed employee cannot be in any better position than one who was actually dismissed by an employer. The tribunal therefore is required to consider whether the dismissal would have been fair in the circumstances of this case.

60. In accordance with section 98 of the Employment Rights Act 1996 it is for the respondent to prove to the tribunal that the reason for the claimant's dismissal was one of those reasons which, potentially, can amount to a fair reason for dismissal. Here the respondent states it could have dismissed the claimant because of a reason that related to his conduct. This is a potentially fair reason for dismissal contained within the Employment Rights Act 1996.

61. Although there is no burden of proof upon him to show another reason for his dismissal, in this matter the claimant has not suggested there is any other reason that the respondent would seek to have ended his employment.

62. Weighing up the evidence therefore the tribunal is satisfied that the respondent had a genuine belief in the claimant's misconduct. For these purposes it does not matter whether the factual basis of the belief is actually correct or even whether it had reasonable grounds so to believe,

as this is a consideration which is considered in the context of the assessment of fairness under section 98(4).

63. In light of this the tribunal is now required to consider whether the respondent had conducted a reasonable investigation. The tribunal has done this by looking firstly at the nature of the investigation with a view to determining whether it accorded with what a reasonable employer would do, and then by considering whether such a hypothetical reasonable employer would have felt able to form a genuine belief that the claimant was guilty of what was presented as being the reasons for his dismissal. As stated above the facts in this matter are largely agreed: the claimant accepted he posted these comments on Facebook. There is little more, therefore, which a reasonable employer would have done in this regard.

64. However, the investigation should not simply cease on that conclusion, as the respondent in submissions contended it should. The accusation for which the claimant was dismissed was that his conduct had damaged the reputation of the respondent. This was covered by the respondent's disciplinary policy, which defined the bringing of the respondent into disrepute as gross misconduct. However, there was no evidence that the reputation of the respondent had, in fact, been so damaged. A reasonable employer conducting a disciplinary investigation into reputational damage should, the tribunal finds, have investigated this point. Such considerations would, as have already been found above, have included a consideration of the number of 'friends' that the claimant had; the fact that he believed his settings to be private; the fact that there had been no commentary or 'likes' in respect of the statement; the fact that there were no identifying features of the profile of the claimant so as to mark him out as an employee of the respondent; the fact that the posts do not appear to have been circulated more widely; and the fact that they were deleted at an early stage.

65. The tribunal then turned to considering whether the respondent's procedure was reasonable in other regards. The tribunal read the minutes of the disciplinary hearing: at the very outset of the minutes the claimant is asked whether he has any mitigation to offer for his conduct. Initially this concerned the tribunal as it may show that the respondent did not enter the hearing with an open mind, which a reasonable employer would do. However, we accept that in these circumstances it was not outside the range of reasonable responses for the respondent to have adopted this approach in the circumstances where the claimant admitted the conduct and the posts were before the employer. We are however concerned that what mitigation that was provided was not necessarily thoroughly considered.

66. In all other regards it appears the respondent complied with the ACAS Code of Practice. Weighing all these factors in the balance however, the tribunal find that the procedure was unreasonable and fundamentally flawed in that a reasonable employer would have obtained evidence of harm being inflicted by the claimant's comments. Accordingly the respondent did not conduct a reasonable investigation.

67. The final question the tribunal must ask itself is whether any dismissal would have been within the range of reasonable responses? It is not up to the tribunal to substitute its own view for that of the reasonable employer. The tribunal is obliged to formulate a view on whether or not the conduct complained of was sufficiently serious to justify dismissal, and thus whether the decision to do so was inside or outside the range.

68. Again, this has been a difficult decision for the tribunal. There was ample evidence that the claimant posted the comments; indeed he had always accepted he did and was apologetic for his actions. Viewed objectively, the fact that a senior employee is making very disparaging comments about his employer's product, in circumstances where he is responsible for managing the sales accounts of that product, might well lead the ordinary man in the street to think that a dismissal was a virtual certainty. Against this, as stated above, must be weighed the fact that there was no evidence of harm actually being caused to the respondent by the claimant's posts.

69. Again, there was no policy which the claimant can be said to have broken by his actions and, therefore no sanction highlighted as flowing from such a breach. There is nothing to suggest that the claimant was informed that private posts in his own time from an account not linked to the respondent could be used to discipline him, and, whilst serious, the nature of the posts is not analogous to the behaviour in *Williams*, ibid. The claimant is a longstanding member of staff of the respondent, was highly regarded with a clean disciplinary record and whose actions can be said to amount to an aberration borne of frustration in an otherwise unblemished career.

70. The tribunal is mindful of the fact that it is judging the decision to dismiss according to the range of reasonable responses open to a reasonable employer, and it should not substitute its judgment for that of the employer on this point. A decision to dismiss in these circumstances would seem perhaps to be harsh but that does not necessarily mean it is outside the range of reasonable responses. However, taking all of the above factors into account, in this matter the tribunal finds that a dismissal of the claimant would have fallen outside the range of reasonable responses in circumstances where no policy existed.

Conclusions on the complaints of unfair dismissal

71. The tribunal finds therefore that the claimant was constructively dismissed and that the respondent would have not have been able to fairly dismiss him in the circumstances of this case. Accordingly the claimant's claim is well founded and succeeds.

72. The matter is therefore to be listed for a remedies hearing in which issues of contributory fault and *Polkey* will have to be addressed. In addition, as the claimant has succeeded in his claims, the parties will be expected to address the tribunal on the imposition of a financial penalty on the respondent, amounting to not more than half of what it is ordered to pay the claimant, up to a maximum of £5,000.00 in accordance with the

Employment Tribunals Act 1996 (as amended) as well as whether the claimant should be repaid the fees he has paid to bring his claim to the tribunal.

Commentary

The judgment above is the culmination of the various commentaries on the earlier documents. Ultimately, and unsurprisingly, the claim was successful, though the question of contributory fault and *Polkey* are left open to at least some extent. The attempt by the respondent to make as a condition of continued employment a blanket prohibition on accessing or using Facebook, even in respect of matters entirely unrelated to the employment of the claimant, amounts to a repudiatory breach of the implied term of trust and confidence, and as a result the resignation amounted to constructive unfair dismissal.

The judgment itself addresses numerous issues relevant to employers, who may find themselves in very similar situations. The remainder of this commentary analyses the judgment and provides some hints and pointers as to where the employer went wrong.

The tribunal commences by setting out the agreed issues and the factual matrix. As will often be the case in social media disputes, the facts themselves are not in dispute; where an employee is confronted with evidence that posts have been made, he will likely have little choice but to accept that the material was in fact placed on his social media account. In some cases there may be a dispute as to how this material came to be posted, and whether the employee is as a result culpable: for example in the *Mason* case the offending tweet was uploaded by Mr Mason's girlfriend, without his knowledge. In such cases, the tribunal may have to consider how a reasonable employer would have treated such information, and may also analyse the ease by which an employee allows posts to be made from his accounts. Often, though, the employee will accept that the posts were made, but seek to argue that he was entitled to make them, or that they did not cause harm, or that they were immediately deleted and were not disseminated. There may also be issues to consider as to how the employer came to know of the posts, which may be relevant to data protection, as considered in Chapter 2.

In this scenario, the employee does not seek to contend that anyone other than he posted the comments, or, in reality, that the content of the posts was not at least potentially harmful. He takes issue with what could be taken to be an over-reaction by his employer. As the tribunal comments in the judgment above, had the employer sought to impose a more reasonable sanction, such as prohibiting the making of posts referencing the employer or its products, or limiting the prohibition to derogatory commentary, a different result might have been reached. It further notes →

that a lay observer might consider that an employee who has acted in the way that Mr Smith did would be shocked to consider that he could bring and win a claim for constructive unfair dismissal. It is likely that this is correct; the tenor of the posts might lead a reasonable objective bystander to consider that dismissal was an appropriate sanction. The conclusion of the tribunal in the case study is deliberately ambiguous on this point. It is a nice distinction between conduct that would allow an employer reasonably to dismiss and that which falls the other side of the line; and the failings by the respondent in the investigation carried out, together with the absence of a social media policy appear to have been the determining factors in this regard. The scenario is designed to highlight that even seemingly outrageous behaviour may result in an employer being adjudged culpable if it fails to take sensible precautions.

That a social media policy is important should by this stage be beyond argument. The tribunal notes repeatedly its surprise that no policy is in place. This echoes views expressed by numerous judicial decisions, most tellingly in the various *Linfox* cases considered by the Australian courts. The quotation set out above from the *Pearson v Linfox* decision is worth repeating in this context:

> [46] Secondly, Linfox's desire to have a policy in place about the use of social media by employees can be understood. The evidence indicated it had been criticised in other proceedings for not having done so. Further, in an employment context the establishment of a social media policy is clearly a legitimate exercise in acting to protect the reputation and security of a business. It also serves a useful purpose by making clear to employees what is expected of them. Gone is the time (if it ever existed) where an employee might claim posts on social media are intended to be for private consumption only. An employer is also entitled to have a policy in place making clear excessive use of social media at work may have consequences for employees.

The Australian courts (and, it is submitted, the Tribunal's of England and Wales) recognise that it is appropriate and legitimate for employers to seek to protect their interests by circumscribing the online interaction of their employees whether at work or in their personal time, and whether from professional or personal accounts. The arguments over personal internet use being private have largely been settled; provided that the employer has a reasonable policy in place that has been communicated and as appropriate employees have received related training, arguments over privacy and personal freedom of expression will not find favour. Conversely, *Williams* demonstrates that behaviour that is self-evidently gross misconduct will still result in a dismissal, but the very fact that the conduct complained of in that case was of a serious nature, and was conducted over workplace email, demonstrates that there is a range of lesser behaviour that may be culpable only when the employer protects itself by implementing an appropriate policy.   →

The authors' seeming obsession with social media policies is therefore justified as a recommendation that employers remove any doubt that social media misconduct will have consequences. As the tribunal found in this case, it is surprising that this company has no social media policy. The policies relied upon are vague, unspecific and clearly amount to an attempt to adapt existing policies to new circumstances. However they do nothing other than state that bringing the reputation of the employer into disrepute may amount to gross misconduct. In modern social media times this is insufficient. Policies need to spell out what is and what is not misconduct; to detail what use, how, when, and where, is acceptable, and the consequences of misuse. It is essential to be clear that the policy applies not just to work hours, work accounts or work equipment, but to posts made in personal time, from accounts that have no bearing on employment, and which may be ill-advised or spur of the moment, potentially fuelled by intoxication. If the policy makes clear that all of those eventualities are covered, it is far more likely that the employer will prevail in any claim in which it becomes involved.

Investigation into harm, actual or potential, is also of essential importance. The respondent is rightly criticised by the tribunal in this scenario for not having carried out any such investigation. The fact of the posts is not disputed; but the evidence of the claimant was that he had a limited social media footprint; that no comments were made in response to his posts; that there were no 'likes' of the post, and that there was in reality no risk to the reputation of his employer. His friends knew where he worked, but also knew that he was keen on the WonderBox as a product, and, he contended, would have taken his comments as they were intended – frustration and banter. The respondent failed to consider any of these matters, and as a result was unsuccessful in arguing that there would have been a dismissal in any event. Once again, had a policy been in place, the employer would likely not have had to carry out such a detailed investigation. The purpose of a policy is to prescribe potentially harmful behavior, and it is breach of that policy which leads to the culpable offence. Whether harm has actually been caused is then a secondary consideration which may go to the reasonableness of the sanction, but the employer is far more protected by having already spelled out in the form of the policy that it considers such actual or potential harm to be a potentially dismissable offence. A significant factor is likely to be the extent of the employee's social media connections and the concomitant increased risk of harm in such circumstances. But, in the absence of such a policy, the employer is required to justify the steps that it took in far more detail in the circumstances presented to it, and a more in-depth consideration of actual or potential harm will likely then be required.

Ultimately, the success of the claimant in this case turns, however, on the entirely inappropriate approach of the respondent to the posting of the messages to Facebook. There is no similar reported case of which the ➡

authors are aware where an employer has sought, as a condition of continuing employment, to prevent an employee from accessing a social media site at all. It is legitimate for employers to ban the use of social media in the workplace, or to limit employees' time to a specified number of minutes or to breaks. It is likewise legitimate for employers to circumscribe the use of social media in a personal capacity even outside of working hours, by, for example, preventing reference to the employer or its products, or by making clear that derogatory, disparaging or inappropriate comments, of the sort posted by the claimant here, will potentially entitle the employer to dismiss. But preventing an employee from using social media at all, even in a personal capacity, is, it is submitted, a step too far, save in highly exceptional cases (such as, as outlined above, where the nature of the employee's work is so sensitive that the employer has identified a risk from any social media presence whatsoever, or for employees in particularly sensitive posts being prevented from joining rival social media platforms). It was never likely that a tribunal would uphold such a blanket provision, and a full consideration of Art 10 rights in particular would likely mean that any such prohibition was unlawful. This is not cured by the fact that the prohibition was deployed as an alternative to dismissal following on from what were clearly inappropriate and culpable posts.

Had the respondent simply dismissed the claimant on the basis that the posts amounted to gross misconduct, it had a far better chance of successfully defending an ensuing unfair dismissal claim. It would still have been criticised for its investigation process, and the consideration in particular of the harm caused to the respondent might have led to a finding of unfair dismissal in any event, though it is suggested that had the respondent either had a policy in place or had detailed the risk of harm from reposts (as recognised by the tribunal) in the course of the dismissal, it would have been difficult for a tribunal to find that such a dismissal was outside the range of reasonable responses. Such an approach is seen in cases such as *Preece* and *Weekes*. The irony here is that in giving the claimant an option to remain employed, the respondent crossed over into acting unreasonably.

14.11   The following table lists some lessons which can be learned from the case study.

Do	Don't
Have a policy! Although this point has already been stressed to breaking point in earlier chapters, the scenario is designed to illustrate the risks to employers who do not address their minds to the risk of social media and do not provide employees with guidance on what is and is not acceptable outside of working hours. In the absence of such a policy employers may find themselves having to justify not just their actions but also the investigations that they have carried out to consider risk and harm.	Rely upon existing policies – these will often not be fit for purpose. In particular it is important to set out consequences relating to personal use and the nature of posts. If an employee is to be disciplined in respect of material posted from a personal account and in personal time, harm will ordinarily be a significant factor. The existence of a policy will go a long way towards demonstrating that the risk of harm has been considered and identified.
Consider at investigatory and disciplinary stages what has been posted, what risks arise, what terms of the policy have been breached, and what an appropriate sanction, taking into account potential mitigation, might be.	Simply assume that harm has been caused and it is for the employee to mitigate. Considerations such as the number of followers, privacy settings and the manner in which posts have been received may be relevant to a reasonable response.
Minute meetings carefully. Employees or Tribunals may still not be familiar with internet or social media terminology or the particular risks that it entails. Ensure that these issues are covered in the minutes of the meetings, which should be as close as possible to verbatim and which should be counter-signed by the employee.	Simply summarise discussions. Leaving out details, particularly when seeking to demonstrate that harm has been caused or could have been caused and in the absence of a policy, leaves the employer open to challenge as to their procedure. It may also omit crucial details relating to social media misuse that may be obvious to employer and employee, but that the tribunal may not understand without explanation.

Do	Don't
Set out why it is considered that harm has or might be caused, in both the witness evidence and the ET3. Although it is likely that most tribunals will be familiar, at least on a rudimentary basis, with common social media sites, it is important to spell out in the evidence why there is a risk of harm to the company from the posts, rather than to leave this to submissions.	Assume that the particular reputational concerns of the employer are self-evident from the fact that an employee has posted inappropriate material on the internet. A failure to set out why harm is or could be caused may be the difference, particularly in the absence of a social media policy, between fair and unfair dismissal.
Be prepared to explain social media and particular social media sites.	Assume knowledge by the tribunal.
Ensure that sanctions imposed are appropriate and proportionate to the harm caused. The dismissal of an employee or the imposition of a final written warning, coupled with the right of the employer to monitor future posts, may well be appropriate or legitimate, rather than a dismissal.	Impose Draconian and inappropriate sanctions, particularly where these impinge on the personal rights outside of work of the employee. Seeking to prevent an employee from accessing particular sites outside of the workplace and/or from personal equipment is unlikely in most cases to be reasonable or proportionate.
Always consider *Polkey* and contributory fault. Although a finding of unfair dismissal is more likely to be avoided by the existence of an appropriate policy, ensure that, as a back up, arguments in this regard can be run.	Forget to consider in disciplinary processes the potential of risk of harm. If an employee is going to be kept on, make clear that their behaviour was unacceptable and must change. But do not seek to prevent them from social media use entirely!

14.12 It should be borne in mind at all times by employers faced with social media misconduct that, at one and the same time, the tribunals are consistently applying well-established principles of employment law to social media misconduct claims, and are developing a new body of case-law. As has been made clear elsewhere in this work, essentially all of the available decisions have been decided on such tried and tested principles, and the higher courts have declined to give any specific guidance on social media cases generally. This may or may not change, though the authors have speculated that the Employment

Appeal Tribunal or more likely the Court of Appeal will take the opportunity in an appropriate case to lay down guidance, most likely in respect of social media restrictive covenants or policies.

14.13 What is almost certain to happen however is the increase in precedent. At the time of writing there are a relatively limited number of reported or available cases concerning social media dismissals in England and Wales. Many cross-refer to other decisions, whilst stressing that the applicable tests are those well-established employment law canards. It is likely that the existing body of case-law will continue to develop and to self-reinforce.

14.14 It may be that the Court of Appeal will at some stage conduct a sweeping consideration of English and Commonwealth jurisprudence in this area, and as a result particular and specific principles will begin to develop. These may include the enforceability of particular terms in policies, and in particular may give rise to a consideration of the balance between the interests of the employer on the one hand, and the right to a private life and to freedom of expression of individual employees in their own time and from their own devices. Commonwealth jurisdictions have demonstrated that challenges to policies that seek to control the behaviour of employees in their personal lives will not prevail where the interests of the employer is or could be damaged as a result (see *Pearson*, and note that the English and Welsh tribunals appear to treat this almost as read notwithstanding *ECHR* provisions). The quote from *Pearson* above makes clear that privacy arguments for personal social media accounts are not likely to find traction.

14.15 The question for employers will always be: where is the line to be drawn? Even if guidance is eventually promulgated, the nature of social media means that most cases will by their nature remain fact-sensitive. Where no policy is in place, the factual considerations will be wide, and will encompass in particular the question of harm. The absence of a policy means that a tribunal is able to delve far deeper into the motivations of the employer for taking disciplinary action and to consider the reasons behind these motivations. Where a policy is in place, an employer is much more readily able to present itself as acting reasonably to react to circumstances which have already been considered to give rise to risk, and to implement appropriate sanctions for conduct which an employee knows or ought to know will lead to such action. An employer that disciplines for a breach which it has anticipated will always be in a far stronger position than one which is simply reacting to circumstances, particularly where the conduct complained of is carried out by the employee in their own time. The legal system has unequivocally accepted that employers are entitled to intervene in the personal affairs of their employees where the same is proportionate, legitimate and justified, and will likely support an employer who takes steps to discipline an employee for actions that are likely to harm its interests. But, likewise, an employer that fails to make clear to its employees that it requires them to consider its interests even when off duty, will struggle to justify a dismissal absent egregious misconduct.

14.16 Ultimately, the purpose of this scenario is to demonstrate that notwithstanding clear employee misconduct, an employer may still find themselves coming unstuck if they have not carried out a proper investigation, particularly where their policies do not seek to circumscribe actions outside of the workplace. As the tribunal in this case study recognised, the line between work and home is increasingly blurred by social media; but if an employer wishes to seek to control the behaviour of their employees online outside of the ordinary workplace, it is necessary for them to make this clear by way of a clearly set out written policy. Any less, and the employer leaves itself open to a successful claim, as the scenario demonstrates.

CHAPTER 15

OTHER MATERIALS

PROTECTION FROM HARASSMENT ACT 1997[1]

England and Wales

1 Prohibition of harassment[2]

(1) A person must not pursue a course of conduct –

    (a) which amounts to harassment of another, and
    (b) which he knows or ought to know amounts to harassment of the other.

[(1A) A person must not pursue a course of conduct –

    (a) which involves harassment of two or more persons, and
    (b) which he knows or ought to know involves harassment of those persons, and
    (c) by which he intends to persuade any person (whether or not one of those mentioned above) –
        (i) not to do something that he is entitled or required to do, or
        (ii) to do something that he is not under any obligation to do.][3]

---

[1] Information: Act reference: 1997 c 40. Royal assent: 21 March 1997. Long title: An Act to make provision for protecting persons from harassment and similar conduct.
[2] Provision details: Commencement: 16 June 1997 (SI 1997/1418).
[3] Amendment: Subsection inserted: Organized Crime and Police Act 2005, s 125(1), (2)(a), with effect from 1 July 2005, (SI 2005/1521, art 3(1)(m)).

(2) For the purposes of this section [or section 2A(2)(c)][4], the person whose course of conduct is in question ought to know that it amounts to [or involves][5] harassment of another if a reasonable person in possession of the same information would think the course of conduct amounted to [or involved][6] harassment of the other.

(3) Subsection (1) [or (1A)][7] does not apply to a course of conduct if the person who pursued it shows –

(a) that it was pursued for the purpose of preventing or detecting crime,
(b) that it was pursued under any enactment or rule of law or to comply with any condition or requirement imposed by any person under any enactment, or
(c) that in the particular circumstances the pursuit of the course of conduct was reasonable.

2 Offence of harassment[8]

(1) A person who pursues a course of conduct in breach of [section 1(1) or (1A)][9] is guilty of an offence.

(2) A person guilty of an offence under this section is liable on summary conviction to imprisonment for a term not exceeding six months, or a fine not exceeding level 5 on the standard scale, or both.

(3) ...[10]

[2A Offence of stalking

(1) A person is guilty of an offence if –

(a) the person pursues a course of conduct in breach of section 1(1), and
(b) the course of conduct amounts to stalking.

(2) For the purposes of subsection (1)(b) (and section 4A(1)(a)) a person's course of conduct amounts to stalking of another person if –

(a) it amounts to harassment of that person,
(b) the acts or omissions involved are ones associated with stalking, and
(c) the person whose course of conduct it is knows or ought to know that the course of conduct amounts to harassment of the other person.

---

[4]   Amendment: Words inserted: Protection of Freedoms Act 2012, s 115(1), Sch 9, Pt 11, para 143(1), (2), with effect from 25 November 2012 (SI 2012/2075).
[5]   Amendment: Words inserted: Organized Crime and Police Act 2005, s 125(1), (2)(b), with effect from 1 July 2005 (SI 2005/1521, art 3(1)(m)).
[6]   Amendment: Words inserted: Organized Crime and Police Act 2005, s 125(1), (2)(b), with effect from 1 July 2005 (SI 2005/1521, art 3(1)(m)).
[7]   Amendment: Words inserted: Organized Crime and Police Act 2005, s 125(1), (2)(c), with effect from 1 July 2005 (SI 2005/1521, art 3(1)(m)).
[8]   Provision details: Commencement: 16 June 1997 (SI 1997/1418).
[9]   Amendment: Words substituted: Organized Crime and Police Act 2005, s 125(1), (3), with effect from 1 July 2005 (SI 2005/1521, art 3(1)(m)).
[10] Amendment: Subsection repealed: Police Reform Act 2002, s 107(2), Sch 8, with effect from 1 October 2002 (Police Reform Act 2002 (Commencement No 1) Order 2002, SI 2002/2306).

(3) The following are examples of acts or omissions which, in particular circumstances, are ones associated with stalking –

(a) following a person,

(b) contacting, or attempting to contact, a person by any means,

(c) publishing any statement or other material –
    (i) relating or purporting to relate to a person, or
    (ii) purporting to originate from a person,

(d) monitoring the use by a person of the internet, email or any other form of electronic communication,

(e) loitering in any place (whether public or private),

(f) interfering with any property in the possession of a person,

(g) watching or spying on a person.

(4) A person guilty of an offence under this section is liable on summary conviction to imprisonment for a term not exceeding 51 weeks, or a fine not exceeding level 5 on the standard scale, or both.

(5) In relation to an offence committed before the commencement of section 281(5) of the Criminal Justice Act 2003, the reference in subsection (4) to 51 weeks is to be read as a reference to six months.

(6) This section is without prejudice to the generality of section 2.][11]

[2B Power of entry in relation to offence of stalking

(1) A justice of the peace may, on an application by a constable, issue a warrant authorising a constable to enter and search premises if the justice of the peace is satisfied that there are reasonable grounds for believing that –

(a) an offence under section 2A has been, or is being, committed,

(b) there is material on the premises which is likely to be of substantial value (whether by itself or together with other material) to the investigation of the offence,

(c) the material –
    (i) is likely to be admissible in evidence at a trial for the offence, and
    (ii) does not consist of, or include, items subject to legal privilege, excluded material or special procedure material (within the meanings given by sections 10, 11 and 14 of the Police and Criminal Evidence Act 1984), and

(d) either –
    (i) entry to the premises will not be granted unless a warrant is produced, or
    (ii) the purpose of a search may be frustrated or seriously prejudiced unless a constable arriving at the premises can secure immediate entry to them.

(2) A constable may seize and retain anything for which a search has been authorised under subsection (1).

---

[11] Amendment: Section inserted: Protection of Freedoms Act 2012, s 111(1), with effect from 25 November 2012 (SI 2012/2075).

(3) A constable may use reasonable force, if necessary, in the exercise of any power conferred by virtue of this section.

(4) In this section "premises" has the same meaning as in section 23 of the Police and Criminal Evidence Act 1984.][12]

3 Civil remedy[13]

(1) An actual or apprehended breach of [section 1(1)][14] may be the subject of a claim in civil proceedings by the person who is or may be the victim of the course of conduct in question.

(2) On such a claim, damages may be awarded for (among other things) any anxiety caused by the harassment and any financial loss resulting from the harassment.

(3) Where –

    (a) in such proceedings the High Court or a county court grants an injunction for the purpose of restraining the defendant from pursuing any conduct which amounts to harassment, and

    (b) the plaintiff considers that the defendant has done anything which he is prohibited from doing by the injunction,

the plaintiff may apply for the issue of a warrant for the arrest of the defendant.

(4) An application under subsection (3) may be made –

    (a) where the injunction was granted by the High Court, to a judge of that court, and

    (b) where the injunction was granted by a county court, to a judge or district judge of that or any other county court.

(5) The judge or district judge to whom an application under subsection (3) is made may only issue a warrant if –

    (a) the application is substantiated on oath, and

    (b) the judge or district judge has reasonable grounds for believing that the defendant has done anything which he is prohibited from doing by the injunction.

(6) Where –

    (a) the High Court or a county court grants an injunction for the purpose mentioned in subsection (3)(a), and

    (b) without reasonable excuse the defendant does anything which he is prohibited from doing by the injunction,

he is guilty of an offence.

---

[12] Amendment: Section inserted: Protection of Freedoms Act 2012, s 112, with effect from 25 November 2012 (SI 2012/2075).

[13] Provision details: Commencement: sub-ss (1), (2): 16 June 1997 (SI 1997/1498); sub-ss (3)–(9): 1 September 1998 (SI 1998/1902).

[14] Amendment: Words substituted: Organized Crime and Police Act 2005, s 125(1), (4), with effect from 1 July 2005 (SI 2005/1521, art 3(1)(m)).

(7) Where a person is convicted of an offence under subsection (6) in respect of any conduct, that conduct is not punishable as a contempt of court.

(8) A person cannot be convicted of an offence under subsection (6) in respect of any conduct which has been punished as a contempt of court.

(9) A person guilty of an offence under subsection (6) is liable –

(a) on conviction on indictment, to imprisonment for a term not exceeding five years, or a fine, or both, or

(b) on summary conviction, to imprisonment for a term not exceeding six months, or a fine not exceeding the statutory maximum, or both.

[3A Injunctions to protect persons from harassment within section 1(1A)

(1) This section applies where there is an actual or apprehended breach of section 1(1A) by any person ('the relevant person').

(2) In such a case –

(a) any person who is or may be a victim of the course of conduct in question, or

(b) any person who is or may be a person falling within section 1(1A)(c),

may apply to the High Court or a county court for an injunction restraining the relevant person from pursuing any conduct which amounts to harassment in relation to any person or persons mentioned or described in the injunction.

(3) Section 3(3) to (9) apply in relation to an injunction granted under subsection (2) above as they apply in relation to an injunction granted as mentioned in section 3(3)(a).][15]

4 Putting people in fear of violence[16]

(1) A person whose course of conduct causes another to fear, on at least two occasions, that violence will be used against him is guilty of an offence if he knows or ought to know that his course of conduct will cause the other so to fear on each of those occasions.

(2) For the purposes of this section, the person whose course of conduct is in question ought to know that it will cause another to fear that violence will be used against him on any occasion if a reasonable person in possession of the same information would think the course of conduct would cause the other so to fear on that occasion.

(3) It is a defence for a person charged with an offence under this section to show that –

(a) his course of conduct was pursued for the purpose of preventing or detecting crime,

---

[15] Amendment: Section inserted: Organized Crime and Police Act 2005, s 125(1), (5), with effect from 1 July 2005 (SI 2005/1521, art 3(1)(m)).

[16] Provision details: Commencement: 16 June 1997 (SI 1997/1418).

(b)   his course of conduct was pursued under any enactment or rule of law or to comply with any condition or requirement imposed by any person under any enactment, or

(c)   the pursuit of his course of conduct was reasonable for the protection of himself or another or for the protection of his or another's property.

(4)   A person guilty of an offence under this section is liable –

(a)   on conviction on indictment, to imprisonment for a term not exceeding five years, or a fine, or both, or

(b)   on summary conviction, to imprisonment for a term not exceeding six months, or a fine not exceeding the statutory maximum, or both.

(5)   If on the trial on indictment of a person charged with an offence under this section the jury find him not guilty of the offence charged, they may find him guilty of an offence under section 2 [or 2A][17].

(6)   The Crown Court has the same powers and duties in relation to a person who is by virtue of subsection (5) convicted before it of an offence under section 2 [or 2A][18] as a magistrates' court would have on convicting him of the offence.

[4A Stalking involving fear of violence or serious alarm or distress

(1)   A person ("A") whose course of conduct –

(a)   amounts to stalking, and

(b)   either –

(i)   causes another ("B") to fear, on at least two occasions, that violence will be used against B, or

(ii)   causes B serious alarm or distress which has a substantial adverse effect on B's usual day-to-day activities,

is guilty of an offence if A knows or ought to know that A's course of conduct will cause B so to fear on each of those occasions or (as the case may be) will cause such alarm or distress.

(2)   For the purposes of this section A ought to know that A's course of conduct will cause B to fear that violence will be used against B on any occasion if a reasonable person in possession of the same information would think the course of conduct would cause B so to fear on that occasion.

(3)   For the purposes of this section A ought to know that A's course of conduct will cause B serious alarm or distress which has a substantial adverse effect on B's usual day-to-day activities if a reasonable person in possession of the same information would think the course of conduct would cause B such alarm or distress.

(4)   It is a defence for A to show that –

---

[17]   Amendment: Reference inserted: Protection of Freedoms Act 2012, s 115(1), Sch 9, Pt 11, para 143(1), (3)(a), with effect from 25 November 2012 (SI 2012/2075).

[18]   Amendment: Reference inserted: Protection of Freedoms Act 2012, s 115(1), Sch 9, Pt 11, para 143(1), (3)(b), with effect from 25 November 2012 (SI 2012/2075).

(a) A's course of conduct was pursued for the purpose of preventing or detecting crime,

(b) A's course of conduct was pursued under any enactment or rule of law or to comply with any condition or requirement imposed by any person under any enactment, or

(c) the pursuit of A's course of conduct was reasonable for the protection of A or another or for the protection of A's or another's property.

(5) A person guilty of an offence under this section is liable –

(a) on conviction on indictment, to imprisonment for a term not exceeding five years, or a fine, or both, or

(b) on summary conviction, to imprisonment for a term not exceeding twelve months, or a fine not exceeding the statutory maximum, or both.

(6) In relation to an offence committed before the commencement of section 154(1) of the Criminal Justice Act 2003, the reference in subsection (5)(b) to twelve months is to be read as a reference to six months.

(7) If on the trial on indictment of a person charged with an offence under this section the jury find the person not guilty of the offence charged, they may find the person guilty of an offence under section 2 or 2A.

(8) The Crown Court has the same powers and duties in relation to a person who is by virtue of subsection (7) convicted before it of an offence under section 2 or 2A as a magistrates' court would have on convicting the person of the offence.

(9) This section is without prejudice to the generality of section 4.][19]

5 Restraining orders[20] [on conviction][21]

(1) A court sentencing or otherwise dealing with a person ('the defendant') convicted of an offence . . .[22] may (as well as sentencing him or dealing with him in any other way) make an order under this section.

(2) The order may, for the purpose of protecting the victim [or victims][23] of the offence, or any other person mentioned in the order, from . . .[24] conduct which –

(a) amounts to harassment, or

---

[19] Amendment: Section inserted: Protection of Freedoms Act 2012, s 111(2), with effect from 25 November 2012 (SI 2012/2075).

[20] Provision details: Commencement: 16 June 1997 (SI 1997/1418).

[21] Amendment: Words inserted: Domestic Violence, Crime and Victims Act 2004, s 58(1), Sch 10, para 43(1), (2), with effect from 30 September 2009 (SI 2009/2501).

[22] Amendment: Words repealed: Domestic Violence, Crime and Victims Act 2004, ss 12(1), 58(2), Sch 11, with effect from 30 September 2009 (SI 2009/2501).

[23] Amendment: Words inserted: Organized Crime and Police Act 2005, s 125(1), (6), with effect from 1 July 2005 (SI 2005/1521, art 3(1)(m)).

[24] Amendment: Words repealed: Domestic Violence, Crime and Victims Act 2004, s 58, Sch 10, para 43(1), (3), with effect from 30 September 2009 (SI 2009/2501).

(b) will cause a fear of violence,

prohibit the defendant from doing anything described in the order.

(3) The order may have effect for a specified period or until further order.

[(3A) In proceedings under this section both the prosecution and the defence may lead, as further evidence, any evidence that would be admissible in proceedings for an injunction under section 3.][25]

(4) The prosecutor, the defendant or any other person mentioned in the order may apply to the court which made the order for it to be varied or discharged by a further order.

[(4A) Any person mentioned in the order is entitled to be heard on the hearing of an application under subsection (4).][26]

(5) If without reasonable excuse the defendant does anything which he is prohibited from doing by an order under this section, he is guilty of an offence.

(6) A person guilty of an offence under this section is liable –

(a) on conviction on indictment, to imprisonment for a term not exceeding five years, or a fine, or both, or

(b) on summary conviction, to imprisonment for a term not exceeding six months, or a fine not exceeding the statutory maximum, or both.

[(7) A court dealing with a person for an offence under this section may vary or discharge the order in question by a further order.][27]

[5A Restraining orders on acquittal

(1) A court before which a person ('the defendant') is acquitted of an offence may, if it considers it necessary to do so to protect a person from harassment by the defendant, make an order prohibiting the defendant from doing anything described in the order.

(2) Subsections (3) to (7) of section 5 apply to an order under this section as they apply to an order under that one.

(3) Where the Court of Appeal allow an appeal against conviction they may remit the case to the Crown Court to consider whether to proceed under this section.

(4) Where –

(a) the Crown Court allows an appeal against conviction, or

(b) a case is remitted to the Crown Court under subsection (3),

---

[25] Amendment: Subsection inserted: Domestic Violence, Crime and Victims Act 2004, s 12(2), with effect from 30 September 2009 (SI 2009/2501).

[26] Amendment: Subsection inserted: Domestic Violence, Crime and Victims Act 2004, s 12(3), with effect from 30 September 2009 (SI 2009/2501).

[27] Amendment: Subsection inserted: Domestic Violence, Crime and Victims Act 2004, s 12(4), with effect from 30 September 2009 (SI 2009/2501).

the reference in subsection (1) to a court before which a person is acquitted of an offence is to be read as referring to that court.

(5) A person made subject to an order under this section has the same right of appeal against the order as if –

(a) he had been convicted of the offence in question before the court which made the order, and

(b) the order had been made under section 5.][28]

6 Limitation

In section 11 of the Limitation Act 1980 (special time limit for actions in respect of personal injuries), after subsection (1) there is inserted –

> "(1A) This section does not apply to any action brought for damages under section 3 of the Protection from Harassment Act 1997."

7 Interpretation of this group of sections[29]

(1) This section applies for the interpretation of [sections 1 to 5A.][30]

(2) References to harassing a person include alarming the person or causing the person distress.

[(3) A 'course of conduct' must involve –

(a) in the case of conduct in relation to a single person (see section 1(1)), conduct on at least two occasions in relation to that person, or

(b) in the case of conduct in relation to two or more persons (see section 1(1A)), conduct on at least one occasion in relation to each of those persons.][31]

[(3A) A person's conduct on any occasion shall be taken, if aided, abetted, counselled or procured by another –

(a) to be conduct on that occasion of the other (as well as conduct of the person whose conduct it is); and

(b) to be conduct in relation to which the other's knowledge and purpose, and what he ought to have known, are the same as they were in relation to what was contemplated or reasonably foreseeable at the time of the aiding, abetting, counselling or procuring.][32]

(4) 'Conduct' includes speech.

---

[28] Amendment: Section inserted: Domestic Violence, Crime and Victims Act 2004, s 12(5), with effect from 30 September 2009 (SI 2009/2501).

[29] Provision details: Commencement: 16 June 1997 (SI 1997/1418).

[30] Amendment: Words substituted: Domestic Violence, Crime and Victims Act 2004, s 58(1), Sch 10, para 44, with effect from 30 September 2009 (SI 2009/2501).

[31] Amendment: Subsection substituted: Organized Crime and Police Act 2005, s 125(1), (7)(a), with effect from 1 July 2005 (SI 2005/1521, art 3(1)(m)).

[32] Amendment: Subsection inserted: Criminal Justice and Police Act 2001, s 44, with effect from 1 August 2001, (Criminal Justice and Police Act 2001 (Commencement No 1) Order 2001, SI 2001/2223.

[(5) References to a person, in the context of the harassment of a person, are references to a person who is an individual.][33]

EQUALITY ACT 2010

Other prohibited conduct

26 Harassment

(1) A person (A) harasses another (B) if –

(a) A engages in unwanted conduct related to a relevant protected characteristic, and
(b) the conduct has the purpose or effect of –
 (i) violating B's dignity, or
 (ii) creating an intimidating, hostile, degrading, humiliating or offensive environment for B.

(2) A also harasses B if –

(a) A engages in unwanted conduct of a sexual nature, and
(b) the conduct has the purpose or effect referred to in subsection (1)(b).

(3) A also harasses B if –

(a) A or another person engages in unwanted conduct of a sexual nature or that is related to gender reassignment or sex,
(b) the conduct has the purpose or effect referred to in subsection (1)(b), and
(c) because of B's rejection of or submission to the conduct, A treats B less favourably than A would treat B if B had not rejected or submitted to the conduct.

(4) In deciding whether conduct has the effect referred to in subsection (1)(b), each of the following must be taken into account –

(a) the perception of B;
(b) the other circumstances of the case;
(c) whether it is reasonable for the conduct to have that effect.

(5) The relevant protected characteristics are –

age;
disability;
gender reassignment;
race;
religion or belief;
sex;
sexual orientation.

---

[33] Amendment: Subsection inserted: Organized Crime and Police Act 2005, s 125(1), (7)(b), with effect from 1 July 2005 (SI 2005/1521, art 3(1)(m)).

FAMILY LAW ACT 1996

41 [...]³⁴ (*repealed*)

NOTES

Amendments–Repealed by Domestic Violence, Crime and Victims Act 2004, ss 2(1), 58(1), Sch 11.

Non-molestation orders

42 Non-molestation orders³⁵

(1)   In this Part a 'non-molestation order' means an order containing either or both of the following provisions–

(a)   provision prohibiting a person ('the respondent') from molesting another person who is associated with the respondent;

(b)   provision prohibiting the respondent from molesting a relevant child.

(2)   The court may make a non-molestation order–

(a)   if an application for the order has been made (whether in other family proceedings or without any other family proceedings being instituted) by a person who is associated with the respondent; or

(b)   if in any family proceedings to which the respondent is a party the court considers that the order should be made for the benefit of any other party to the proceedings or any relevant child even though no such application has been made.

(3)   In subsection (2) 'family proceedings' includes proceedings in which the court has made an emergency protection order under section 44 of the Children Act 1989 which includes an exclusion requirement (as defined in section 44A(3) of that Act).

(4)   Where an agreement to marry is terminated, no application under subsection (2)(a) may be made by virtue of section 62(3)(e) by reference to that agreement after the end of the period of three years beginning with the day on which it is terminated.

[(4ZA)   If a civil partnership agreement (as defined by section 73 of the Civil Partnership Act 2004) is terminated, no application under this section may be made by virtue of section 62(3)(eza) by reference to that agreement after the end of the period of three years beginning with the day on which it is terminated.]³⁶

[(4A)   A court considering whether to make an occupation order shall also consider whether to exercise the power conferred by subsection (2)(b).

---

³⁴   Amendments: Section repealed: Domestic Violence, Crime and Victims Act 2004, ss 2(1), 58(1), Sch 11, with effect from 5 December 2005 (SI 2005/3196).

³⁵   Provision details: Commencement: 1 October 1997 (SI 1997/1892).

³⁶   Amendment: Words inserted: Civil Partnership Act 2004, s 82, Sch 9, Part 1, para 9, with effect from 5 December 2005 (SI 2005/3175).

(4B) In this Part 'the applicant', in relation to a non-molestation order, includes (where the context per-mits) the person for whose benefit such an order would be or is made in exercise of the power conferred by subsection (2)(b).][37]

(5) In deciding whether to exercise its powers under this section and, if so, in what manner, the court shall have regard to all the circumstances including the need to secure the health, safety and well-being–

(a) of the applicant ...[38]; and
(b) of any relevant child.

(6) A non-molestation order may be expressed so as to refer to molestation in general, to particular acts of molestation, or to both.

(7) A non-molestation order may be made for a specified period or until further order.

(8) A non-molestation order which is made in other family proceedings ceases to have effect if those proceedings are withdrawn or dismissed.

NOTES

Amendments–Civil Partnership Act 2004, s 82, Sch 9, Part 1, para 9; Domestic Violence, Crime and Victims Act 2004, s 58(1), (2), Sch 10, para 36(1), (2), (3).

[42A Offence of breaching non-molestation order

(1) A person who without reasonable excuse does anything that he is prohibited from doing by a non-molestation order is guilty of an offence.

(2) In the case of a non-molestation order made by virtue of section 45(1), a person can be guilty of an offence under this section only in respect of conduct engaged in at a time when he was aware of the existence of the order.

(3) Where a person is convicted of an offence under this section in respect of any conduct, that conduct is not punishable as a contempt of court.

(4) A person cannot be convicted of an offence under this section in respect of any conduct which has been punished as a contempt of court.

(5) A person guilty of an offence under this section is liable –

(a) on conviction on indictment, to imprisonment for a term not exceeding five years, or a fine, or both;
(b) on summary conviction, to imprisonment for a term not exceeding 12 months, or a fine not exceeding the statutory maximum, or both.

(6) A reference in any enactment to proceedings under this Part, or to an order under this Part, does not include a reference to proceedings for an offence under this section or to an order made in such proceedings.

---

[37] Amendment: Sections inserted: Domestic Violence, Crime and Victims Act 2004, s 58(1), Sch 10, para 36(1), (2), with effect from 1 July 2007 (SI 2007/1845).
[38] Amendment: Words repealed: Domestic Violence, Crime and Victims Act 2004, s 58(1), (2), Sch 10, para 36(1), (3), with effect from 1 July 2007 (SI 2007/1845).

'Enactment' includes an enactment contained in subordinate legislation within the meaning of the Interpretation Act 1978 (c 30).][39]

Further provisions relating to occupation and non-molestation orders

43 Leave of court required for applications by children under sixteen[40]

(1) A child under the age of sixteen may not apply for an occupation order or a non-molestation order except with the leave of the court.

(2) The court may grant leave for the purposes of subsection (1) only if it is satisfied that the child has sufficient understanding to make the proposed application for the occupation order or non-molestation order.

44 Evidence of agreement to marry [or form a civil partnership][41][42]

(1) Subject to subsection (2), the court shall not make an order under section 33 or 42 by virtue of section 62(3)(e) unless there is produced to it evidence in writing of the existence of the agreement to marry.

(2) Subsection (1) does not apply if the court is satisfied that the agreement to marry was evidenced by –

    (a) the gift of an engagement ring by one party to the agreement to the other in contemplation of their marriage, or

    (b) a ceremony entered into by the parties in the presence of one or more other persons assembled for the purpose of witnessing the ceremony.

[(3) Subject to subsection (4), the court shall not make an order under section 33 or 42 by virtue of section 62(3)(eza) unless there is produced to it evidence in writing of the existence of the civil partnership agreement (as defined by section 73 of the Civil Partnership Act 2004).

(4) Subsection (3) does not apply if the court is satisfied that the civil partnership agreement was evidenced by –

    (a) a gift by one party to the agreement to the other as a token of the agreement, or

    (b) a ceremony entered into by the parties in the presence of one or more other persons assembled for the purpose of witnessing the ceremony.][43]

NOTES

Amendments–Civil Partnership Act 2004, s 82, Sch 9, Part 1, para 10.

[39]   Amendment: Section inserted: Domestic Violence, Crime and Victims Act 2004, s 1, with effect from 1 July 2007 (SI 2007/1845).

[40]   Provision details: Commencement: 1 October 1997 (SI 1997/1892).

[41]   Amendment: Words inserted: Civil Partnership Act 2004, s 82, Sch 9, Part 1, para 10(2), with effect from 5 December 2005 (SI 2005/3175).

[42]   Provision details: Commencement: 1 October 1997 (SI 1997/1892).

[43]   Amendment: Subsections inserted: Civil Partnership Act 2004, s 82, Sch 9, Part 1, para 10(1), with effect from 5 December 2005 (SI 2005/3175).

## 45	Ex parte orders[44]

(1)	The court may, in any case where it considers that it is just and convenient to do so, make an occupation order or a non-molestation order even though the respondent has not been given such notice of the proceedings as would otherwise be required by rules of court.

(2)	In determining whether to exercise its powers under subsection (1), the court shall have regard to all the circumstances including–

(a)	any risk of significant harm to the applicant or a relevant child, attributable to conduct of the respondent, if the order is not made immediately;

(b)	whether it is likely that the applicant will be deterred or prevented from pursuing the application if an order is not made immediately; and

(c)	whether there is reason to believe that the respondent is aware of the proceedings but is deliberately evading service and that the applicant or a relevant child will be seriously prejudiced by the delay involved–

   (i)	where the court is a magistrates' court, in effecting service of proceedings; or

   (ii)	in any other case, in effecting substituted service.

(3)	If the court makes an order by virtue of subsection (1) it must afford the respondent an opportunity to make representations relating to the order as soon as just and convenient at a full hearing.

(4)	If, at a full hearing, the court makes an occupation order ('the full order'), then–

(a)	for the purposes of calculating the maximum period for which the full order may be made to have effect, the relevant section is to apply as if the period for which the full order will have effect began on the date on which the initial order first had effect; and

(b)	the provisions of section 36(10) or 38(6) as to the extension of orders are to apply as if the full order and the initial order were a single order.

(5)	In this section–

'full hearing' means a hearing of which notice has been given to all the parties in accordance with rules of court;

'initial order' means an occupation order made by virtue of subsection (1); and

'relevant section' means section 33(10), 35(10), 36(10), 37(5) or 38(6).

## 46	Undertakings[45]

(1)	In any case where the court has power to make an occupation order or non-molestation order, the court may accept an undertaking from any party to the proceedings.

---

[44]	Provision details: Commencement: 1 October 1997 (SI 1997/1892).

[45]	Provision details: Commencement: 1 October 1997 (SI 1997/1892).

(2)   No power of arrest may be attached to any undertaking given under subsection (1).

(3)   The court shall not accept an undertaking under subsection (1) [instead of making an occupation order][46] in any case where apart from this section a power of arrest would be attached to the order.

[(3A)   The court shall not accept an undertaking under subsection (1) instead of making a non-molestation order in any case where it appears to the court that –

(a)   the respondent has used or threatened violence against the applicant or a relevant child; and
(b)   for the protection of the applicant or child it is necessary to make a non-molestation order so that any breach may be punishable under section 42A.][47]

(4)   An undertaking given to a court under subsection (1) is enforceable as if [the court had made an occupation order or a non-molestation order in terms corresponding to those of the undertaking][48].

(5)   This section has effect without prejudice to the powers of the High Court and the county court apart from this section.

NOTES

Amendments–Domestic Violence, Crime and Victims Act 2004, s 58(1), Sch 10, para 37.

47   Arrest for breach of order[49]

(1)   ...[50]

(2)   If –

(a)   the court makes [an occupation order][51]; and
(b)   it appears to the court that the respondent has used or threatened violence against the applicant or a relevant child,

it shall attach a power of arrest to one or more provisions of the order unless the court is satisfied that in all the circumstances of the case the applicant or child will be adequately protected without such a power of arrest.

---

[46]   Amendment: Words inserted: Domestic Violence, Crime and Victims Act 2004, s 58(1), Sch 10, para 37(1), (2), with effect from 1 July 2007 (SI 2007/1845).

[47]   Amendment: Subsection Amendment inserted: Domestic Violence, Crime and Victims Act 2004, s 58(1), Sch 10, para 37(1), (3), with effect from 1 July 2007 (SI 2007/1845).

[48]   Amendment: Words substituted: Domestic Violence, Crime and Victims Act 2004, s 58(1), Sch 10, para 37(1), (4), with effect from 1 July 2007 (SI 2007/1845).

[49]   Provision details: Commencement: 1 October 1997 (SI 1997/1892).

[50]   Amendment: Subsection repealed: Domestic Violence, Crime and Victims Act 2004, s 58(1), Sch 10, para 38(1), (2), Sch 11, with effect from 1 July 2007 (SI 2007/1845).

[51]   Amendment: Words substituted: Domestic Violence, Crime and Victims Act 2004, s 58(1), Sch 10, para 38(1), (3), with effect from 1 July 2007 (SI 2007/1845).

(3)   Subsection (2) does not apply in any case where [the occupation order][52] is made by virtue of section 45(1), but in such a case the court may attach a power of arrest to one or more provisions of the order if it appears to it –

(a)   that the respondent has used or threatened violence against the applicant or a relevant child; and

(b)   that there is a risk of significant harm to the applicant or child, attributable to conduct of the respondent, if the power of arrest is not attached to those provisions immediately.

(4)   If, by virtue of subsection (3), the court attaches a power of arrest to any provisions of [an occupation order][53], it may provide that the power of arrest is to have effect for a shorter period than the other provisions of the order.

(5)   Any period specified for the purposes of subsection (4) may be extended by the court (on one or more occasions) on an application to vary or discharge [the occupation order][54].

(6)   If, by virtue of subsection (2) or (3), a power of arrest is attached to certain provisions of an order, a constable may arrest without warrant a person whom he has reasonable cause for suspecting to be in breach of any such provision.

(7)   If a power of arrest is attached under subsection (2) or (3) to certain provisions of the order and the respondent is arrested under subsection (6) –

(a)   he must be brought before the relevant judicial authority within the period of 24 hours beginning at the time of his arrest; and

(b)   if the matter is not then disposed of forthwith, the relevant judicial authority before whom he is brought may remand him.

In reckoning for the purposes of this subsection any period of 24 hours, no account is to be taken of Christmas Day, Good Friday or any Sunday.

(8)   [If the court –

(a)   has made a non-molestation order, or

(b)   has made an occupation order but has not attached a power of arrest under subsection (2) or (3) to any provision of the order, or has attached that power only to certain provisions of the order][55],

then, if at any time the applicant considers that the respondent has failed to comply with the order, he may apply to the relevant judicial authority for the issue of a warrant for the arrest of the respondent.

---

[52]   Amendment: Words substituted: Domestic Violence, Crime and Victims Act 2004, s 58(1), Sch 10, para 38(1), (4), with effect from 1 July 2007 (SI 2007/1845).

[53]   Amendment: Words substituted: Domestic Violence, Crime and Victims Act 2004, s 58(1), Sch 10, para 38(1), (3), with effect from 1 July 2007 (SI 2007/1845).

[54]   Amendment: Words substituted: Domestic Violence, Crime and Victims Act 2004, s 58(1), Sch 10, para 38(1), (4), with effect from 1 July 2007 (SI 2007/1845).

[55]   Amendment: Words substituted: Domestic Violence, Crime and Victims Act 2004, s 58(1), Sch 10, para 38(1), (5), with effect from 1 July 2007 (SI 2007/1845).

(9)   The relevant judicial authority shall not issue a warrant on an application under subsection (8) unless –

(a)   the application is substantiated on oath; and
(b)   the relevant judicial authority has reasonable grounds for believing that the respondent has failed to comply with the order.

(10)   If a person is brought before a court by virtue of a warrant issued under subsection (9) and the court does not dispose of the matter forthwith, the court may remand him.

(11)   Schedule 5 (which makes provision corresponding to that applying in magistrates' courts in civil cases under sections 128 and 129 of the Magistrates' Courts Act 1980) has effect in relation to the powers of the High Court and a county court to remand a person by virtue of this section.

(12)   If a person remanded under this section is granted bail (whether in the High Court or a county court under Schedule 5 or in a magistrates' court under section 128 or 129 of the Magistrates' Courts Act 1980), he may be required by the relevant judicial authority to comply, before release on bail or later, with such requirements as appear to that authority to be necessary to secure that he does not interfere with witnesses or otherwise obstruct the course of justice.

NOTES

Amendments–Domestic Violence, Crime and Victims Act 2004, s 58(1), Sch 10, para 38.

48   Remand for medical examination and report[56]

(1)   If the relevant judicial authority has reason to consider that a medical report will be required, any power to remand a person under section 47(7)(b) or (10) may be exercised for the purpose of enabling a medical examination and report to be made.

(2)   If such a power is so exercised, the adjournment must not be for more than 4 weeks at a time unless the relevant judicial authority remands the accused in custody.

(3)   If the relevant judicial authority so remands the accused, the adjournment must not be for more than 3 weeks at a time.

(4)   If there is reason to suspect that a person who has been arrested –

(a)   under section 47(6), or
(b)   under a warrant issued on an application made under section 47(8),

is suffering from [mental disorder within the meaning of the Mental Health Act 1983][57], the relevant judicial authority has the same power to make an order under section 35 of [that Act][58] (remand for report on accused's mental

[56]   Provision details: Commencement: 1 October 1997 (SI 1997/1892).
[57]   Amendment: Words substituted: Mental Health Act 2007, s 1(4), Sch 1, Pt 2, para 20(1), (2)(a), with effect from 3 November 2008 (SI 2008/1900).
[58]   Amendment: Words substituted: Mental Health Act 2007, s 1(4), Sch 1, Pt 2, para 20(1), (2)(b), with effect from 3 November 2008 (SI 2008/1900).

condition) as the Crown Court has under [that section][59] in the case of an accused person within the meaning of that section.

NOTES

Amendments–Mental Health Act 2007, s 1(4), Sch 1, Pt 2, para 20.

49 Variation and discharge of orders[60]

(1) An occupation order or non-molestation order may be varied or discharged by the court on an application by –

    (a) the respondent, or
    (b) the person on whose application the order was made.

(2) In the case of a non-molestation order made by virtue of section 42(2)(b), the order may be varied or discharged by the court even though no such application has been made.

(3) If [B's home rights are, under section 31,][61] are a charge on the estate or interest of the other spouse or of trustees for [A][62], an order under section 33 against [A][63] may also be varied or discharged by the court on an application by any person deriving title under [A][64] or under the trustees and affected by the charge.

(4) If, by virtue of section 47(3), a power of arrest has been attached to certain provisions of an occupation order …[65], the court may vary or discharge the order under subsection (1) in so far as it confers a power of arrest (whether or not any application has been made to vary or discharge any other provision of the order).

NOTES

Amendments–Civil Partnership Act 2004, s 82, Sch 9, Part 1, para 11; Domestic Violence, Crime and Victims Act 2004, s 58(1), Sch 10, para 39, Sch 11.

. . .

---

[59] Amendment: Words substituted: Mental Health Act 2007, s 1(4), Sch 1, Pt 2, para 20(1), (2)(c), with effect from 3 November 2008 (SI 2008/1900).

[60] Provision details: Commencement: 1 October 1997 (SI 1997/1892).

[61] Amendment: Words substituted: Civil Partnership Act 2004, s 82, Sch 9, Part 1, para 11(a), with effect from 5 December 2005 (SI 2005/3175).

[62] Amendment: Reference substituted: Civil Partnership Act 2004, s 82, Sch 9, Part 1, para 11(b), with effect from 5 December 2005 (SI 2005/3175).

[63] Amendment: Reference substituted: Civil Partnership Act 2004, s 82, Sch 9, Part 1, para 11(b), with effect from 5 December 2005 (SI 2005/3175).

[64] Amendment: Reference substituted: Civil Partnership Act 2004, s 82, Sch 9, Part 1, para 11(b), with effect from 5 December 2005 (SI 2005/3175).

[65] Amendment: Words repealed: Domestic Violence, Crime and Victims Act 2004, s 58(1), Sch 10, para 39, Sch 11, with effect from 1 July 2007 (SI 2007/1845).

General

62 Meaning of 'cohabitants', 'relevant child' and 'associated persons'[66]

(1) For the purposes of this Part –

(a) 'cohabitants' are [[two persons who are neither married to each other nor civil partners of each other but are living together as husband and wife or as if they were civil partners;][67] and][68]

(b) ['cohabit' and 'former cohabitants' are to be read accordingly, but the latter expression][69] does not include cohabitants who have subsequently married each other [or become civil partners of each other][70].

(2) In this Part, 'relevant child', in relation to any proceedings under this Part, means –

(a) any child who is living with or might reasonably be expected to live with either party to the proceedings;

(b) any child in relation to whom an order under the Adoption Act 1976[, the Adoption and Children Act 2002[71] or the Children Act 1989 is in question in the proceedings; and

(c) any other child whose interests the court considers relevant.

(3) For the purposes of this Part, a person is associated with another person if –

(a) they are or have been married to each other;

[(aa)they are or have been civil partners of each other;][72]

(b) they are cohabitants or former cohabitants;

(c) they live or have lived in the same household, otherwise than merely by reason of one of them being the other's employee, tenant, lodger or boarder;

(d) they are relatives;

(e) they have agreed to marry one another (whether or not that agreement has been terminated);

---

66 Provision details: Commencement: 1 October 1997 (SI 1997/1892).

67 Amendments: Words substituted: Civil Partnership Act 2004, s 82, Sch 9, Pt 1, para 13(1), (2)(a), with effect from 5 December 2005 (SI 2005/3175).

68 Amendments: Words substituted: Domestic Violence, Crime and Victims Act 2004, s 3, with effect from 5 December 2005 (SI 2005/3196).

69 Amendments: Words substituted: Domestic Violence, Crime and Victims Act 2004, s 58(1), Sch 10, para 40, with effect from 5 December 2005 (SI 2005/3196).

70 Amendments: Words substituted: Civil Partnership Act 2004, s 82, Sch 9, Pt 1, para 13(1), (2)(b), with effect from 5 December 2005 (SI 2005/3175).

71 Amendment Words inserted: Adoption and Children Act 2002, s 139(1), Sch 3, paras 85, 86(a), with effect from 30 December 2005 (SI 2005/2213).

72 Amendments: Paragraph inserted: Civil Partnership Act 2004, s 82, Sch 9, Pt 1, para 13(1), (3), with effect from 5 December 2005 (SI 2005/3175).

[(eza) they have entered into a civil partnership agreement (as defined by section 73 of the Civil Partnership Act 2004) (whether or not that agreement has been terminated;][73]

[(ea) they have or have had an intimate personal relationship with each other which is or was of significant duration;][74]

(f) in relation to any child, they are both persons falling within subsection (4); or

(g) they are parties to the same family proceedings (other than proceedings under this Part).

(4)   A person falls within this subsection in relation to a child if –

(a) he is a parent of the child; or

(b) he has or has had parental responsibility for the child.

(5)   If a child has been adopted or [falls within subsection (7)][75], two persons are also associated with each other for the purpose of this Part if –

(a) one is a natural parent of the child or a parent of such a natural parent; and

(b) the other is the child or any person –
  (i)   who had become a parent of the child by virtue of an adoption order or has applied for an adoption order, or
  (ii) with whom the child has at any time been placed for adoption.

(6)   A body corporate and another person are not, by virtue of subsection (3)(f) or (g), to be regarded for the purposes of this Part as associated with each other.

[(7)   A child falls within this subsection if –

(a) an adoption agency, within the meaning of section 2 of the Adoption and Children Act 2002, has power to place him for adoption under section 19 of that Act (placing children with parental consent) or he has become the subject of an order under section 21 of that Act (placement orders), or

(b) he is freed for adoption by virtue of an order made –
  (i)   in England and Wales, under section 18 of the Adoption Act 1976,
  (ii)   . . . [76]
  (iii) in Northern Ireland, under Article 17(1) or 18(1) of the Adoption (Northern Ireland) Order 1987[, or

---

[73] Amendments: Paragraph inserted: Civil Partnership Act 2004, s 82, Sch 9, Pt 1, para 13(1), (3), with effect from 5 December 2005 (SI 2005/3175).

[74] Amendment: Paragraph inserted: Domestic Violence, Crime and Victims Act 2004, s 4, with effect from 1 July 2007 (SI 2007/1845).

[75] Amendment: Words substituted: Adoption and Children Act 2002, s 139(1), Sch 3, paras 85, 86(b), with effect from 30 December 2005 (SI 2005/2213).

[76] Amendment: Paragraph repealed: Adoption and Children (Scotland) Act 2007 (Consequential Modifications) Order 2011, SI 2011/1740, art 2, Sch 1, Pt 3, with effect from 15 July 2011.

(c) he is the subject of a Scottish permanence order which includes provision granting authority to adopt.][77][78]

[(8) In subsection (7)(c) 'Scottish permanence order' means a permanence order under section 80 of the Adoption and Children (Scotland) Act 2007 (asp 4) (including a deemed permanence order having effect by virtue of article 13(1), 14(2), 17(1) or 19(2) of the Adoption and Children (Scotland) Act 2007 (Commencement No 4, Transitional and Savings Provisions) Order 2009 (SSI 2009/267)).][79]

NOTES

Amendments–Adoption and Children Act 2002, s 139(1), Sch 3, paras 85, 86, 87; Civil Partnership Act 2004, s 82, Sch 9, Pt 1, para 13; Domestic Violence, Crime and Victims Act 2004, ss 3, 58(1), Sch 10, para 40; SI 2011/1740.

Prospective amendments–Domestic Violence, Crime and Victims Act 2004, s 4

DEFAMATION ACT 2013

Sections 1, 8, 13

1 Serious harm

(1) A statement is not defamatory unless its publication has caused or is likely to cause serious harm to the reputation of the claimant.

(2) For the purposes of this section, harm to the reputation of a body that trades for profit is not 'serious harm' unless it has caused or is likely to cause the body serious financial loss.

****

8 Single publication rule

(1) This section applies if a person –

(a) publishes a statement to the public ('the first publication'), and
(b) subsequently publishes (whether or not to the public) that statement or a statement which is substantially the same.

(2) In subsection (1) 'publication to the public' includes publication to a section of the public.

(3) For the purposes of section 4A of the Limitation Act 1980 (time limit for actions for defamation etc) any cause of action against the person for

---

[77] Amendment: Paragraph and preceding word inserted: Adoption and Children (Scotland) Act 2007 (Consequential Modifications) Order 2011, SI 2011/1740, art 2, Sch 1, Pt 1, para 5(a), with effect from 15 July 2011.

[78] Amendment: Subsection inserted: Adoption and Children Act 2002, s 139(1), Sch 3, paras 85, 87, with effect from 30 December 2005 (SI 2005/2213).

[79] Amendment: Subsection inserted: Adoption and Children (Scotland) Act 2007 (Consequential Modifications) Order 2011, SI 2011/1740, art 2, Sch 1, Pt 1, para 5(b), with effect from 15 July 2011.

defamation in respect of the subsequent publication is to be treated as having accrued on the date of the first publication.

(4)   This section does not apply in relation to the subsequent publication if the manner of that publication is materially different from the manner of the first publication.

(5)   In determining whether the manner of a subsequent publication is materially different from the manner of the first publication, the matters to which the court may have regard include (amongst other matters) –

(a)   the level of prominence that a statement is given;
(b)   the extent of the subsequent publication.

(6)   Where this section applies –

(a)   it does not affect the court's discretion under section 32A of the Limitation Act 1980 (discretionary exclusion of time limit for actions for defamation etc), and
(b)   the reference in subsection (1)(a) of that section to the operation of section 4A of that Act is a reference to the operation of section 4A together with this section.

****

13   Order to remove statement or cease distribution etc

(1)   Where a court gives judgment for the claimant in an action for defamation the court may order –

(a)   the operator of a website on which the defamatory statement is posted to remove the statement, or
(b)   any person who was not the author, editor or publisher of the defamatory statement to stop distributing, selling or exhibiting material containing the statement.

(2)   In this section 'author', 'editor' and 'publisher' have the same meaning as in section 1 of the Defamation Act 1996.

(3)   Subsection (1) does not affect the power of the court apart from that subsection.

HUMAN RIGHTS ACT 1998

Legislation

3   Interpretation of legislation

(1)   So far as it is possible to do so, primary legislation and subordinate legislation must be read and given effect in a way which is compatible with the Convention rights.

(2)   This section –

(a) applies to primary legislation and subordinate legislation whenever enacted;

(b) does not affect the validity, continuing operation or enforcement of any incompatible primary legislation; and

(c) does not affect the validity, continuing operation or enforcement of any incompatible subordinate legislation if (disregarding any possibility of revocation) primary legislation prevents removal of the incompatibility.

. . .

Schedule 1
The Articles

PART I
THE CONVENTION – RIGHTS AND FREEDOMS

. . .

Article 8
Right to respect for private and family life

1 Everyone has the right to respect for his private and family life, his home and his correspondence.

2 There shall be no interference by a public authority with the exercise of this right except such as is in accordance with the law and is necessary in a democratic society in the interests of national security, public safety or the economic well-being of the country, for the prevention of disorder or crime, for the protection of health or morals, or for the protection of the rights and freedoms of others.

Article 9
Freedom of thought, conscience and religion

1 Everyone has the right to freedom of thought, conscience and religion; this right includes freedom to change his religion or belief and freedom, either alone or in community with others and in public or private, to manifest his religion or belief, in worship, teaching, practice and observance.

2 Freedom to manifest one's religion or beliefs shall be subject only to such limitations as are prescribed by law and are necessary in a democratic society in the interests of public safety, for the protection of public order, health or morals, or for the protection of the rights and freedoms of others.

Article 10
Freedom of expression

1 Everyone has the right to freedom of expression. This right shall include freedom to hold opinions and to receive and impart information and ideas

without interference by public authority and regardless of frontiers. This Article shall not prevent States from requiring the licensing of broadcasting, television or cinema enterprises.

2 The exercise of these freedoms, since it carries with it duties and responsibilities, may be subject to such formalities, conditions, restrictions or penalties as are prescribed by law and are necessary in a democratic society, in the interests of national security, territorial integrity or public safety, for the prevention of disorder or crime, for the protection of health or morals, for the protection of the reputation or rights of others, for preventing the disclosure of information received in confidence, or for maintaining the authority and impartiality of the judiciary.

DATA PROTECTION ACT 1998

Schedules 1, 2, 13

Schedule 1
The data protection principles

PART I
THE PRINCIPLES

1 Personal data shall be processed fairly and lawfully and, in particular, shall not be processed unless –

(a) at least one of the conditions in Schedule 2 is met, and
(b) in the case of sensitive personal data, at least one of the conditions in Schedule 3 is also met.

2 Personal data shall be obtained only for one or more specified and lawful purposes, and shall not be further processed in any manner incompatible with that purpose or those purposes.

3 Personal data shall be adequate, relevant and not excessive in relation to the purpose or purposes for which they are processed.

4 Personal data shall be accurate and, where necessary, kept up to date.

5 Personal data processed for any purpose or purposes shall not be kept for longer than is necessary for that purpose or those purposes.

6 Personal data shall be processed in accordance with the rights of data subjects under this Act.

7 Appropriate technical and organisational measures shall be taken against unauthorised or unlawful processing of personal data and against accidental loss or destruction of, or damage to, personal data.

8 Personal data shall not be transferred to a country or territory outside the European Economic Area unless that country or territory ensures an adequate level of protection for the rights and freedoms of data subjects in relation to the processing of personal data.

PART II
INTERPRETATION OF THE PRINCIPLES IN PART I

The first principle

1

(1) In determining for the purposes of the first principle whether personal data are processed fairly, regard is to be had to the method by which they are obtained, including in particular whether any person from whom they are obtained is deceived or misled as to the purpose or purposes for which they are to be processed.

(2) Subject to paragraph 2, for the purposes of the first principle data are to be treated as obtained fairly if they consist of information obtained from a person who –

    (a) is authorised by or under any enactment to supply it, or

    (b) is required to supply it by or under any enactment or by any convention or other instrument imposing an international obligation on the United Kingdom.

2

(1) Subject to paragraph 3, for the purposes of the first principle personal data are not to be treated as processed fairly unless –

    (a) in the case of data obtained from the data subject, the data controller ensures so far as practicable that the data subject has, is provided with, or has made readily available to him, the information specified in sub-paragraph (3), and

    (b) in any other case, the data controller ensures so far as practicable that, before the relevant time or as soon as practicable after that time, the data subject has, is provided with, or has made readily available to him, the information specified in sub-paragraph (3).

(2) In sub-paragraph (1)(b) 'the relevant time' means –

    (a) the time when the data controller first processes the data, or

    (b) in a case where at that time disclosure to a third party within a reasonable period is envisaged –

        (i) if the data are in fact disclosed to such a person within that period, the time when the data are first disclosed,

        (ii) if within that period the data controller becomes, or ought to become, aware that the data are unlikely to be disclosed to such a person within that period, the time when the data controller does become, or ought to become, so aware, or

        (iii) in any other case, the end of that period.

(3) The information referred to in sub-paragraph (1) is as follows, namely –

    (a) the identity of the data controller,

(b) if he has nominated a representative for the purposes of this Act, the identity of that representative,

(c) the purpose or purposes for which the data are intended to be processed, and

(d) any further information which is necessary, having regard to the specific circumstances in which the data are or are to be processed, to enable processing in respect of the data subject to be fair.

3

(1) Paragraph 2(1)(b) does not apply where either of the primary conditions in sub-paragraph (2), together with such further conditions as may be prescribed by the [Secretary of State] by order, are met.

(2) The primary conditions referred to in sub-paragraph (1) are –

(a) that the provision of that information would involve a disproportionate effort, or

(b) that the recording of the information to be contained in the data by, or the disclosure of the data by, the data controller is necessary for compliance with any legal obligation to which the data controller is subject, other than an obligation imposed by contract.

NOTE

Paragraph 3 is amended by SI 2003/1887.

4

(1) Personal data which contain a general identifier falling within a description prescribed by the [Secretary of State] by order are not to be treated as processed fairly and lawfully unless they are processed in compliance with any conditions so prescribed in relation to general identifiers of that description.

(2) In sub-paragraph (1) 'a general identifier' means any identifier (such as, for example, a number or code used for identification purposes) which –

(a) relates to an individual, and

(b) forms part of a set of similar identifiers which is of general application.

NOTE

Paragraph 4 is amended by SI 2003/1887.

The second principle

5

The purpose or purposes for which personal data are obtained may in particular be specified –

(a) in a notice given for the purposes of paragraph 2 by the data controller to the data subject, or

(b) in a notification given to the Commissioner under Part III of this Act.

6

In determining whether any disclosure of personal data is compatible with the purpose or purposes for which the data were obtained, regard is to be had to the purpose or purposes for which the personal data are intended to be processed by any person to whom they are disclosed.

The fourth principle

7

The fourth principle is not to be regarded as being contravened by reason of any inaccuracy in personal data which accurately record information obtained by the data controller from the data subject or a third party in a case where –

(a) having regard to the purpose or purposes for which the data were obtained and further processed, the data controller has taken reasonable steps to ensure the accuracy of the data, and
(b) if the data subject has notified the data controller of the data subject's view that the data are inaccurate, the data indicate that fact.

The sixth principle

8

A person is to be regarded as contravening the sixth principle if, but only if –

(a) he contravenes section 7 by failing to supply information in accordance with that section,
(b) he contravenes section 10 by failing to comply with a notice given under subsection (1) of that section to the extent that the notice is justified or by failing to give a notice under subsection (3) of that section,
(c) he contravenes section 11 by failing to comply with a notice given under subsection (1) of that section, or
(d) he contravenes section 12 by failing to comply with a notice given under subsection (1) or (2)(b) of that section or by failing to give a notification under subsection (2)(a) of that section or a notice under subsection (3) of that section.

The seventh principle

9

Having regard to the state of technological development and the cost of implementing any measures, the measures must ensure a level of security appropriate to –

(a) the harm that might result from such unauthorised or unlawful processing or accidental loss, destruction or damage as are mentioned in the seventh principle, and
(b) the nature of the data to be protected.

10

The data controller must take reasonable steps to ensure the reliability of any employees of his who have access to the personal data.

11

Where processing of personal data is carried out by a data processor on behalf of a data controller, the data controller must in order to comply with the seventh principle –

    (a) choose a data processor providing sufficient guarantees in respect of the technical and organisational security measures governing the processing to be carried out, and

    (b) take reasonable steps to ensure compliance with those measures.

12

Where processing of personal data is carried out by a data processor on behalf of a data controller, the data controller is not to be regarded as complying with the seventh principle unless–

    (a) the processing is carried out under a contract –

        (i) which is made or evidenced in writing, and

        (ii) under which the data processor is to act only on instructions from the data controller, and

    (b) the contract requires the data processor to comply with obligations equivalent to those imposed on a data controller by the seventh principle.

The eighth principle

13

An adequate level of protection is one which is adequate in all the circumstances of the case, having regard in particular to –

    (a) the nature of the personal data,

    (b) the country or territory of origin of the information contained in the data,

    (c) the country or territory of final destination of that information,

    (d) the purposes for which and period during which the data are intended to be processed,

    (e) the law in force in the country or territory in question,

    (f) the international obligations of that country or territory,

    (g) any relevant codes of conduct or other rules which are enforceable in that country or territory (whether generally or by arrangement in particular cases), and

    (h) any security measures taken in respect of the data in that country or territory.

14

The eighth principle does not apply to a transfer falling within any paragraph of Schedule 4, except in such circumstances and to such extent as the [Secretary of State] may by order provide.

NOTE

Paragraph 4 is amended by SI 2003/1887.

15

(1) Where –

(a) in any proceedings under this Act any question arises as to whether the requirement of the eighth principle as to an adequate level of protection is met in relation to the transfer of any personal data to a country or territory outside the European Economic Area, and

(b) a Community finding has been made in relation to transfers of the kind in question,

that question is to be determined in accordance with that finding.

(2) In sub-paragraph (1) 'Community finding' means a finding of the European Commission, under the procedure provided for in Article 31(2) of the Data Protection Directive, that a country or territory outside the European Economic Area does, or does not, ensure an adequate level of protection within the meaning of Article 25(2) of the Directive.

Schedule 2
Conditions relevant for purposes of the first principle: processing of any personal data

1

The data subject has given his consent to the processing.

2

The processing is necessary –

(a) for the performance of a contract to which the data subject is a party, or

(b) for the taking of steps at the request of the data subject with a view to entering into a contract.

3

The processing is necessary for compliance with any legal obligation to which the data controller is subject, other than an obligation imposed by contract.

4

The processing is necessary in order to protect the vital interests of the data subject.

5

The processing is necessary –

  (a)　for the administration of justice,
  [(aa)for the exercise of any functions of either House of Parliament,]
  (b)　for the exercise of any functions conferred on any person by or under any enactment,
  (c)　for the exercise of any functions of the Crown, a Minister of the Crown or a government department, or
  (d)　for the exercise of any other functions of a public nature exercised in the public interest by any person.

NOTE

Paragraph 5 is amended by the Freedom of Information Act 2000, s 73, Sch 6, para 4.

6

(1) The processing is necessary for the purposes of legitimate interests pursued by the data controller or by the third party or parties to whom the data are disclosed, except where the processing is unwarranted in any particular case by reason of prejudice to the rights and freedoms or legitimate interests of the data subject.

(2) The [Secretary of State] may by order specify particular circumstances in which this condition is, or is not, to be taken to be satisfied.

NOTE

Paragraph 6 is amended by SI 2003/1887.

Schedule 3
Conditions relevant for purposes of the first principle: processing of sensitive personal data

1

The data subject has given his explicit consent to the processing of the personal data.

2

(1) The processing is necessary for the purposes of exercising or performing any right or obligation which is conferred or imposed by law on the data controller in connection with employment.

(2) The [Secretary of State] may by order –

  (a)　exclude the application of sub-paragraph (1) in such cases as may be specified, or
  (b)　provide that, in such cases as may be specified, the condition in sub-paragraph (1) is not to be regarded as satisfied unless such further conditions as may be specified in the order are also satisfied.

NOTE

Paragraph 2 is amended by SI 2003/1887.

3

The processing is necessary –

(a) in order to protect the vital interests of the data subject or another person, in a case where –
    (i) consent cannot be given by or on behalf of the data subject, or
    (ii) the data controller cannot reasonably be expected to obtain the consent of the data subject, or
(b) in order to protect the vital interests of another person, in a case where consent by or on behalf of the data subject has been unreasonably withheld.

4

The processing –

(a) is carried out in the course of its legitimate activities by any body or association which –
    (i) is not established or conducted for profit, and
    (ii) exists for political, philosophical, religious or trade-union purposes,
(b) is carried out with appropriate safeguards for the rights and freedoms of data subjects,
(c) relates only to individuals who either are members of the body or association or have regular contact with it in connection with its purposes, and
(d) does not involve disclosure of the personal data to a third party without the consent of the data subject.

5

The information contained in the personal data has been made public as a result of steps deliberately taken by the data subject.

6

The processing –

(a) is necessary for the purpose of, or in connection with, any legal proceedings (including prospective legal proceedings),
(b) is necessary for the purpose of obtaining legal advice, or
(c) is otherwise necessary for the purposes of establishing, exercising or defending legal rights.

7

(1) The processing is necessary –

(a) for the administration of justice,

[(aa) for the exercise of any functions of either House of Parliament,]
(b)   for the exercise of any functions conferred on any person by or under an enactment, or
(c)   for the exercise of any functions of the Crown, a Minister of the Crown or a government department.

(2) The [Secretary of State] may by order –

(a)   exclude the application of sub-paragraph (1) in such cases as may be specified, or
(b)   provide that, in such cases as may be specified, the condition in sub-paragraph (1) is not to be regarded as satisfied unless such further conditions as may be specified in the order are also satisfied.

NOTE

Paragraph 5 is amended by the Freedom of Information Act 2000, s 73, Sch 6, para 5; SI 2003/1887.

[7A

(1) The processing –

(a)   is either –
  (i)   the disclosure of sensitive personal data by a person as a member of an anti-fraud organisation or otherwise in accordance with any arrangements made by such an organisation; or
  (ii)   any other processing by that person or another person of sensitive personal data so disclosed; and
(b)   is necessary for the purposes of preventing fraud or a particular kind of fraud.

(2) In this paragraph 'an anti-fraud organisation' means any unincorporated association, body corporate or other person which enables or facilitates any sharing of information to prevent fraud or a particular kind of fraud or which has any of these functions as its purpose or one of its purposes.]

NOTE

Paragraph 7A is inserted by the Serious Crime Act 2007, s 72.

8

(1) The processing is necessary for medical purposes and is undertaken by –

(a)   a health professional, or
(b)   a person who in the circumstances owes a duty of confidentiality which is equivalent to that which would arise if that person were a health professional.

(2) In this paragraph 'medical purposes' includes the purposes of preventative medicine, medical diagnosis, medical research, the provision of care and treatment and the management of healthcare services.

9

(1) The processing –

    (a) is of sensitive personal data consisting of information as to racial or ethnic origin,

    (b) is necessary for the purpose of identifying or keeping under review the existence or absence of equality of opportunity or treatment between persons of different racial or ethnic origins, with a view to enabling such equality to be promoted or maintained, and

    (c) is carried out with appropriate safeguards for the rights and freedoms of data subjects.

(2) The [Secretary of State] may by order specify circumstances in which processing falling within sub-paragraph (1)(a) and (b) is, or is not, to be taken for the purposes of sub-paragraph (1)(c) to be carried out with appropriate safeguards for the rights and freedoms of data subjects.

NOTE

Paragraph 9 is amended by SI 2003/1887.

10

The personal data are processed in circumstances specified in an order made by the [Secretary of State] for the purposes of this paragraph.

NOTE

Paragraph 10 is amended by SI 2003/1887.

INDEX

References are to paragraph numbers.